FOURTH EDITION

CASE STUDIES IN ABNORMAL BEHAVIOR

Robert G. Meyer
University of Louisville

Allyn and Bacon

Boston   London   Toronto   Sydney   Tokyo   Singapore

Series editorial assistant: Jessica Barnard
Manufacturing buyer: Suzanne Lareau

Library of Congress Cataloging-in-Publication Data

Meyer, Robert G.
    Case studies in abnormal behavior / Robert G. Meyer. — 4th ed.
      p.   cm.
    Includes bibliographical references and index.
    ISBN 0-205-28624-0
    1. Mental illness—Case studies.
  RC465.M44   1998
  616.89'09—dc21   95-4459
                                         CIP

Printed in the United States of America
10 9 8 7 6 5 4 3 2 1   02 01 00 99 98

To Monika Meyer Hubbard:
Still quite a case and still delightful

CONTENTS

PREFACE

Research articles in abnormal psychology necessarily focus on specific theories and experiments; texts in this area are concerned with integrating a vast array of literature on historical, descriptive, research, diagnostic, and treatment issues. Some texts do a good job of bringing in "chunks" of case material to demonstrate particular points. However, textbooks cannot do justice to their other goals if they provide any significant number of cases in depth. *Case Studies in Abnormal Behavior* fills this niche. This book helps the reader regain a sense of how the whole person experiences and reacts to the diverse factors studied in abnormal psychology. The abstract and conflicting concepts of this field can thus be seen in the context that eventually counts—the totality of an actual person who has the disorder.

Some of the cases are people who are well known for one reason or another, like Princess Diana, or who have played an important role in the evolution of the field of psychology, like Anna O. A number of these and other cases presented here are based on actual, recent cases, although in those cases not in the public record, identifying details have, of course, been changed to protect people from even a small chance that they would be recognized. Aside from those in the public record, most cases originated in the experience of the author or were donated by colleagues. I have also included a couple of cases published in journals, which either make an original point or demonstrate a particular point of view, as in the cases of Hans, Albert, and Peter in Chapter 3.

Readers will note that cases that are provided by the author and that are not public cases or reprints from journals are assigned names with a logical or mnemonic relationship to the syndrome being studied; for example, Agnes—Agoraphobia. While this may seem corny, I have found it to be a helpful technique for most readers. Students have said this device adds clarity to classroom discussion and enhances the remembrance of the cases if needed during a test.

The reader may note the high number of case studies in this book. Feedback from my students and from other professors and their students indicated that case studies in most other books were too long and included irrelevant detail (and in some cases were much too short). The cases in this book contain the full details of background material that are relevant to etiological, diagnostic, and therapeutic considerations, and yet (I hope) they are not overly long. This allows me to provide a full spectrum of case studies, perhaps more than in any previous case study book. It also allows me to detail cases from all categories of the *Diagnostic and Statistical Manual (DSM-IV)* of the American Psychiatric Association, to provide contrast cases within the major categories, and to present some other cases that deal with other important patterns.

Relevant and detailed family and social history data are presented in almost all of these case studies, to give the reader a clearer idea about how specific behavior patterns were generated and maintained. A few of the case studies have little background data, such as in the case of Harry (in Chapter 15), in which an abrupt organic trauma is the focus of disorder, or if it seems highly probable that genetic factors dominated the development of the disorder, as in the case of Virginia Woolf (Chapter 7). In cases such as Harry's, I present more detailed information on present behavior and the responses in psychological evaluations.

All cases go through to a natural conclusion, even though it may not always be termed a success. As in most experiences, much can be learned from failure.

The author wishes to thank those who helped with this book. Much appreciation is extended to Sean Wakely, my Allyn and Bacon editor, for his support and advice. I would also like to acknowledge the very helpful input from Susan Leavenworth in writing some of these cases, and also input from Lisa Thomas in the cases of Betty Ford and Elvis Presley, as well as the extensive help in organizing and typing this book provided primarily by Georgette Moore and Sandy Garcia.

R.G.M.

INTRODUCTION
AND HISTORY

*If you always think the way you always thought
you'll always get what you always got.*

—Anonymous

The field of abnormal psychology has evolved through many theoretical orientations. In the first half of this century the Freudian psychoanalytic model, already developing a more broad-spectrum *psychodynamic* orientation (Schwartz et al., 1995; Kohut, 1977), clearly dominated the study of abnormal psychology in North America. At the same time, the seminal behavioral studies of John Watson and Mary Cover Jones established behaviorism as an important influence in the study of abnormal behavior. While behaviorism—more specifically, behavior therapy—was coming into bloom in the 1950s and 1960s (Wolpe, 1958; Ayllon and Azrin, 1968) and then merging with the cognitive therapies in the 1980s and 1990s, a third force also was emerging, marked by diverse theories, many new psychotherapies (Garfield, 1981), and a varying and differing interest in diagnosis and etiology. At the same time, psychodynamic theory was further diversifying and showing a renewed concern for experimental verification (Wachtel, 1997; Schwartz et al., 1995; Silverman and Weinberger, 1985). Behavior therapy meanwhile was becoming (1) less wedded to theory (Lazarus, 1971), (2) was also expanding its concern back to at least some aspects of the mind under the influence of the cognitive behavior modifiers (Meichenbaum, 1977; Beck et al., 1990), (3) was developing into a broader perspective on environmental variables under the social learning theorists (Bandura and Walters, 1963; Mischel, 1969), (4) was forced by the pressure of managed care and national health insurance issues into an emphasis on shorter-term and more focused therapies, and (5) helped facilitate the overall trend in the mental health field toward a greater emphasis on the experimental verification of assessment and intervention techniques (Meyer and Deitsch, 1996).

Teachers and practitioners alike have reflected the increasing sophistication that is inherent in this maturing and diversification process. Very few would now argue that any one technique or theoretical approach answers all or even most of the diagnostic, etiological, and treatment questions that arise. Certain theories and techniques have more relevance to certain disorders. In this vein, it is interesting that the "sphere of relevance" of an approach is most closely centered on the original group that was studied or treated when the approach came into being.

Freud's specific theories became less relevant as society lost some of the repressions of the Victorian era (possibly only to take on repressions in other dimensions). Carl Jung's treatment techniques, which focus on uncovering "spiritual" yearnings and on creating a sense of meaning, arose primarily in the therapy of middle-age males who had "made it big" financially and in their careers but who lived the feelings expressed in the songstress Peggy Lee's classic refrain "Is that all there is?" Just as the client-centered therapy techniques of Carl Rogers seem most appropriate to bright, "psychologically minded," and introspective clients (similar to the graduate ministerial and psychology students Rogers first worked with), the behavior therapist's "token economy" is most effective when dealing with clients who are institutionalized and who show marked deficits in basic social and interpersonal skills.

Concomitant with this growing awareness that no one theory or technique holds all the answers is the concept that a number of diverse techniques may be necessary to handle any one case most efficiently. This multimodal approach, first thoroughly developed as a concept by Arnold Lazarus, is an underlying assumption in this book; it is dramatically emphasized in the case of Roger, discussed in the upcoming section on theories and techniques.

The eclecticism inherent in the ideas stated here is another assumption in this book. Optimally, this allows a broad-based acceptance of many causal paths to disorder, as well as a more comfortable melding with most specific theories, and an absence of an "in-group" language.

In order to put some of these comments in perspective and to provide a historical framework for the book, a synopsis of important historical developments related to mental disorder is offered next.

> *The only reason I have dabbled in psychology here is to demonstrate to you that you can use it to arrive at whatever conclusions suit you best. It all depends on who uses it. Psychology tempts even the most responsible and serious people to create fictions, and they cannot really be blamed for that....*
>
> —Defense attorney Fetyukovich's closing argument from Fyodor Dostoyevsky's novel *Brothers Karamazof*

Major Historical Developments Related to Mental Disorder

1. Western Society

Early Greeks: Hippocrates (460–377 BC) provides a focus on the brain as the site of disorder and emphasizes life stressors.

Romans: Galen (second century AD) conceptualizes the hospital as a treatment center and posits the first thorough classification of disorders.

Age of Crusades: Physicians obtain higher-status social class and greater intellectual influence; Greek and Roman texts are rediscovered; and contact with Near Eastern and Oriental influences offer new perspectives on abnormal behavior.

1347: From this year to the end of the fourteenth century, the Black Death ravages Europe, destroying not only lives but also the "medieval period" in its primary reliance on theological explanations of everyday behavior.

Renaissance (1500–1650): There is a beginning rejection of witchcraft; naturalistic explanations of emotional disorder attain wider acceptance; and in the late fifteenth and early sixteenth centuries former leprosariums are converted into the first asylums or "madhouses."

Enlightenment (1700–1800): More humane care becomes prevalent, as well as keeping of case histories and rudimentary statistics.

Late 1700s—Jean-Baptiste Pussin and then Phillipe Pinel free mental patients from their chains at LaBicetre, a hospital in Paris.

1865: Gregor Mendel publishes his influential theories of genetics.

1879: Wilhelm Wundt, a professor of physiology at the University of Leipzig in Germany, establishes the first laboratory for the experimental study of psychology.

1883: Emil Kraeplin's influential textbook on psychiatry likens mental disorder to physical disease.

1891: The first description of psychosurgery is published by Dr. Gottlieb Burckhardt, director of a Swiss asylum. His techniques were popularized in the 1930s by Dr. Egas Moniz, a Portuguese psychiatrist.

1893: Sigmund Freud, with Josef Breuer, publishes the first chapters of *Studien uber hysterie.* Hypnosis is used to produce spontaneous verbalizations, which are theorized to break down psychological repressions, leading to catharsis and "cure." These concepts parallel the earlier theories of Johann Christian Heinroth (1773–1843), who asserted that mental illness springs from the conflict between unacceptable wishes and the guilt generated by these wishes.

1905: The first true IQ scale, the Binet-Simon Scale, is published.

1921: The first description of the Rorschach Test is published. Hermann Rorschach, a Swiss psychiatrist, had noticed while riding in the country that what his children saw in the clouds reflected their personalities.

2. United States

Early colonial period: There is a regression to witchcraft and demonology.

1693: This was the peak of the witch-hunting trials in Salem, Massachusetts.

1773: The first hospital specifically for mental patients is opened in Williamsburg, Virginia.

Late 1700s: "Moral therapy" becomes popular.

1812: Benjamin Rush, a signer of the Declaration of Independence and the "father of American psychiatry," writes the first American textbook on psychiatry. He also invents the "tranquilizing chair," a kind of immobile straitjacket.

1842: Dorothy Dix takes a position as a schoolteacher in a prison. The conditions she encounters prompt her to become the major reformer of the mental health movement in the nineteenth century.

Approximately 1850: The hospital reform movement begins to generate more humane treatment.

Late 1800s: The medical model increases its influence.

1892: The first meeting of the American Psychological Association (APA) is held. The APA incorporates in 1925 (and eventually adopts its first formal ethics code in 1953).

1892: Responding to an invitation from William James to direct the psychological laboratory at Harvard, Hugo Munsterberg, who had been a student of Wilhelm Wundt, engages in activities that arguably earn him the title "Father of Forensic Psychology" in the United States. Although controversial and self-promoting, he makes some worthwhile contributions in the areas of experimental and forensic psychology, including his 1908 book *On the Witness Stand.*

1896: Lightner Witmer establishes the first psychological clinic in the United States at the University of Pennsylvania.

Ca. 1900: Morton Prince pioneers the use of hypnosis in reintegrating (i.e., "fusing") a multiple personality in his case of "Miss Beauchamp."

Early 1900s: The Freudian model increases its influence, stimulated by Freud's lectures delivered at Clark University in 1912.

1907: Clifford Beers writes *A Mind That Found Itself,* the story of his long-term struggle with his own mental illness and the treatments he encountered. The widespread popular response to his book furthered the reform movement inherited from the efforts of Dorothy Dix.

1913: John Watson publishes his influential manifesto, "Psychology as a Behaviorist Views It." Watson argues that psychology should abandon the study of consciousness, laying the groundwork for the behavior therapists and for later theorists like B. F. Skinner.

Early to mid 1900s: The behavioral model increases its influence.

1923: In *Frye* v. *United States* (295 F.1013(D.C. Cir.)), a federal appeals court establishes the standard of "scientific acceptance" for the admission of information-based opinions from an expert witness into trial testimony. (This will remain the standard until 1993, when the Supreme Court, in *Daubert* v. *Merrill Dow Pharmaceuticals,* allows a much less stringent "helpfulness" standard in federal trials.)

1936: The first psychosurgery in the United States, a frontal lobotomy, is performed by Dr. James Watts and Dr. Walter Freeman in Washington, DC.

1939: The Wechsler-Bellevue Intelligence Scale is published, the predecessor of the various Wechsler measures of intelligence, the most popular forms of the IQ test.

1943: The first version of the Minnesota Multiphasic Personality Test (MMPI), devised by Starke Hathaway and Jovian McKinley, is published. (It will be revised as MMPI-2 in 1989.)

1952: The first edition of the *Diagnostic and Statistical Manual of Mental Disorders* is published by the American Psychiatric Association.

1950s and 1960s: The humanistic and cognitive models increase influence; and the advent of a new class of psychotropic drugs, the phenothiazines, for example, chlorpromazine (Thorazine) for the first time allow chemical control of psychotic behavior.

Early 1960s: The Community Health Act of 1963 and the mental health centers that are subsequently developed change care delivery structure; the related "deinstitutionalization" of patients generates an exodus from the centralized state hospital systems.

1980s–2000: These decades give rise to the "corporatization" of mental health care delivery and the advent of "managed care." Those who pay for services (or their administrators—e.g., health maintenance organizations [HMOs] and preferred provider organizations [PPOs]) capture the system from those who deliver the services. There is movement toward universal health care, with modest coverage for mental health.

> *America is one of the few places where the failure to promote oneself is widely regarded as arrogance.*
>
> —Gary Trudeau, cartoonist author of *Doonesbury*

An Outline of the Cases

The first chapter's case, that of O. J. Simpson, highlights the social, legal, and political issues inherent in defining abnormality and subsequently applying that label to an individual. The second chapter, on theories and techniques, first presents the case of Danielle, who manifests a persistent though not constant moderate level of anxiety, several simple phobias, and some allied mild depression. After Danielle's case is detailed, there is an analysis of the etiology and treatment that could be expected from the six major overall theoretical viewpoints: psychoanalytic-psychodynamic, behavioral, cognitive, information processing and systems theory, humanistic-existential, and biological. The chapter closes by describing a multi-modal treatment approach, wherein techniques from a variety of theoretical perspectives are blended together to treat a case of exhibitionism.

The third chapter, (the first to focus on a specific syndrome) is concerned with the anxiety disorders. After a discussion of those three little fellows (Hans, Albert, and Peter) who are classic, early cases in the psychodynamic and behavioral traditions, more severe cases are presented, specifically agoraphobia and the obsessive-compulsive disorder. This chapter closes with a relatively recent but often used addition to the *DSM,* posttraumatic stress disorder, which is considered as an anxiety disorder.

Chapter 4 presents both the dissociative disorders and sleep disorders, as the altered state of consciousness in each provides some interesting contrasts. The dissociative disorders are exemplified by the case of Anna O., considered the first case in the psychoanalytical tradition and here seen not so much as a case of hysteria but as a case of multiple personality. The sleep disorders are represented first by a sleepwalking case and then one that combines a disturbance of the sleepwake cycle with insomnia. Chapter 5 looks at the somatization disorder (in the case of Empress Alexandra Fedorovna) and the psychogenic pain disorder, commonly observed subtypes of the somatoform disorders.

Chapter 6 is concerned with severely disruptive syndromes: the schizophrenic and paranoid disorders, as seen in cases of undifferentiated schizophrenia, paranoid schizophrenia (here exemplified in Freud's classic case of Daniel Paul Schreber), and the paranoid personality disorder. Schizophrenia is a subgroup within the overall conceptual category of "psychosis," which essentially designates a loss of reality contact. The two schizophrenia cases allow a contrast between paranoid schizophrenia, the most well-integrated form, and undifferentiated schizophrenia, in which functioning has deteriorated. These two forms are then compared with the nonpsychotic paranoid personality disorder pattern. The other category of very severe disorders, the affective disorders, is detailed in Chapter 7 in cases of major depressive disorder (the case of Joseph Westbecker—a workplace violence case that was also the first major civil trial focusing on the drug Prozac) and bipolar disorder (the case of Virginia Woolf, a famous writer and a pioneer in the women's movement); again, both of these are often psychotic-level disorders.

In combination with the case of exhibitionism from Chapter 2, the spectrum of the psychosexual disorders is seen in Chapter 8. In addition to a classic paraphiliac (the case of Jeffrey Dahmer) and a pedophile (Jesse Timmendequas), cases of both male and female sexual dysfunction are noted, as well as a case of transvestism. Then Chapter 9 (Addictive Disorders) discusses three of the most common disorder patterns in our society, alcohol dependence (in the case of Betty Ford), prescription drug abuse (in the case of Elvis Presley), and nicotine dependence (in the case of Dr. S.).

Complementing the discussion of addictive patterns in Chapter 9, Chapter 10 discusses the eating disorders, with the case of Karen Carpenter focusing on anorexia nervosa and that of Princess Diana on bulimia nervosa. Chapter 11 has three of the more important personality disorders: the histrionic, antisocial, and schizoid patterns. Ted Kaczynski, known more popularly as the Unabomber, illustrates the schizoid personality disorder. The antisocial diagnosis is discussed in the case of Theodore Bundy. This complements the discussion of the paranoid personality disorder in Chapter 6. Somewhat related issues are then found in Chapter 12 in the disorders of impulse control, seen in cases of pathological gambling, and kleptomania. Violence patterns are found in several cases throughout this book, for example, in the cases of O. J. Simpson (Chapter 1), Jeffrey Dahmer (Chapter 8), and others. In Chapter 13 the issue of violence and its causes is specifically addressed in the case of Jack Ruby and then in two cases of family violence. In Chapter 14, cases of developmental language disorder, attention-deficit disorder with hyperactivity, and early infantile autism illustrate three of the most critical disorders that emerge in childhood. The oppositional disorder and separation anxiety disorder (associated with school phobia) cases then document two common maladaptive channels for the strivings for identity and independence that are often a concern in middle childhood and adolescence. The last case focuses directly on the identity crises and identity disorder.

Chapter 15 offers two cases in which a clearly defined organic factor has caused psychological symptomatology. The first case documents a person's disorder and then virtually complete recovery of psychological functioning subsequent to having an entire half of the brain surgically removed. The second case focuses on Alzheimer's disease, illustrated by the plight of former president Ronald Reagan.

Chapter 16 is concerned with the interaction of psychological disorder and legal issues. Providing a transition from the prior chapter, the first case discusses the evaluation of an elderly woman's legal competence to handle her affairs. The second case, that of John Hinckley, who attempted to assassinate President Reagan, examines the legal concepts of insanity, incompetency to stand trial, and involuntary civil commitment as it relates to predicting dangerousness. Chapter 17 focuses on the development of positive mental health.

The full spectrum of cases provided by this book should develop an awareness of the diversity inherent in the modern study of abnormal psychology.

1

Concepts of Abnormality

Adultery: Consensual non-monogamy.

Corrupt: Morally challenged.

Looters: Nontraditional shoppers.

Drug addicts/alcoholics: People of stupor.

Sadomasochists: The differently pleasured.

—A few entries from *The Official Politically Correct Dictionary and Handbook,* by Henry Beard and Christopher Cerf

The first case in this book, that of O. J. Simpson, dramatically highlights some of the problems inherent merely in defining abnormal behavior. A traditional method of defining abnormal behavior has been to use statistical norms. However, this only establishes extremes and does not per se discriminate between positive and negative patterns or characteristics. Also, some widespread patterns, for example, drunk driving, anxiety, may be labeled as normal because of their commonness.

Defining abnormality as the absence of optimal or ideal characteristics is another possibility. The problem is then simply shifted, what is "optimal," and who decides? Also, most normal individuals are not that close to "ideal."

In any case, most people will generally agree that abnormal behavior is behavior that significantly differs from some consensually agreed upon norm and which is in some way harmful to the differently behaving person or to others. More specifically, components of a judgment of abnormality often include the following descriptors:

deviant
Deviant refers to behavior that differs markedly from socially accepted standards of conduct. In many cases the word has negative connotations.

different
Different also suggests behavior that varies significantly, at least statistically, from the accepted norm, but it does not usually have negative connotations.

disordered
Disordered implies a lack of integration in behaviors; the result may be impairment of a person's ability to cope in various situations.

bizarre
Bizarre suggests behavior that differs extremely from socially accepted norms. In addition, it connotes inadequate coping patterns and disintegration of behavioral patterns.

If we like a man's dream, we call him a reformer;
if we don't like his dream, we call him a crank.
—William Dean Howells, Writer (1837–1920)

The DSM's

The general framework for this book is in the diagnostic terminology of *DSM-IV* (American Psychiatric Association, 1994). Even though there are valid criticisms of the DSM approach, the manual is the official document of the American Psychiatric Association, is approved by the American Psychological Association, and is well respected by all varieties of mental health workers, both nationally and internationally. The first *DSM* was published in 1952, *DSM-II* in 1968, *DSM-III* in 1980, and *DSM-III-Revised* in 1987. There were numerous changes from *DSM-III-R* to *DSM-IV*, published in 1994. Indeed, the simple listing of changes took up twenty-eight pages in the *DSM-IV* book. Concisely, some of the more important changes are as follows: only the Personality Disorders and Mental Retardation remain on Axis II; Rett's Disorder, Childhood Disintegrative Disorder, and Asperger's Disorder have been added as Childhood Disorders; there is no separate category of Attention Deficit Disorder, it is subsumed under ADHD; there is now a separate overall category of Eating Disorders; there are now two separate Bipolar Disorders, with Bipolar Disorder II referring to the traditional, severe form, where both recurrent manic and depressive patterns are observed; the phrase "outside the range of normal human experience" has been deleted as a criteria for PTSD, and the related category of Acute Stress Disorder has been added; the term Multiple Personality Disorder has been changed to Dissociative Identity Disorder; Passive-Aggressive Personality Disorder has been deleted as an Axis II Personality Disorder but has been retained in revised form as a "Criteria Set . . . for further study"; two new patterns in "other conditions that may be a focus of clinical attention" are "Religious or Spiritual Problem" and "Acculturation Problem."

Rates of Mental Disorders

There have been many efforts over the last several decades to effectively apply definitions of abnormality to determine overall rates of mental disorder. Earlier endeavors provided some useful data, but all prior efforts pale in comparison to the landmark study developed by the National Institute of Mental Health (NIMH), which was initially reported on in a series of six articles in the October 1984 issue of the *Archives of General Psychiatry,* as well as in numerous follow-up articles, and was then summarized by Robins and Regier (1990).

The sheer scope of the NIMH study was unprecedented. Over 17,000 representative community residents (virtually a five-fold increase over the most exhaustive previous studies of this research quality) were sampled at five sites (Baltimore; New Haven, Connecticut; North Carolina; St. Louis; and Los Angeles). These subjects were administered a thorough and standardized structured interview, using the Diagnostic Interview Schedule, and were then followed up a year later with a reinterview. Unlike many earlier studies, this research was not restricted to reporting only on hospitalized mentally disordered persons, or only on prevalence of treatment, or on current symptoms or level of impairment.

The researchers first measured the groups from the five sites from the perspective of 6-month prevalence rates—that is, how many people showed a particular disorder at some time in the 6 months during which the population was assessed (Robins and Regier, 1990). They found that about 19% of adults over age 18 suffered from at least one mental disorder during a given 6-month period. Somewhat different results were obtained by taking the perspective of lifetime prevalence rates—that is, how often a disorder occurs percentage-wise in the population. The lifetime prevalence of any mental disorder in the general population is about 33%, but only 22% if alcoholism and substance abuse are excluded. More common disorders, based on lifetime prevalence in the general population, are anxiety disorders (15%, particularly phobias, 13%); alcoholic disorders (13%); affective disorders (8%, particularly major depressive episodes, 6%); and drug disorders other than alcoholism (6%, particularly marijuana dependence or abuse, 4%). Some disorders were much more common than previously thought. These include dysthymia (3%); obsessive-compulsive disorder (2%); and posttraumatic stress disorder (1%, with a 15% prevalence in Vietnam vets). For schizophrenia, the lifetime prevalence rate in these studies was 1.0–1.5%, and for the antisocial personality disorder the rate was 2.5%.

The NIMH study also looked at differences in the incidence of mental disorders among those who lived in urban central city areas, in suburbs, and in small towns and rural areas. For schizophrenia, organic brain disorder, alcoholism, drug abuse, and antisocial personality, the rates were highest in the central city, at the middle level for suburban areas, and lowest in the rural and small town populations. Incidence was relatively even throughout these three areas for major depressions and phobias, although somatization disorders, panic disorders, and some affective disorders were a bit higher in rural and small town areas than elsewhere. The only disorder that was found to be higher in the suburbs was the obsessive-compulsive disorder; not surprising, given that many of the characteristics of this disorder have functional value in a competitive society.

Overall median age of onset is less than 25 years of age. There has been an increasing prevalence of emotional disorder in persons born after World War I, especially for affective disorders. Also, it is estimated that about 20–30% of those diagnosable as mentally ill never receive any treatment. And only about 20% of those treated receive care from mental health specialists; most receive it from medical practitioners other than psychiatrists.

Issues relevant to these points, issues, and statistics will occur throughout this book, and several are especially evident in this first case of O. J. Simpson.

A Presumably Normal Person Potentially Viewed as Pathological

> *"Is Adolf Hitler Crazy?" Bohner asked eventually—the sort of damn-fool question too many people ask as soon as they hear a man is a psychologist. (p. 136)*
> —Len Deighton, *Goodbye Mickey Mouse* (1982)

The famous, or infamous, case of O. J. Simpson highlights many of the conceptual and diagnostic dilemmas that often confront mental health professionals. What sort of psychopathology, if any, led to his behavior within the episode of June 17, 1994? Was he a psychopath? Did he deteriorate into some sort of psychotic state at some point? On what dimension(s) is he reasonably construed as normal or abnormal?

The Case of O. J.

O. J. Simpson literally and figuratively ran to the forefront of the American consciousness. We first knew him as a dazzling running back at the University of Southern California where he won the Heisman Trophy. Then he went to the pros with the Buffalo Bills and the San Francisco 49ers where he was the first running back to gain 2000 yards in one season and was named to the Pro Football Hall of Fame in 1985. We next saw him running through airports in Hertz Rent-A-Car commercials, during the time when he also had some previously forgettable roles in movies like *The Towering Inferno* and *The Naked Gun* and was a commentator on ABC Sports Monday Night Football. However, he had become an American icon, or, as one television executive commented, "He was Michael Jordan before Michael Jordan."

Tragically, the last time his running was highlighted in our consciousness was when we saw him running on Friday night June 17, 1994; when the nation watched the police pursue him in his white Ford Bronco, along with his friend Al Cowlings, in an almost funereal passage down a Los Angeles freeway. In sum, until June 17, 1994, the public's perception of O. J. Simpson, in addition to appreciation of his substantial athletic talent, was of an easy-going, articulate individual, that is, as normal, if not much more normal, as anyone in the public eye. After that date, information kept accumulating to suggest a very different picture.

He was born on July 9, 1947, and was named Orenthal James Simpson, the name Orenthal coming from an obscure French actor. His early childhood appears to have been relatively unremarkable, although his father had abandoned the family when O. J. was just a toddler. A reaction against his awareness that his father was both gay and dysfunctional may in part explain O. J.'s alleged "macho" patterns. His mother, Eunice, a strong and supportive figure throughout his life, raised O. J. and his three siblings by working as an orderly on a psychiatric ward.

Ironically, the boy who was to grow up to be one of the greatest running backs in football history was called "Pencil Legs" as a child and had to wear leg braces until age 5 because of a diagnosed case of rickets along with a calcium deficiency. He remained pigeon-toed and bowlegged, and his deformed extremities contrasted with his large head, subjugating him to taunts like "Headquarters" and "Waterhead."

However, as O. J. developed into adolescence, he moved from defense to offense. Although he was probably never a hard-core delinquent, he came close. In junior high school he became a bully, and at age 14, he joined a "fighting gang," the Persian Warriors. He received his sexual initiation from the gang's "ladies auxiliary," and also managed to get caught stealing from a local liquor store. The myth is that a talk with baseball legend Willie Mays pushed him back onto a positive path. Reality is that his mother's directing him toward a small Catholic school placed him with a much more positive peer group and also allowed him to attain a more positive identity by demonstrating his emerging athletic skills. He did so, leading the city in scoring his senior year.

Recruiters came flocking. But, contrary to image, O. J. was never overly bright, nor was he a good student, and he didn't have adequate grades for a major college. So he enrolled in the City College of San Francisco. He starred in football and was able to earn grades that were at least adequate (and, in those days, adequate wasn't much) to accept a scholarship at USC. Here he became an All-American, won the Heisman Trophy in 1968, and gained "polish." He learned to dress well, to talk well, and to communicate an amiable and easy-going image. However, he was not a student-scholar and dropped out before earning his degree. But he went on to stardom as a pro and then gradually developed into an American icon, a beloved and almost universally recognized hero.

His private life was less admirable. He was reputed as a chronic womanizer, but he told us that his devout Baptist wife "brings the Lord into our house and helps me when I sway" (and he swayed a lot). Although he stayed married for 11 years to Marguerite, the marriage was marked by several separations and by O. J.'s womanizing. He also reportedly abused Marguerite. He denied this. He was believed.

He reportedly had a drug problem. He clearly did use marijuana. A Buffalo television station reported that the owner of a bar that Simpson frequented stated that O. J. had been snorting coke during his years with the Bills and twice came very close to being busted. But, O. J. was believed to be drug-free—at least by the NFL. He told *Playboy* magazine that he had experimented with drugs (marijuana) only once, as an adolescent, but that he "just pretended to take a hit." Even President Bill Clinton didn't try to say he "only pretended," just that he didn't inhale. Clinton was not believed; O. J. was.

In the most publicized abuse incident, on New Year's Eve of 1989, during his second marriage, a hysterical and severely bruised Nicole came out of the bushes in a bra and underpants to report "He's going to kill me" to the officers responding to a 911 call.

When O. J. came out, he said, "I got two women and I don't want that woman anymore," shouted at the officers, and drove off. But Nicole later refused to testify, and charges were dropped. O. J. told Hertz CEO Frank Olsen (who paid O. J. a great deal as their advertising spokesperson), and the public that it was only an argument and was "no big deal and there was nothing to it." Olsen, Hertz, and the public believed. We all wanted to believe, and our behavior may have been a form of abnormal behavior, as it is certainly maladaptive.

O. J. had met his second wife, Nicole Brown, then 18 years old, in June 1977 at a nightclub where she was waiting tables. This was just before celebrating his tenth wedding anniversary with Marguerite, who was carrying their third child. O. J. and Nicole were quickly involved, but O. J. and Marguerite were not divorced until later, in 1980. The relationship with Nicole was stormy from the beginning, as he was very controlling (and she no doubt contributed in some fashion) and was easily made jealous although he was reportedly already consistently unfaithful to her. When Nicole became pregnant in 1985, they worked out a complex prenuptial agreement and were married. The child was born on October 17, 1985. Nine days before, the police made their first documented response to a distress call at 360 Rockingham. O. J. had knocked the front window out of the car with a baseball bat, and the responding officer found Nicole sitting on the hood of the car. Nothing came of it. During the next 4 years, until the New Year's episode, Nicole made at least eight and perhaps as many as thirty distress calls (it's unclear how many there were because no charges were filed).

After the New Year's episode the marriage went further downhill, marked by drug and alcohol abuse by both and by public and private conflict. The divorce was finalized in October 1992. Nevertheless, O. J. and Nicole periodically reconciled and split up from that time until Nicole was killed late on the night of Sunday, June 12, 1994.

There is evidence that just prior to the killings, O. J. was getting clear messages from Nicole that there was no longer any chance of a reconciliation. Also, at 7:00 A.M., 15 hours before the killings, Paula Barbieri, a model who was dating O. J., left a message on his phone recorder that his relationship with her was also over. Another model, Gretchen Stockdale, testified during the first trial, but outside the jury's presence, that O. J. had left her a phone message about three hours before the slayings, saying he was "finally . . . totally unattached with everybody."

Much of the data would at least suggest that O. J. killed Nicole, along with Ronald Goldman, who was returning a pair of sunglasses she had left at a restaurant. Goldman was also a friend, and possibly a lover.

Standards of Proof

As most readers are aware, Simpson was unanimously found "not guilty" (note that a criminal suspect is never formally found to be "innocent") of the criminal charge of murder and then subsequently was unanimously found legally responsible in the civil trial by a different jury for the deaths of the two victims. Some commentators have argued that race played a factor since the jury in the criminal trial was largely black, while the jury in the civil trial was all white. Although that may be the case, certainly a factor was the different standards of proof required, that is, "beyond a reasonable doubt" for most criminal trials and "preponderance of evidence" for civil trials; most assume this means just over 50%. O. J. Simpson's difficulties in the child custody area highlight the third legal standard of proof, that is, "clear and convincing evidence." This third standard is intended to fall between the other two and thus applies to quasi-criminal procedures, that is, where there is an imposed loss of one's constitutional rights. This standard could only apply to such procedures as the termination of parental rights—upheld in the 1982 Supreme Court case of *Santosky* v. *Kramer* (455 U.S. 745), later dramatized in the movie "Kramer vs. Kramer" starring Dustin Hoffman and Meryl Streep—or in civil commitment cases, where one is placed in a mental hospital after having been found to be both mentally ill and imminently dangerous to self or others.

Diagnoses and Syndromes

Whether he did kill Nicole or not, O. J.'s overall behavior was certainly abnormal at times. Did it warrant a formal *DSM-IV* diagnosis? Both O. J. and Nicole probably suffered from substance abuse and co-dependency. There is evidence that both experienced periods of significant depression and/or anxiety, and that O. J. was evidently suicidal after the incident. In addition to a *DSM-IV* diagnosis, patterns of abnormality, or syndromes (as opposed to *DSM-IV* diagnoses), may apply "the battered spouse syndrome," "co-dependency." A *DSM-IV* diagnosis is generally accepted as having more credibility and validity than a syndrome.

Many such syndromes have appeared (or been publicized) in recent years. Some, such as the battered spouse syndrome (BSS) have at least stood the test of time. Others have surfaced only momentarily, to quickly disappear.

BSS (then the battered *woman* syndrome) defense was first successfully employed in 1977 in *State* v. *Grieg*. The court in Yellowstone County, Montana allowed testimony about the violence a woman had experienced in her marital relationship and how this might have made her psychologically unable to leave her husband. The jury voted to acquit, on self-defense. Since that time the BSS has been used in numerous cases, with varying success. It has often been intermingled with the concept of the *DSM-IV* diagnosis Post-Traumatic Stress Disorder (PTSD)(Melton et al., 1997) (see Chapter 3). The early use of PTSD (a diagnosis, i.e., accepted in the *DSM's*), and to a lesser extent, of BSS (a syndrome) in the legal arena often portrayed the victim client as severely disordered, almost psychotic-like at times, as a result of the trauma. More recently both PTSD and BSS have been portrayed as "normal" or expected responses to a severe trauma (Meyer and Deitsch, 1996).

A syndrome is defined in *Webster's Third International Dictionary* as "(1) a group of symptoms or signs typical of a disease, disturbance, condition or lesion in animal or plants; (2) a set of concurrent things: concurrent." Various other definitions of *syndrome* contain most of the same elements, with the general idea being that a syndrome is a group of behaviors or events that are consistently reported or observed. For the specific issues here, syndromes are reports of observed patterns of behavior that are predictably precipitated by some event.

There are conceptual difficulties with defining behaviors as abnormal in any syndrome. First, there is the clear implication that in some way and/or in some degree, a consequent critical behavior has been compelled. For example, when establishing the BSS in an assault or murder case, the clear purpose is to void some degree or even all of the perpetrator's responsibility for the behavior. The standard argument, at least by implication, is that the establishment of the syndrome's existence de facto mutes or voids responsibility. At the same time, it is evident that (1) only a minuscule percentage of battered spouses ever criminally assault or murder their abusers, (2) there is no clear variable or set of variables that differentiates those who do from those who don't, and (3) if there is a valid case for the behavior as self-protection, the availability of the more legally acceptable self-defense claim negates the need for the establishment of a syndrome.

To highlight the positives and problems of syndromes as a quasi-diagnosis, I have presented on several occasions (Meyer and Deitsch, 1996) for consideration the issue of the possible validity of the "estranged spouse syndrome." One of the clearest and best-known examples that appears to demonstrate this syndrome is O. J. Simpson, as all of the essentials of the syndrome are seemingly found in his case: (1) one spouse (A = O. J.) is evidently still in love with or emotionally dependent upon the other (B = Nicole); (2) B is disengaging from A, but because of ambivalence, concern for A's feelings, fear of A and so on; B provides mixed messages; (3) some event or series of events transforms A's intellectual understanding that there is a disengagement into an emotional or "gut-level" awareness that it is "over"; (4) A becomes severely emotionally disrupted by a sense of loss, often confounded by feelings of shame, humiliation, betrayal, jealousy, and so on; (5) depression, anxiety, and anger grow in A in a variable admixture; (6) in some cases, personality predispositions of A (and often to some degree in B as well) combine with a catalytic event, such as seeing B with a new lover or losing another important relationship (possibly facilitated by easy access to means and the use of disinhibiting substances), causing emotional arousal and disruption to peak, and very likely to spill into anger and on occasion into homicidal and/or suicidal ideation and behavior.

The point is that one can argue that the ESS, and for that matter, a number of other patterns of behavior, show the consistency required of a syndrome. I also believe one could establish that the ESS shows a consistency that is at least equal to that of the BSS (Meyer and Deitsch, 1996). The dilemma then is whether or not "consistency" of behavior should allow an inference that the behavior was to some degree "compelled," and in turn, to allow a perpetrator to argue less or even an absence of responsibility for a related act. Legal cases have generally accepted this "compulsion based on consistency" in clear cases of BSS, but not often in most other syndromes. The dilemma is confounded by the fact that there is little truly scientific data to allow definitive conclusions; thus, political issues may dominate. (See the discussion, later in this chapter, on the admission of scientific evidence into the legal arena.)

Perceptions of Abnormality

It is interesting that our sociopolitical assumptions are often critical to a judgment of abnormality. In earlier times, certain similar behaviors in a person of prestige might be termed "romantic" rather than abnormal. For example, although the renowned music composer Hector Berlioz composed his *Symphonie Fantastique* out of his love for the Irish actress Harriet Smithson, he had not succeeded in meeting her by the time that work was introduced in December 1830. He became engaged to a 19-year-old pianist, Camille Marie Moke, just before he left for Italy as a Prix de Rome fellow early in 1831. In April he received an unpleasant letter from his fiancee's mother, announcing Camille Marie's marriage to another man. Berlioz wrote in his memoirs that he was so outraged that he determined to return in disguise and kill them all: "As for subsequently killing myself, after a coup on this scale it was of course the very least I could do." People saw this as a demonstration of Berlioz's romanticism rather than abnormality, in part because of the attitudes of the time and also because he didn't ever actually do it. In fact he eventually married Harriet. Truly, there are times when a judgment as to deviance is "in the eye of the beholder."

Guidelines for Judging Abnormality

Applied Psychology will ... become an independent experimental science which stands related to the ordinary experimental psychology as engineering to physics. Politicians, military officers, and even clergymen have awakened to the utility of psychology; the lawyer alone is obdurate. . . . The lawyer and the judge and the juryman are sure that they do not need the experimental psychologist. They go on thinking that their legal instinct and their common sense supplies them with all that is needed.

—Hugo Munsterberg, *On the Witness Stand* (1908)

General guidelines have evolved throughout history, modern research studies, and across most cultures that are consistently relevant to a judgment of abnormality. These criteria can be summarized as follows:

- Some recurring behaviors that seem indicative of potential, developing, or existent mental disorder are: (1) inability to inhibit self-destructive behaviors, (2) seeing or hearing things that others in the culture agree are not there, (3) sporadic and/or random outbursts of violence, (4) consistent inability to relate interpersonally in an effective manner, (5) persistent academic and/or vocational failure, (6) anxiety and/or depression, and (7) inability to conform to codes of behavior whether one verbalizes a desire to do so or not.

- The most consistent criteria for deciding whether or not any specific individual is abnormal are: (1) the deviance (or bizarreness) of behavior from the norms of that society, (2) the continuity and/or persistence of disordered behavior over time, and (3) the resulting degree of disruption in intrapersonal and/or interpersonal functioning.

- The continuum of behavior ranges from clearly normal adjustment to definitely abnormal adjustment. Many people's behavior belongs in that middle area where judgments about abnormality are difficult.

- The causes of any one abnormal behavior pattern are usually multiple. A specific abnormal behavior pattern is seldom inherited genetically, but genetic factors may play a part in predisposing a person to abnormality of one sort or another. Indicators of abnormality are not necessarily obvious or flagrant. In many cases the signs are uncommon and/or subtle. Both long-term and transient social value systems affect judgments as to whether or not a person is abnormal.

- A psychological handicap often has a more negative effect on interpersonal relationships than does a physical handicap. The label of psychological abnormality often remains with a person even after the disorder no longer exists. Such a label, which shapes people's expectations and responses, may prolong the psychological disorder.

- In most societies there is a substantial overlap between judgments of mental abnormality and criminal behavior; that is, the same specific behavior may receive either label, depending on who is doing the labeling.

The Scientific Method

I am starved for love and I almost believe wicked science is guilty.

—Letters of Albert Einstein

A prominent change relevant to mental health that has evolved especially in modern times is the recognition of the need for scientifically valid information. As Table 1–1 shows, all research methods can be useful. For an excellent example of how a natural event observation can be scientifically valid, see the section on etiology in Alzheimer's Disease in Chapter 15. In most instances, the idea, or model or paradigm, must eventually be validated through a well-designed experiment.

The evolution of scientific knowledge is within the following sequence: (a) general ideas and insights; (b) observations, often in clinical cases; (c) initial theories; (d) hypotheses; (e) operational definitions; (f) experiments; (g) new theories and models or paradigms; (h) new hypotheses; (i) further experiments; and (j) new models or paradigms, and revised theories.

A theory is a statement about the probable relationship among a set of variables. It organizes existing knowledge of a phenomenon, provides a tentative explanation for the phenomenon, and generates predictions (hypotheses) about the phenomenon. A hypothesis is a prediction of some relationship between variables, or of an experimental result. After data has been collected, a theory may be arrived at inductively. Induction/Inference is the process of drawing a general conclusion from a set of specific instances or statements, that is, the process of using events or statements to draw a conclusion that is *probably* true.

TABLE 1–1 Positive and Negative Aspects of Research Methods

Method	Positive Aspects	Negative Aspects
Case Study	a. Generates new theories b. Records rare situation c. Inexpensive and easy to carry out	a. Highly subject to selective and observer bias b. Can't generalize the results c. Can't determine any true cause
Natural Event Observation	a. Allows study of major event and over-all cause b. Is not artificial	a. May introduce observer bias and/or disturb a natural event b. Can't repeat the event; difficult to generalize any results
Correlational Design	a. Allows quantification and replication b. Need not be artificial, although often is	a. Cannot define the specific cause
Experiment	a. May control, insulate, and define specific causes b. Allows manipulation of variables, repetition, and generalization	a. May become overcontrolled or too focused, thus becoming artificial and missing the reality of the issue b. The control that is available is subject to unethical methods and abuse of subject rights
Model or Paradigm	a. Provides new insights and hypotheses and coherence between specific issues	a. Attachment to model may blind one to data that are contradictory

After a theory has been constructed, hypotheses are arrived at deductively. Deduction is the process of drawing specific conclusions for a general statement, that is, the process of using events or statements to draw a conclusion that must be true. In deduction, if the premises are true the conclusion must be true; if the conclusion is false, then at least one premise is not true; if the conclusion is true, the premises *might* be true. Hypotheses may be tested with research. If the hypotheses are not borne out, the theory has been deductively *falsified* (the theory, as it is, cannot be true). If the hypotheses are borne out, the theory has been inductively supported (the theory is consistent with the new data, but some other theory may also predict the same results). Logically, a theory can be falsified, or proven wrong, but can never actually be truly and definitively confirmed. In summary, a good theory . . . (1) accounts for most or all available data; (2) predicts new findings; (3) is subject to testing and falsification; and (4) is *parsimonious,* that is, it should be as simple as possible.

Issues about the validity of various research studies are common in most fields, certainly including psychology. The following suggest ways one might go about obtaining more valid research.

Replication—A major fault in many fields is the acceptance of findings from unreplicated studies (or worse, only from clinical case observation), especially when the original finding was obtained by someone with a vested interest in that finding and/or a related theory. Science makes much of its progress in a plodding fashion, not just by dazzling insights and innovative research.

The Use of Adequate Control Groups—Indeed, some research has only an assumed control group. Often, more than one type of control group is needed, but is often not included.

Adequate Sample Size—If sample size is not adequate, a few extreme responses can distort the data so as to make it appear there is a group effect of some significance, even if most of the group changed only minimally.

Representative Samples—Using Psychology 101 students is defensible in many states of research. However, samples that represent society as a whole need to be considered before any significant generalizations can be attempted.

The Confusion of Type I and Type II Errors—If they are confusing to you, you may feel like the old sea captain who, on each and every morning out at sea would arise, have a cup of coffee, open a small drawer in his desk to which only he had a key, peruse a piece of paper, and then take the helm. This went on for over 40 years. Then, one day, he gracefully died at the wheel. The other ship's officers rushed to his room and forced open the drawer only to find a piece of paper on which it was written "starboard is to the right, port to the left." In any case, a Type I error, or false positive, tells you that something, such as a treatment technique, works when it doesn't. A Type II error, a false negative, says a procedure doesn't work when it actually does.

"Blind" Participants—One of the biggest problems in psychological research is the relative lack of experimenters who are blind to the purpose of the study. This lack may be acceptable at the initial stages of a research program, but it should be controlled for in later stages. To the degree feasible, and within the constraints of reasonable informed consent, subject should also be blind to the purpose of the study.

Dualistic Thinking—It is always tempting to simplify things by separating mind and body, psychology and biology. The Law of Parsimony does tell us that if two hypotheses are equally powerful in explaining data, we should prefer the simpler hypothesis. But many times, not only in science, but in areas such as courtroom trials, we accept the less explanatory but simpler physiological reasoning. An excellent example of a study demonstrating mind-body interdependence is that of Schwartz, et al., (1996) as discussed in the case of Bess in Chapter 3.

Reasonable Levels of Significance—The traditionally accepted .01 and .05 levels of significance were not set in stone by some god of research, but are accepted as a result of consensus decision rules. As such, they may not always work well. For example, in an exploratory study using a small N, reaching a significance level of only .15 may be valuable, as it can be used to refine the research to a point where a higher significance level may be appropriate.

Clinical Versus Statistical Significance—While empirically validated findings are much more valuable than clinical case-generated findings, the difference between "statistical" significance and "clinical" significance is sometimes overlooked. For example, a relaxation technique may produce an average decrease of two points of blood pressure, hardly of clinical significance. But, if sample size is huge, this will attain "statistical" significance, and may confer some undeserved validity on the relaxation technique.

Research and the Courts

A critical societal issue is how the findings of science are brought to bear on issues in the courtroom, such as the acceptance of DNA evidence, or the rejection by most courts of the results of polygraph tests. The standard that has dominated this issue is the "Frye Rule," established by a Federal Appeals court in 1923, which says that evidence is admissible if the science supporting it "is sufficiently established to have gained general acceptance in the particular field to which it belongs."

In 1993, in *Daubert* v. *Merrill Dow Pharmaceuticals* (113 S.Ct. 2786), the Supreme Court established a new, less stringent standard, verbalized as a "help-fulness standard," under which the decision rule is whether the information is viewed by the judge as helpful to the trier of fact. This standard is mandatory in Federal courts. Although it has been adopted by some state courts, states may retain the more restrictive "scientific acceptance" standard. The more restrictive standard does help juries avoid having to cope with the questionable value of "fad" or "junk science" findings.

2

Theories and Techniques

There are today a diversity of approaches to the assessment and treatment of mental disorders. As will be evident in the second case in this section (Roger, an exhibitionist), many of these treatment techniques can be blended into multimodal individualized intervention programs. However, in the first case, that of Danielle, we will begin by discussing the particulars of her case history and then examine how the major theories of mental disorders would explain how these problem patterns came about and what each would propose as the primary treatment plan.

Multiple Theoretical Views on Moderate Anxiety, Depression, and Simple Phobias

The Case of Danielle

Complaining that he suffered from acrophobia, which is the abnormal fear of heights, the athlete said, "I went to Paris and visited the Eiffel Tower last year. I started going up and then I quit. I couldn't stand the height."

The athlete was Billy Olson, who had just set a world indoor pole vault record of 19 feet 5-1/2 inches.

—Sarasota Herald Tribune, Feb. 11, 1996

The case of Danielle is concerned with a most common pattern, one that includes some simple phobias as well as persistent although not constant moderate anxiety and depression. Many people at one time or another suffer from similar disorders. However, many do not seek professional treatment, for a variety of reasons ("It costs too much to see a shrink"; "I don't think they could help me"; "That kind of stuff is only for people who are really crazy"; "Nobody in my family has ever gone to a psychologist so I just couldn't go to one"; etc.). Such attitudes are especially unfortunate here, as the prognosis for controlling problems such as Danielle's is good.

After the presentation of Danielle's case history, we will consider how the major theories (psychoanalytical-psychodynamic, behavioral, cognitive, information processing systems, humanistic-existential, and biological) would approach the etiology and treatment of her disorder.

The Case of Danielle

Danielle, who has just turned 26, presented herself to a university-based psychology clinic with complaints of problems with her work and marriage, as well as just being generally unhappy.

A structured interview and several psychological tests were administered. What emerged was a picture of a young woman who had suffered from a variety of phobias as well as varying degrees of depression and anxiety throughout most of her life. Yet, from most perspectives, she has usually functioned within the normal range on most dimensions. She had a normal childhood, and both Danielle and her parents would have characterized her as reasonably well adjusted and happy. Her grades were above average throughout grade school and high school, and although Danielle struggled academically in college, she did manage to graduate with a business degree, with a major in marketing. She started to work on her MBA but felt "just burnt out" with school. So she quit to take a lower-echelon job in the marketing department of a large firm in a major city about 300 miles from the area where she grew up and went to college.

She was introduced to her future husband shortly after moving to that city and they were married after a brief but intense courtship of 4 months. This intensity waned almost immediately after the marriage ceremony, and they settled into a routine marked neither by contentment nor by obvious problems. They seldom fought openly, but they developed increasingly "parallel lives," wherein interactions (including sexual ones) were pleasant but minimal.

Embedded in this overall life structure were the difficulties that had moved Danielle to come to the clinic. Ever since she had been little, Danielle had been afraid of snakes and insects, especially spiders, and from her high school years onward she became anxious if closed in for any length of time in a small room (claustrophobia). She also reported that she occasionally experienced periods during which she would feel anxious for no reason that she could put her finger on ("free-floating anxiety") and then, more rarely, would become depressed. Once, when in college, the depression became severe enough that she considered suicide. Fortunately her roommate was sensitive to the crisis. She made sure Danielle went over to the campus counseling center, and Danielle's upset diminished quickly enough for her to quit therapy after three sessions.

More recently, Danielle had experienced the episodes of anxiety and depression more consistently, and it was clear that her husband didn't have much interest in hearing about this. Also, she still had the phobias. She could live with the fears of the snakes and spiders, although they substantially reduced her ability to enjoy outdoor activities. But the claustrophobia had worsened, making some of the meetings required by her job very difficult for her.

Danielle's history was not grossly abnormal in any dimension, but there were aspects that could be related to her developing problems. Although Danielle's birth was normal, she was noted to be a "fussy" child who seemed to startle more easily than did her two younger brothers. Also, her mother was a rather anxious person and on a few occasions had taken to her bed, obviously somewhat depressed, blaming it on "female problems." Both parents obviously loved and cared for all the children, but Danielle's father was not one to show affection often. He demanded good performance, in both the academic and social areas, and a lack of performance usually meant some form of direct punishment as well as emotional distance from him.

Case Analysis

We'll now turn to an analysis of this case from the perspective of each of the major theories, and some other details that emerged in Danielle's case will be discussed as appropriate. The discussion of each of these theoretical perspectives on etiology and treatment will not be presented in great detail. Also, the most commonly accepted theories and treatments for anxiety and depression will be discussed again in the later sections of this book that focus on those problems.

The Psychoanalytic-Psychodynamic Perspective. Psychoanalysis is the approach originally devised by Sigmund Freud and elaborated by his early and more orthodox followers. As changes in theory or technique were introduced by persons who still followed the essential points of Freudian theory, these splinter schools (developed first by individuals such as Adler and Jung and later by Klein, Horney, and Sullivan and more recently by Kernberg, Gill, Bion, Ricoeur, Arieti, Silverman, Shafer, Kohut, Mahler, and others) were usually termed psychodynamic (Wachtel, 1997; Schwartz et al., 1996).

However, virtually all of those theorists would see Danielle's problems as developing out of an inadequate resolution of conflicts that could have developed in one of the hypothesized stages of development that each person, as represented through the "ego," must proceed through to reach maturity (the oral, anal, phallic, latency, and genital stages). Conflicts in the Oedipal phase (a prelude to the genital stage), interpreted as the male child's desire to sexually possess the mother and get rid of the father (the Electra phase is analogous in the female) are seen as crucial to a number of patterns. (See the discussion in Chapter 3 of Little Hans.) Underlying tension leaves the person anxious without an explanation for this feeling (Fenichel, 1945)—the free-floating anxiety experienced by Danielle.

As regards depression, Karl Abraham's early classic papers (Abraham, 1916) provided the basis for the orthodox psychoanalytic view. He theorized that depressed individuals, unable to love, project their frustrated hostility onto others and believe themselves to be hated and rejected by other people. Abraham related depression to orality and explained loss of appetite and related symptoms in terms of an unconscious desire to devour the introjected love-object. Thus, introjection (rather than the projection that psychoanalysts see as central to the paranoid process) is the psychopathological process, and the depressive's self-reproach can therefore be seen as an attempt to punish those newly incorporated components of the self.

Silvano Arieti and Jules Bemporad (1978) later presented a version of the traditional psychodynamic position. They view the depressed person as one who has suffered some great loss in childhood, for example, a first child who experienced "paradise lost" when a new sibling near in age grabbed the heretofore undivided attention of the mother—a situation that, it turns out, occurred with Danielle. Other such losses could include early parental death (although this does not always produce depression) or abandonment or an abrupt parental decision to prohibit any type of childish behavior and to insist that the child now act "grown up."

Arieti and Bemporad believe that the depressive persistently strives to regain what has been lost by trying to please others, particularly "dominant others." Not surprisingly, the self-generated expectancies often exceed capabilities; thus failure follows, while self-blame increases and self-esteem lessens.

Psychoanalytic treatment involves techniques like (1)"free association" (having the person say whatever comes to mind, without censoring it—a more difficult task than it may initially appear); (2) the analysis of dreams; (3) analysis of the feelings the client develops toward the therapist (transference); and (4) attempts to develop insight into the sources of the anxiety and depression. Orthodox analytic treatment, which is practiced by few therapists today, would have the analyst sitting behind the client who is on a couch, seldom confronting or responding to the client at any length. To the degree the therapy is less orthodox, and thus more likely to be termed psychodynamic, the therapist is more likely to face the client, confront issues more directly, and in general interact more. The insights that are attained, along with the accompanying release of emotion (catharsis), theoretically act to decrease the anxiety and depression and thus allow the development of more mature and effective coping patterns.

A unique psychodynamic therapy has been put forward by Lloyd Silverman and Joel Weinberger (1985). Based on the psychoanalytic thesis that there are powerful unconscious wishes for a state of symbiotic oneness with the "good mother of early childhood," the concept is that gratification of such desires enhances positive psychological functioning (and those who are anxious and depressed are especially needy in this regard). The major support for this thesis comes from experiments in various laboratories employing the subliminal psychodynamic activation method with over forty groups of subjects from varied populations. These studies have reported that 4-millisecond exposures (a speed that does not allow conscious visual recognition of the stimulus, that is, subliminal) of stimuli intended to activate these unconscious symbiotic-like fantasies (usually the phrase "Mommy and I are one") do produce a positive effect on psychological functioning. Some variation of this technique could have been used as one part of a treatment plan for Danielle.

The Behavioral Perspective.   Early efforts by behaviorists to explain the development of anxiety and phobias were essentially efforts to translate psychoanalytic thought into the language of learning theory. However, beginning with John Watson and Mary Cover Jones (see the discussions of Little Albert and Little

Peter in Chapter 3), early practitioners such as Joseph Wolpe and Arnold Lazarus, and later theorists such as Clark Hull and B. F. Skinner, the explanation of the development of anxiety and phobias was in terms of conditioning principles (Maultsby, 1998). Thus, anxiety is a learned response that now is unpleasant but which was appropriate at the time of learning. However, the avoidance inherent in the response prevents the corrective learning of newer, more adaptive responses.

The two major ways in which the anxiety responses and phobic patterns are learned are *modeling* and *direct experience learning,* which are then amplified by mental and behavioral rehearsal. An examination of Danielle's history revealed that modeling played a significant role in the development of her anxiety and phobic responses in response to snakes and insects. As is the case with most people who have such fears, there was no actual, naive traumatic encounter with one of these creatures. Rather, Danielle's mother, as well as her aunt who often babysat her, would shriek with horror at the sight of a spider, or at even the suggestion that a snake might be in the vicinity. Danielle at some level of consciousness assumed that if these gigantic and all-powerful adults (from the perspective of a small child) were so afraid of these creatures, she ought to be too. Her responses copied from her models were accepted and reinforced by those around her. Note that the differential stereotypical reaction to such responses in boys may explain why such patterns are not so usually evident in males. Also, boys are more likely to be encouraged to have actual encounters with these potential phobia sources. In any case, while modeling can often be an efficient way of learning, as it does save the time and possible pain of trial-and-error learning, sometimes, as with Danielle, modeled patterns may promote maladaptive behavior.

The simple phobias, of which Danielle's fears of snakes and spiders are good examples, often have simple and specific targets. Some of these fears probably had an evolutionary value for the human species (e.g., avoidance of poisonous snakes, etc.), and some theorists believe this is evidence that there is a greater *preparedness* to associate anxiety responses to these stimuli, and this contributes along with the modeling to the overall learning process here.

On the other hand, direct experience learning was critical to the origin of Danielle's claustrophobic pattern. When she was young, punishments were spanking, being made to stand in the corner, or a withdrawal of reinforcers (staying up, TV, etc.). However, if she really upset her mother, Danielle would be forced to stay in a small, dark closet until she was quiet and her mother felt calmed down. On a couple of occasions this took several hours. The anxiety and discomfort of the situation, compounded by Danielle's fear of the dark and sense of uncertainty about what was going to happen to her, produced a panic response. Panic includes a sense of loss of control, the most anxiety-generating experience of all. Direct experience learning is a potent factor in the development of many phobias.

Regarding depression, the general theories of the early behaviorists were first refined into an overall theory by Ferster in 1965; the general concept is that depression can result from either of two processes (Ferster and Culbertson,

1982), which do not necessarily exclude parallel biological issues. In the first, an environmental change (e.g., loss of job, death in the family) sharply lessens the level of incoming reinforcement, and no new methods of obtaining reinforcement have developed. Danielle's college depression immediately followed a breakup with her boyfriend. They had always spent a great deal of time together, so this abrupt loss of reinforcement precipitated the depression in that instance.

Behaviorists also note that depression can occur from a pattern of avoidance behavior. This is when a person's attempts to avoid aversive situations have become so strong that they preclude behaviors that bring reinforcement; that is, these behaviors are used to avoid anxiety.

From a treatment perspective, behavior therapists have pioneered some of the most successful treatments for phobias and anxiety, even using such approaches as group therapy (Chambless, et al., 1996). The most commonly used technique, however, has been exposure therapy, especially in the specific form of systematic desensitization therapy (SDT). Typically, the therapist first develops a relaxation response, sometimes through drugs but more commonly and controllably through some form of relaxation training. A hierarchy of anxiety-producing stimuli is then presented (Wolpe, 1973), and may be enhanced by virtual reality techniques. For Danielle, the hierarchy involved closed spaces, snakes, and spiders.

In each case, Danielle would be asked to describe the most anxiety-arousing situation she could think of. That scene (e.g., "snakes crawling over my body") would receive a score of 100. A scene that brings on little or no anxiety ("hearing my professor mention snakes") would receive a 0. While remaining relaxed, the client is gradually moved through each hierarchy in imagination, or "in vitro," and then some live tasks ("in vivo") may be introduced (e.g., asking Danielle to handle a snake or sit for a period of time in a small closed room).

An alternative behavioral technique for treating phobias or anxiety is flooding, or implosion therapy, which attempts to maximize anxiety, rather than minimize it as is done in SDT. Usually carried out in a few longer-than-usual sessions, the technique asks the person to image more and more anxiety-producing scenes (e.g., snakes crawling in and out of body orifices). Virtual reality procedures are used to enhance this method. The theory is that the anxiety will eventually peak and then extinguish, with the consequence that the phobia gradually lessens.

As for Danielle's depression, behavior therapists would emphasize getting her in touch with more interpersonal contacts and sources of positive reinforcement. This could mean returning to active sports and learning social skills so that she could have more rewarding interpersonal interactions. Because depressives tend to be overwhelmed by tasks, breaking a goal down into subtasks and short-term goals, the "graded-task" approach, is useful.

Also, behavior therapists would help Danielle survey her present range of activities. Depression tends to simultaneously lessen activity in general and increase the percentage of nonpleasurable activities. Contracting, modeling, and stimulus-control techniques could help to reverse this process.

Morita therapy, developed by a Japanese professor named Morita, is an approach that combines both behavioral and cognitive elements, as is evident in these two quotes from David Reynolds (1984), one of the foremost interpreters of Eastern psychotherapy techniques to Western cultures.

> Behavior wags the tail of feelings. Behavior can be used sensibly to produce an indirect influence on feelings. Sitting in your bathrobe doesn't often stimulate the desire to play tennis. Putting on tennis shoes and going to the courts, racket in hand, might. (p. 100)

> Awareness, awareness, awareness. That is where we live. That is all we know. That is life for each of us. (p. 4)

A Morita therapist would attempt to bring a regular routine into Danielle's life; would de-emphasize talking about the historical antecedents to her problems; would emphasize the growth possibilities in all experiences, including pain and failure; would try to get her to begin to function "as if" she was psychologically healthy and competent; and would emphasize bringing both attention and awareness into all facets of her day-to-day functioning.

The Cognitive Perspective.   Since cognition refers to a person's thinking pattern, any theorists who talk about disordered thinking patterns as critical to the development of psychopathology can be considered to be cognitive theorists. In that general sense, psychoanalytic and psychodynamic theorists also have a cognitive perspective (Wachtel, 1997).

However, a more focused emphasis on cognition as central to the development of anxiety is found in the pioneering works of people like Albert Ellis and George Kelly and later therapists like Donald Meichenbaum. Kelly's theory of "personal constructs" notes that people develop certain beliefs, of which they may be consciously unaware, that cause them anxiety. Cognitive-behavior therapists such as Ellis similarly comment on how we adopt belief-rules like "I must reach a high point of success in whatever I undertake"; "If I ever show aggression or upset to those people close to me, they won't love me." Not surprisingly, no one can ever fully live up to such standards, and anxiety and depression quite naturally ensue.

Aaron Beck focused on the development of depression from cognitive beliefs, and the theory evolved from an initial study (Beck and Valin, 1953) that indicated that themes of self-punishment occurred with great frequency in the delusions of psychotically depressed clients. Beck would not disagree with the psychodynamic theorists that an early traumatizing event could predispose an individual to depression. However, the major focus is on distorted thought patterns. Beck and others note that depressives have developed thought processes that simultaneously (1) *minimize* any positive achievements; (2) *magnify* problems with "catastrophic expectations," that is, "making mountains out of molehills"; and (3) also tend to view issues in extremes, that is, to *polarize* their ideas, seeing only in black or white, no greys; as well as (4) *overgeneralizing* to a conclusion based on little data, for example, one or two events. These tendencies are often compounded by a sense of "learned helplessness," a view that one cannot do anything to really control or change one's world. Low self-esteem, lessened activity, negative mood, and self-punitiveness follow (Alford and Beck, 1997; Beck and Valin, 1953; Barrett and Meyer, 1992).

As for intervention, Albert Ellis (1983) who was functioning as a cognitive-behavior therapist before anyone even used that term, would directly challenge his client's irrational beliefs. For example, Danielle believed that she could never again be happy, and that if she were to leave the marriage, no one would ever find her attractive again. He would directly confront these beliefs, exploring what the implications and consequences would be if indeed these irrational hypotheses were true. This is then followed by challenges to act in accord with the more rational beliefs that the client has now labeled as more likely to happen.

Beck also tries to help clients bring their beliefs and expectations into consciousness and/or clearer focus, although he is a bit less confrontational than Ellis in this process. He then helps them explore new beliefs. Donald Meichenbaum (1986) goes a step further by first helping clients eliminate negative subvocal verbalizations such as, "When things in my life do not go the way I want them to, it is bad or terrible." He then helps the clients develop alternative sets of positive self-statement, "When things don't go my way, it may be unpleasant, but it's not the end of the world. Sometimes things do go my way; sometimes they don't," to consciously and periodically repeat to themselves. Such therapists readily agree with the clients' protests that they won't believe what they are saying. However, if they persist, the repetition of positive self-statements does have an effect. Helping clients engage in positive imaging of successful and competent behaviors, possibly through hypnosis, can help here as well.

Information Processing and Systems Theory. Modern variations of the cognitive approach, pioneered by people like Noam Chomsky, Walter Mischel, George Kelly, and James Grier Miller, are information-processing modeling, sociocultural, and systems theory, and they often overlap. They are obviously influenced by evolving concepts from computer science and from interdisciplinary studies, and they share a belief in two seemingly paradoxical concepts: (1) Emotional disorder is a universal human experience, even in many of its specific manifestations; and (2) the pattern and experience of emotional disorder can be strongly influenced by the amount and types of information that are obtained from the persons, families, and society around that individual, while the diagnosis and treatment are likewise affected by that information. Consider this example described by Walter Mischel (1986):

> A boy drops his mother's favorite vase. What does it mean? The event is simply that the vase has been broken. Yet ask the child's psychoanalyst and he may point to the boy's unconscious hostility. Ask the mother and she tells you how "mean" he is. His father says he is "spoiled." The child's teacher may see the event as evidence of the child's "laziness" and chronic "clumsiness." Grandmother calls it just an "accident." And the child himself may construe the event as reflecting his "stupidity." (pp. 207–208)

Information theorists use the terms of computer science, for example, "*hard-wired* for sex," (it's built in genetically) or "brain software" (information provided from the outside that is developed into what George Kelly referred to as a "personal construct," a personal myth about life, such as "Your family are the only people that you can really trust").

Psychological disorders are discussed as disorders of input (e.g., faulty perception), storage (e.g., amnesia from brain trauma), retrieval (e.g., selective recall as in paranoia), manipulation of information (e.g., via defense mechanisms), or output (e.g., the "flight of ideas" in mania). There is also a focus on how individuals encode information. For example, aggressive young males as well as those who watch a large amount of violent programming on television (and these groups do overlap somewhat) are more likely to encode neutral behaviors of others as threatening. Similarly, when males receive messages from their environment, like "When women say 'no' and they don't appear very angry, they really mean 'yes,'" they may be more likely to misinterpret signals or statements from women they are interested in, a fertile situation for date rape.

Sociocultural theorists like Thomas Szasz, who pioneered the concept of the "myth of mental illness," and R. D. Laing take the theory of input disorder a step further to propose that the cause of abnormal behavior is to be found in society rather than in the individual who manifests a disorder. They look to the conflict and stress engendered by social problems, for example, poverty, discrimination, social isolation, or the messages embedded in a society's overall structure, as the explanation for psychological disorder. For example, Laing often speaks of "unjust societies" as creating psychological disorder in the oppressed. The weakness of the sociocultural perspective has always been trying to explain why certain individuals in the same conditions are affected with manifest disorder, while others are not.

The Humanistic-Existential Perspective. From a humanistic viewpoint, anxiety and depression are a result of cultural and social structures that impede the full expression of the personality (May, 1980; Maslow, 1954; Rogers, 1961). The psychodynamicist sees these emotions as determined early in development and maintained by defense mechanisms. The behavioral therapist argues that they are a function of experience with a variety of conditions that result in patterns being learned, unlearned, and relearned throughout life. However, the humanist sees anxiety and depression as inevitable as long as societies thwart a person's goodness and inborn drive for self-actualization. Anxiety and depression are therefore functions of the society and will continue until the right kind of social atmosphere is made available.

Two conditions often implicated by the humanists are a repressive society and/or poverty. Poverty obviously limits the options a person can take, not only in development of the self, but also in remedying disorder and deficit. Within a repressive society, fear of self-expression forces the individual to adopt constricted or disordered response patterns, with anxiety or depression as a common response.

Because of the limitations and constraints of society, the pure humanist does not focus much on the concerns of an individual client. The humanist would contend that because the individual is forced to sacrifice to social demands that are inconsistent and arbitrary, the defense strategies that he or she adopts reflect the irrational nature of the society. Anxiety and depression may therefore be a prerequisite for existence in a chaotic world (May, 1981).

Humanists feel their energy is thus better directed at righting the original causes. Indeed, Carl Rogers, the founder of nondirective, or client-centered, therapy, virtually ceased doing any individual therapy in favor of working with whole subgroups from the perspective of a humanistic educator and social engineer. Directly attacking conditions generated by poverty would not be relevant with Danielle, although it might be with some other cases in this book (e.g., see the case of Abby in Chapter 13 on family violence and child abuse). It is true that some aspects of Danielle's problem might be relevant to change by humanistic social engineering, but it's unlikely there would be enough benefits to directly help her in any immediate sense.

Some parts of the community psychology movement are quite consistent with the humanistic approach. The idea here is that a change in social conditions, through educational efforts or a redirection of social variables, will change the level of disorder (or more likely, act to prevent emergence of that disorder in persons vulnerable to it in the future).

Existential psychotherapists like Viktor Frankl and Medard Boss are more concerned about the individual "choices" of the client. Like cognitive therapists, they would directly confront the distorted beliefs of the client, probably placing more emphasis on the absurdity or paradoxes inherent in the particular individual's conditions in the world (Frankl, 1975). At the same time, they might well change the focus of the problem from the original causal conditions, be they social forces, biological disorder, early environment, or whatever, toward the choices the individual has to make in the here and now (Boss, 1963). This focus on the present is also a constant theme in Gestalt therapy, which has strong existential and cognitive components (Bongar and Beutler, 1995).

While existential theories are most closely associated with European philosophy and psychology, it is not unknown in other cultural traditions. For example, the Akan people of Ghana believe that all people are endowed with the capacity for correct thought and correct action, and emphasize that each individual is ultimately responsible for his or her own life situation, a central tenet of existentialism. A technique termed Sunsum, or NTU, is a primary principle of the Bantu people that focuses on personal responsibility, and a related saying, "Mmo'denbo' Bu Musuo Abasa So," translated as "If you try hard, you will always break the back of misfortune" was the central theme of the 1997 International Convention of the Association of Black Psychologists.

With Danielle an existential therapist would likely point out that preoccupation with her anxiety and depression allows her to escape responsibility for making choices in her world. The parallel life that has been established in her marriage could go on indefinitely, as in many "conflict-habituated" marriages.

Making authentic choices can change these and similar patterns. But those choices leave the chooser open to the burden of responsibility for their consequences. An existential therapist would try to get the individual to stop evading any important choices and their consequences (Frankl, 1975).

Existentialists are also likely to have their clients squarely face the responsibility for past choices or, as is often the case, the results of avoiding a choice (Boss, 1963). This commonly entails "guilt," and existentialists emphasize the difference between neurotic guilt and true guilt. Neurotic guilt is the experience of anxiety and depression from situations that the person had no part in bringing about, for example, restrictive early parenting practices. True guilt entails the acceptance of responsibility for conscious choices or a lack of choosing and the willingness to live with a full acceptance and awareness of the consequences that cannot be changed, with efforts now being made to right any negative effects that can be changed. Here anxiety and depression, especially the free-floating anxiety that Danielle occasionally experienced, are seen as possible symptoms of the avoidance of authentic choices and true guilt.

The Biological Perspective. Anxiety and depression from the biological perspective are seen as conditioned by a person's physiology. Also, some physiological conditions may be genetically determined. In Danielle's case there are indicators that she may have had some genetic disposition to developing anxiety responses; she was a "fussy" child, was easily startled, and had an anxious mother.

The fact that Danielle's mother had apparently been depressed would lead to the suggestion that Danielle's occasional depression had a strong genetic component (although of course this would have allowed Danielle to model the behavior as well). The major biological theories of depression are typically a variation on the theme that depression reflects an alteration in the level of brain transmitters (chemicals that facilitate nerve transmission to the brain) such as norepinephrine or serotonin. However, it should be remembered that a variety of external or psychological conditions (e.g., situationally generated stress or anxiety, prolonged inactivity, prolonged low sunlight conditions, or various substances such as caffeine and the "beta-blockers" used to treat high blood pressure and heart pain) can produce physiological changes that in turn generate depression (Nathan et al., 1995). Evidence does show that genetic variables play a part in significant endogenous (internally generated) depression. However, all indications are that the major components of Danielle's depression were exogenous, or reactive to the situational problems in her world.

The biological treatment for anxiety emphasizes chemotherapy with the drugs usually referred to as the "minor tranquilizers," for example, the propanadiols such as meprobamate (Equanil) or the benzodiazepenes such as diazepam (Valium). Psychological techniques, such as relaxation training, can also be effective in reducing even the physiological components of anxiety.

The biological theorist has traditionally used one of two major chemotherapies, the MAO inhibitors and the tricyclics, for any significant depression. Both have significant side effects (MAO inhibitors—toxic cardiovascular and liver reactions, problematic interactions with certain foods; tricyclics—dizziness, heart and gastrointestinal disorders). Both require trial-and-error adjustments (titration) on dosages, and both take from several days up to several weeks to show an effect. Some believe that these drugs deal with differentially generated depressions (i.e., the tricyclics for norepinephrine-based depression, MAO inhibitors when it's serotonin-based). Also, tricyclics seem to work better with depressives who show some delusional characteristics. Other newer drugs, for example, the selective serotonin reuptake inhibitors (SSRI's) such as Prozac offer fewer side effects and different modes of action (see Table 7-1 in Chapter 7). In any case, research indicates that all of these drugs, when they are effective, act almost exclusively to increase the frequency of activity-related behaviors, and they only indirectly and unpredictably change interpersonal and cognitive components (Nathan et al., 1995).

Because not all severe depressions react positively to chemotherapy, and because it is a delayed reaction even when they do, electroconvulsive therapy (ECT) or, less commonly, psychosurgery are sometimes used for depression. These interventions seem to be useful with severe, acute depressions, especially where there is a suicidal component, and the delay in the developing effects of the antidepressants is even more problematical. Even in the relatively small proportion of cases in which ECT and psychosurgery are effective, one needs to balance any gain with the irrevocable nature of this type of intervention and the several potentially severe side effects.

The Multicutural Perspective. Some disorders, for example, schizophrenia, show a remarkable consistency across cultures. In others the content of the pattern is affected by one's culture, for example, the named characters, like Jesus Christ, Allah, in a delusional system (see Chapter 6). It's also true that in some instances, both the pattern and content of a disorder are set by the culture, as in the following table.

Some mental health care (often not enough) is provided in virtually all cultures. For example, in Bregbo, a fishing village near Abidjan, Ivory Coast, in Africa, there is a monument to Albert Atcho, a legendary healer known as the Prophet. With his large starfish-shaped rings, Mr. Atcho, who died in 1990 at the age of 84, is said to have cured thousands of people, sons and daughters of the rich and poor alike, who streamed to his home from far and wide. Although Mr. Atcho's powers were considered by his constituents to be a gift of God, his techniques actually blended a warm and supportive acceptance much like Carl Rogers' "unconditional positive regard," hypnotic-like suggestions, and the facilitation of catharsis and commitment by way of a lengthy confessional process. We'll now consider the various types of mental health providers found in the United States and most Western countries.

The Various Mental Health Professionals

Just as there are various theories and techniques of mental disorders, there are a variety of mental health professionals. This can be confusing to laypersons and even professionals, such as judges. For example, in *Jaffee* v. *Redmond* (116 S.

Culture-Bound Syndromes

Numerous patterns of aberrant behavior and troubling experience are recognized mostly in specific localities or societies, and may not be linked to an official diagnostic category. Here are some of them:

Pattern	Where Recognized	Description
Amok	Malaysia; similiar patterns elsewhere	Brooding followed by a violent outburst; often precipitated by a slight or insult; seems to be prevalent only among men.
***Anorexia Nervosa**	United States and some other Western cultures	The culture-bound aspect is reflected in the disproportionate occurrence in upper-middle and upper-class, white females (Ch. 10).
Ataque de nervios ("attack of nerves")	Latin America and Mediterranean	An episode of uncontrolled shouting, crying, trembling, heat in chest rising to the head, verbal or physical aggression.
Bilis, colera, or muina	Many Latin groups	Rage perceived as disturbing bodily balances, causing nervous tension, headache, trembling, screaming, etc.
Boufee delirante	East Africa and Haiti	Sudden outburst of agitated and aggressive behavior, confusion and mental and physical excitement
Brain fag	West Africa; similar symptoms elsewhere	"Brain tiredness," a mental and physical reaction to the challenges of schooling.
Dhat	India; also in Sri Lanka and China	Severe anxiety and hypochondria associated with discharge of semen and feelings of exhaustion.
Falling out or blacking out	Southern United States and Caribbean	Sudden collapse; eyes remain open but sightless; the victim hears but feels unable to move.
Ghost sickness	American Indian Tribes	Preoccupation with death and the dead, with bad dreams, fainting, appetite loss, fear, hallucinations, etc.
Hwa-byung	Korea	Symptoms attributed to suppression of anger, like insomnia, fatigue, panic, fear of death, depression, indigestion, etc.
Koro	Malayasia; related conditions in East Asia	Sudden intense anxiety that sexual organs will recede into body and cause death; occasional epidemics.
Latah	Malaysia; Indonesia, Japan, Thailand	Hypersensitivity to sudden fright, often with nonsense mimicking of others, trancelike behavior.
Locura	United States and Latin America	Psychosis tied to inherited vulnerability and/or life difficulties; incoherence, agitation, hallucinations, possibly violence.
Mal de ojo ("evil eye")	Mediterranean and elsewhere	Sufferers, mostly children, are believed to be under influence of "evil eye," causing fitful sleep, crying, sickness, fever.
***Multiple Personality Disorder** (MPD)	United States	Though a controversial position, many experts view MPD as a culture-bound phenomenon (see Ch. 4).
Pibloktoq	Arctic and subarctic Eskimo communities	Extreme excitement, physical and verbal violence for up to 30 minutes, then convulsions and short coma.

Culture-Bound Syndromes *Continued*

Pattern	Where Recognized	Description
Qi-gong psychotic reaction	China	A short episode of mental symptoms after engaging in Chinese folk practice of qi-gong, or "excercise of vital energy."
Shen-k'uel or shenkul	Taiwan and China	Marked anxiety or panic symptoms with bodily complaints attributed to life-threatening loss of semen.
Sin-byung	Korea	Syndrome of anxiety and bodily complaints followed by dissociation and possession by ancestral spirits.
Spell	Southern United States	A trance in which individuals communicate with deceased relatives or spirits; not perceived as a medical event.
Susto ("fright" or "soul loss")	Latin groups in United States and Caribbean	Illness tied to a frightening event that makes the soul leave the body, causing unhappiness and sickness.
Taijin kyofusho	Japan	An intense fear that the body, its parts or functions displease, embarrass, or are offensive to others.
Zar	North Africa or Middle East	Belief in possession by a spirit, causing shouting, laughing, head banging, etc.; not considered pathological.

Adapted in part from "Diagnostic and Statistical Manual of Mental Disorders," Fourth Edition (American Psychological Association)

*Included in the official *DSM-IV* system

Ct.; 64 L.W. 4490, June 13, 1996), the Supreme Court created a new "evidentiary privilege" that supported confidentiality for psychotherapy clients. The Court agreed that this should also apply to clinical social workers. They did not support it for other types of social workers, or any type of counselor, citing lack of definition of the speciality and/or weak credentialing–training requirements. In any case, the following is a list of some mental health professionals and their credentials.

Clinical Psychologists	Have a master's degree and a Ph.D. in psychology (or in some cases a Psy.D., which has a lesser emphasis on research training), with specialized training in assessment techniques (including psychodiagnostic tests) and research skills.
Counseling Psychologists	Have a Ph.D. or Psy.D in psychology. Typically work with adjustment problems (e.g., in student health or counseling centers) not involving severe emotional disorder.
Experimental Psychologists	Have a Ph.D. in psychology. Provide much of the basic and applied research data that allow us to progress in the study of human behavior.

Psychiatric Social Workers	Have a master's degree in social work, sometimes a B.A., and very occasionally a Ph.D., with a specialized interest in mental health settings.
Psychiatrists	Have an M.D. with a specialization in emotional disorders, just as other physicians might specialize in pediatrics or family medicine.
Psychoanalysts	Usually have either an M.D. or Ph.D., with a training emphasis in some form of psychoanalytic therapy.
Psychiatric Nurses	Have an R.N., sometimes with an M.A., with specialized training for work with psychiatric patients.
Pastoral Counselors	Have ministerial degree with some additional training in counseling techniques, to help clients whose emotional difficulties center on a religious or spiritual conflict.
Specialty Counselors	The technicians of the mental health field. Often have no higher than a bachelor's degree, and sometimes less than that, but with specific training to assist in the treatment of a specific focus problem, for example, alcohol or drug abuse.

A Multimodal Treatment Program

The Case of Roger, an Exhibitionist

"That's nice" she said. But seeing him struggle she wanted to laugh. What a misshapen and ridiculous thing the penis was! Half of them didn't even work properly and all of them looked pathetic and detachable, like some wrinkled sea creature—like something you'd find goggling at you and swaying in an aquarium. (p. 140)

—Paul Theroux, *Doctor Slaughter* (1984)

This case was treated by E. Mitchell Hendrix, Ph.D., while under the supervision of the author. Dr. Hendrix deserves the majority of credit for his creative and integrative treatment of a difficult problem. This case shows how a variety of different treatment techniques can be blended into a treatment package designed for a specific problem. This is usually referred to as a "multimodal" approach, an approach first formally developed in detail in the writings of Arnold Lazarus (1971).

The Case of Roger

Social History Data

The important features of this particular selection are the treatment issues. However, certain aspects of Roger's earlier development should be mentioned because they are consistent with the observations noted in other exhibitionists.

Like many exhibitionists, Roger did not have a consistent and positive relationship with a father or father-substitute. Roger's father abandoned the family when Roger was about 7 years old. He has only vague memories of his father, none of which are positive. Roger is an only child. Following the abandonment by his father, Roger's mother reacted to the demands of the single parent role by becoming overprotective and dominating. Although she did not directly reinforce any effeminate behavior in Roger, she always emphasized "dangers" in the world and generally made conservative decisions about any potential risks that Roger might encounter. As a result, Roger feared risking, not only in physical activities, but in interpersonal areas as well.

He did have friends as he grew up, some of whom were close to him, although he never effectively interacted with women. He was seduced when he was 12 years old by a 16-year-old cousin. She made Roger disrobe in front of her, played with him until he had an erection, and then masturbated him to orgasm while fondling herself. On later occasions she had Roger attempt penetration, although this never led to a satisfying sexual experience for either of them.

Roger began to date with regularity when he entered his senior year in high school. He had intercourse on two occasions during that year, but neither was particularly satisfying to either himself or his partner. He reported that he got more enjoyment out of masturbating in front of his partner than he did actually having intercourse with her, although he insisted that he wished he enjoyed intercourse more.

He first exhibited himself in his junior year in high school when he encountered two younger girls in a field near his school. He had been urinating and did not see the girls until they were very close. He turned and the girls looked, screamed, and ran away. Roger reports he became terribly aroused, and when he came home that evening, he masturbated several times with the images of exhibiting himself. He tried to repeat the pattern regularly, often using the ploy of pretending to be urinating into bushes at spots where he knew women would pass by. He would now masturbate as soon as the woman had passed by him, and this of course further reinforced the pattern. In one sense, this was a wise choice. The victim was always in the bind of deciding whether or not the exhibitionism had been intentional or accidental, and for that reason there was seldom a report to the police. But Roger is a bright individual, who knew the risks he was taking. When he came very close to being caught, he referred himself to the psychological training clinic at his school.

Treatment

Roger had been sexually exposing himself to females five to seven times weekly for several weeks, and this was the most intense the problem behavior had been in its 7-year history. He estimated his total number of exposures to be between six and seven hundred. Incredibly, he had not been criminally apprehended.

Although aversive conditioning techniques might have been considered appropriate, the therapist felt that a more comprehensive approach was warranted. Further exploratory sessions with the client revealed a history of adequate heterosexual functioning apart from his exhibitionism. Very active sexually since puberty, Roger had had a brief marriage and a series of interpersonally superficial sexual partnerships.

Roger was seen for thirty-two sessions within a 6-month period. The problem was first reconceptualized as an inappropriate response to heterosexual stimuli rather than sexual deviancy. A very goal-directed and hard-driving individual, Roger could trace sources of tension to his busy schedule, his relationship with his current girlfriend, and to his work. He felt that exposing himself and later masturbating provided him momentary release of frustration and "time out" from tension, although guilt feelings typically followed. Hence, the next step involved progressive relaxation training in the office as a self-control technique and a means of interrupting tension-building response sequences.

He was then given cassette tapes of the relaxation instructions and asked to practice frequently on his own, recording the time of relaxation and degree of experienced calmness. Autogenic training was later used as an adjunct. Roger was asked immediately to keep a daily log of his sexual behavior, describing in appropriate detail the precipitating conditions and results of both desirable and undesirable sexual responses. Self-control was emphasized as the rationale for use of relaxation approaches, the home practice, and the record keeping.

Another aspect of treatment involved desensitization to several hierarchies of interactions with females. Key dimensions were imagined females' attractiveness, dress, ages, and interpersonal styles, as well as the extent of imagined interaction. Cognitive restructuring was also employed in an attempt to have the client broaden his range of expected positive outcomes.

In-session work was complemented by in vivo desensitization and practice in interpersonal interactions. On several occasions the therapist accompanied Roger to interaction settings such as the campus snack shop. There they jointly analyzed situations and discussed interactions as the client conversed with other students, particularly females. His perceptions of other persons' styles were examined and alternative perceptions were proposed by both client and therapist. An additional homework assignment asked Roger to monitor the frequency, nature, and degree of satisfaction of his interactions with others. Behavioral contracts were then negotiated that called for him to interact with others with increasing frequency, and progress was monitored.

A technical matter to be dealt with was that Roger had typically only felt the urge to expose himself if he was farther than ten feet from the target female. If he found himself within that radius, he did not lose sexual interest, but he was disinclined to act inappropriately. With close monitoring, a technique combining general relaxation and self-instructions to be calm and behave cordially was designed and implemented. In vivo use of this technique, coupled with desensitization to approaching attractive females, eventually enabled Roger to interact much more frequently with women. He reported a corresponding decrease in both his felt hostility and the urge to expose himself. Positive coping imagery was also used during therapy meetings and by Roger when he practiced relaxation on his own. His developing ease in the company of attractive females allowed him to elicit more and more positive responses from them.

Roger's high rate (almost daily) of indecent exposure declined dramatically shortly after the onset of therapy, but he continued to occasionally expose himself. He was trained to analyze situations in which the opportunity for exhibitionism was great and to administer subvocal self-instructions on how to deal with these temptations. Initially the strategy was to have him masturbate in seclusion (a response already in his repertoire) instead of actually exposing himself. Later, when it was clear that this response had supplanted the indecent exposure, he worked on fixing the sexual image in his mind and removing himself to a more private setting to masturbate. Finally he was able to either delay responding to sexual stimuli or to respond in a more socially appropriate manner, such as engaging the female in a conversation. This succession of graded steps seemed to be a major facet of the treatment. At each step, associated fears were extinguished as new skills were developed.

Because it was expected that temptations would sometimes override Roger's self-control abilities, a provision was made for him to call the therapist at the clinic or at his home or to stop by the office during periods of difficulty. This variant of delay therapy (Meyer, 1973) offered support and interrupted the exhibitionistic response chain.

At Roger's request, an attempt was made to enhance sexual attraction to his current girlfriend. The therapist suggested that Roger substitute an enticing sexual image of his girlfriend for whatever fantasies he might be imagining during masturbation. At first the substitution was made just before ejaculation. Gradually the substitution was made earlier and earlier. Correspondingly, some suggestions from the developing work of Masters et al. (1970, 1994) were offered to enhance actual sexual relations with his girlfriend. Assertiveness training at this point also proved helpful. Feedback from Roger indicated success.

Interspersed among Roger's periods of tension were feelings of pessimism and depression, and he would speak in the bitter tones of a cynic. Experiential focusing invariably related these feelings to the avoidance of practical decisions that he needed to make. Later in therapy, Roger was well aware of this trap and worked to confront issues in his life more squarely. Another technique involved replaying sections of earlier therapy tapes. For instance, when he occasionally became discouraged and cynical about the treatment, the therapist played back Roger's earlier comments in which he expressed pride in his progress in himself. Much of the last few sessions was then spent listing alternative courses of career action for Roger's immediate future.

Follow-Up and Comment

Roger was followed for another year after treatment was terminated, and he showed no return to the exhibitionist pattern. However, the very high rate of recidivism in exhibitionists indicates that there should always be a long follow-up.

In summation, a presenting problem that might have been dealt with primarily (if not exclusively) via aversive conditioning was handled here with a mélange of techniques, the "standard of care" in modern psychotherapies. Over the course of a 6-month active interaction between client and therapist the following techniques were selectively applied: extensive historical interviewing and client expression of feeling; progressive relaxation (with home practice), autogenic training, self-monitoring and record-keeping, environmental manipulation, assertive training, self-instruction, operant and respondent shaping procedures, desensitization (with in vivo exercises), cognitive restructuring, client-therapist meetings in real world settings, behavioral rehearsal, imagery delay therapy, Masters and Johnson techniques, experiential focusing, joint review of transcripts of previous therapy sessions, and active follow-up agreements. These techniques were not applied mechanistically, but rather in the context of a helping relationship marked by a caring therapist and mutual respect and commitment to honesty and responsibility.

We will soon turn to those patterns of disorder in which the central issue is too much anxiety, that is, the anxiety disorders, the first of the sections on specific disorder patterns, that make up the rest of this book. Now, however, we will look at a model of change behaviors that is applicable to many disorders.

**An Overall
Perspective
on
Treatment
Change**

Continuing in the traditions of the early studies of psychotherapy by such people as Tim Leary (yes, the Timothy Leary of LSD 1960s notoriety) and the first meta-analytic studies of psychotherapy (Smith, Glass, and Miller (1980). Seligman (1995) and others have reviewed these studies, including a massive study by *Consumer Reports*, to conclude that: (a) psychotherapy is effective, (b) long-term treatment is better than short-term treatment, (c) no specific treatment modality is clearly better for most disorders, (d) medication plus psychotherapy is not usually significantly better than psychotherapy alone, (e) the curative effects of psychotherapy are often more long-term than those of medication, (f) the effective use of psychotherapy can reduce the costs of physical disorders, (g) there is no clear evidence that psychologists, psychiatrists, and social workers differ in treatment effectiveness, (h) all three of these groups are more effective than counselors or long-term family doctoring, and (i) clients whose length of therapy or choice of therapy was limited by insurance or managed care did worse than those without such limits.

Prochaska, DiClemente, and Norcross (1992) provide a useful model for change behaviors. Although designed originally to respond to substance abuse behaviors, it is helpful for responding to virtually all disorders. They conceptualize change as occurring in five stages:

1. Precontemplation: The person avoids any confrontation of true issues and generally denies realistic consequences.

2. Contemplation: There is at least some acknowledgment of responsibility and problematic consequences and at least a minimal openness to the possibility of change, although effective change has not yet been instituted.

3. Preparation: This is the decision point. There is enough acknowledgment of problematic behaviors and consequences that the person can make the required cognitive shift to initiate change.

4. Action: There is a higher sense of self-liberation or willpower, generating sets of behaviors toward positive coping and away from situations that condition the undesired behavior.

5. Maintenance: Efforts are directed toward remotivation and developing skills and patterns that avoid relapse and promote a positive lifestyle.

The following, adapted from Prochaska, DiClemente, and Norcross (1992), lists the major change processes that are embedded in various treatments and theories. They are listed in the order in which they occur in the overall change process: Consciousness raising is more likely to occur in the precontemplation and contemplation stages, and self-disclosure and trust are more likely to be central to action and maintenance processes.

Process	*Definitions: Interventions*
Consciousness raising	Increasing information about self and problem: observations, confrontations, interpretations, bibliotherapy

Dramatic relief	Experiencing and expressing feelings about one's problems and solutions: psychodrama, grieving losses, role playing
Environmental reevaluation	Assessing how one's problem affects physical environment: empathy training, documentation of effects
Self-reevaluation	Assessing how one feels and thinks about oneself with respect to a problem: value clarification, imagery, corrective emotional experience
Choice and commitment	Choosing and commiting to act or belief in ability to change: decision-making therapy, New Year's resolutions, logotherapy techniques, commitment-enhancing techniques
Reinforcement management	Rewarding oneself or being rewarded by others for making changes: contingency contracts, overt and covert reinforcement, self-reward
Self-disclosure and trust	Being open and trusting about problems with someone who cares: therapeutic alliance, social support, self-help groups
Counter conditioning	Substituting alternatives for problem behaviors: relaxation, desensitization, assertion, positive self-statements
Stimulus control	Avoiding or countering stimuli that elicit problem behaviors: restructuring one's environment (e.g., removing alcohol or fattening foods), avoiding high-risk cues, fading techniques
Sociopolitical	Increasing alternatives for nonproblem behaviors available in society: advocating for rights of repressed, empowering, policy interventions

3

The Anxiety Disorders

We all experience anxiety at one time or another. In the anxiety disorders, anxiety is either consistently experienced or at least occurs when the person attempts to suppress or otherwise control the symptoms. Some disorders formerly referred to as transient situational disturbances are now included among the anxiety disorders in the Posttraumatic Stress Disorder and Acute Stress Disorder (a new addition in *DSM-IV*) categories. In addition, these are the categories of Agoraphobia, Social Phobia, Simple Phobia, Panic Disorder, Generalized Anxiety Disorder, and Obsessive-Compulsive Disorder. Agoraphobia, as seen in the case of Agnes, the second separate case in this section, is a fear of being left alone or finding oneself in public places in which one could be embarrassed and/or not able to find help in case of sudden incapacitation. In a social phobia, people fear and avoid situations in which they might be open to scrutiny by others. They are afraid of being embarrassed or humiliated and often avoid such situations as public speaking or being called on in class. The simple phobia diagnosis is often referred to as a specific phobia, and is the focus in the first set of cases, "The Three Little Boys." In a panic disorder the person experiences recurrent, unpredictable panic attacks. The generalized anxiety disorder is characterized by consistent physiologically experienced anxiety without a primary syndrome manifesting phobias, panic attacks, obsessions, or compulsions. The diagnostic emphasis is on muscle tension, apprehension, and autonomic overreactivity. The obsessive compulsive disorder, discussed in detail in the case history of Bess, is a relatively common and debilitating disorder that is often difficult to treat.

The posttraumatic stress disorders are reactions to psychologically traumatic events that would elicit symptoms in most people (e.g., rape, or assault, kidnapping, military combat, and disasters). The characteristic response involves reexperiencing the traumatic event, depression and/or withdrawal, and a variety of autonomic symptoms, and it is described in the case of the "Postman" found at the end of this section.

A Study on Anxiety

**The Three
Little Boys:
Hans, Albert,
and Peter**

*Fear has many eyes and can see things
underground.*

—Miguel de Cervantes (1547–1616)

Hans, Albert, and Peter are all young boys who became famous in the mid-1920s as a result of being experimental-clinical subjects of Sigmund Freud, John Watson, and Mary Cover Jones, respectively. Freud published his theory of the origin and cure of anxiety based on information learned from Little Hans, while Little Albert and Little Peter were used to demonstrate the origins and cure for anxiety according to learning theory.

Freud's study of Hans (Fernald, 1984), a 5-year-old boy born in 1903, was the first published case analysis of a child. Freud used the case of Hans published in 1909 to illustrate his theory of childhood sexuality, the Oedipal complex, and the origins of neuroses. Freud only later postulated an aggressive drive; he used this case of Hans to demonstrate that "the motive force" of all neurotic symptoms of later life was based on conflicts around the sexual drive. Before Hans, Freud's theory was only applied to adults. By studying a child, Freud strengthened his conviction that people are born with universal conflicting urges that form the basis of neuroses. Just as Freud's theory explained the origin of Hans's phobia, Freud believed the phobia was cured when Hans was presented with and understood the reasons for his fears. Thus, Freud's theory both explained and cured Hans of his phobia (in theory).

The Case of Little Hans

Even though Hans was one of Freud's most significant case studies, he only saw the boy in person once. Responding to Freud's encouragement to provide information about those who have neuroses, Hans's father wrote Freud numerous letters detailing his son's behavior and statements. The more salient facts are recounted here.

At age 3, when Hans showed an interest in his "widdler" (penis), his mother told him if he touched it she would have it cut off. Later, responding to his unclothed mother who asked him why he was staring at her, Hans said he wanted to see if she had a penis, which he thought would be as big as a horse. His mother indicated that she did have a penis. Still at age 3, Hans witnessed the circumstances surrounding the birth of his little sister. Hans heard his mother groaning and saw bedpans full of blood. He said, "But blood doesn't come out of *my* widdler" (Fernald, 1984).

Numerous accounts described Hans's preoccupation with the penis. He commented that his baby sister had an extremely small one, which Freud construed as meaning it had possibly been cut off. When Hans was 4 he asked his mother why she did not touch his penis when powdering him, to which she responded that it was not proper. He answered, "But it's great fun."

Finally, at age 5, Hans had developed "a nervous disorder." He protested having to walk on the streets because he feared that a horse would bite him. Freud responded to this report that what Hans really wanted was to sleep with his mother, whose bed he occasionally shared. Hans's father told Hans that horses do not bite, to which Hans responded that he overheard his friend's father warning his friend not to touch the white horse or it will bite. Eventually Hans was afraid of all large animals. He told his father that his fear was so great that he touches his penis every night. His father told him to stop touching his penis and his fear would disappear. When Hans said he stopped touching his penis, his father retorted "But you still want to." Hans agreed.

Freud referred to the information that Hans's father shared with his son about his penis and wishing to sleep with his mother as "enlightenment," which Hans needed simply to accept in order to recover. As the facts about Hans's case unfold, it becomes apparent that his father planted Freud's notions into his mind and reinforced his son for reporting facts that concurred with the theory. When Hans said he was afraid of the horse's black bridle, Freud interpreted this as being afraid of the father's black moustache. An ensuing conversation from father to son was as follows: "You'd like to be Daddy and married to Mummy; you'd like to be as big as me and have a moustache; and you'd like Mummy to have a baby.... Would you like to be married to Mummy?" Hans replied, "Oh, yes."

Freud and Hans's father, who was one of Freud's most devoted followers, only paid attention to information from Hans that supported the psychoanalytic theory. An extreme example of this was when Hans told his father that his younger sister was white and lovely. In order to fit this statement into Freud's concept of sibling rivalry, his father construed Hans's statement as hypocritical and insincere.

Even though Freud was aware of the contrived nature of the information, he interpreted Hans's phobia as an Oedipal conflict that came out when Hans did not touch his penis. The more intense sexual arousal that followed is the genesis of Hans's phobia. The libidinal longing is transformed into anxiety.

In summary, Freud interpreted Hans's story as originating in desire for sex with his mother, and when his father prevented this, he hated, feared, and wished to murder his father. Because there was no way to express it, Hans's sexual desire for his mother turned into anxiety. The anxiety also served the purpose of keeping Hans near his mother. Afraid that his father would cut off Hans's penis if his desires were known, Hans transferred his fear of his father to a fear of horses. Finally, and most remarkably, Hans's anxiety finally disappeared because he became aware of and understood his Oedipus complex.

The Case of Little Albert

Not to be outdone by Freud, an American psychologist in the 1920s known as the Father of Behaviorism, John Watson, performed his own anxiety-inducing experiment (Watson and Rayner, 1920), after being awarded a grant of $100 in 1917 to study reflexes and instinct in human infants. Watson called the infant "Little Albert" so that he would be compared with Little Hans. Watson's article on Albert is the earliest known explanation of anxiety that is clearly based on learning theory.

Before conducting his experiment, Watson exposed 9-month-old Albert to various stimuli to see his reaction. Albert showed no distress at a rat and a rabbit; however, he was upset at the noise of a hammer hitting a steel bar behind his back. Then when Albert was 11 months old, Watson startled him with the same distressing loud noise behind Albert's back whenever he played with a small white laboratory rat. After the noise was paired with the rat an unreported number of times, Albert became upset in the presence of the rat even when there was no noise (when not allowed to suck his thumb). In addition, because Albert also exhibited this anxiety when exposed to a sealskin coat (and other objects—a Santa Claus mask and a rabbit and dog), Watson concluded that the fear extended to other furry animals and objects. Many accounts of Watson's study state that Albert's fear of the rabbit was later removed. In reality, Albert's mother terminated her son's involvement in the experiment, so there was never any chance to remove the phobia. Additionally, Watson knew ahead of time that she planned to do this and yet did nothing to remove the phobia.

Watson declared the experiment a success because he produced a phobia in a child solely through the use of conditioning. He chose to overlook the fact that Albert showed no signs of fear if permitted to suck his thumb and also that punishment was included in this approach. Critics pointed out that generalizing Albert's phobia to all furry objects may have been too broad a conclusion when all that occurred was Albert "fretting" around a sealskin coat. Watson never exposed Albert to a cotton coat to compare the reactions. Others who tried to replicate Watson's results have generally failed. Despite this, the contribution made by Little Albert to the field of psychology was demonstrating that anxiety could be conceptualized in terms of classical conditioning.

Curiously, John Watson went on to become a pioneer in a totally different area, as his academic career ended abruptly in 1920. He reportedly had a number of extramarital affairs, but then fell hopelessly in love with his research assistant, Rosalie Raynor, whom he later married. His wife at that time discovered the affair, and the ensuing divorce and scandal led the president of Johns Hopkins to dismiss Watson. In a commentary on the different ethical perspective of those times, the dismissal was based on the divorce rather than the affair with a student; today, it would be the latter that could be the cause for dismissal. In any case, Watson joined the J. Walter Thompson advertising agency of New York, which still operates today. As he was in psychology, he was a creative innovator here as well. He is credited with devising the coffee break, in order to increase the sales of Maxwell House Coffee. He was also the first to offer free samples in return for filling out questionnaires, and the first to employ demographic surveys of target populations of potential consumers. At times his approach was a bit heavy-handed; in one campaign for the Scott Paper Company, Watson had a picture of a surgical team at work, with the caption, "And the trouble began with harsh toilet tissue." On a more negative note, he is also reputed to have developed the advertising that was successful in encouraging women to smoke cigarettes.

The Case of Little Peter

Behavior therapy proceeded with publications by Mary Cover Jones (1924) who, with guidance from Watson, experimented with classical conditioning to cure phobias. Jones treated Peter, one of her most serious cases, for 2 months on a daily basis. She called him "Little Peter" to join the Freud-Watson line of research and sought to show that the conditioning process could be used to eliminate fears. Peter, a 3-year-old boy, had a fear of white rats, rabbits, fur, cotton, wool, and similar items. During his first session, Peter, while sitting in a high chair, was eating candy when a rabbit in a cage was placed four feet away from him. Peter immediately began crying and begging that the rabbit be taken away. After 3 minutes he again started crying about the rabbit, and it was removed.

Gradually the duration of "rabbit time" increased and the proximity of the rabbit to Peter decreased as he exhibited an increasing tolerance to the rabbit's presence. Two months later, in Peter's last session, his behavior was markedly different. Standing in a high chair while looking out of a window, Peter asked, "Where is the rabbit?" (Jones, 1924, p. 389). The experimenter placed the rabbit at his feet. Peter patted the rabbit and tried to pick it up but it was too heavy. With help from the experimenter Peter was able to hold and play with the rabbit. After treatments ended, Peter continued to show no fear when exposed to similar small animals.

Jones cautioned that this method is delicate because just as she was able to pair food, a positive stimulus, with the rabbit, a negative stimulus, the opposite result could have occurred, attaching the anxiety associated with the rabbit to the sight of food. Although Jones acknowledged the fact, it was seldom mentioned in subsequent accounts that prior to the first formal session with Peter, Jones introduced Barbara, a child who played with the rat without fear, and then in the next 7 treatment days, Peter played with three children who manifested no fear of a rabbit. Thus, social imitation is certainly a factor in addition to this early form of exposure therapy.

Summary

Hans provided Freud with a psychoanalytic basis to explain both cause and cure for anxiety; Albert was Watson's source for explaining anxiety through classical conditioning; and Peter provided information to support classical conditioning as a way to extinguish anxieties. Today there are multiple theories about the origins and preferred treatments of the various types of anxiety. We have seen here the psychoanalytic and behaviorist theories applied to anxiety. In addition, cognitive therapy utilizes schemata and the concept of thought distortion as the fundamentals for change.

The origins of Albert's phobia can be attributed directly to the classical conditioning performed by Watson. In general it appears that environmental stimuli play a large part in the development and maintenance of anxiety. Some modern theories assert that Hans and Peter's phobias probably started with a negative reaction to an environmental stimulus, while others pursue more genetic and biological origins.

"Exposure" treatments such as systematic desensitization (SDT) are commonly used and are effective with a wide variety of phobias. SDT can be adapted to group treatment and does not require a substantial number of sessions. If SDT is done in a group, the experience has the added advantage of providing real-life modeling from the other members of the group. Cognitive-behavior modification, social skills training, anxiety management techniques, and "exposure" treatments are most commonly used, as well as psychotropic medication (Whybrow, 1997).

Occasionally other symptomatology surfaces after behavioral treatments have dealt with the specific referral symptom. This need not be considered an indication of symptom substitution, because in most instances, the other pathology has always been there. When the more debilitating primary symptoms are relieved, the person can turn his or her attention to other problems. Secondary gain patterns also often occur with the phobias. For example, Hans received a great deal of attention and reinforcement from his father for reporting his sexual urges and other symptoms of his phobia.

/ *Agoraphobia*

The Case of Agnes

The problem with television is that people must sit and keep their eyes glued to a screen: The average American family hasn't the time for it. TV will never be a serious competitor of broadcasting [radio].

—The New York Times (1939)
(Television was introduced April 30, 1939)

Agoraphobia is marked by an irrational fear of leaving one's home and its immediate surroundings. It is often preceded and accompanied by various panic attacks. The specific *DSM-IV* diagnoses are Agoraphobia without History of Panic Attack, Panic Disorder, and Panic Disorder with Agoraphobia. Agoraphobia is specifically defined as the avoidance (or endurance with distress) of any situation, particularly being alone, in which people fear they would be embarrassed and/or could not be helped or get in touch with help in the event of a panic attack or having panic-like symptoms (Zuercher, 1996). These fears pervade their worlds, and they avoid being alone in open spaces or avoid public places. As a result, their normal behavior patterns and experiences are severely disrupted.

The *DSM-IV* offers the specific diagnoses of Panic Disorder with Agoraphobia or without Agoraphobia. To diagnose either type of panic disorder, the *DSM-IV* requires (1) recurrent unexpected panic attacks and (2) at least one of these attacks being followed by at least a month by one or more of (a) persistent anticipatory concern about attacks, (b) worry about implications or consequences of having an attack, or (c) a resultant significant change in behavior.

In order to diagnose a panic "attack," the *DSM-IV* requires the fear-discomfort and presence of at least four of the following symptoms during most of the attacks: (1) palpitations, pounding heart, or accelerated heart rate; (2) chest discomfort; (3) choking sensations; (4) feeling faint or dizzy; (5) feelings of unreality or depersonalization; (6) paresthesia (numbness or tingling); (7) hot or cold flashes; (8) sweating; (9) shaking or trembling; (10) nausea or abdominal distress; (11) fear of dying; or (12) fear of going crazy or losing control.

On occasion, panic attacks may last for hours, although attacks are typically for a period of about 15 minutes during which the person literally experiences terror. They present a high suicide risk (Fawcett, 1992). About one-third to one-half of such individuals develop agoraphobic patterns. The disorder seldom first emerges after age 45 or before age 14, and modal ages of onset are late adolescence or the mid-30s. Genetic factors play a part. The disorder is recurrent and episodic, with about half of these cases becoming chronic.

The Case of Agnes

Agnes is a thin, reasonably attractive 43-year-old white female who was brought to the community mental health center in the eastern seaboard city in which she lived. Her 22-year-old daughter brought her, stating that Agnes was driving her crazy with requests that she accompany her everywhere. Agnes reports that she has always been a "tense" person, has experienced agoraphobic symptoms off and on during the last 7 years, but the intensity has increased substantially in the last 6 months.

For the past 4 years, Agnes has also suffered with what she refers to as "heart disease." She has often taken herself to a cardiologist, complaining of rapid or irregular heartbeats. The physician always reassured her that he saw no pathology and stated he felt that it was probably a result of anxiety and tension. He advised her to exercise regularly and prescribed tranquilizers for any severe episodes of anxiety. Agnes occasionally uses the tranquilizers, but not to any significant extent. It is interesting that she has never experienced any of the symptoms at home, even though she does rather heavy housework without any assistance.

The agoraphobic pattern took a severe turn for the worse 6 months ago during the middle of winter, while Agnes was visiting her daughter. Her daughter had taken her own child to a movie, leaving Agnes alone in their home. There had been a severe snowstorm the day before. It was difficult for cars to get about, and Agnes became fearful that she was isolated. She tried to call her sister who lives in a nearby city, only to find that the phone was dead. At this point she began to panic, noticed her heart beating rapidly, and thought she was going to have a heart attack. When Agnes's daughter eventually came home after the movie and some shopping, Agnes was extremely distraught. She was lying on the couch crying and moaning and had started to drink to try to lose consciousness. After her daughter returned, Agnes continued to drink, and with the added reassurance of her daughter, she managed to fall asleep. When she awakened, she felt better and refused to seek help for her fears. In the last 6 months she has had other similar experiences of near panic at the thought of being alone.

Agnes's husband, who is a sales representative for a national manufacturing company, spends a lot of time on the road. When he is home, he is no longer willing to listen to Agnes's complaints. But the problem is not as apparent then, since Agnes relaxes considerably when her husband accompanies her on outings. Although she can acknowledge that her behaviors are absurd and not warranted by demands in her environment, Agnes is still compelled to perform within this pattern. As is often the case with agoraphobia, Agnes shows an accompanying level of depression, as she has a sense of helplessness about controlling the events of her world. In that sense, she reflects the phenomenon referred to as "learned helplessness."

Agnes did not have a difficult or unhappy childhood. Her father was very authoritarian and discouraged rebellion in his children, although he was otherwise warm and affectionate with them. He had a moderate drinking problem and was prone to whip

Agnes's older brother when he was intoxicated. This older brother was the one family member who was overtly rebellious and independent. Her mother was passive and submissive and manifested mild agoraphobia herself, although she would never have been allowed to seek professional help for her condition.

Throughout her school years, Agnes was described as a "good student" and "teacher's pet." She had one or two girlfriends with whom she could talk about her worries, but she was not active socially. She did not participate in school activities and was not outgoing with other students. Because Agnes was somewhat plain in appearance, she was not "pulled out" of her withdrawal by any males who might have shown some interest. When free of school and schoolwork, she assisted her mother in domestic duties.

Following high school graduation, Agnes took a job as a secretary with hopes of saving money for college. She did not make enough at first and had to remain at home. When she was 20 years old, she met her future husband at a church gathering, and they were married within the year. She continued her work as a secretary in order to help him finish his last year of college. Her husband was stable and undemonstrative and, like her father, was a bit authoritarian. Agnes thus found it easy to become passive and dependent in response to him. She continued to long for a college degree but never made any real efforts to pursue it. After the birth of her daughter she had another pregnancy that ended in a miscarriage. This upset her so much that she refused to think of becoming pregnant again. Throughout the early years of her marriage, Agnes was stable in her functioning and only occasionally showed nervousness or anxiety. Yet, as noted, in recent years she has shown increased problems.

Etiology

A number of factors in Agnes's background make it understandable that she would eventually develop an agoraphobic response. First, she had always been timid and shy; it is probable that genetic temperament factors at least partially influenced her development in this pattern (Amir, 1998). But the pattern was also facilitated by her parents. Her father was clear in what types of behaviors he expected. He did not want any rebellious behaviors, particularly from his daughter, and was quick to suppress any show of such behavior. On the other hand, he was affectionate, and his affection was clearly reserved for times when deference to his authority was apparent. Agnes's mother was a classic model for agoraphobic behavior. She was deferent and passive and at the same time showed anxiety-coping patterns that had an agoraphobic quality to them. She also kept Agnes involved in domestic activities through late adolescence, which did not encourage her to experiment with new and independent roles.

Agnes's lack of physical attractiveness precluded being drawn out of her developing withdrawal patterns by attention from males, and her lack of social or athletic interests reinforced her lack of attention from peers. When Agnes eventually married, her husband's similarity to her father's authoritarianism facilitated passive and dependent behaviors. Although she hoped someday to return to college and develop a career, she never made any efforts to bring this to fruition. It is probable that her husband would have quashed this desire.

Agnes's miscarriage precipitated her first panic-like response, but it was controlled by the structure of the hospital and the sedative medication she received. The miscarriage was a tremendous threat, because it was in the area of child care that she had found her primary source of self-definition. She carried a fear of re-experiencing this panic and as a result avoided future pregnancies while throwing herself into the care of her home and daughter. It is interesting that while Agnes's husband demanded passivity in his wife, he allowed and reinforced independent and even masculine behaviors in his daughter. Such behaviors provided him with a companion in fishing and golf, skills his wife had never considered developing. This allowed the daughter to escape the cycle that had been passed to Agnes from her mother and probably from other women in the family history before her. Her daughter's independence, however, stressed Agnes because it threatened her own sense of being needed. As her daughter became more independent, Agnes became more liable to anxiety, which then channeled into agoraphobic responses. The heart palpitations and slight arrythymias that naturally accompany anxiety in many individuals provided her with another focus for her anxiety. However, she was not classically hypochondriacal (Meister, 1980) since she did not seek out a variety of physicians to look at her symptoms, she did not present a wide variety of symptoms, and in general she attended to the comments and advice of her physician.

Once she had experienced a true panic reaction, she was then sensitized to anticipate a fear of helplessness, a frightening feeling. As a result, she engineered a wide variety of behaviors to keep her from re-experiencing panic. The patterns she developed were initially successful, as remaining at home kept her calm. But such a pattern requires giving up much in the world, including the support of her husband and daughter, who increasingly found her behaviors tedious and irritating. As this occurred, Agnes became more isolated, thus coming closer in actuality to the feeling of being alone emotionally and to the consequent panic she feared so much.

The specific diagnosis that Agnes received was Agoraphobia with Panic Attacks. Incidentally, it should be noted that some of her behaviors might also have suggested the diagnosis of Avoidant Personality Disorder. But there is little concern about the symptoms in the avoidant personality. The person may be socially isolated and passive yet seems less concerned about this behavior and evidences little apparent desire to change it.

Treatment Options

A number of treatments are potentially useful in dealing with agoraphobia. Cognitive-behavioral and the behavioral treatments have received the most research attention and support in treating all of the anxiety disorders. This is especially so for those referred to as "exposure treatments," which have a common goal of eliminating maladaptive anxiety by exposing the client to fear-producing stimuli (Chambless et al., 1996). An exposure program for agoraphobia would help the client gradually enter those situations, such as specific enclosed places, shopping malls, bridges, tunnels, and the like, that such clients typically avoid the most.

A specific form of relaxation, applied relaxation, can be useful with the panic component. After a relaxation technique such as progressive muscle relaxation is learned, any word, for example, spoon, is conditioned to become a cue for the relaxation, so that eventually the effects of the well-learned relaxation pattern work as a counterconditioning procedure to anxiety. Also the passivity and timidity common to agoraphobia make assertiveness training a helpful adjunct.

Medication can be helpful, especially for the panic component (see Table 3–1). The benzodiazepenes, tricyclic antidepressants (especially imipranine and clomipranine), and the nonoanine oxidase inhibitors (MAOs) have been proven effective, although the problematic side effects of the MAOs make them a less common choice. Unfortunately, without other interventions, there is a substantial relapse rate for the panic component within 6 to 12 months after discontinuance of the medications.

Secondary gain patterns especially occur with agoraphobia. For example, Agnes's controlling response toward her daughter is this kind of side effect. Insight-oriented psychotherapy can be helpful in breaking the dependence roles that so often interfere with the agoraphobic's development of new responses.

Agoraphobia is difficult to treat. Two of the more effective traditional exposure techniques for it are implosion (or imaginal exposure) therapy and flooding (now termed in vivo exposure therapy). Graduated exposure therapy is also commonly used now; in this technique the goal is to keep exposing the individuals to the feared stimulus, allowing them to experience as much anxiety as they can tolerate, until they can begin to make both approach and mastery responses. Because the treatment process is likely to be a long one, group treatment techniques, along with bibliotherapy (reading specified self-help books) can be helpful (Zuercher, 1996). Since the spouse of an agoraphobic may have a vested interest in the client staying agoraphobic (although this is typically denied consciously or unconsciously), marital or family therapy may be necessary.

TABLE 3–1 Antianxiety Drugs

**Name
(Generic/Trade)**

Benzodiazepines	Nonbenzodiazepines
diazepam (Valium)	buspirone (Buspar)
chlordiazepoxide (Librium)	propanolol (Inderal)
chlorazepate (Tranxene)	
prazepam (Centrax)	
halazepam (Paxipam)	
lorazepam (Ativan)	
alprazolam (Xanax)	
oxazepam (Serax)	
clonazepam (Klonipin)	

The goal of implosion or imaginal exposure therapy is to maximize anxiety, whereas SDT attempts to keep anxiety at a minimal state while the person gradually confronts the feared stimuli. G. Gordon Liddy, former Watergate personage and now an author and radio commentator, in an interview in the October 1980 issue of *Playboy*, gives a vivid description from his youth of a self-administered flooding technique:

> For example, to conquer my fear of thunder, I waited for a big storm and then sneaked out of the house and climbed up a seventy-five foot oak tree and latched myself to the trunk with my belt. As the storm hit and chaos roared around me and the sky was rent with thunder and lightening, I shook my fist at the rolling black clouds and screamed, "Kill me! go ahead and try! I don't care! I don't care!"...I repeated this kind of confrontation over a period of years, mastering one fear after another. I was afraid of electricity, so I scraped off an electrical wire and let ten volts course through me.

The Treatment of Agnes

The "exposure" treatments of implosion therapy (imaginal exposure) or flooding (in vivo exposure therapy) are ideal for agoraphobics such as Agnes, who already shows a moderate ongoing level of anxiety. Implosion therapists attempt to maximize anxiety and yet keep the person in continued confrontation with the feared stimuli so that the anxiety peaks, or in the language of the behaviorist, "extinguishes." A cognitive explanation for the extinction phenomenon asserts that the person has simply discovered that the expected catastrophic events do not occur, even under maximal stimulus conditions. As a result, the agoraphobic becomes aware that there is nothing that warrants their extreme fear and they gain an increased sense of control.

Agnes was scheduled for an open-ended implosion session, one without a built-in time limit, which is standard because it is difficult to predict how long it will take the anxiety to peak. Agnes was asked to imagine different variations of her greatest fears, such as being left alone, being helpless, and going into a panic. The therapist then used graphic and vivid language throughout the session to maximize the images in Agnes's imagination. Agnes had been told ahead of time that this technique would bring on anxiety, but she had to commit herself to stay with it, with the assurance that the therapist would be there with her. She did so, and even when the scenes produced intense anxiety, she continued to hold the scenes in her imagination. If she had not done so, the result would have been counterproductive rather than simply neutral. The following dialogue is excerpted from her first treatment session:

> *Therapist:* Agnes, keep imagining the scenes just like you have been doing—you're doing very well. I want you to imagine yourself at your daughter's house. It is a cold, bleak day. The wind is howling and all of a sudden the electricity goes out. Imagine that intensely. You rush to the phone and pick it up only to realize the phone is also dead. Now you realize that with the electricity off, the furnace will not turn on and it is gradually getting much colder.

Agnes: I'm scared, I don't want to see that. Can't we stop?

Therapist: No, remember you must go on and keep these images in your mind. You're feeling colder. It's getting darker and now your heart starts to beat wildly. It's not beating right. You can feel it going wrong. You're really scared now and you know that no one's coming back home.

This type of suggestion, along with scenarios of being abandoned as an old person, a lonely death, and having another miscarriage, were suggested throughout the three sessions it took for Agnes to begin to be able to face her fear and make some new, positive steps. Her anxiety peaked and then lessened several times in those three sessions, as more than one peak and fading phase is usually required. Once Agnes began to feel more confident, she was included in group therapy and also had a few marital therapy sessions with her husband. She recovered significantly over a period of 5 months. Although over the years she is likely to have occasional return bouts of at least a mild form of the agoraphobia, her increasing confidence and positive behaviors predict that she will be able to bounce back and handle those situations.

Comment

In Agnes's case the following factors contributed to her debilitating agoraphobia: (1) a probable temperamental predisposition toward excessive organismic arousal to stress, (2) her mother's modeling of mild agoraphobic symptoms, and (3) her father's contingent affection. Against these historical factors, Agnes's response to the miscarriage in her second pregnancy was her first experience with extreme anxiety. She was frightened by the magnitude of her experienced distress and immediately decided to avoid (with certainty) another experience of overwhelming helplessness by refusing to become pregnant again. The typical mild anxiety that pervades the agoraphobic's life between panic episodes was exacerbated in Agnes's case by her own daughter's independence, which threatened Agnes's sense of being needed. These variables combined with Agnes's limited social development and resulted in an inability to cope with her loneliness and anxiety, except through increased withdrawal and fearfulness. Her family's impatience with Agnes's symptoms increased her isolation and encouraged her manipulation of her daughter's affection.

Obsessive-Compulsive Disorder

The Case of Bess

Shoelaces had to lie flat against his shoes. Going on or off the field he would run by the right side of the goalpost only. First step up the stairs had to be with the left foot. Before going into a game the first time he'd have somebody slap his shoulder pads exactly three times. The long white sleeve of the sweatshirt we wear under our jerseys always had

to be visible. He always sat in the last row of the plane—claimed it was safer... shall I go on?
—William Kienzle, *Sudden Death* (1985)

For Obessive-Compulsive Disorder (OCD) the *DSM-IV* requires evidence of either obsessions (recurrent and persistent thoughts, images, or impulses experienced at some point as inappropriate and intrusive; absorb at least 1 hour a day; cause distress; are not just an excessive response to real-life issues; persist despite attempts to resist; and the thoughts are recognized as one's own), or compulsions (repetitive behaviors that are somehow a product of an obsessional pattern, accompanied by behaviors designed to change the situation, and these behaviors are not realistic for the situation). The obsessions or compulsions must then be recognized as excessive or unreasonable. OCD is often chronic and accompanied by some disruption in personal functioning. The prognosis is guarded, since close to 50% will persist in some of their symptomatology, even with treatment. A common co-morbid pattern is depression.

In 1660, the English bishop, Jeremy Taylor, provided an excellent description of a developing obsessive-compulsive pattern in referring to William of Osery as having "read two or three books of Religion and devotion very often... [he] had read over those books three hours every day. In a short time, he had read over the books three times more... [He] began to think... that now he was to spend six hours every day in reading those books, because he had now read them over six times. He presently considered that... he must be tied to 12 hours every day" (Pitman, 1994, p.4).

About 50% of OCDs show some symptoms by age 15, and by the age of 25, more than half of the treated obsessive-compulsives have already shown clear symptoms. The lifetime prevalence rate of OCD is approximately 2.5%. About 25% are clear obsessionals.

As Freud emphasized in his comment (1906–1908) that "Sufferers from this disorder are able to keep their suffering a private matter," OCD is often hidden. As a result, OCD has traditionally been thought to be relatively rare, but more recent estimates suggest it occurs at about a 2.5% lifetime prevalence rate in the general population. Many who might be willing to report phobic anxiety would be more distressed to disclose that they think and act in ways they cannot control.

The most common symptom clusters are (1) washers, (2) sinners/doubters, (3) checkers, (4) counters/organizers, and (5) hoarders. The severe perfectionism found in some OCDs can be a risk factor for suicide, especially in crisis. The most common obsessions seen by clinicians are repetitive thoughts of contamination or of violence, extreme scrupulousness and/or doubts about religion and one's duties, and self-doubts. The most common compulsions include checking behaviors, repetitive acts, and handwashing. OCD does not include compulsions to perform behaviors that are inherently pleasurable, such as alcohol indulgence or overeating.

OCD is occasionally initially confused with Tourette's Syndrome, which is marked by a seemingly compulsive utterance of various words (often obscene) or grunts. It has been asserted that the composer, Wolfgang Amadeus Mozart, suffered from Tourette's because his letters often included curses focused on the buttocks and defecation. Others have noted that it would have to be proven that this behavior was "out of control" to establish Tourette's.

Obsessive-compulsives tend to be more intelligent and to come from a higher social economic class than do other neurotics. This makes sense, as the minor variants of this disorder, such as meticulousness and persistence, are efficient and productive, particularly in a society that is immersed in the idea of external achievement (van Oppen, Hoekstra, and Emmelkamps, 1995). They do not resonate to the idea that "Only seekers find, but never while seeking."

The Case of Bess

Bess is an attractive 27-year-old upper middle class woman. She lives by herself in a well-kept apartment in one of the best sections in town. Yet she has few friends, and social activities play a small role in her life. Most evenings she works rather late and then comes home, fixes her own dinner, and reads or watches television until she is ready to fall asleep. Frequently she needs alcohol and a sleeping pill to get to sleep. She is an only child; her parents were divorced when she was 10 years old. She was primarily raised by her demanding mother, having only sporadic contact with her father. Bess is a successful accountant for a large manufacturing firm and spends a lot of time at her work. She is a perfectionist, but of course this is generally functional in accounting.

Bess's mother often expressed her love for her and spent a great deal of time with her. At times it was as if she had no other activities in her world that could give her a sense of meaning. Yet Bess does not recall the time with her mother as filled with warmth or fun. Rather, her mother focused on activities in which Bess could "improve herself." She was constantly setting up lessons for Bess to take, and they would usually fight over whether Bess was trying hard enough at these lessons. When home, her mother consistently emphasized the virtues of cleanliness and neatness. They struggled over these issues. Her mother constantly nagged her for not having the things in her room "in order." Bess would work at this task when she was ordered to do so, but the minute her mother took her attention away, Bess would allow things to get disorderly. Her mother continually emphasized to her that this attitude would hurt "when she got older," yet she never made it clear how.

Her mother showed an inordinate concern about cleanliness. She made sure that Bess washed her hands thoroughly each time Bess went to the bathroom or for any reason touched herself in the genital area. Her mother was repulsed by the smell of the bathroom and had a variety of deodorants and incense candles available to counteract odors. Anything rotten or dirty was lumped into this category of repulsiveness and was immediately cleaned and deodorized.

Like most individuals, Bess had times as a child when she felt unhappy. When she expressed these feelings to her mother, she would immediately try to talk Bess out of the feelings. Her major point seemed to be "I love you so much, and spend so much time with you, so how can you be unhappy?" If Bess further expressed her unhappiness, it quite clearly upset her mother.

Bess enjoyed visiting her father, who lived in a nearby city. He was more relaxed about the world, although he had not been very successful and had moved through a series of jobs. He was generally a happy person and attended to Bess when she was there, although he seldom kept in contact when she was absent. Her mother was never happy when Bess went to see her father and subverted this contact whenever possible. She never failed to take the chance to point out to Bess how her father's "laziness" had brought him nothing from the world and she implied that he did not support them the way he should.

Bess in various ways resisted her mother at home, but she lived out her mother's value system in school. She worked very hard and was meticulous in her preparation of assignments. Because she was higher than average intellectually, she consistently succeeded in school. At the same time, she was seen as a "do-gooder" and was not popular with her peers. She did not get involved in class activities; she spent most of her time preparing her lessons and then doing chores around the house.

She also was quite active in the Methodist church, in which her mother raised her. This was generally a positive experience for her, although there were occasions when she became upset about whether she had been "saved" or whether she was a "sinner." The upset usually passed quickly as Bess pushed herself further into her schoolwork or any activity prescribed by her church for dealing with these concerns. As Bess moved into late adolescence, she became more and more beset by erotic fantasies. She was never totally sure that this was against the rules of her church, but she supposed it was. Bess tried to control the fantasies through repetitive tasks or other kinds of activities that distracted her attention. She particularly became a fan of crossword puzzles and jigsaw puzzles. These would occupy her for hours, and her mother was happy to buy her the most complex available. But occasionally the erotic fantasies arose at a time when Bess had few defenses available, and she would then engage in orgiastic bouts of masturbating.

Bess had surprisingly little difficulty interacting with males on a friendship basis. Yet she never seemed to know how to deal with the romantic and sexual issues. As a result, she seldom dated anyone for any length of time. She did become enamored of a boy at a nearby college when she was a senior in high school. He constantly pressed her for sex, and she refused. However, one night she gave in when they had had too much to drink at a party. They then had sex virtually every day for a couple of weeks, at which time Bess began to fear pregnancy. It turned out her fears were well founded, to the horror of her mother when she was told. She immediately arranged an abortion, never allowing Bess to think out whether this was what she wanted. After the abortion, she took Bess on a trip to Europe, during which time she strictly chaperoned her. When they returned, the boyfriend had found another lover, as Bess's mother had hoped.

Bess slipped into the role of "top student," received many honors, and then easily moved into the role of "up-and-coming young career woman." Her job absorbed most of her time, and it was clear that she was a rising star in the firm she worked for. Bess continued to have vague anxieties about dating, marriage, having a family, and other related issues. She handled these anxieties by throwing herself even harder into her work. At the same time, however, she began to experience symptoms that focused around the issue of cleanliness, a pattern not dissimilar from her mother's.

This concern with cleanliness gradually evolved into a thoroughgoing cleansing ritual, which was usually set off by her touching of her genital or anal area. In this ritual, Bess would first remove all of her clothing in a preestablished sequence. She would lay out each article of clothing at specific spots on her bed and examine each one for any indications of "contamination." She would then thoroughly scrub her body, starting at her feet and working meticulously up to the top of her head, using certain washcloths for certain areas of her body. Any articles of clothing that appeared to have been "contaminated" were thrown into the laundry. Clean clothing was put in the spots that were vacant. She would then dress herself in the opposite order from which she took the clothes off. If there were any deviations from this order, or if Bess began to wonder if she might have missed some contamination, she would go through the entire sequence again. It was not rare for her to do this four or five times in a row on certain evenings.

As time passed, she developed a variety of other rituals and obsessive thoughts, usually related to using the toilet, sexual issues, or the encountering of possible "contamination in public places." As her circle of rituals widened, her functioning became more impaired, as the rituals consumed enormous amounts of time and psychic energy. She was aware of the absurdity of these behaviors but at the same time felt compelled to go through with them and did not constantly question them. Finally the behaviors began to intrude on her ability to carry out her work, the one remaining source of meaning and satisfaction in her world. It was then that she referred herself for help.

Etiology

From a biological perspective, studies using brain scans, typically PET scans, find that four brain structures "lock together" in OCDs; that is, they become overactive in unison. One structure is the orbital frontal cortex, situated just over the rear of the eye socket, which operates as the brain's error-detection circuit. The orbital frontal cortex alerts the rest of the brain when something is wrong and needs to be taken care of. In obsessive-compulsive disorder it's hyperactive, so they keep correcting what they think is not right, like checking to see the stove is turned off over and over.

Connections to the caudate nucleus and the cingulate gyrus, structures deep in the brain's core, give one the feeling something is deadly wrong. They make the heart pound and the gut churn with anxiety. The thalamus, the brain's relay station for sensory information, also tends to act in unison. When one of these brain structures becomes more active metabolically, the other three do too; which is not the case in healthy people. The caudate nucleus is usually over active in people with obsessive-compulsive disorder. Patients who respond positively to selective serotonin reuptake inhibitors like Prozac or Luvox, often the medications of choice, show a lessening of activity in the caudate nucleus. Just as important, the caudate nucleus also becomes less active in OCD clients who respond to psychotherapy (Schwartz et al., 1996).

Freud's view of obsessive-compulsive individuals was that these persons were still functioning at the anal-sadistic stage of development and that conflicts over toilet training were critical in their development. This theory has some face validity (or apparent truth) in many cases, including Bess's. However, these common concerns about dirt related to toilet training could occur simply because this is one of the first arenas in which parent and child struggle for control of the relationship. It is also usually the first period in which whole sequences of parental behavior are integrated and modeled by the developing child. Hence, it is easy for these types of concerns to become the content of obsessive-compulsive features. It is also clear that these issues are not relevant to a substantial number of obsessive-compulsives.

Obsessive-compulsives usually model much of their behavior from parents (Amir, 1998). A common learned defense against anxiety for the obsessive-compulsive is intellectualization (talking around the core issue of a conflict in order to avoid its gut level impact). This pattern is effective in many areas, such as school and work. But when it is used to deal with anxiety, it is not effective in the long run, as it does not actually serve to gain corrective information and because these rituals require large amounts of time and energy.

Bess's development shows most of these factors. Her mother was a good model for obsessive-compulsive behavior, and Bess had no significant access to other models. Her mother was also adept at inculcating guilt, and she voided Bess's attempts to dissipate her conflicts by voicing and sharing her concerns and upset. Bess's pattern of religious involvement furthered the development of guilt, and, as is common with most adolescents, sexual concerns provided a ready focus for the conflicts.

The rituals that the obsessive-compulsive develops serve to distract the individual from fully confronting the experience of anxiety or the feeling of a loss of control (van Oppen et al., 1995). Bess had long ago learned that involvement in academic subjects not only brought her inherent rewards, but at the same time distracted her from her conflicts and impulses. She feared that if she gave in to the unacceptable impulses, she could not control her behavior. As a result, she often vacillated between over control of impulses and constant indulgence, as was evident in her masturbation patterns. Like many obsessive-compulsives, Bess feared that if she let down her guard and followed her impulses, she might never again regain control, and "control" is important to obsessive-compulsives. Hence, any activities that served to distract her were welcomed. Her obsessive interest in crossword and jigsaw puzzles is an instance of an individual's trying to distract herself in activities that are often pleasant accompaniments to a full life. Her ritual cleansing was another way of distracting herself from the void of meaning in her world and from the anxiety that was always at the edge of her awareness. Yet, as she most feared, she gradually lost control of these patterns and they began to dominate her world even to the point of interfering with the area that had always provided meaning and satisfaction to her—her work.

Treatment Options

A wide variety of treatments have traditionally been applied to the obsessive-compulsive personality. In actuality, none have achieved spectacular success, as OCD is difficult to treat, probably because the conflicts and anxiety have already been well covered over by the obsessive-compulsive patterns. Also, such individuals seem to fear the passivity (i.e., loss of control) implied by the "patient role."

Psychoanalysts have had some success with the obsessive-compulsive personality. However, the danger with this psychoanalysis is that the obsessive-compulsive individual has had a long history of using intellectualization as a defense mechanism, and the technique of free association in psychoanalysis easily lends itself to the abuse of intellectualization. Only if the therapist can skillfully keep the client away from this pattern can psychoanalysis be helpful (Wachtel, 1997).

Psychosurgery is traditionally reputed to be successful in some cases of obsessive-compulsive disorder, but, in actuality, it is seldom effective. Medication has been increasingly used, and is often necessary, especially with severe cases. Cloimipramine has been the treatment of choice.

However, most therapists (Chambless et al., 1996; van Oppen et al., 1995) recommend a clear and consistent program of *response prevention* (e.g., taking all soap and towels away from a handwasher) combined with constant *exposure in vivo* to the eliciting stimuli to promote extinction in the context of firm and consistent support. A demanding but affirming therapy relationship is the core of an effective treatment program for the compulsive aspects of the disorder. An additional behavioral technique that has been helpful is "thought stopping," presented in more detail in the case history of Randy, the transvestite.

Cognitive-behavior modification can also be effective. Schwartz et al., 1996) confirmed that cognitive-behavior modification can reverse the OCD's physiological "locking up" of brain structures, especially in the connections of the caudate nucleus to the orbital frontal cortex, as described earlier in the section on etiology. Clients learned to relabel their obsessive urges as such, rather than simply giving in to them. Instead of saying, "I have to wash my hands again," they were trained to say, "I'm having an obsessive urge or a compulsion again." Clients were instructed to explain to themselves why the urges and the sense of dread persisted, reminding themselves that they had a disorder that caused the feelings and thoughts. Then, instead of giving in to the urge, they intentionally engaged in 15 minutes of an activity they could be absorbed in and found enjoyable or productive. They might practice a musical instrument, or take a walk, or knit. This shifted their attention away from the compulsion, a step that is crucial in altering the brain's circuitry. The therapy, in which sessions were held once or twice a week for 10 weeks, often culminated in clients' being able to dismiss their urges as symptoms as soon as they felt them. Finally, the urges themselves diminished. The benefits lasted in at least 80% of the cases. This study (Schwartz et al., 1996) is also especially noteworthy in its demonstration that psychological techniques can produce physiological changes in the brain, as shown by positron emission topography (PET).

In some cases, "paradoxical techniques" have been used. For example, the client is asked to purposefully proceed with the unwanted thoughts and behaviors, but to exaggerate them. Doing these behaviors on purpose, in varying patterns, seems to give the client a greater sense of control over the behaviors, and therapy can build upon this developing sense of control.

Medication is often useful, especially where depression is a co-morbid pattern. Clomipranine was the first drug to win official FDA approval for the treatment of OCD, and it is still usually the drug of choice, although it has more side effects than most other drug options here, that is, SSRIs such as fluoxetine, fluroxamine, sertraline, and paroxetine (Lydiard et al., 1996).

Bess's Therapy

*If you mean to keep as well as possible, the less
you think about your health the better.*
—Oliver Wendell Holmes, *Over the Teacups*

Although the classic regimen for OCD is response prevention and exposure, Bess's therapist chose to start the treatment with cognitive-behavior modification combined with thought stopping, which can be construed as a form of response prevention. In the thought stopping, he first asked Bess to let the obsessions just flow freely, and to raise her hand to let the therapist know when she was doing so. Some time after Bess had raised her hand, the therapist shouted "Stop" and then asked Bess to examine her consciousness. Naturally, the train of obsessions had been disrupted. They did this several times, and then the therapist asked Bess herself to shout "Stop" whenever she felt herself in the midst of these obsessions. She was then asked to practice this in her own natural world and was given a small portable shock unit to amplify the effect. Whenever Bess shouted "Stop" to herself, she also gave herself a moderately painful electric shock from this unit, which she had strapped inconspicuously under her dress. This thought stopping demonstrated to Bess that her obsessions could actually be controlled. In that sense it was the basis on which her therapist could train her in new, positive behaviors.

Together, these techniques helped Bess substantially diminish the obsessive-compulsive patterns within 4 months. She and the therapist also worked on the void of positive activities in Bess's life. She was in therapy for approximately 2 years before she achieved what she considered to be an adequate success. Even so, at various times in the ensuing years, Bess occasionally experienced a reemergence of the concerns that she had experienced. Once, she returned for several therapy sessions in order to work these through, although she was usually able to deal with any residual patterns using the skills she had learned in the original therapy sessions, plus training in new skills to cope with these impulses.

Comment

The obsessive-compulsive disorder is at least initially experienced as a distressing loss of control over one's thoughts and actions and is usually somewhat incapacitating. However, a degree of obsessiveness can be productive, and balancing that productiveness against losses in other areas of life is a cost–benefit decision. For example, Dom Capers, a head coach of the National Football League Carolina Panthers, is a productive obsessive. The description of his earlier years as the defensive coordinator with the Pittsburgh Steelers indicated that he worked 100-hour weeks, up to 20 hours daily, during the football season. He arrived at the office each morning at 6:30. The only night he left before 10:00 was Friday— "date night" with his wife. Steelers players called him a workaholic, an exacting perfectionist.

His mother said Capers had been that way since he was born. His brother recalled Capers precisely mowing neighbors' lawns in their hometown of Buffalo, Ohio, trimming the sidewalks by hand with a fork. Capers is an obsessive organizer, a stickler for even the most minute details. For at least 14 years, he has chronicled everything he has done every day, neatly printing every word in a leather-bound calendar book. He has recorded the date, time, and specifics of every team meeting, practice, and game during his stays as an assistant coach with Ohio State, the defunct U.S. Football League's Philadelphia-Baltimore Stars, the NFL's New Orleans Saints, and the Steelers. He has also written down every movie he's seen, every jog, plane trip, church visit, and meal. "It's the only way I know how to do things," Capers said. He always emphasized that nothing should be left to chance, the obsessives' credo as they try to gain certainty in an uncertain world.

Posttraumatic Stress Disorder

The Case of Ryan, the "Postman"

The one thing I remember about Christmas was that my father used to take me out in a boat about 10 miles offshore on Christmas Day, and I used to have to swim back. Extraordinary. It was a ritual. Mind you, that wasn't the hard part. The difficult bit was getting out of the sack.

—John Cleese, British comedian

The essence of *traditional* posttraumatic stress disorder (PTSD) is a delayed distress response pattern to a very atypical and significantly traumatic event, an event that would elicit in most people very negative and disturbed responses. However, the modern concept downplays the "delayed" and "very atypical" concepts. PTSD clients generally re-experience the stressor in intrusive thoughts and dreams, and depression and anxiety are common. Delayed disturbances in combat veterans—as from the Vietnam conflict, which was a spur to the modern conceptualization of this disorder—are often appropriately diagnosed here (Briere, 1997).

The requirements for a *DSM-IV* diagnosis of PTSD are quite complex, possibly reflecting the combination of high controversy, use in the legal arena, and potential common usage of the diagnosis. The *DSM-IV* requires (for at least a month; if less than 4 weeks, the diagnosis of Acute Stress Disorder may be appropriate): (1) exposure to a traumatic event in which there is actual or threatened serious trauma or threat to self or others *and* there is intense fear, helplessness, or horror (or at least disorganized or agitated behavior in children); (2) persistent re-experiencing of the event as evidenced by at least one of (a) recurring and intrusive distressing recollections, (b) recurrent distressing dreams, (c) acting or feeling as if the event is recurring, or (d) intense psychological distress at cues (internal or external) that symbolize or resemble the event, (e) as in #4, but physiological reactions to such cues; (3) persistent avoidance of stimuli associated with the event and a numbing of responsiveness as evidenced by three of these: (a) efforts to avoid related feelings or thoughts, (b) efforts to avoid related activities, places, or people, (c) inability to recall an important event component, (d) reduced participation in significant activities, (e) feelings of detachment or estrangement from others, (f) restricted affect range, (g) sense of a foreshortened psychological or physical future; (4) two persistent, post-trauma symptoms of arousal, from (a) difficulty falling or staying asleep, (b) irritability or anger outbursts, (c) difficulty concentrating, (d) hypervigilance, (e) exaggerated startle responses. A critical predictor of a later PTSD is evidence of dissociation, such as blanking out, reporting or appearing to be "in a daze," at the time of trauma, and this dissociation may appear to onlookers to be a calm, nonstressed response. In addition, evidence of lower intelligence, prior patterns of social withdrawal, irritability and/or impulsivity, general patterns associated with major depression and/or a family history of depression, substance abuse, significant delay before seeking treatment, secondary gain, and detachment or denial patterns suggest a greater likelihood of developing PTSD and a more negative prognosis.

The Case of Ryan, the "Postman"

Ryan, known by his friends in the army as the "Postman," was a 21-year-old white man first seen by staff psychologists at the Veterans Administration hospital in the fall of 1970. At that time he quietly stated that he was seeking help at the "request" of his fiancee, who had threatened to break off their engagement unless he did so.

A check into his background revealed that he had been honorably discharged from the army the previous summer following a tour of duty in Vietnam. He had been reserved and aloof on his return home, and his family and friends had simply assumed this was a natural reaction to readjustment to civilian life, noting that he was obviously happy to be home.

About a month after his return, to no one's surprise, he announced his engagement to his high school sweetheart. However, he did raise a few eyebrows by taking a job at a local factory instead of returning to college to obtain his degree in forestry, which had been his lifelong dream. He seemed dissatisfied with the job from the beginning. He worked lethargically, became irritable at the slightest frustration, and remained detached from his fellow workers. It was also about this time that he experienced his first panic-filled dissociative state.

His roommate, an old friend with whom he shared an apartment, recalled that one night, after a particularly rough day at work, Ryan had fallen into a light sleep in a chair while watching television. After turning off the television, his roommate walked across the room to lock the front door. Just as he shoved home the bolt of the dead lock, Ryan awakened and hit the ground yelling something unintelligible. His eyes were wide open, as he rapidly scanned the room. He appeared to be having difficulty breathing, was trembling, and was sweating profusely. After calming down somewhat, he complained of dizziness and "feeling odd," and swore his roommate to secrecy about the incident.

Ryan recalled that in the days following that first incident his irritability and anger grew even worse and he began to have nightmares. The only people with whom he retained even a semblance of closeness were his family and fiancee, and even those relationships lacked their characteristic warmth and spontaneity. In an attempt to break him out of an ever-increasing depression, his fiancee finally convinced him to join her and his grandfather in a stroll through some of the woods on his parents' property. This was a formerly enjoyable activity, but since returning home he had declined to go along. Ryan remembered that during the walk, after some initial apprehension, he had actually felt relaxed for the first time in a long while. However, when a helicopter suddenly flew over, he dropped to a crouched position, frantically scanning the woods and shouting orders. After getting him back to the house, his grandfather and fiancee watched helplessly as he broke down crying, admitting that this was the second such occurrence. It was at this point that his fiancee responded to his objections to seeking help with the threat of terminating their engagement.

Ryan's History
Ryan was the oldest of two boys and a girl raised in a small town 15 miles outside a large northwestern city. His father was a physician who was already 40 when Ryan was born, and his mother, 8 years younger than his father, dedicated all of her time to her firm and protective upbringing of the children. The family was of "good stock," and serious illness and premature death were unfamiliar to Ryan as he grew up.

He was polite, bright, and happy as a young boy, and while he enjoyed the company of other people, he also loved being by himself sometimes, especially outdoors. The family owned several hundred acres, and he spent many weekend afternoons in the woods with his favorite grandfather, who taught him how to hunt and to appreciate nature. Ryan also proved to be quite athletic; he lettered in high school basketball and baseball, although he never developed an interest in football, somewhat in respect for his mother's worry that it was "too violent."

By the summer of 1968, Ryan was 19 years old, standing 6 feet tall and weighing 175 pounds. He had grown into a rather independent, yet surprisingly sensitive young man, with an easy-going laugh and a sparkle in his eyes. Although friendly to everyone, he considered himself to have only two or three close friends, along with his steady girlfriend, whom he had dated since his sophomore year in high school. A good student, he had just finished his first year at a state university working toward a degree in forestry when he received his draft notice. Although understandably unhappy about the 2-year interruption in his life plans, he accepted the notice as a responsibility he had to fulfill.

Following a tearful farewell and what seemed like a whirlwind training period, Ryan found himself in an Army Ranger unit operating in the Central Highlands of Vietnam. He was a member of a six-man squad that would spend anywhere from 4 to 12 weeks at a time out in the field. Their mission was to make contact with enemy forces, at which point they would engage the enemy or radio their position for an air strike and fall back. Like most men newly rotated into such a squad, he was initially the radio operator. This position was "inherited" by most newcomers due to (1) the weight and cumbersomeness of the radio and (2) the danger involved in carrying it, since the enemy would naturally make a high priority of knocking the radio out to prevent notification of their position.

Two other positions usually "inherited" were those of the "point" and "slack" men. These two men would walk approximately 15 yards ahead of the other four, with the point man in the lead checking the ground for booby traps, while the slack man followed close behind scanning the cover immediately ahead for any hint of "Charlie." It was the position of point for which Ryan was being groomed, due partly to recognition of his field skills previously developed by his grandfather. It was also around this time that he was no longer known as Ryan, but rather as the "Postman," a nickname resulting from the quantity of mail he received from home, most of which he would carry into the field in his helmet.

In writing home, the Postman found it hard to find the right words to express his experiences, although words such as *scared, cold, hot, wet,* and *lonely* certainly applied. However, one word seemed to sum up the totality of the whole experience: *waiting.* The very nature of the job dictated that something was going to happen, yet there was absolutely no way of knowing when it would occur. Compound this with the added knowledge of the point man that if he missed as much as one small clue his next step could be his last, and one can begin to understand the Postman's experience. However, as the Postman tried to explain in his letters, one had to live through it to understand the nature of combat in Vietnam.

The only bright spot in his ordeal was a friendship that developed with Winston, a fellow draftee who had rotated into the squad shortly after the Postman's arrival. The friendship was based on their complementary interests in nature. The Postman had all the instincts and knowledge of a pathfinder, Winston's specialty was in the area of botany, his major in college. The two seemed to enter into almost a mutual information exchange when time allowed, each teaching the other his special knowledge.

Unfortunately, this ad hoc nature seminar had an unhappy ending about 2 weeks after Winston succeeded the Postman at point. Possibly some aspect of the Southeast Asian flora caught Winston's eye when he should have been concentrating on the ground ahead. The Postman never had a chance to find out; both Winston and the slack man were blown apart by a grenade booby trap.

The Postman's withdrawal from reality following the death of his friend proved extensive enough to warrant his temporary removal from his squad for treatment of "combat fatigue." The application of the crisis intervention principles of immediacy, proximity, and expectancy (discussed later in this case) had drastically improved the success rate of the treatment of combat fatigue in Vietnam. Indeed, the Postman was back with his squad within a week, although his sparkle and spontaneity were gone.

Following his return, the Postman kept himself rather distanced from other squad members. In addition, he strongly objected to anyone other than himself taking the position of point for the remaining 5 months of his tour of duty, even as it approached its end, a time when most men understandably became very protective of themselves. It is a tribute to his skill, however, that his squad experienced no death or injury related to booby traps during this period.

> *The trouble about always trying to preserve the*
> *health of the body is that it is so difficult to do*
> *without destroying the health of the mind.*
> —G. K. Chesterton, *On the Classics*

Etiological Factors

Several key factors were involved in the Postman's development of a posttraumatic stress disorder, the most obvious of which was the nature of the stressor. Military combat has long been recognized as an extremely stressful experience, and combat in Vietnam proved to be extremely so due to the guerrilla-style "hit and run" fighting. There were no "front lines" behind which one was safe. Death could come from an unseen sniper, a booby-trapped trail, and even from "innocent" women and children. This was particularly true of action in the field, with survival literally depending on hyperalertness. Such an attitude had to be maintained virtually 24 hours a day, for anywhere from 30 to 90 days at a time, particularly in such positions as point and slack.

There was also a certain trade-off in the rotation system that was used in Vietnam. The policy of rotation after 12 months of duty was a factor in the decrease in cases of combat exhaustion during that conflict, apparently as a result of the establishment of a DEROS (date of expected return from overseas), recognizable as a clear point at which the stress would cease. However, at the same time, the system usually had men returning home within 48 to 72 hours of the end of their tour of duty, offering them little in the way of "decompression" from their traumatic experience.

Experience with posttraumatic stress suggests that decompression is a natural and necessary process for many individuals following such an extreme stressor. Decompression involves a gradual "coming to grips" with the traumatic event and the eventual acceptance and integration of the experience into the self. As with civilian disasters, this process often necessitates a rehashing of the experience, a process that many returning servicemen find almost impossible to go through, for several reasons. First of all, the system of rotation was highly individualized in the sense that a soldier rarely returned home with his buddies, a situation in which common experiences could at least be shared and discussed. Second, the swiftness of the return allowed little time for adjustment to the inevitable culture shock generated by moving from the pressures of jungle warfare back into the alternative pressures of a highly technological society. In addition, far from the respect and gratitude expected, many returning veterans were aghast at finding themselves bearing the hostility generated by the nation's growing dissatisfaction with the war effort. Rather than offering the supportive environment so necessary and listening to the horrors these men had experienced, people rejected or at best chose to ignore these veterans. With no outlet for their pent-up frustrations, anxieties, problems of conscience, and emotional confusion, it is small wonder that many such veterans (both men and women) developed, and continue to develop, problems in adjusting to civilian life.

As acknowledged in the *DSM*, predisposing individual characteristics may play a role in the development of a posttraumatic stress disorder. This often refers to the existence of prior psychopathology. However, in the Postman's case, any predisposing "weakness" probably came from the absence of any emotional or stress "inoculation" in his life history; for example, no threatening illness, his rather protected upbringing by somewhat older parents, and the small size of his hometown. Thus, when confronted with the extreme stress of warfare in Vietnam, he lacked a substantial arsenal of adaptive coping methods that might have been learned from lesser stressors and that would have prepared him for response to later stress.

Lacking this psychological toughness, the Postman's already pressed defenses had been overwhelmed by the horror of seeing a close friend blown to bits. This shock to his unprotected system was so severe that it forced a temporary "shutdown" of reality processing, with consequent development of an extremely "thick" emotional insulation. Such a defense was probably furthered to a degree by his already introspective nature. The cost of such protection was the suppression of all of his feelings and emotions arising from the incident, particularly the guilt. For not only did he experience the common "survivor's" guilt of "why him and not me?" but he also felt that his own skills should not have let something like that happen. This feeling was reinforced when his guilt-induced claim to the point resulted in no further casualties for the remainder of his tour. Thus, he agonized, if he had never originally relinquished that position, the deaths would not have occurred.

Even though such feelings were initially kept out of consciousness, the Postman's return to the intimate relationships with his family and fiancee created problems. The emotional base and depth of those relationships slowly wore through his tough insulation. The return of feelings also meant the return of painful memories. As the feelings slipped closer to consciousness, such strong cues as the sound of a helicopter or a metallic sound similar to the click of a rifle bolt elicited the hidden emotions, much as occurs in posthypnotic suggestions.

Flashbacks, or vivid re-experiencing of the traumatic event, are commonly reported in cases of PTSD. But they can be malingered in order to bring a claim of PTSD into the legal arena. The dramatic quality of flashback symptoms is certainly impressive; the difficulty is in deciphering the veracity of such reports. The following criteria are typically characteristic of true flashbacks:

- The flashback is sudden and unpremeditated.
- The flashback is uncharacteristic of the individual.
- There is a retrievable history of one or more intensely traumatic events that are re-enacted in the flashback.
- There may be amnesia for all or part of the episode.
- The flashback lacks apparent current and specific motivation.
- The current trigger stimuli reasonably resemble the original experiences.
- The individual is at least somewhat unaware of the specific ways he or she has re-enacted some of the prior traumas.
- The individual has, or previously had, other believable symptoms of PTSD.

Treatment

Based on a comparison of psychodynamic, behavioral, and biochemical treatments for PTSD, it appears that direct therapeutic exposure to the trauma (e.g., via systematic desensitization or flooding or even focused group discussion) and cognitive reframing have emerged as the most important factors in treatment (Briere, 1997; Chambless et al., 1996). A working-through process in which the client's world—beliefs, overall cognitive schemata, are modified in accord with the traumatic memory is often necessary for successful treatment.

A somewhat controversial treatment, EMDR (eye-movement desensitization and reprocessing therapy) has received support for its use with various anxiety disorders, though it has most commonly been applied to PTSD. EMDR has been compared with exposure therapy because it requires clients to recall traumatic memories that cause problems such as nightmares, intrusive thoughts, flashbacks, anxiety, depression, and relationship problems. Unlike the process of exposure therapy, however, EMDR clients hold an image of the memory in mind as the therapists prompt them into 20 to 30 seconds of rapid, side-to-side eye movement. The clients then report the memories, feelings, or thoughts that emerge. This sequence continues until troubling emotions no longer accompany the memory. In some studies in which EMDR and exposure therapy obtained comparable results, both therapists and clients showed some preference for EMDR because exposure therapy is more emotionally difficult for both groups.

The principles of crisis intervention noted earlier that have been employed in cases of combat exhaustion in the field, immediacy, proximity, and expectancy, also provide an excellent framework within which to treat posttraumatic stress syndromes. In this case, *immediacy* refers to the early detection and treatment of the disorder, with an emphasis on returning individuals to their typical life situations as quickly as possible. *Proximity* emphasizes the need to treat them in their ongoing world by avoiding hospitalization. Lastly, *expectancy* is the communication of the therapist that while their reaction is quite normal, it still does not excuse them from functioning adequately; the "sick role" is not reinforced (Meyer and Deitsch, 1996). An overall supportive atmosphere of warmth, understanding, and whatever empathy is possible is also important. Since the environment to which these individuals return should be similarly supportive, sessions with family and friends can be beneficial.

Treatment of Ryan

An alert staff member at the VA hospital where Ryan originally inquired about help noted his strong attachment to both his father and grandfather, so he referred Ryan to a rather "fatherly" therapist. True to the hunch, rapport was easily established despite the somewhat coercive nature of the referral. After some trust was developed, Ryan was induced to attend weekly "rap sessions" held for veterans at the hospital, which, although painful, did help him to face the memories he had for so long attempted to suppress.

The individual and group sessions emphasized the recognition that the disorder was an understandable reaction and that the resulting anxieties had to be approached and dealt with if a desired level of adjustment was ever to be attained. Ryan's specific focus eventually turned to his guilt over the circumstances of his friend's death, a guilt that permeated the memory of everything associated with his Vietnam experience. The therapies allowed him to realize that despite the injustice of the deaths, he himself had not failed in any responsibility to the two men killed. Relaxation training also played an important role in dealing with the generalized anxiety that had resulted from the guilt. Such anxiety is problematic in many cases of PTSD, as it often persists despite the recognition of its irrationality.

Another focus of attention at this point were the cues that had apparently triggered his dissociative states. Discovering these to be the sounds of a helicopter or a metallic click similar to the click of a rifle bolt, an SDT was employed. Ryan was urged to use a controlled relaxation response in handling his fears and anxieties associated with the particular sound through the progressive stages of: (1) imagining the sound in different situations, (2) listening to a recording of the sound, and (3) eventually having in vivo experiences with the source of the sound. This last stage consisted of an actual ride in an army helicopter and several sessions of having a rifle randomly bolt-loaded and fired near him. Therapy could not entirely eliminate a fear response to these cues, but it did extinguish their ability to elicit a dissociative state. Just as importantly, it showed Ryan a method by which he could adaptively handle such anxiety when it occurred.

Another factor that played a vital role throughout his treatment and subsequent recovery was the supportive, caring atmosphere provided by his family and fiancee. Involved from the beginning, they attended several sessions, both with and without Ryan, in an effort to gain an understanding of the problems he faced and to learn what role they could play in his recovery. This revived the former intimacy of their relationships with Ryan and also taught them how to be supportive without reinforcing the sick role.

4

Dissociative and Sleep Disorders

The dissociative disorders are marked by a sudden disruption or alteration of the normally integrated functions of consciousness. This disturbance is almost always temporary, although it may wax and wane, particularly in amnesia and fugue. With the exception of the depersonalization disorder, the dissociative disorders occur rarely, and consideration must be given to the faking of this type of disorder in order to avoid some social or moral responsibility (Melton et al., 1997).

The *DSM* subcategories are: Psychogenic Amnesia, an acute disturbance of memory function; Psychogenic Fugue, a sudden disruption of one's sense of identity, usually accompanied by travel away from home; Dissociative Identity Disorder (Multiple Personality Disorder), the domination of the person's consciousness by two or more separate personalities (the classic and in many ways the most severe of the Dissociative Disorders as demonstrated in the case of Anna O.); and Depersonalization Disorder, a disturbance in the experience of the self in which the sense of reality is temporarily distorted.

There is also a category referred to as Other Dissociative Disorders, simply a residual category. The patterns most commonly included in this diagnosis are those of persons who experience a sense of unreality that is not accompanied by depersonalization and who also show some trance-like states.

It can be argued that the Depersonalization Disorder, also referred to as the Depersonalization Neurosis, is not appropriately included in this general category, as there is no substantial memory disturbance. Yet there is a significant disturbance, albeit temporary, of the sense of reality, and thus the identity is certainly affected.

The sleep disorders are included in this chapter because they are analogous to the dissociative disorders in that they also involve an altered state of consciousness. Sleep, although an altered state, is of course a normal process, and the disruptions are usually not as severe as they are in the dissociative processes.

There are a wide variety of possible disturbance patterns, and the cases here deal with the most common and important patterns: Sam, sleepwalking and Ilse, insomnia.

The Multiple Personality Disorder

Introduction

You want to go where everybody knows your name.

—From the theme song of Cheers

The *DSM-IV* uses the term Dissociative Identity Disorder; we'll use the more universally recognized term of Multiple Personality Disorder (MPD). *DSM-IV* defines MPD as the presence of two or more distinct personalities within one person, each of which is relatively complete and integrated and maintains its own pattern of behavior, thinking, and social relationships. Each of these entities may be dominant and control behavior at different times or in different situations. MPD is the most extreme of the dissociative disorders. While persons exhibiting psychogenic fugue typically experience only one "switch" to another personality, multiples experience many personality alternations over an extended period of time. The alternate personalities generally serve important functions the core personality cannot manage for itself. Unfortunately, many people believe that MPD is closely related to schizophrenia, possibly because this latter term literally means "split mind."

No disorder has proven more fascinating to the public than MPD. Two books dealing with the topic, *The Three Faces of Eve* and *Sybil* became best-sellers and were made into movies. Despite the attention that such popularizations have received, MPD remains one of the least understood psychological disorders, in part because reliable reports in the professional literature are quite rare.

It is difficult to judge the incidence of MPD. After the celebrated case of Mary Reynolds, described by S. L. Mitchell in 1817, only 76 cases were reported in the ensuing 127 years (Taylor and Martin, 1944). Since 1944, the number of reported cases increased somewhat, with Winer (1978) finding over 200 documented cases. A few modern theorists have suggested that a significant proportion of all psychiatric patients are multiples, but most researchers or clinicians would find this figure unbelievable. Thigpen and Cleckley (1984), as well as Weissberg (1993), have suggested that much of the apparent increase here may be due to the glamour that accrues to both patients and therapists claiming the disorder, as well as attempts by clients to escape accusations of criminal behavior by presenting themselves as "split personalities." Of the cases documented to date, the majority, up to 90%, are women.

An additional complicating factor stems from the nature of MPD. In most cases the core personality is completely unaware of the alternates, though the reverse need not be true (Kluft, 1998). Because the alternates usually have specific roles, they are unlikely to seek treatment on their own. The core personality is often aware of "blackouts" or lost time but is unlikely to discuss these problems with anyone. When multiples do enter treatment it is often for reasons other than the primary disorder, such as suicide attempts or criminal behavior. The most common diagnoses initially given are major depression and schizophrenia. Most multiples are only identified as such after some extended contact with mental health specialists who eventually observe one or more of the alternates in vivo.

A history of having suffered amnesia or other dissociative experiences or borderline personality disorder pattern is mildly predictive of a future multiple personality disorder, as is a history of physical or sexual abuse (especially repeated, traumatic incest). Stress and/or significant personal loss is an important precipitating factor, as are difficult developmental or social transition points. New personalities are usually a crystallization into a personality of opposite facets from the original one.

Anna O. is critical to the development of psychoanalytic theory and then the later psychodynamic therapies; indeed, she is considered the first patient of psychoanalysis. Specifically, she is the first patient with whom the cathartic method was employed. In light of the evolution of modern diagnostic concepts, it is increasingly evident that Anna O. suffered from MPD, in addition to or instead of the traditional diagnosis of Anna as "hysteric" (Weissberg, 1993).

Also, although even many professionals believe Anna O. was a patient of Freud's, he never saw her. Rather, she was a patient, for about 18 months between November 1880 and June 1882, of Josef Breuer, Freud's early mentor and collaborator. Breuer and Freud both viewed Anna O. as a classic case of hysteria. However, Weissberg (1993) argues persuasively that although there are hysteric components, she is most accurately seen as a multiple personality, with the possibility that the MPD was at least in part induced by Breuer's treatment. Some difficulties in assessing this case stem from the fact that Breuer did not write up the case until 10 years after he had terminated treatment with her.

Breuer, one of the most famous physicians of his time, already had a scientific reputation for his discovery of the automatic control of breathing by the vagus nerve, thereafter termed the Hering–Breuer reflex, thus also honoring Ewald Hering, the professor who had started him on that research. Breuer also made another permanent scientific contribution with his finding that the semicircular canals control equilibrium. Curiously, Breuer waited 5 months after the conclusion of the therapy with Anna to discuss his "talking cure" with Sigmund Freud. That date, November 18, 1882, is considered by many to be the founding point of modern psychotherapy.

The Case of Anna O.

Anna (actually Bertha Pappenheim), an unmarried 21-year-old woman from a prominent Jewish family in Vienna, first consulted with Breuer at the end of November 1880. The initial complaint was a persistent cough, and he used hypnosis to elicit memories to reconstruct the events that led up to referral. This included Anna's reaction to childhood and more recently, to her distress around caring for her father while his health gradually failed. In July 1880, he developed a pleuritic abscess, probably caused by tuberculosis, the possible cause of Anna's symptoms as well.

As is often the case with seriously disordered individuals, any success and/or acceptance of the initial complaint allows elaboration into numerous allied symptoms; in Anna's case, vision and hearing problems, neck weakness, headaches, and anesthesia of her right arm and leg. She then became mute for 2 weeks, and soon thereafter revealed two distinct personalities that apparently switched back and forth without warning. Anna's first or usual personality was a bit melancholy, in part because, as is common with MPDs, she experienced gaps in consciousness, mood swings, and even possible hallucinations. As is also often the case with MPDs, the second personality (that Breuer called her "alienated state" or "condition seconde") had a more antisocial quality, what Anna termed "naughty." It was also often abusive toward others, and occasionally generated odd, rebellious behaviors like tearing buttons off of bedclothes.

After Anna's father's death on April 5, 1881, she (1) stopped recognizing anyone except Breuer, (2) would only communicate in English (her second language), and (3) would eat only if fed by Breuer. As is evident, this first Freudian was hardly orthodox in his therapeutic technique. Every day Anna would become somnolent in the afternoon (probably autohypnotically), and after sunset Breuer would formally hypnotize her or she would do the autohypnosis. She would recount her hallucinations—dreams of that day and then awaken "calm and cheerful."

Yet, her condition worsened, and she became suicidal. On June 7, 1881, she was moved to a house outside Vienna where she could be monitored more closely. Breuer now visited her most days, occasionally resorting to pleading to get her to talk. She would sometimes only talk after thoroughly feeling Breuer's hand to make sure it was him, asserting she could not recognize him visually. Although her symptoms had at first worsened, they now calmed somewhat. Anna attributed this to the "talking cure" of reliving her memories under hypnosis, and Anna moved back to Vienna.

However, Anna's personalities again changed dramatically, and Breuer could now elicit a personality shift by showing her oranges (the only food she would eat during the first part of her illness). It was in this period that after avoiding water for 6 weeks, Anna, while hypnotized, recalled her disgust when she saw a dog drink from a water glass, and then when she awakened, her hydrophobia disappeared. Breuer now had the insight to recognize this as *catharsis,* a basic principle of psychoanalytic technique, and systematically used it on her many other symptoms. Most disappeared and in the process Breuer discovered they had all started the summer her father fell ill. Breuer and Freud later theorized that Anna's feelings about this had been "strangulated" (later termed "repressed"), only to then come out in her various symptoms and then to be relieved by "insight" as well as "working through" by analyzing dreams and talking into "abreaction" and eventual catharsis, bringing a cure.

Although many of Anna's symptoms cleared, her alter personality appeared again in spring 1881, something Breuer called a "disagreeable event." Breuer last saw her in June 1882 and stated she now enjoyed "complete health." But, possibly reflecting his Victorian ethics, his pride, his reported panic, or all three, he neglected to note that in their last session Anna had told him she was pregnant with his baby. After calming her down by inducing a hypnotic trance, Breuer arranged for his own immediate departure to Venice with his wife for a second honeymoon. Anna was not pregnant. Freud later used his belief that Breuer had misunderstood Anna's sexual attraction to Breuer to develop his concepts of transference and countertransference.

Documents were later obtained from Anna's file at the Bellevue Sanatorium in Kreutzlingen, where she was hospitalized in July 1882 for morphine addiction, indicating periodic inability to speak German, her first language, absences of consciousness, and feelings of "time missing." Anna also showed two separate personality states at least 5 years after termination and 6 years after her second personality was discovered.

Consistent with the concept that abuse is often (but not always) found in the histories of those who later manifest MPD, there were indications that Anna had been sexually abused, and that she was certainly emotionally abused by her mother. As an adult in her social work career she showed a consistent preoccupation with and active efforts against Jewish men who abused women. She was also generally emotionally abused, in that her needs to be independent were stifled first by her father, also by the family's Orthodox Jewish practices, by her mother and brother who eventually even excluded her from the care of her dying father, and then by society's repressive attitude at that time toward bright and intellectually curious women. Ironically, Anna maintained a lifelong disdain for psychoanalysis, and the Nazis later used Anna's journalistic exposé of wealthy Jewish slave traders as anti-Jewish propaganda.

However, Anna did eventually recover and overcome her addiction. In 1895, she became the director of a Jewish orphanage in Frankfurt, Germany. She never married, but traveled widely and campaigned to improve the conditions of women. In 1904, she founded a League of Jewish Women, the first organization of its kind. And in 1907, she began a home for unwed mothers. Committed to the causes of women and children, she can be considered an early feminist. She wrote, "If there is any justice in the next life, women will make the laws and men will bear the children!" In 1954, the West German government issued a commemorative postage stamp in her honor, one of a series entitled "Helpers of Humanity."

MPD Controversies

Most experts believe there are true MPDs, with these qualifications (Spanos, 1996; Weissberg, 1993; Thigpen and Cleckley, 1984):

- While a few therapists seem to come up with many "multiples" in their practice, most therapists seldom see such cases.
- Not only have there been significantly more reports of cases of MPD, but in recent decades MPDs report a significantly greater number of secondary personalities, or "alters."
- The diagnosis of MPD is to some degree culture-bound, and the great bulk of cases have been observed in the United States.
- The diagnosis has another possible culture-bound bias in that the vast majority of MPD cases are female.
- In the majority of cases the diagnosis of MPD only emerges after a period of therapy, usually employing hypnosis (and often self-hypnosis) and with a therapist who is sympathetic to (if not an active advocate for) the idea of multiples.
- Many proponents of MPD argue that separate "alters" or personalities may influence the MPD's general behavior without actually emerging or being

observable to others, thus making any kind of independent corroboration impossible. If so, the concept of MPD must be placed in the realm of philosophy or religion rather than of science.

- As in the case of Anna O., the great majority of information derives from anecdotal testimony and case reports and remains unverified by scientific methods. However, much of this information is repeated often enough to take on the veneer of truth.

- Some of the supposed scientific findings about MPD that are commonly repeated by believers are spurious. For example, advocates consistently assert that different personalities show different physiological patterns, for example, in EEG patterns and in psychological test response patterns. However, normals can show similar differences when they are in different emotional states, and persons who attempt to simulate different personalities show EEG differences similar to those found in different MPD personalities. Also, some scientific findings, for example, that many MPDs report a history of childhood abuse, are generalized to the point of becoming inaccurate; for example, "many" becomes "most" or even "virtually all"; or a history of abuse becomes specified as a history of sexual abuse, and so on.

Etiology

Dissociative processes are a part of normal functioning, although the propensity for their use varies among individuals. Many kinds of stressful events, such as natural disasters and combat fatigue, can produce extreme dissociative phenomena. The extreme manifestations seen in some cases of MPD stem from long-term stress, often associated with severe trauma and/or abuse.

MPD can also be seen as a learned response within the family. Research suggests that in most instances at least one parent is severely disturbed, as was the case with Anna O. Many multiples report the dissociation of the first alternate in early childhood, often before the age of 6. This first dissociation establishes a pattern wherein sudden stresses elicit further alternates that arise to meet new challenges. Cases of "super-multiples" with over 100 alternates have been reported but are understandably given little credence in professional circles.

Individuals are especially susceptible to developing a multiple personality if they (1) were abused as children; (2) are under significant stress; (3) have had somewhat contradictory personality factors; (4) have experienced maternal rejection; (5) are impressionable, suggestible, and/or dependent; (6) tend toward over-dramatic behaviors; and (7) have unrealistically high standards of performance.

Many persons find it difficult to imagine the underlying mechanism of dissociation. It seems implausible that truly distinct personalities could share the same neural patterns. The most promising explanation for this phenomenon appears to be a state dependent learning (SDL) model. An organism's state at any given time is a function of conditions in the environment as well as physical and psychological conditions. Information learned under certain conditions is best recalled in the exact same state and may be inaccessible under a different state. Idiosyncratic cues, such as the oranges in Anna O.'s case, may then call out an alternate personality. Thus, dissociation is an extreme form of SDL. Multiples may acquire memories and behaviors while in a state of extreme stress and are later amnesic for this information while in a more normal state. When the stressful state is reinstituted, the memories and behavior return and may appear to belong to a different person. This model would help explain why alternate personalities tend to be emotionally responsive while the core personality seems affectively blunted or drained. It would also explain why alternates seem to have specific functions and tend to appear only in situations that call for their functions.

Treatment Options

The classical treatment approach with MPD (indeed, in that sense originating with Anna O.) makes extensive use of hypnotic techniques (Weissberg, 1993; Meyer, 1992). Because hypnosis is often viewed as a structured or purposeful form of dissociation, it can help to make the transition from one alternate or ego state to another more predictable and manageable. An alternative explanation holds that the hypnosis merely produces a placebo effect, giving the client a rationale to give up dissociative symptoms. The usual strategy is to elicit each of the alternates, while audio- or videotaping, and discover their peculiar memories and characteristics to gain a working knowledge of the elaborately divided self-system of the client. Next the therapist negotiates with each alternate for some kind of therapy contract. This process often meets with considerable resistance, because some alternates may be hostile, destructive, or negativistic, while others may be immature, egocentric, or seductive toward the therapist. Eventually, all must be convinced that they stand to gain from being integrated into a whole person.

The process of fusion, or joining of two or more alternates, is often dramatized in popular accounts of MPD. It can be seen as a more elaborate effort to help the client reconcile conflicting motives and ideas, as is common in many types of therapy. Hypnosis may be used to contact the alternates and encourage them to become active at the same time. Some clinicians make videotapes of the alternates and show them to the others during a waking state. The order of fusion generally follows two patterns. Alternates that dissociated at the same time or serve similar roles are brought together first. The therapist then attempts to reconcile remaining personality fragments with the core personality in roughly the order in which they split off. This process may involve hypnotic age regression of the core personality to the appropriate time period.

While some therapists have attempted to use anti-psychotic drugs in treating multiples, these efforts have had limited success. Anti-anxiety medications may be useful during periods of extreme stress as the process of fusion is underway.

Comment

Many clinicians have noted that MPD can often be an iatrogenic disorder, one that is superimposed on a variety of amorphous complaints by the therapist's suggestions that multiplicity would explain the client's condition (Spanos, 1996;

Weissberg, 1993). Many of these persons are frightened by their experiences, and might be particularly vulnerable to such suggestions. A second reason for skepticism about the concept of MPD stems from the occasional attempts of malingerers to escape criminal responsibility by presenting themselves as "split personalities." Most clinicians do accept the notion of MPD in principle, but most would argue that this disorder is very rare and difficult to diagnose (Weissberg, 1993; Thigpen and Cleckley, 1984). Unfortunately, the rise in reports has stemmed primarily from the work of a relatively small number of clinicians and researchers who have much of their professional identity invested in the concept. Our knowledge of this puzzling disorder would be greatly enhanced by increased involvement of mainstream psychologists and psychiatrists who could bring more diverse perspectives to bear on the problem.

Sleep Disorders

The little girl did not want to go to sleep in a neighbor's house unless the bedroom door was left open. "Why, you're not afraid of the dark—a big girl like you?" the neighbor teased.

"Yes, I am," the little girl cried.

"But you're not afraid of the dark at your house."

"I know," answered the little girl, "but that's my dark."

—Anonymous story

Sleep is a most important event. People sleep for different lengths of times at different ages. Newborns need from 13 to 16 hours of sleep, and after that the need, on the average, starts to decrease so that those who are past 50 years of age need about 7 hours. Also, we require more sleep when we are sick, stressed, or have been involved in strenuous activities, and women need more during menstruation and pregnancy (Harsh and Ogilvie, 1995).

There is great variety in sleep disorders, just as there is in normal sleep patterns. Many adults will suffer a period of chronic insomnia at some point in their lives. In the *DSM-IV* the sleep disorders are divided into (1) Sleep Disorders Related to Another Mental Disorder, for example, a mood or anxiety disorder, (2) Sleep Disorder Due to a General Medical Condition, (3) Substance-Induced Sleep Disorder, and (4) the focus of this chapter, Primary Sleep Disorder. The Primary Sleep Disorders are subdivided into the Dysomnias (abnormalities in the sleep cycle's amount, quality, or timing) and the Parasomnias (sleep-related abnormal events, such as nightmares).

The Dysomnias include (1) Primary Insomnia (307.42), at least 1 month of difficulty initiating or maintaining sleep, with life impairment, and not better explained by other sleep or other disorders; (2) Primary Hypersomnia (307.44), at least a month of excessive sleepiness, less if recurrent, and life impairment, and so on; (3) Narcolepsy (347), at least 3 months of daily and irresistible attacks of refreshing sleep that include at least either catalepsy or recurrent intrusions of REM sleep into the sleep wakefulness transition, (4) Breathing-Related Sleep Disorder (780.59), evidence of a sleep-disrupting breathing condition, (5) Circadian Rhythm Sleep Disorder (307.45), impairing and persistent or recurring excessive sleepiness or insomnia due to a mismatch of the sleep–wake cycle to the individual's circadian rhythm and/or environment requirements, which can be further specified as "Delayed Sleep Phase Type," "Jet Lag Type," "Shift Work Type," or "Unspecified Type", and (6) Dysomnia NOS (307.47).

The Parasomnias are Nightmare Disorder (307.47), impairing and repeated sleep awakenings, with recall of extended and very frightening dreams, with rapid reorientation upon awakening; Sleep Terror Disorder (307.46), impairing sleep awakenings, usually with a panicky scream, intense fear with related autonomic signs, relative unresponsiveness to comforting, with little recall of the dream; Sleepwalking Disorder (307.46), impairing repeated sleepwalking episodes, with unresponsivity in the episode, relatively quick reorientation, and amnesia for the episode; and Parasomnia NOS (307.47).

The critical diagnostic recommendation is that any apparently serious sleep disorder should be evaluated at a sleep disorder center; a thorough evaluation should include some observation and physiological monitoring, ideally of at least a couple of nights of sleep.

We will now present two cases that detail three of the most important and common patterns: sleepwalking disorder in the first case and chronic insomnia and disruption of the sleep–wake cycle in the second. The first case, of Sam, focuses on sleepwalking.

Little or no research has been done on the control of sleepwalking, although as early as 1968, Silverman and Geer eliminated one patient's nightmares by systematic desensitization. Most people do not view sleepwalking as more than an unavoidable nuisance. Even in the case presented, it was not the sleepwalking per se that was the problem, as the patient had walked in his sleep at a regular and high rate for 9 years.

> It is no small art to sleep: to achieve it one must
> keep awake all day.
>
> —Friedrich Nietzsche, *Thus Spake Zarathustra* (1885)

The Case of Sam

Sam, a 24-year-old white male, came in at the instigation of his wife. During a recent act of sleepwalking he took down a shotgun, loaded it, and prepared to fire at imaginary burglars. His wife awakened to find herself looking into the end of the gun. Luckily, her screaming did not stimulate him to fire but rather woke him up. She insisted that he see someone the very next day. He had previously walked in his sleep four to five times a week without incident ever since he was 15 years old. His wife had tolerated this, only occasionally complaining of being awakened by his fumbling about.

Indications given by Sam and his wife were that Sam had a very normal and happy childhood. He had no more than the usual childhood diseases, was obviously loved and well cared for by his parents, and never showed any childhood maladjustment.

Sam did casually mention that since his first year of college he had always suffered anxiety before taking tests and had resorted to tranquilizers with little success. He said he was now becoming more anxious as time loomed for his bar examination.

Associated Features

There is no indication that psychological disorder is common in the background of persons with a sleepwalking disorder (Pressman and Orr, 1997). However, as with Sam, episodes become more frequent when the person is under stress or is fatigued. The incident with the shotgun brought Sam to treatment, but similar aggressive or destructive incidents were never observed in Sam's history. Such incidents seldom happen with sleepwalkers.

Similar to Sam's, most sleepwalking episodes usually last anywhere from a couple of minutes up to 30 to 40 minutes. Episodes usually occur in the nonrapid eye movement period, that component of sleep that typically contains the EEG delta activity (sleep stages 3 and 4).

Sleepwalkers often just sit up, make a few movements, and then go back to sleep; only occasionally does the episode proceed to actual walking. When they do walk, they show a blank stare (which can appear eerie or frightening), are poorly coordinated, can see and maneuver around objects, and usually are amnesic for the experience, which is the dissociative component.

Sleepwalking usually begins in and is most common in childhood, and approximately 15–20% of the population have sleepwalked at least once. There may be a genetic component, as the disorder does tend to run in families, and it is more common in males (Pressman and Orr, 1997; Harsh and Ogilvie, 1995).

Sam's Treatment

The following recommendations, as adapted in part from Gilmore (1991), were presented to Sam in a handout to take home:

1. Use no drugs, alcohol, or caffeine, and use no psychotropic medications unless prescribed by a physician who is aware of the potential of such medications to exacerbate sleepwalking. Avoid any over-the-counter cold remedies or diet pills that contain stimulants.

2. Remove and/or dismantle any lethal weapons from access by the sleepwalker.

3. Take special precautions, such as placing locks on doors and windows, tying one's ankle to the bedpost, and placing a "kiddie fence" by the bedroom door.

4. Sleep on the ground floor.

5. Get treatment for depression and/or other concurrent emotional problems.

6. Learn stress management skills and obtain skills and reassurance to lower anxiety, and consider marital counseling for related stress.

7. Maintain a regular sleep–wake cycle and get adequate sleep at regular intervals.

8. Get a complete assessment by an expert in sleep disorders who can monitor physiological measurements.

Relaxation techniques were employed, as there seemed to be a possible relationship of the gun incident to the test anxiety. A seven-item hierarchy of anxiety-arousing situations was agreed upon, ranging from "hearing about a friend who has a test," through "trying to study several days before the tests," up to the most anxiety-ridden item "receiving the test paper and looking it over."

Sam said his wife was a light sleeper and often awakened during the sleepwalking because her bed was close to his, and the only exit from his bed was along a narrow aisle between the beds. He agreed to have her bed moved into contact with his so that he would have to wake her by crawling over her. His wife purchased a loud whistle, which she was instructed to keep by the bed and to blow anytime she was awakened by his sleepwalking. She was to chart each act of sleepwalking and how long it took him to react to the whistle.

Sam's bar exam was 1 month away, so he was seen twice a week for systematic desensitization (see the case of Danielle in Chapter 2). He was seen for a total of ten sessions (5 weeks). In the meantime, he had dismantled the firing pin of his shotgun.

Sam sleepwalked four times during the first week. His wife immediately blew the whistle and woke him. He sleepwalked five times the second week, twice the third, and no more from the fourth week on. He had no negative reaction to the whistle.

During the first week he was unable to study effectively. However, in the second week he accomplished the amount of studying he felt necessary. This change persisted, and there was a minimum of felt anxiety. He passed his bar exam with a mark somewhat higher than he expected even under optimal conditions.

At a 3-month follow-up he reported he had walked in his sleep twice more, but each time, when his wife blew the whistle, he awoke immediately. At a 1-year follow-up, he reported only two more such incidents. He had had no problem studying or concentrating in his law work.

We now turn to an even more common problem, insomnia and the disruption of the sleep cycle.

> *Mr. Answer Man, what is the existential equivalent of infinity?*
>
> *Why, insomnia, Sandy, good old insomnia.*
>
> —Norman Mailer, *Of a Fire on the Moon* (1970)

The Case of Ilse

Ilse is 42 years old and has two well-adjusted children, ages 21 and 19. The older is married and lives across town from her, and the younger is a sophomore at the state university some 90 miles from the medium-size eastern seaboard city where Ilse lives.

Ilse married while in college and almost immediately became pregnant with their first child, but she did finish her B.S. and R.N. degrees. The marriage had its problems but had been generally satisfying to her and lasted until Ilse was 34. At that time her husband rather abruptly announced that he had become involved with another woman and did not want to continue the marriage.

Ilse was shattered by this, but within a year she recovered. She had been working part-time as a nurse, but she immediately took a full-time job. As the children grew older, she added some occasional part-time jobs, and with the aid of child support and judicious investing has become financially stable. She has developed a wide range of outside interests and a number of good, close friends and would be considered happy by both herself and her friends.

However, since adolescence Ilse has been troubled by occasional bouts of disturbed sleep, which have increasingly bothered her over the last several years. Most often she goes to sleep without much trouble, but awakens after 90 minutes or so. She then is unable to get back to sleep easily, sometimes going the rest of the night without any decent sleep. At other times, she can't even get to sleep in the first place and spends the night moving about, getting only snatches of sleep. Also, during especially stressful periods in her life, for example, change of work hours or problems with her boyfriend or one of her children, she has a nightmare, often awakening with a scream from a vivid and frightening dream, usually shaking and in a cold sweat.

She consulted with her physician, an internist. She gave Ilse an array of physical tests, told her she was fine, and gave her a prescription for some sleeping pills that she advised her to take only if she needed them (see Table 4–1). They did prove useful when she took only one on a particularly stressful night, for example, before leaving town on a long trip. But Ilse would occasionally take them for a number of nights in a row. They would knock her out the first night or two, then would do little more than make her sleep deeply for 3 or 4 hours, after which she had even more consistent difficulty returning to sleep than she had experienced before using the pills.

She returned to her internist, who told her there was really nothing more that she could do, and she referred Ilse to a neurologist. The neurologist gave her several other tests, told her she was fine, and prescribed another brand of sleeping pill, with much the same result as before.

Ilse was disappointed and upset. She tried several techniques that she had read about in nursing journals. Unfortunately, she was also siphoning off a few sleeping pills at a time for her own use from the patients on the general medicine ward where she was a supervisor, and occasionally took these for a few nights in a row. Almost nothing helped here, probably because she was randomly mixing pills and techniques.

The sparse follow-up data available suggest that Ilse's problems continued. From her own subjective perspective, she is likely to see her problems as worsening, as she will need somewhat less sleep anyway as the years go by. It is regrettable that Ilse's case occurred before clinics specifically designed to treat sleep disorders became more common. It is likely that if there had been one to refer her to, the outcome would have been more positive. Such clinics would have given Ilse advice and counseling much like that following Table 4–1.

TABLE 4–1 Sedative-Hypnotic Drugs

Name (Generic/Trade)	
Benzodiazepines	**Barbiturates**
Flurazepam (Dalmane)	Secobarbital (Seconal)
Temazepam (Restoril)	**Other Sedative-Hypnotics**
Triazolam (Halcion)	
Estazolam (ProSom)	Chloral hydrate (Noctec)
Quazepam (Doral)	Zolpidem tartrate (Ambien)

Treatment possibilities

Although Ilse has occasionally experienced nightmares, the primary issues are her delayed or advanced phase sleep cycle disorder (i.e., awakening after 3–4 hours of sound sleep with problems going back to sleep) and her insomnia (the inability to get to sleep in the first place). Such sleep disorders can be secondary to other psychopathology or be caused at least in part by externals such as allergies, aging, types of food eaten (e.g., too much caffeine), or side effects of medications (Harsh and Ogilvie, 1995), but none of these appears applicable to Ilse.

The humorist and old-time movie star W. C. Fields once said that the best way to get a good night's sleep was to go to bed. He should have added "at a regular time every night, and within a regular routine." He should have also advised that if you do not fall asleep within 15 to 30 minutes, you should get up, and only come back to bed when you actually feel sleepy. The important point is to consistently associate the bed with falling asleep. People with problems like Ilse's should not work in bed or read or watch TV for long periods of time. They should establish a set routine and stay with it.

A sleep clinic would then have looked at other issues with Ilse. After an initial interview and review of medical records, a physical exam and a battery of questionnaires and psychological tests are given, along with a polysomnogram. A polysomnogram, through electrodes attached to the face and head during an actual sleep period, records brain waves, muscle movements, and eye movements. Data from all of these pinpoint any abnormalities. If no great abnormality is located, then eating, exercise, and napping patterns are considered, and suggestions for other potentially useful techniques are made.

As noted, the first goal would be to help someone like Ilse establish a regular bedtime routine. Regarding eating patterns, Ilse would be advised that a late heavy meal often has a negative effect, but a small portion of food at bedtime is positive for most people, especially certain types of food. Specifically, foods that are high in the amino acid L-tryptophan (such as milk products, poultry, tofu, and eggs) have been found to aid sleep. Also, sweet, starchy foods high in natural carbohydrates, such as bread, bananas, and figs, help liberate the L-tryptophan. The process is even further facilitated by a small portion of foods high in both fat and carbohydrates, such as, peanuts, walnuts, and avocados.

Napping and exercise patterns also need to be assessed. Napping has been defined as an unconscious 25-minute rest without pajamas, and it does seem to be an aspect of the body's natural biorhythms. It helps those who need it to catch up on their sleep, but naps late in the day can facilitate an insomniac pattern. A disrupted biorhythm leading to sleep disorder can often be evened out by controlled exposure to intense light or dosages of melatonin. It is also helpful to get in the habit of not only going to bed at the same time every night, but also getting up at the same time every morning.

People who take little or no vigorous exercise are more prone to insomnia and sleep cycle disorders. Good vigorous exercise three or four times a week, at least 3 to 5 hours before bedtime, helps develop more restful sleep patterns, and it is even better if it is carried out in the late afternoon or early evening.

Other techniques have been found useful with certain people, for example: (1) yoga or other slow stretching exercises and/or a warm bath 2 hours before bed (as the body temperature naturally returns to normal, one tends to become drowsier); (2) a period of "quiet time" before bed; (3) slow, repetitively melodic music; (4) repetitive sound, such as a white noise machine; (5) a nose bandage facilitates breathing, especially if allergies are a factor; (6) a distracting, repetitive internal dialogue (i.e., "counting sheep"); (7) certain herb teas, like chamomile, skullcap, kava-kava, periwinkle; and (8) use of certain vitamins, especially the B vitamins, and calcium, magnesium, and potassium. Medication (see Table 4–1) can be helpful as a short-term mechanism. Relaxation training and/or biofeedback training may also be instituted by a therapist, and psychotherapy can reduce the stress and conflicts that lead to sleep disruptions similar to those that Ilse experienced.

5

The Somatoform Disorders

Persons with somatoform disorders, like those with the factitious disorder (see Chapter 16) manifest complaints and symptoms of apparent physical illness for which there are no demonstrable organic findings to support a physical diagnosis, thus an accurate diagnosis in this group of disorders can be difficult (Escobar, 1998; Katon, 1993). However, the symptoms of the somatoform disorders are not under voluntary control, as are those of the factitious disorders. The diagnosis of somatoform disorder is made when there is good reason to believe that the person has little or no control over the production of symptoms. While factitious disorders are more common in men, somatoform disorders occur more frequently in women.

> *There's a fly to deep center field. Winfield is going back, back. He hits his head against the wall! It's rolling toward second base!*
>
> —San Diego Padres broadcaster Jerry Coleman

Somatoform Disorder Subcategories

There are five major subcategories of the somatoform disorders: Somatization Disorder, Undifferentiated Somatoform Disorder, Conversion Disorder, Psychogenic Pain Disorder, and Hypochondriasis. There is also a catch-all category, Atypical Somatoform Disorder, in which individuals are placed if they fit the general criteria for somatoform disorder but not the specific criteria of the other four major categories.

Somatization Disorder

The chronic though cyclic multiple somatic complaints that mark the Somatization subcategory of the somatoform disorders are not primarily due to any physical illness. Yet they may be mixed with other symptoms derived from an actual disease, so arriving at this diagnosis is initially difficult. This disorder is discussed in the first case in this chapter, along with the Undifferentiated Somatoform Disorder.

The symptoms of both of these disorders are often presented in a vague but exaggerated fashion. Incidentally, this dramatic component was the linkage between the traditional diagnostic terms *hysterical neurosis* and the *hysterical personality*. Fortunately, the *DSM-IV* terminology did away with some of the confusion inherent in these labels. Hysterical personalities are now referred to as having a histrionic personality disorder (see the case of Hilde, Chapter 11). Hysteria is typically subsumed under one of the somatoform disorders, usually as a conversion disorder that is still sublabeled the Hysterical Neurosis, Conversion Type.

Conversion Disorder

The Conversion Disorder pattern is similar in many respects to the Somatization Disorder. The difference is that in the Conversion Disorder there is a specific symptom or a related set of symptoms, and these symptoms are either used for the attainment of some secondary gain or they express a psychological conflict. Conversion symptoms are not under voluntary control. Psychogenic Pain Disorder, which is discussed in detail in the upcoming case of Pam, can be considered a subcategory of Conversion Disorder in which the specific symptom is simply pain.

With some of the psychosexual dysfunctions (see Chapter 8), it may be difficult to decide whether the problem directly expresses a psychological issue and is thus technically a Conversion Disorder or whether it is a physiological response to anxiety. In actuality, it may be a mixture of both. For these reasons, as well as for convenience, all of these cases are included in the psychosexual disorders.

A Conversion Disorder is still referred to as a "hysterical neurosis, conversion type," and such individuals are said to manifest *la belle indifférence,* an attitude in which there is little concern about the apparent serious implications of the disorder. Persons with a Conversion Disorder appear to be aware at some level that their complaints do not predict the dire consequences that others might infer from them. Although indifferent to their presenting symptoms, a pattern of emotional "ups and downs" (lability) in response to other stimuli is commonly noted. *La belle indifférence* is not found in all Conversion Disorders. Some people develop their symptoms under extreme stress and manifest that stress quite directly. Yet, even in these individuals, anxiety seems to dissipate over the duration of the disorder in favor of a focus on physical symptoms.

Hypochon-driasis   Hypochondriacs unreasonably interpret normal or relatively unimportant bodily and physical changes as indicative of serious physical disorder. They are constantly alert to an upsurge of new symptomatology, and as the body is constantly in physiological flux, they are bound to find signs that they can interpret as suggestive of disorder.

In one sense, hypochondriacs do not fear being sick; they are certain they already are. Hypochondriasis is a relatively common pattern from adolescence to old age. It is seen most frequently in the 30- to 40-year age range for men and the 40- to 50-year age range for women (Meister, 1980). Meister also believes that there are many "closet hypochondriacs," who do not constantly go to physicians yet are heavily involved in health fads, checking of body behaviors, and discussion of their concerns with close friends (who may relish the quasi-therapist role). These closet hypochondriacs would not earn a formal *DSM* diagnosis, as they do not fit some of the specific requirements, such as seeking out medical reassurance and going through physical examinations. Nonetheless, they manifest the disorder.

A number of common factors have been observed in the development of hypochondriasis:

- Most hypochondriacs have a background marked by substantial experience in an atmosphere of illness. This could include identification with a significant other who was hypochondriacal or early exposure to a family member who was an invalid.

- Hypochondriacs often have had a strong dependency relationship with a family member who could express love and affection normally or intensely during periods when the hypochondriac was ill, yet was distant or nonexpressive at other times.

- Hypochondriacs often channel their psychological conflicts and their needs for existential reassurance into this pattern. The hypochondriac pattern of behavior may mask a mid-life crisis or some other challenge that is not being met effectively.

- A certain subgroup of hypochondriacs are postulated as having a predispositional sensitivity to pain and body sensation. This could be stimulated by prior physical disorder in systems in which the hypochondriacal pattern is now manifest.

All of these factors are naturally facilitated by reinforcement of the hypochondriasis in the client's world. Avoidance of tasks or demands because of being sick is often noted here. A most entertaining portrayal of this disorder is presented by Woody Allen in his 1986 movie *Hannah and Her Sisters*.

Now let us turn to to a case on the Somatization Disorder, and then to a common pattern within the somatoform disorders, the Psychogenic Pain Disorder.

Somatization Disorder

> Father Theodosius, representative of the Russian
> Ecclesiastical Mission in Jerusalem was pictured in
> a white robe and a black headdress, was asked
> about the afterlife, he said, "When I die, I'll go to
> heaven. That's what I'm working on. What do you
> think I'm dressed like this for?"

The Case of "Alix " —Empress Alexandra Fedorovna

Alix Victoria Helena Louise Beatrice, Princess of Hesse-Darmstadt, was born on June 6, 1872, in Darmstadt, a medieval German city near the river Rhine. She was named "Alix," the closest euphonic rendering of "Alice" in German. She was named after her mother, Princess Alice of England, the third of Queen Victoria's nine children.

Her mother, in a letter to the queen, described Alix as a "sweet merry little person, always laughing," and everyone quickly took to Alix's nickname of "Sunny." Her godparents were Tsar Alexander III of Russia and the future King Edward VII of England, so it is not surprising she had an early entree into contact with royalty across Europe as well as the Russian imperial family.

At least until age 6, Alix had the idyllic childhood people fantasized was characteristic of nobility. When she was 6, an outbreak of diphtheria swept through the palace where she lived, eventually killing her 4-year-old sister. Then, apparently stressed from taking care of her sick children, Alix's mother, Princess Alice, fell ill and died at age 35. After the tragic death of her mother, Alix's sunny disposition darkened, and henceforth a hard shell of aloofness often covered her emotions.

She first met her future husband, Nicholas, the future Tsar Nicholas II of Russia (of the Romanov family), when at age 12 she traveled to St. Petersburg, Russia, for the marriage of her sister to the younger brother of Tsar Alexander III. Five years later, in 1889, when she visited her sister in St. Petersburg, Alix and Nicholas met again, and apparently fell in love.

Although still somewhat aloof with groups of people, Alix was a generally happy person whose life was normal and unpretentious, at least for a princess. In 1889, she rejected the marriage proposal of Prince Albert Victor, heir to the throne of England, who later died tragically at age 28. In 1894, she accepted the marriage proposal of Nicholas II.

In October 1894, Tsar Alexander III reported distress from headaches, insomnia, and weakness in his legs. At first there was little concern. But he worsened and less than 2 weeks later, on November 1, 1894, he died at age 49. Nicholas, now age 26, and Alix were married on November 26, 1 week after the funeral. After a long period of mourning and preparation, Nicholas was crowned Tsar (actually "Emperor and Autocrat of All the Russias") on May 26, 1896. Alix became the Empress Alexandra Fedorovna.

There was intense pressure and expectancy that Alexandra would produce a son, as only a male could be an heir to the throne. In mid-November 1895, Alexandra went into labor, and cannons were fired, 300 cannon shots to announce the birth of a boy. They stopped firing at 101, announcing the birth of Grand Duchess Olga. At 2- year intervals, three more daughters were born: Tatiana; Marie; and then Anastasia, in 1901, the same year as the death of Queen Victoria of England.

Then, on August 12, 1904, Tsar Nicholas II was able to write in his diary, "A great never-to-be-forgotten day when the mercy of God has visited us so clearly. Alix gave birth to a son at one o'clock. The child has been called Alexis." The joy in the royal family was unbounded, but only until 6 weeks later when Nicholas II wrote "A hemorrhage began this morning without the slightest cause from the navel of our small Alexis." Within months the terrifying suspicion of both parents was fulfilled; Alexis had hemophilia. Some historians would later argue that this defect in this tiny infant would be the critical factor in toppling imperial Russia.

Hemophilia is an inherited blood-clotting deficiency, transmitted in a sex linked recessive Mendelian pattern. Thus, while women carry the defective genes, they almost never suffer from the disease. The disease has been recognized since ancient times, for example, in the Egypt of the Pharaohs a woman was forbidden to bear more children if her firstborn son bled to death from a minor wound. It has been termed "the royal disease," and Queen Victoria, who was grandmother, aunt, and so on, to most of Europe's royalty turned out to be a hemophilia carrier.

Alexis was a charming, chubby, blonde youngster. He was constantly attended by guards, restricted from many activities; and doted on continuously, especially by his mother who felt enormous guilt over "producing" his condition. Crisis after crisis occurred, after the slightest bump or fall, with Alexis often enduring great pain and/or being near death. In 1912, an injury was exacerbated by the trauma from the jolts of a carriage ride, and he again almost died. He was allegedly saved through the intervention of the monk, Father Gregory Efimovich (known as Rasputin, from a Russian word for "dissolute"). Rasputin eventually gained great power with the royal family, especially with Alexandra. Rasputin allegedly controlled Alexis's bleeding through hypnosis, but criticism of his influence over Alexandra was a rallying cry for revolutionaries. Nicholas was apparently not as taken by Rasputin as some have believed, but he was willing to put up with it, once commenting, "Better one Rasputin than 10 fits of hysterics a day," reflecting Alexandra's deepening emotional disorder.

Many factors took an emotional toll on Alexandra. She suffered from sciatica, a severe pain in the back and legs that she had periodically experienced since childhood. Her pregnancies were all difficult. But all of this paled before the emotional battles with her son's hemophilia. During the crises, she would sit all day and night with Alexis, often observing him in great pain. After a crisis, she would collapse, lying on a bed or couch for weeks, moving only in a wheelchair. In 1908, she began having episodes marked by hyperventilation, anxiety, and/or fatigue. She reported a variety of other physical symptoms at other times, including headaches and nausea, and also fainted on several occasions. She attributed virtually all of these symptoms to "an enlarged heart" and "a family weakness of blood vessels." Episodes were common. In 1911, she wrote, "I have been ill nearly all the time." Evidence for this pattern continued periodically until her death.

The political upheaval fomented by revolutionaries such as Alexander Kerensky and carried through by Vladimir Ilyich Ulyanov (known as Lenin), gradually swept the revolutionaries into power. In mid-March, 1917, Tsar Nicholas II abdicated in favor of his brother, who in turn almost immediately abdicated. Tsar Nicholas II and his family were exiled to Siberia.

On July 17, 1918, apparently in order to destroy any lingering hopes of a return of the Romanov dynasty or any royalty, the imprisoned Tsar and his family were executed, along with four retainers who had shared the family's captivity: a cook, a valet, a maid, and the Romanov's physician. Yakov Yurovsky, the Bolshevik officer in charge of the

Romanov's captivity, was a photographer by vocation. He asked the eleven prisoners to stand in two rows against the wall of the room, as if for a family portrait. Satisfied with his arrangement, he then called in the killer squad (six Latvians, five Russians) who immediately crowded into the narrow doorway that faced the captives. As Yurovsky finished reading a brief statement that ended with the words "the Ural Executive Committee has decided to execute you," the shooting began. The brutality and sadism of the carnage are unequaled in the recent annals of royal executions.

The tzar was killed on the spot, as were the empress and Grand Duchess Olga, neither of whom could finish making the sign of the cross. Other members of the group were less fortunate. Because the czarevitch and the three remaining sisters wore corsets thickly sewn with some seventeen pounds of jewels, for long moments bullets fired at their chests continued to ricochet around the tiny room like hail, failing to kill them. First mystified, then enraged, the executioners, in a mayhem of billowing gun smoke, blood, and shouts of terror, finished off their victims with bayonets and rifle butts—so viciously that some of the imperial party's skulls, in the words of a forensic expert, were "crushed as though a truck drove over them."

In 1992, the remains were exhumed from shallow graves in a forest near Yekaterinburg, the city in the Urals where they were executed. Definitive DNA tests in Britain and the United States identified the remains of Nicholas, Alexandra, and three daughters. The bones of both Alexis and either Anastasia or Marie (it is not clear which one's set of bones is the one that is missing) have not been clearly identified. Legends identify it as Anastasia, spawning numerous books and movies based on claims by various women to be the true Anastasia. On July 17, 1998, 80 years to the day they were massacred, the remains of the family were reburied in St. Catherine Cathedral in St. Petersburg, Russia.

The Diagnosis

It is not surprising that Queen Victoria is associated with this case. The somatoform disorders were common in the Victorian era and were the source of much of Sigmund Freud's theorizing in that period.

Let's first consider which specific somatoform disorder would apply here. In order to diagnose a Somatization Disorder, the *DSM-IV* requires evidence of a history of physical complaints occurring over several years, resulting in seeking treatment or a significant life impairment, with evidence that the physical symptoms began before the age of 30. The clients must also show, at some time in the course of disorder, four pain symptoms, two gastrointestinal symptoms, one sexual symptom, and one pseudoneurological symptom, and either (1) these symptoms cannot be directly explained by a medical condition or substance, or (2) if there is a relevant medical condition, the response is excessive, and it is not a Factitious Disorder (see Chapter 16). The Somatization Disorder is thought to be diagnosed rarely in males, but approximately 1% of females are alleged to have this disorder at some point in their lives.

On the other hand, in order to diagnose the Undifferentiated Somatoform Disorder the *DSM-IV* requires only one physical complaint, again not directly explainable by a substance or a general medical condition, or being an excessive response if there is a medical condition; a life impairment resulting from the complaint; duration of at least 6 months; and no other mental disorder diagnoses that better account for the symptoms.

Alix's condition would at least warrant the diagnosis of Undifferentiated Somatoform Disorder. She showed numerous physical symptoms not attributable to any true medical condition and these symptoms persisted over many years. It is probable that she would also earn the more specific diagnosis of Somatization Disorder. There is no evidence that Alix ever showed a sexual symptom within this pattern, but a lack of disclosure in this regard would be consistent with the tenor of those times. In any case, Alix quite clearly suffered some form of a classic somatoform disorder.

Causes

As to the possible causes of this disorder in Alix, several factors likely played a part (Escobar, 1998). The psychological trauma from her mother's death and the atmosphere of illness that surrounded this episode no doubt influenced her in this direction. Her periodic bouts of sciatica also set the stage.

Significant stressors after the engagement and marriage were periodic rejection by the Russian people because she was "German" and the intense expectancy that she would produce a son. The precipitants were followed by the crushing disappointment upon learning of Alexis's hemophilia. Then, for the rest of her life, there were the constant crises around her son's health that required huge expenditures of both physical and emotional energy.

Lastly, in the Victorian period, people communicated about their distress through the vehicle of descriptions of physical disorder, a pattern still observed today in many elderly patients. There were no "shrinks" or counselors as we know them today. People were not encouraged to talk about their emotional feelings or problems; indeed, more often they were discouraged from doing so.

All of this was certainly a fertile ground for the production of a somatoform disorder. Factors such as (1) childhood or adolescent trauma within an atmosphere of illness, (2) experience with an actual physical illness, (3) depression, (4) major physical and emotional stressors, and (5) the inability to articulate or communicate one's distress in psychological terms are still common precipitants.

Treatment

Today a treatment regimen for any of the somatoform disorders, and especially the Somatization Disorder, could include various components, for example psychotherapy, biofeedback, group or support group therapy, and so on. But, whatever techniques are employed, the following core principles (Katon, 1993) should govern the treatment plan: (1) the suffering should be accepted as real though real does not always mean a physical cause. It's often hard to find a treating physician with this attitude; (2) there should be regularly scheduled visits for "treatment," so that production of a new disorder is not required as an "admission ticket"; (3) after a thorough physical, constant recourse to more and more obscure lab tests should be avoided; (4) antianxiety or sleeping medications should seldom be prescribed, especially as they can be addicting; (5) never prescribe pain medications "as needed"; only prescribe them for short, defined periods; (6) above all, get the client moving psychologically and physically. Never prescribe rest, and help the client to understand that resting and inactivity are always counterproductive; and (7) families should be involved in the treatment. They can be taught to help get the actual client to exercise and avoid inactivity. They can learn to respond supportively yet without encouraging "pain" or "disease" talk.

These principles can also be effective in the treatment of the next disorder discussed, that is, pain disorder.

Psychogenic Pain Disorder

The Case of Pam

They breathe truth that breathe their words in pain.
—William Shakespeare, *Richard II* (1596)

Psychogenic pain disorders are similar to conversion symptoms that center on an experience of pain for which there is no plausible physiological explanation. Often the pain may be initiated by some real traumatic event, such as an accident. In other cases the pain merely asserts itself gradually until it is entrenched in the sufferer's lifestyle (Katon, 1993).

Conversion disorders differ from the factitious disorders in that the conversion sufferer is not consciously aware that the symptoms experienced are unreal, that is, have no physical basis. The notion that pain, sometimes serious and debilitating pain, is all in one's head is difficult to accept. It is important to note that the experience of pain takes place not at the perceived site of discomfort, but in the brain, and a variety of central nervous system operations may influence pain experiences. Techniques such as Lamaze (for childbirth) are based on the assumption that appropriate attitudes and emotions can minimize pain. Psychogenic pain often seems to be the flip side of this process, with conversion-prone persons experiencing intense symptoms with minimal provocation.

Until the last century a variety of florid conversion disorders were relatively common. Some patients would mysteriously lose sensation in all their extremities or suffer sudden seizures. Recent advances in medicine have made it possible to easily debunk these extreme displays, and they have nearly disappeared. Relative to these sorts of conversion disorders, the incidence of psychogenic pain has increased dramatically, perhaps because vague, diffuse pain symptoms are far more difficult to identify as inaccurate. The Psychogenic Pain Disorder thus presents a special diagnostic challenge that requires the collaboration of psychologists with medical specialists, who are often the first to encounter the psychogenic pain symptoms.

Look for a long time at what pleases you, and for a longer time at what pains you.
—Collette, French novelist (1873–1954)

The Case of Pam

Pam was 38 years old when first seen at the pain clinic. She reported that she had suffered with recurrent hip pain since her early teens, linked to a car accident that occurred when she was 17. Her regular physician, a gynecologist, had referred her to an orthopedic surgeon but this evaluation yielded no conclusive explanation for the ongoing pain. Her hip pain was sporadic, sometimes confining her to bed for a day or two. On the other hand, she and her husband had recently taken a skiing vacation with no ill effects.

Pam also reported frequent headaches, which she characterized as "migraines, definitely." Like her hip pain, the headaches were an intermittent problem, sometimes being quite severe while later disappearing altogether for several weeks. The headaches had begun about 2 years previously, shortly after Pam and her family had moved into the area. Again, Pam was referred to a medical specialist, a neurologist, for evaluation. The neurologist noted that her description of the headaches did not correspond to a typical migraine pattern, and he was unable to find a plausible explanation for them. He initiated the referral to the pain clinic in cooperation with Pam's gynecologist.

Finally, Pam had recently seen a daytime television show that described premenstrual stress (PMS), and she suggested that this would explain both of her problems as well as several new infirmities. The gynecologist reported that this possibility had already been considered and did not account for Pam's problems. Hence, "functional" or psychogenic factors would need to be evaluated.

Etiology

At the pain clinic, Pam was seen by several health care personnel. Thorough medical, psychological, and social histories were taken, and numerous psychological and medical tests performed. Finally, a multidisciplinary team reviewed all the available data and found that a variety of psychological factors probably served as the primary sources of both the headaches and the hip pain.

Pam was the second youngest of four children, a position that ensured that she received little individual attention from her parents. Her younger sister was pampered as the baby of the family, while her older brother excelled in sports. Because he was several years older, his achievements seemed to overshadow the younger children's. This effect was heightened by the attitudes of Pam's parents, who felt that males should be competitive and outgoing and rewarded this behavior in a variety of ways. They also expected their daughters to strive for success, but in more traditional female roles, such as music and academics. Pam came to adopt a traditionally feminine view of herself and confined herself to these outlets.

Pam described her parents as cool and aloof. They rarely showed affection toward one another or toward their children. On the whole the family had little social contact with others in the community, except for formal events centering on church and school activities. Pam and her siblings found that emotional displays of any kind made their parents uncomfortable, and so they learned to hide their feelings. Pam recalled that her parents seemed more caring and tender toward her whenever she suffered a childhood illness, such as measles.

Pam's father spent little time with the family, instead devoting himself to his career. The children were troubled by their father's absence, but Pam's mother quashed any complaints. She shamed the children for complaining while their father was working so hard to be a good provider. While the children suspected that their mother also resented the father's absence, she never expressed this directly. Instead, she behaved with superficial charm toward her husband. Whenever he did wish to spend time with her, she suddenly became tired or ill, thus frustrating his limited attempts at intimacy. Pam adopted her mother's style of suppressing frustrations with others, only to express them in indirect ways. This pattern depended in part on her expectation that she would be made to feel guilty if she voiced her discontent overtly.

Pam reported that her mother suffered a variety of gynecological problems and that she frequently consulted her physician. On occasion her vague complaints would require that she stay off her feet for several days. During these episodes the father would demand that the children do nothing to upset their mother, thus indicating that he believed the illnesses were stress-induced. He behaved solicitously toward his wife until she felt better, then frantically threw himself back into work to "catch up." A predictable cycle was established, with the mother becoming ill and dominating the family briefly, only to have things return to normal as soon as she felt better. Pam learned first-hand that ill behaviors could be effective in gaining attention (and control) from otherwise disinterested family members.

Pam was an attractive girl who reached puberty rather early. She was initially pleased by her resulting popularity and became involved in a variety of school-related activities. Upon entering high school, she hoped to begin dating, viewing this as a logical extension of her social life. Consistent with her parents' reluctance to confront many aspects of human intimacy, they did not discuss sexuality with her, and she was quite naive about the role it might play in dating. Despite her parents' attempts to screen her boyfriends, Pam inevitably dated boys who pressured her to become sexually active. Surprised by these advances, she resisted anything more than light petting at first. Eventually she became involved in a long-term relationship and in this context she felt less inhibited. She found the warmth and intimacy of these interludes a welcome change from the emotional coldness of her family. While she began to enjoy more sexual experimentation, she had moral reservations about these activities and experienced considerable emotional conflict as a result. Ultimately Pam and her boyfriend progressed to having intercourse in the back seat of his car. Following one of their initial encounters, when Pam was 17, they were involved in a car wreck on the way to her parents' home. Each sustained a variety of minor injuries, and Pam complained that her right hip was stiff and sore. Physicians found no sign of injury and suggested that the pain would go away in a few days.

Despite these predictions, Pam's hip pain continued and came to interfere with many of her activities, including dating. After several months the boyfriend began dating someone else, and Pam's pain gradually subsided. This relationship had produced considerable conflict for Pam, but her "injury" provided her with an indirect means of escape. She did not have to break off the relationship herself or insist that the boyfriend stop pressuring her for sex. It is not unusual for conversion symptoms, including psychogenic pain, to symbolically reflect the underlying anxieties that they mask; in this case, Pam's hip pain had localized near the genital area.

After high school, Pam continued to live at home while attending a local community college. Her grades would have permitted her to attend a more prestigious institution, but her parents preferred that she remain within their control. Pam resented the implication that her educational advancement should give way to their wishes, but she protested little. She met her husband through the community college, and they married after a brief romance. In many respects, this liaison served as an escape from her parents' domination, and it was particularly effective as they did not approve of her husband-to-be.

Pam reported that her husband, John, is a conventional, hard-working individual. He has an M.B.A. and works for a local bank in an administrative capacity. Like Pam's father, John puts in considerable overtime and seems to have little involvement with his family. His expectation is that Pam will take care of all the domestic duties while he will be the "breadwinner." The couple have three children ranging in age from 9 to 15. The children participate in athletic and artistic activities in addition to attending a private school. The family is comfortably upper middle class. Pam perceives the demands placed on her as onerous and would like to escape some of them. Her pain experiences may help her to do this.

When asked about the strengths and weaknesses of her marriage, Pam had difficulty in identifying strengths, other than that she believes her husband is "substantial." She feels that their relationship lacks much real emotional commitment. Pam was able to identify one area of conflict. The family had moved every 2 to 3 years because John felt that it was necessary to advance his career. At present, Pam is very comfortable with her home and social circle. While she finds it difficult to make friends, she has become close to several people in the community and is resistant to another move.

She was uncharacteristically adamant about her position when John once again mentioned "moving on" approximately 2 years ago. She felt guilty for this outburst and resolved not to act so hotheaded in the future. Her recurrent headaches began shortly thereafter. Pam now has some realization that she can tell when John wants to discuss moving, and it appears that her headaches serve to preempt these overtures. They may also provide an escape from the many demands her children place on her.

Treatment Options

Recall that the treatment principles discussed in the preceding case of a Somatization Disorder are equally applicable here. Because a broad range of factors may contribute to psychogenic pain, many types of interventions have been employed with some success (Escobar, 1998; Katon, 1993). One group of approaches centers on confronting the lack of a plausible physiological explanation for the pain while pointing up the psychological "rewards" for the pain experience. Techniques associated with reality therapy and confrontation-insight therapy may be useful. Such confrontations must be carefully managed, however, to prevent flight from treatment. Because these persons often find intense relationships anxiety provoking, they instinctively withdraw from therapists who attempt to cut through their superficial defenses.

Behavioral techniques provide a second major line of attack. Merely changing the clients' environments to eliminate secondary gains may serve to reduce the frequency or intensity of psychogenic pain experiences. Also, biofeedback has been found to help alleviate many types of pain, even if no clear pathophysiology exists. Contracting with clients to increase the number of activities they attempt may divert attention and energy away from the pain experience. These efforts are consistent with the finding that many persons experiencing psychogenic pain may be clinically depressed. Depressed persons also tend to benefit from attempting a wider range of activities.

A third general approach entails training clients to relate to others in more positive and explicit ways. Often their pains and illnesses serve to gain attention and caring from others or to absolve clients of responsibilities they find overwhelming. Assertiveness or social skills training may help the individuals express their needs clearly, thus reducing the need for more manipulative behavior. Work on problem solving or related issues may help clients manage demands adequately.

Pam's Treatment

Pam's evaluation at the pain clinic took weeks to complete. During this period she was asked to keep a journal of her pain experiences and a variety of other activities and events. Once the team had determined that her pain was primarily, if not entirely, psychogenic, the journal data were helpful in pointing out many contributing factors. She was gently but firmly confronted with the possibility that her hip pain and headaches served several purposes of which she was unaware.

During the initial phase of therapy, Pam was encouraged to explore several characteristics of her early life that predisposed her to pain disorder. She came to recognize that her passivity and dependency, inability to confront negative emotions, and guilt proneness stemmed from the family milieu in which she was raised. Subsequently she was encouraged to explore ways in which she might be re-enacting the patterns of behavior her mother had used in her own marriage.

Homework assignments for Pam initially focused on increasing positive activities outside her usual domestic drudgery. Special emphasis was placed on health-related behaviors such as exercise and diet. Subsequently she felt healthier and more energetic, factors that greatly reduced her expectations that she would be ill or in pain. Biofeedback was useful in giving her more of a reality-based perception of physical sensations and symptoms. She also contracted to increase contacts with her friends. It was far more inconvenient to have a headache or sore hip when it would conflict with a luncheon engagement or some other pleasurable activity.

Pam's skills in relating to others came under scrutiny in the course of therapy. Social skills and assertiveness training methods were used to enhance her ability to make appropriate requests of others, to express her opinions openly, and to refuse requests politely.

The husband was also brought into the therapy effort. It was noted that he shared a number of his wife's attributes, including difficulty expressing emotions and passivity in confronting problems. It became apparent that the family's repeated moves had been motivated not so much by career necessity as by John's inability to confront normal difficulties in the workplace. With this brought into awareness, the ongoing but veiled conflict over an impending move was subsequently reduced. A brief but intensive course of couples therapy helped both Pam and John become better able to work out potential problems quickly, rather than experiencing ongoing anxiety over their lack of resolution. The couple also found that their relationship became more emotionally passionate, and John found that he wanted to spend more time with his wife. Pam's need to gain attention through incapacity was thus negated.

Ultimately Pam made a successful recovery from two recurrent and debilitating problems. Her treatment was facilitated by the multidisciplinary nature of the pain clinic. Many persons experiencing psychogenic pain have been told by an acquaintance or family member that "it's all in (their) head," and hence refer themselves to a variety of medical specialists in an attempt to validate their pain experience. These persons often receive treatments that they do not need, such as analgesic medications, which are basically ineffective. They easily habituate to or even become addicted to medications, so they should never receive medications "as needed," but only for short, circumscribed periods. Side effects and iatrogenic health problems may be the result. As with the Factitious Disorder (see the case of Frank in Chapter 16) it is important that these persons be identified rather than left to flounder in the conventional medical system.

Comment

Persons who suffer with psychogenic pain seem to fall along a continuum ranging from those whose pain is primarily a reflection of some type of psychological conflict to those whose symptom production is dominated by secondary gain. Most conversion disorders involve each motif to some degree, as was the case with Pam. Her hip pain initially arose as a result of intense internal conflict. It was apparently prolonged because it was so effective in eliciting secondary gains. Once the pattern of illness behavior and concessions from the environment is established, it is common for these persons to acquire additional symptoms. New complaints often arise in the face of new demands or if the old symptom is discredited somehow. Also, complaints that are difficult to verify empirically may serve as the "raison d'être" for conversion symptoms.

The Nocebo Effect

The "nocebo effect" could be implicated in at least part of the symptom picture seen in some cases of somatization (including pain) disorder. Experts have long recognized the placebo effect; that patients improve because they believe they will; the opposite (nocebo) effect may be equally powerful: patients get sick because they believe they will.

The nocebo phenomenon may also be responsible for occasional outbreaks of what has been called "epidemic hysteria," in which numerous people in a group such as students in school suddenly begin to experience similar symptoms of illness, although no physical cause is found. Seventy-eight such outbreaks of illness were documented in Quebec between 1872 and 1972. The fact that the symptoms are triggered by patient beliefs does not make them less real or less costly to the patients, and the possibility that expectations could be a major factor in illness should be taken seriously.

6

The Schizophrenic and Delusional (or Paranoid) Disorders

Especially severe forms of psychopathology, characterized by perceptual, cognitive, affective, communicative, motor, and motivational disturbances and specifically denoted by a loss of contact with reality, are termed psychoses. Some psychotic reactions are obviously associated with brain disruption due to physical causes such as diseases of the nervous system, brain tumors or injuries, toxic drug or chemical reactions, or circulation disturbances. More prevalent are the functional psychoses that do not stem fully and directly from a known physical trauma to the brain, although a biological factor (e.g., genetic) may be an important or even a primary cause. There are three major classifications of functional psychoses: Mood (Affective), Schizophrenic, and Paranoid. The Mood (Affective) Psychotic Disorders, which are discussed in the next chapter, are characterized by extreme fluctuations of mood, with related disturbances in thought and behavior. The *DSM-IV* also includes the Schizoaffective Disorder, in which schizophrenic and affective symptoms are both prominent and develop at about the same time.

The primary focus here is on the *DSM-IV* diagnostic categories of the Schizophrenic Disorders and the Delusional (or Paranoid) Disorders. The major symptoms of schizophrenia involve withdrawal from reality, with flat or inappropriate emotional reactions and marked disturbances in thought processes. Delusions, hallucinations, and stereotyped mannerisms are common.

> *All issues are political issues, and politics itself is a mass of lies, evasions, folly, hatred, and schizophrenia.*
>
> —George Orwell (1903–1950)

Schizophrenia has been recognized as a disorder since Benedict Morel's (1857) description of a 13-year-old whose intellectual, moral, and physical functions gradually and inexplicably deteriorated over time. Morel used the term *demence précoce* (mental deterioration at an early age); he thought the deterioration was caused by hereditary factors and was virtually irreversible. Several modern theories of the disorder do not differ much from Morel's views. *Dementia praecox*, the Latin form of Morel's term, was used by Emil Kraeplin (1899) to refer to the rather large class of disorders that have features of mental deterioration beginning early in life. Eugen Bleuler (1911) introduced the term *schizophrenia* (split mind) to indicate his belief that the disorder chiefly involved a lack of integration between thoughts and emotions and a loss of contact with reality.

To apply the overall diagnosis of schizophrenia, the *DSM-IV* requires evidence of two of the following: (1) delusions; (2) hallucinations; (3) grossly disorganized or catatonic behavior; (4) disorganized speech; or (5) negative symptoms, such as affective flattening, alogia, or avolition. But if hallucinations involve voices commenting consistently or voices conversing with each other, or if delusions are bizarre, only one of the symptoms is required. The symptoms must be present for at least 1 month, and some signs of the disorder must continue for at least 6 months with or without a prodomal or residual phase. Typical delusions of schizophrenics include somatic delusions, delusions of being controlled, thought broadcasting, and grandiose delusions. Five subtypes of schizophrenia listed in the *DSM-IV* are Paranoid, Disorganized, Catatonic, Undifferentiated, and Residual.

Disorganized Schizophrenia (previously termed Hebephrenia) is marked by disorganized speech and behavior and flat or inappropriate affect (often in the form of random giggling). Catatonic Schizophrenia is manifested by extreme psychomotor disturbance or withdrawal or excitement patterns. Undifferentiated Schizophrenia, as in this chapter's case of Sally, involves a variety of symptoms and is often the eventual diagnosis applied to chronic cases. Paranoid Schizophrenia, as in the case of Daniel Paul Schreber, is the least overtly disturbed form of schizophrenia. This pattern is contrasted with the case of Lloyd, diagnosed as a Paranoid Personality Disorder. Although disturbed, Lloyd does not show the thought disorder, disorganized behavior, or hallucinations that are seen in Schreber. The paranoid disorders are compared in Table 6–1.

The Delusional Disorder (Paranoia) is a psychotic disorder characterized by the gradual development of a complex, intricate, and elaborate delusional system, in contrast to the more fragmented delusions of Schreber (a paranoid schizophrenic) or the nonpsychotic paranoid pattern seen in Lloyd. The delusional systems in a Delusional Disorder (Paranoia) are usually based on misinterpretations of actual events. Once this (inaccurate) premise is established, other aspects of the delusion logically follow. However, an extensive interview with a paranoid patient may reveal no marked abnormalities if the areas of delusional material are not mentioned. Five subgroups (based on type of delusion) are recognized in *DSM-IV*: Erotomanic, Grandiose, Jealous, Persecutory, and Somatic. For example, persons with delusions of grandeur believe they are some exalted being, such as Jesus Christ or the president. Erotomanics believe someone, usually of higher

TABLE 6–1 Paranoid Schizophrenia Compared

Paranoid Schizophrenia	Other Paranoid Disorders
The delusional system is poorly organized and may contain a number of delusions that change over time; schizophrenia and belief system disorder are both fundamental to the abnormality	The irrational beliefs may not be so severe as to constitute a delusion, or, when existent, there are fewer of them and they don't often change; a belief system disorder is the fundamental abnormality
A generally bizarre appearance and attitude	Appearance of normality
Problems in reality contact	Relatively good reality contact
Wide-ranging delusions, including persecution, jealousy, grandiosity, irrelevant thoughts	The delusions are usually of persecution or non–reality-based jealousy
Develops later in life	More consistent relation to early developmental patterns
Biological factors are generally the significant contributing causes	Psychological factors are generally the primary causes
Depression is not very common	Depression or other mood disorder is more common
Develops later in life	First manifestations occur in adolescence or late adolescence
More common in males	Approximately equal incidence in males and females
Often some reasonably normal-appearing outward behaviors	Less disoriented or withdrawn appearance
Higher intellectual ability than other schizophrenics	Often of average intelligence
Rare occurrence in many rural, non-Western cultures	Approximately equal occurrence across cultures
Proportionately shorter hospital stays	Tend toward few periods of hospitalization
Tend toward mesomorphic body build (the body of the powerful athlete)	No specific body build

status, is in love with them. Somatic delusions are very irrational beliefs that one has some physical deficit or general medical condition. Individuals who have delusions of persecution feel they are targets of various conspiracies against them.

We now present the first case, Sally, in which we see Undifferentiated Schizophrenia, a particularly severe level of disorder.

Undifferentiated Schizophrenia

**The Case
of Sally**

*"Your secret dreams that grow over the years like
apple seeds sown in your belly, grow up through
you in leafy wonder and finally sprout through*

your skin, gentle and soft and wondrous, and they
have a life of their own. . . . "

"You've done this?"

"A time or two."

—W. P. Kinsella, *Shoeless Joe* (1982)

Schizophrenia exacts a tremendous cost from both society and the person who suffers from it. Occurrence is approximately equal across sex, although there is frequently a milder course in women as well as a mean later onset of 6 years. Onset typically occurs between mid-teens to mid-twenties. About 1 out of every 100 people in the United States will be diagnosed as schizophrenic at least once in their lifetime. This 1% rate has been consistent across cultures and also across the years within our own culture (Robins and Regier, 1990).

The case of Sally is an example of Undifferentiated Schizophrenia. As we see with Sally, a person who eventually shows an undifferentiated pattern often has shown earlier disorganized, catatonic, or even paranoid patterns. Most long-term schizophrenics show various symptoms at different times and usually eventually show a mixed and/or varying pattern of symptoms, thus earning a diagnosis of Undifferentiated Schizophrenia (American Psychiatric Association, 1994).

The Case of Sally

Sally did not start life with the best roll of the dice. In spite of her physician's warning, her mother persisted in her two-pack-a-day smoking habit even while she was carrying Sally. Also, Sally's mother suffered a severe bout of the flu when she was 5 months pregnant with Sally.

There is also reason to believe Sally may have inherited some vulnerability to schizophrenia. Her maternal grandfather had always been known in the family as an "eccentric," while people less fond of him preferred to call him "crazy" or "nuts." He had developed a number of unique religious beliefs and also was known in the community for having placed unusual mechanisms on the roofs of his barns, supposedly to bring in "electromagnetic energy" to help his livestock grow. Farming in those days did not demand the organizational and financial skills that it does today, so it provided plenty of room for odd and/or person-avoidant behaviors. He was never brought to the attention of any mental health professionals—indeed, he thought *they* were "nuts."

Sally was generally slow to develop. She walked and talked late, but at the same time was an active child. She was never formally diagnosed as "hyperactive" but clearly was above average on this dimension.

Sally's parents had a marriage filled with conflict, even separating for almost 10 months when Sally was 2 years old. But they reunited, to enter into what would best be termed a long-term conflict-habituated marriage.

They were both devoted to Sally, especially since after two miscarriages after Sally's birth they were advised not to have any more children. Sally's father traveled quite a bit because of his position as a sales coordinator for a farm machinery company.

When he was home, he played with Sally a lot. But he could be quite critical if he thought she was not behaving (and later achieving) at the level he thought she should be. Her mother, on the other hand, developed an intense, almost symbiotic relationship with Sally.

Sally was of above-average intelligence. However, in spite of her mother's intense coaching and Sally's withdrawal into studying (and fantasy behavior), her grades were only average or lower in most subjects. It was always as if her thought processes were, as one teacher put it, "just a bit off center."

Sally did have an occasional friend. But her mother's overprotection and Sally's occasional odd behaviors and thought processes kept her out of the flow of activities, and she never made long-term, deep friendships. In fact, when it appeared that Sally had any possibility of having a deep friendship, her mother's intrusions became more pronounced, and the promise of that relationship was destroyed.

Sally was a quiet and mildly shy child. Also, because she did not have the feedback inherent in friendships and an active social life, she developed even more odd interests and mannerisms. These in turn further distanced her socially.

She did graduate from high school and was allowed to board at a nearby college. However, the stress of being in new surroundings was too much for her. She started talking to herself, and her assigned roommate quickly managed to be moved to another room. One afternoon the dorm counselor found Sally in her room sitting in a chair, staring at the floor. Sally was unresponsive, and her limbs could be moved about and would then stay in place, almost as if she were a plastic doll.

Sally was in a withdrawn catatonic state, marked by a condition referred to as "waxy flexibility." She was hospitalized and improved fairly rapidly. She tried to return to school but became more and more reclusive, now often skipping classes. Her mother brought her back home "to take care of her," and Sally degenerated even further, at one point showing a pattern of almost totally unresponsive behavior, interrupted occasionally by periods of giggling and rocking behavior, traditionally termed a hebephrenic pattern.

Sally's father finally insisted that Sally return to the hospital. She did, but when she showed some improvement, her mother again brought her home and did not continue the recommended outpatient treatment. Sally was able to get a part-time job as a clerk in a nearby store that did a low-volume business, which did not place great demands on her. She spent almost all of her free time at home, doing some jobs around the house and spending the rest of the time in her room.

About this time her father suffered a fatal heart attack, making Sally's mother even more dependent on her daughter. Sally had now taken to wandering about on her way home from work, possibly as a defense against the intensity of her mother's needs. Her behaviors were also becoming more bizarre. One day the police found her walking in the shallows of a pond in the town park, muttering to herself. They took her to the local hospital, and she was then transferred to a nearby mental hospital.

Etiology

Just as there are a variety of symptoms in schizophrenia, so also may a number of causes contribute to an eventual case of schizophrenia. In one case certain factors may be primary, whereas in another case other factors may be more critical.

It is important to remember that there are various types of causes for schizophrenia. The several possible "original" causes for schizophrenia are termed *generic variables*; for example, genetics are one possible generic cause. The most immediate manifestation of the disorder is an information-processing deficit, evident in problems in attention, perception, and memory (Knable, Kleinman, and Weinberger, 1995). The variables that subsequently produce these symptoms are labeled *mediating variables*. It is also important to note that there are *maintenance variables*, that is, variables that do not generate the disorder or the symptoms but which later serve to maintain and even increase the symptoms of the disorder (Walker, 1998; Whybrow, 1997).

Various generic, or, original, causes of schizophrenia have been proposed. There is good evidence that there is a genetic (hereditary) predisposition to schizophrenia, which may operate as a compelling cause in some individual cases and may only be a contributing factor in others (Knable, Kleinman, and Weinberger, 1995; Gottesman and Shields, 1972). It is very possible that Sally's eccentric grandfather actually suffered from schizophrenia, although there never was any formal diagnosis.

A critical problem in this case is likely the severe bout of flu that Sally's mother suffered when she was 5 months pregnant with Sally. Research indicates that trauma from a virus, or even malnutrition or some other systemic disruption in the second trimester increases markedly the risk for schizophrenia. The theory is that such an event disrupts the migration of cells resulting from the breaking-up of the neural subplate, which typically first forms in the second trimester of pregnancy and then usually dissipates almost entirely within the first month of life, having performed its task of aiming neurons toward their proper location in the cortex. By far the major migration of cells through that neural subplate occurs during the second trimester, so any disruption at that time is potentially problematic. It can result in an unusual distribution of "guidepost" cells in the brain, leading to atypical and/or faulty neural connections, that is, more of a "bad wiring" than a "bad seed" or "bad environment" hypothesis.

Because of the nature of the symptoms of schizophrenia, any potential cause of brain disorder (genetic problems, birth disorder, trauma, viral or infectious disorder, etc.) may contribute. Even her mother's heavy smoking during the pregnancy could have generated some mild asphyxiation, a combination of anoxia (a loss of oxygen to brain tissue) and increased carbon dioxide tension in the blood and tissues, which leads to an acidic metabolic condition that could result in some tissue damage. Any of these original causes can in turn lead to neurological disorder, or imbalances of brain chemicals such as dopamine, serotonin, or norepinephrine.

Psychological disorders, such as early psychological conflict or family disorder, can also be a critical variable in the development of schizophrenia. While most theorists do not see the psychological factor as an original cause in and of itself, it can certainly be very important in the development, amplification, and maintenance of schizophrenia. For example, research (Miklowitz et al., 1986) indicates that two environmental factors, intrafamilial expressed emotion and communication deviance, are especially contributory, and they both appear to be operative in Sally's case. Expressed emotion refers to a family situation in which parents are emotionally overinvolved and overprotective (as was Sally's mother) or are highly critical (as was her father, at least on occasion).

Communication deviance is a measure of the degree to which an individual is unable to establish and maintain a shared focus of attention with someone while in a dialog. This could of course result from brain disorder, but it could also result from early conflict or familial disorder. Communication deviance was also evident in Sally's history.

Premorbid Factors in Schizophrenia

Even with the potential multicausal background of schizophrenia, there are also various premorbid factors that predict to the emergence of schizophrenia, and a common sequence of what often takes place in the development of schizophrenia.

Premorbid factors are those factors associated with, but not necessarily causal to, the later development of schizophrenia. Only a few of the factors listed here may be noted in any one case, but they are common across cases.

1. A schizophrenic parent or parents or the presence of other schizophrenic blood relatives is a less potent variable. (There is approximately a fifteen times greater chance of developing schizophrenia when a nuclear [blood relation] family member is schizophrenic.)

2. A history of prenatal disruption; birth problems; or viral or bacterial infections or toxic situations in pregnancy, especially if these occur in the second trimester

3. Slowed reaction times in perception (such as slowness in becoming aware of a stimulus) or very rapid recovery rate of autonomic nervous system after stress or novel stimulus

4. Developmental and/or central nervous system dysfunction (such as convulsive disorder), hyperactivity, or enlarged cerebral ventricles (the spaces between brain tissue)

5. Low birth weight and/or low IQ relative to siblings

6. Early role as odd member of family or scapegoat

7. Parenting marked by inconsistency and by emotionally extreme responses (both positive and negative) and double messages; parental rejection, particularly when one parent's negative effect is not countered by corrective attention and care from the other parent

8. Rejection by peers, especially if accompanied by odd thinking patterns, ambivalent and labile emotional responses, or a lack of response to standard pleasure sources

9. Rejection by peers in childhood or adolescence; being perceived by both teachers and peers as more irritable and more unstable than other children

10. An inability to form stable, committed relationships, especially for men (For example, never married men have almost fifty times higher odds of devel-

oping schizophrenia than men who have married; for women, it is about fifteen times higher for never married over married.)

Treatment Options

Given the multi-symptom nature of schizophrenia, it is not surprising that a variety of treatments are needed just to stop and/or reverse the course of the disorder. Total cures are rare. But many schizophrenics can be returned to a level of at least adequate functioning in their job and community.

Administration of psychotropic medication (see Table 6–2), most often the phenothiazines (such as chlorpromazine/Thorazine), the butyrophenones, or the thioxanthenes, is virtually always essential. While extremely helpful in most instances, there are disadvantages to the various chemotherapies: (1) They don't work at all with a sizeable minority of schizophrenics; (2) they work best with "positive" or more benign symptoms but are less effective with the "negative" symptoms (see following discussion); (3) getting the dosage right is difficult, and overmedication can result; and (4) significant side effects are common, especially with long-term use—and long-term use is required in most cases (Walker, 1998; Buckley and Meltzer, 1995).

A variety of other physical treatments are occasionally employed for schizophrenia: electroconvulsive treatment (ECT), dialysis, psychosurgery, and megavitamin therapy. However, there are little data to indicate that these are of any significant help in the treatment of schizophrenia, and there are potentially negative side effects with all of these interventions.

Supportive individual and group psychotherapies, possibly abetted by family or marital therapies in certain cases, are usually parts of any overall treatment program for schizophrenics. They help to reduce excess expressed emotion, thus allowing a lower dosage of maintenance medication, and they also help to ensure the schizophrenic is compliant in taking medication. It is also not well under-

TABLE 6–2 Anti-Psychotic Drugs

**Name
(Generic/Trade)**

Phenothiazines
  chlorpromazine (Thorazine)
  thioridazine (Mellaril)
  fluphenazine (Prolixin)
  fluphenazine decanoate (Prolixin D)
  perphenazine (Trilafon)
  trifluoperazine (Stelazine)

Butyrophenones
  haloperidol (Haldol)
  chlorprothixene (Taractan)

Thioxanthenes
  thiothixine (Navane)

Other anti-psychotic drugs
  loxapine (Loxitane)
  molindone (Moban)
  clozapine (Clozaril)
  risperidone (Risperdal)
  pimozide (Drop)
  olanzapine (Zxprexa)

stood, even by many clinicians, that there is a high rate of suicide in schizophrenia—about ten times higher than in normals—so this must be accounted for. To the degree that schizophrenics are at a low level of overall functioning, confrontive techniques may also be helpful in getting them to at least respond. Also, with severely deteriorated schizophrenics, token economies are useful in modifying a wide range of behaviors, including some of the bizarre mannerisms that distance others, and are also useful in promoting more positive social skills. Milieu therapy (unfortunately at times just a euphemism for the hospital environment) is also helpful in reorienting schizophrenics to more appropriate social behaviors. Other adjunct therapies, such as biofeedback, occupational and expressive therapies, and environmental and nutritional planning, can also be useful. Training in more appropriate cognitive strategies and in ways to avoid the information-processing distortions that occur with schizophrenia are necessary as well.

A most critical step is aiding schizophrenics to make an effective transition back into their family and community. Indeed, it makes little sense to put forth significant time and effort when the problem first comes to the attention of social agencies or treaters and then to provide only a minimum of attention when they return from the hospital to the community. Proactive efforts by an aftercare "case manager," that is, consistent contact, monitoring, and support, sometimes referred to as "assertive community treatment" (ACT), can be effective, although it is seldom applied. It works by helping the client stabilize during crises, apply already learned and new social and coping skills, and make more positive social and vocational contacts.

Negative Symptoms

Negative symptoms (affective flattening, alogia, avolition/apathy, anhedonia/asociality, and attentional impairment) have been found to be directly correlated with a high rate of remission, slow onset, and higher probability of permanent disability for schizophrenics. Positive symptoms—positive in the sense that they are marked by their existence, rather than their absence as in negative symptoms—(hallucinations, delusions, formal thought disorder, and bizarre behavior) respond best to the anti-psychotic medications. Unfortunately, the positive symptoms are relatively weak and unspecific as predictors of other variables. Two negative symptoms, anhedonia and affective flattening, are the strongest independent predictors of negative outcome. Patients with the poorest long-term outcome tend to show greater increases in negative symptoms during the early years of their illness. Early and progressive negative symptoms may signal a process leading to long-term disability.

Positive Prognostic Signs in Schizophrenia

Assuming that some effective treatment is occurring, the following positive prognostic signs predict to an adequate remission once schizophrenia is diagnosed (Walker, 1998; Knable et al., 1995). These variables should be considered as correlated factors rather than necessarily explicit causes of such remission.

- Sexual-marital status: married, or at least a prior history of stable sexual-social adjustment
- The degree to which negative symptoms are absent, especially the degree they are absent early in the symptom picture
- A family history of affective rather than schizophrenic disorder
- Presence of an affective response (elation or depression) in the acute stage of the disorder
- Abrupt onset of the disorder; clear precipitating factors at onset
- Onset later than early childhood
- Minor or no paranoid trends in the disorder
- Higher socio-economic status
- Adequate premorbid school and/or vocational adjustment
- Premorbid competence in interpersonal relationships
- Short length of stay in hospital
- No history of ECT treatment
- Tendency to be stimulation-receptive rather than stimulation-avoidant
- Lower levels of hostility, criticism of others, and emotional overinvolvement (expressed emotion) upon hospital release

Sally's Treatment

Sally's mother subverted any real treatment during Sally's first two hospitalizations. Thus, Sally was not effectively treated until late in the process of her disorder, a not uncommon occurrence with schizophrenics. In her third hospitalization, Sally was immediately put on chemotherapy, in this case Thorazine. She was included in an inpatient therapy group and talked to her psychiatrist for a half hour or so about twice a week.

She showed some fairly rapid improvement on some of the more obvious symptoms, such as talking constantly to herself, sometimes obviously responding to voices she heard. However, some of her "negative" symptoms, specifically her disturbances in attention and thinking, remained. Eventually she was released back to her mother's care, which meant that, in spite of attempts to deal with her large overlay of social deficits through outpatient therapy procedures, Sally made little progress.

There were several relapses; indeed, the relapses began to be more common. The symptoms were now many and varied, although not always so flamboyant as in some of the earliest episodes, thus now earning her the diagnosis of Undifferentiated Schizophrenia. At the last contact with her therapists, Sally was in the hospital. The prognosis for any substantial cure was very poor, and it is probable that she will continue the pattern of going in and out of hospitals and aftercare.

Paranoid Schizophrenia

The Case of Daniel Paul Schreber

Ninety-nine percent of the people in the world are fools and the rest of us are in great danger of contagion.

—Thornton Wilder, *The Matchmaker* (1954)

Paranoid schizophrenia is an interesting and severe disorder. In order to apply a *DSM* diagnosis of Paranoid Schizophrenia, the person must first meet the overall criteria for schizophrenia. The disorder is specifically labeled as Paranoid Schizophrenia when the symptom picture is dominated by preoccupation with grandiose or persecutory delusions, delusions of jealousy (erotomania), or hallucinations (auditory) with a delusional content. See Table 6-1 at the front of this chapter for a comparison of paranoid schizophrenia with the other schizophrenias and with the other paranoid disorders.

A Classic Case of Paranoia

Daniel Paul Schreber gained permanent status as a famous psychiatric patient by virtue of the attention given to him by Freud. The only source of information used by Freud in his renowned analysis of Schreber was a book authored by Schreber himself describing his thoughts and beliefs. Before Freud discovered Schreber's book, he had kept a woman with a classic case of paranoia in psychoanalysis even though he believed she was unable to benefit from therapy, in order to learn about her condition. When Freud discovered Schreber's work, he became consumed with writing Schreber's case history as a classic example of paranoia.

Freud was captivated by the eloquence with which Schreber wrote of his condition. Phrases used by Schreber to describe his condition such as "soul murder" and "nerve contacts" delighted Freud, who introduced them into his written communications. Every page of Schreber's grandiose descriptions of his affairs and the universe was an opportunity for Freud to amplify the sexual aspects of his psychoanalytic theory. Freud believed Schreber's paranoia caused him to explain the universe as a survival mechanism.

The Case of Daniel Paul Schreber

Daniel Paul Schreber was born on July 25, 1842, as the second son and the third of five children into a family of many generations of professionals. There is little direct evidence of what occurred in Schreber's childhood. It is known that he was gifted as a student. His father, Dr. Schreber, was a successful and well-known physician and reformer. One of many books written by Dr. Schreber had to do with how to raise children between infancy and adolescence. Dr. Schreber's first advice in that book, which he asserts with pride that he used on his own children, is to put as much pressure as possible on children during the earliest years of their lives in order to avoid trouble later. Dr. Schreber stated that infants should be bathed in cold water to toughen them up, and, to make sure children never cry, parents must startle children from crying by knocking on the bed or simply punish them by physical beatings, until no emotion is again shown. He stated that children should undergo intense physical training and learn to restrain their emotions.

One of Dr. Schreber's favorite topics was making the child have perfect posture at all times. Between ages 2 and 8 especially, children should wear an orthopedic device made of iron intended to create an extremely erect and straight posture. He emphasized that this must be maintained while the child is sleeping, and he created a device with iron rings and a chain to ensure the child's sleeping posture.

In addition to extremely rigorous restraints and exercises, Dr. Schreber's philosophy was to control every waking moment of a child's day. The child should be completely organized and well groomed at all times. If the child does not perform each activity for the exact and entire time interval alloted to it, the child is to be denied the next scheduled meal for that day. Harsh physical punishment was recommended if the child deviates from the schedule at all. When being punished, the child must hold out his or her hand to the person who is administering punishment, to ensure that the child will not be bitter. He said a list must be maintained on the child's wall detailing every act of disobedience, and at the end of each week the child should be punished accordingly. This was also to ensure that the child will not grow up to masturbate.

As a result of the views of their father, Schreber and his siblings likely grew up in complete passivity, and Schreber was described as nervous in his childhood. In 1858, when Schreber was 16, Dr. Schreber's head was injured when a ladder fell on him. After that he was known to have severe headaches, hallucinations, and stated homicidal intentions. Dr. Schreber was never the same; some believe that his peculiar behavior following the accident was a nervous breakdown. Three years later, when Schreber was 19, his father died.

Schreber became a successful lawyer and later an esteemed judge. His older brother Gustav committed suicide when Schreber was 35 years old. At age 42, Schreber was defeated in a race for political office. It was after this defeat that he suffered his first mental breakdown. He started having hypochondriacal delusions such as believing he was emaciated and that he was going to die of a heart attack. During this first hospital stay, which lasted 6 months, Schreber had speech impediments, two suicide attempts, hypersensitivity to noise, and high emotionality. Even when Schreber was discharged, he believed he had lost 30 pounds (when in fact he had gained 2 pounds).

After his discharge, Schreber spent the next 8 years happily with his wife. His only disappointment was that they had no children. He reached the top of his profession when he was appointed presiding judge of the country's highest court. Immediately before this appointment, Schreber dreamed his mental illness had returned. When his insomnia and anxiety became worse, Schreber contacted Dr. Paul Emil Flechsig, his former psychiatrist. Schreber's condition worsened and he was again hospitalized, this time for 8 years. Schreber was 51, the same age of his father when he suffered the blow to the head from which he never fully recovered.

It is during this second hospitalization that Schreber wrote *Memoirs of My Nervous Illness*, a book recording his thoughts, delusions, and hallucinations, written "to acquaint my wife with my personal experiences and religious ideas" so that she would understand his "various oddities of behavior." It is from this book that we have information about Schreber's psychological condition. Schreber's medical records reflect that when he began his second hospitalization he feared he would soon die and had delusions of persecution. He believed he was a woman and his penis had been twisted off with a nerve probe. He had constant auditory and visual hallucinations. He believed he was being tortured to death and that God spoke openly to him.

Schreber often screamed out of his window statements such as "The sun (or God) is a whore." His thoughts about his body began to change from death and destruction to flowering into the body of a female, which made him pleased to show his doctor his naked chest. He became preoccupied with sexual thoughts.

While Schreber was spending much of his time with ribbons over his naked body in front of a mirror, he was able to write letters to his wife and family wherein he spoke of his illness with amazing insight. In addition, when he was 53, Schreber filed and ultimately won an appeal of his permanent commitment, which had been done without his knowledge. Schreber argued he had a nervous illness that resulted from problems that were objectively true. The court found that Schreber was mentally ill but agreed with him that mental illness was not determinative, as Schreber was able to convince the court he could care for himself. In response to the argument that Schreber's intention to publish his *Memoirs* was evidence of his lack of judgment, the court ruled that the publication might be financially beneficial to Schreber and that, despite the obvious lack of reality in the book, it did reflect a genuine interest in finding the truth.

The content of Schreber's *Memoirs* alternated between three levels: (1) the history of his illness and his efforts to appeal his order of involuntary commitment, (2) his personal experiences, and (3) his analysis of the cosmos. Schreber received information about the cosmos from souls that spoke to him, but unfortunately not in complete sentences, forcing Schreber to do so, which he said caused him to think compulsively:

> I meet a person I know by the name of Schneider. Seeing him the thought automatically arises "This man's name is Schneider" or "This is Mr. Schneider." With it "But why" or "Why because" also resounds in my nerves.
>
> When humans die God appears and sucks the nerves out of the body to return and be purified. Sometimes God, who sees all humans as corpses, makes a mistake and attaches Himself to living humans. When this occurs, there is danger because some living human nerves have such a powerful attraction that God will not be able to disconnect Himself. If this happened, God would cease to exist and there would be a rip or tear in the cosmic order.

The process of being transformed into a woman was one of Schreber's continuing preoccupations. Even though he believed this process was initiated by Flechsig, as a soul murder, with an intent to make him a prostitute, Schreber says that through a series of miracles he agrees to become a woman to ensure his survival. Schreber describes this transformation in terms of many attacks on his body, for example, the destruction and replacement of his internal organs, the pumping out of his spinal cord from his body through the assistance of little men in his feet, and the saturation of his body with female nerves. When he ultimately surrenders to this force, Schreber refers to himself as a joint of pork, and said his ultimate goal was to become pregnant by God.

Schreber's second stay in the hospital ended when he won his appeal of the permanent commitment. Eight years after entering the hospital, at age 60, Schreber went home. He lived there for 5 years. His mother, with whom he had been living, died, and soon after his wife had a stroke and died. After his wife's death, Schreber re-entered the hospital at age 65 and stayed there until his death at age 69, the same year that Freud's essay on paranoia based on Schreber's *Memoirs* was published.

Schreber's last position was as the president of a panel of judges at the court of appeals in Dresden, and throughout his life, Schreber protested the devices his father used on him.

Freud's Analysis of Schreber

Freud interpreted Schreber's delusions as a manifestation of paranoia caused by homosexuality that Schreber denied or rejected. Freud used Schreber's writings to formulate a theory of paranoia. The foundation of this paranoia, repression of his homosexuality, took other forms so that Schreber would not recognize his own wishes. Freud believed Schreber transferred his love for his brother and father to Flechsig and God. Freud used Schreber's *Memoirs* to develop his psychoanalytic theory of paranoia. Freud interpreted Schreber's desire to become a woman as a justification for his loss of masculinity and termed this the "father-complex," viewing homosexual fixation such as Schreber's as the result of unresolved Oedipal conflict. The threat of castration by Schreber's father caused him to abandon his mother's love but at the same time identify with her.

Etiology

The onset of schizophrenia late in Schreber's life is consistent with symptoms he displayed of paranoid schizophrenia. The extreme steps taken by Schreber's father to control his children and inhibit normal functioning and expression of feelings likely resulted in this condition. There were no other known schizophrenics in Schreber's family history, thus placing Schreber into that small percentage of schizophrenics who may have acquired the syndrome during his life. Schreber's delusions were grandiose and bizarre and his hallucinations were constant during his episodes of schizophrenia. His preoccupation with turning into a woman, his involvement with God and nerves, and his compulsive thinking as a result of messages from souls all are part of the classical symptoms of paranoid schizophrenia.

What is interesting is that even during his most extreme episodes, Schreber was able to function sufficiently to meet his needs. For instance, he was able to write a logical, meaningful letter to his wife describing his illness while he was experiencing constant hallucinations and delusions. Also, Schreber's successful appeal of his permanent commitment was seemingly remarkable. These events are not unusual, however, for the paranoid type of schizophrenics, who are often able to present themselves in a reasonably normal-appearing way. Schreber's high level of intelligence also is not uncommon in the paranoid type of schizophrenia.

A factor in Schreber's background that is common in the history of the development of paranoid behavior is the use of harsh and shaming techniques by his parents to discipline him. As Kenneth Mark Colby (1977) notes, the paranoid individual learns very early to use "symbol-processing procedures to forestall a threatened unpleasant affect experience of humiliation, detected as shame signals. . . . In preventing humiliation, the procedures use a strategy of blaming others for wronging the self" (p. 56). Shaming techniques particularly predispose an individual to learn to anticipate the possibility of humiliation and to engage in numerous mechanisms to protect the ego from this experience.

Paranoids do differ from normals in terms of how they process information, that is, in their use of projection. Projection was initially hypothesized by Freudian theorists, in part based on Schreber's case, although they were specifically referring to projection of concern about conflict over homosexuality. More recent formulations have pointed out that it is not necessary to hypothesize a homosexual conflict; indeed, some paranoids are overtly homosexual, which directly contradicts this Freudian theory. On the other hand, the Freudian hypothesis of projection as an abstract concept has held up well through the years, and it is clear that many of the paranoid's delusions are projections of internal ruminations and concerns.

Treatment Options

Persons with a paranoid disorder of any sort are seldom likely to be involved in treatment unless coerced in some way, such as imprisonment, hospitalization, or pressure from a spouse. This is not surprising. Paranoids are inherently suspicious of many people and trust few. Also, most therapies, particularly for interpersonal problems, eventually require a degree of self-disclosure and the client's willingness to admit vulnerability. These behaviors are the antithesis of those qualities that make a person paranoid. Paranoids strongly fear allowing others to see their vulnerabilities and other foibles, as they are then open to a much feared shame experience or even to attack (especially if they have delusions of persecution). Thus, the critical first step is gaining the trust of the client.

Paranoids who are severely disturbed, and thus either dangerous or somewhat disorganized, are likely to be hospitalized. Some clinicians have administered electroconvulsive therapy (ECT) to paranoids, possibly from the notion that the paranoids will subsequently forget the content of their delusions. This treatment has shown little success, which is not surprising as paranoids greatly fear any sense of increased vulnerability and/or loss of control over the self, which is a probable effect of ECT. Secondly, there is not much evidence that ECT is of any therapeutic value, except possibly for acute severe depression, and there is also some risk of short- and long-term memory loss as well as of brain damage from any long-term ECT administration. The same problems and the lack of positive results have generally been found in the application of psychosurgery to paranoid disorders. However, chemotherapy strategies have been effective in reducing the more bizarre components, and more so with persecutory delusions than with somatic or erotomanic delusions (Buckley and Meltzer, 1995). Long-term psychotherapy is difficult because the very nature of most treatment approaches (increased self-disclosure and confrontation of the self) involves the things the paranoid most fears. Any significant cure depends on the therapist's ability to generate trust in one who is inherently untrusting.

Paranoid Personality Disorder

**The Case
of Lloyd**

*Before I built a wall I'd ask to know what I was
walling in or walling out.*

—Robert Frost, American poet (1874–1963)

The paranoid personality disorder is marked by chronic suspiciousness, emotional detachment and isolation from others, and a tendency to be litigious or even pugnacious under stress (Meyer, 1998b). The personality disorders are discussed at length in Chapter 11, and the reader is referred to the introduction of that chapter for a discussion of the general characteristics of those patterns. However, even though Lloyd has a personality disorder rather than a paranoid disorder, the case is presented here because the etiological concepts and treatments dovetail with those presented in the case of Daniel Schreber. At the same time, the symptomatology, etiological considerations, and outcome differ, and these contrasts should help in elaborating an overall understanding of paranoid thinking.

The case of Lloyd involves a young man for whom projection (see discussion in prior case) became a lifelong defensive strategy. Not only was the strategy counterproductive, but it also predisposed the social environment to respond to him hostilely. Met with social isolation throughout his childhood and adolescence, Lloyd found enough evidence to support his belief in his "superiority" and his jealousy of others. Eventually his functioning declined as his paranoid ideation interfered with objective self-evaluation and prohibited personal growth and satisfaction.

The Case of Lloyd

Lloyd was an only child whose mother died of childbirth complications when he was 3 months old. He was mainly cared for by the family's housekeeper until he went to college. When he was 3, his father remarried, but Lloyd's relationship with his stepmother was never better than amiable indifference. She was active in church and civic organizations and left the rearing of Lloyd to the housekeeper and his father.

Lloyd's father was a senior executive with a large, competitive business firm. He often discussed his work-related problems and frustrations during dinner. He was demanding of his employees and quickly fired them if they did not meet his standards. Also, he was critical of himself and often attributed setbacks in the business to his professional weaknesses. Similar demands were made of Lloyd. His father analyzed all of Lloyd's actions and attributed any instance of less-than-perfect achievement to Lloyd's weak efforts. The stepmother usually agreed with his father, although she placed no demands on Lloyd. Lloyd's memory of the housekeeper was that she was affectionate toward him and cared for him responsibly. Yet they were not close and Lloyd did not regard her as a parent.

Lloyd did not attend nursery school or kindergarten and presented behavior problems in the first grade. When his teacher corrected his work, he was resentful and angry.

On occasion, Lloyd would scream at the teacher, tear his papers, and refuse to work any longer. When his parents were informed of such behavior, they accused the teacher of picking on Lloyd and expecting too much of him. However, they did get tutoring for Lloyd, which helped bring him to the level of first-graders who had been to kindergarten and/or nursery school. This served to reduce the intensity of Lloyd's response to criticism. Nevertheless, Lloyd's resentment when corrected was noted by each of his elementary and junior high school teachers.

The family had few close or intimate friends, mainly because of their condescending social attitudes. Lloyd's playmates were carefully screened. As he grew older and brought schoolmates home, his father criticized anyone who was not considered "worthwhile." When his parents thought a friend was unacceptable (most of the time), they were rude and later criticized Lloyd for choosing that friend. Aside from church on Sundays, there were few family activities. Lloyd's father and stepmother were socially active with church- and business-related functions, but Lloyd was seldom included in these functions, and he was sent to visit his (natural) maternal grandparents when his parents vacationed each summer.

Apparently taking his father's lead, Lloyd was domineering and condescending toward his classmates. They naturally resented Lloyd's constant bragging about his grades and assertions of genius, as well as the fact that he was a "snitch." These social problems were brought to his parents' attention, but they criticized the school and assured Lloyd that the other students avoided him because they were jealous of his superior ability. Lloyd internalized these attitudes and used the jealousy explanation to rationalize his subsequent unsuccessful interactions with his peers. This attitude further generalized to all areas of accomplishment. The fault always lay with unreasonable expectations, unclear instructions, and/or other external circumstances beyond his control.

Aside from a few superficial lunch and study buddies, Lloyd had almost no peers with whom he interacted by the time he entered high school. He spent most of his time alone in his room, studying or working with his stamp collection. He graduated with honors from high school and college, and he developed a regional reputation when he began to exhibit his stamp collection.

After college, Lloyd took a managerial position with the firm for which his father worked. He worked hard and advanced to regional supervisor within 3 years. At this point he began dating a young lady of whom his parents approved. They were engaged and married within the year. The marriage was met with more apparent enthusiasm by the parents of the bride and groom than by the newlyweds themselves. Lloyd's wife, Ellen, was quiet and agreeable although plain and "colorless." Apparently her parents had become concerned that Ellen would not attract a suitable (or any) husband and were relieved when Lloyd proposed. Lloyd, on the other hand, was flattered by Ellen's uncritical acceptance and minimal expectations of him. The marriage evolved into a nearly platonic and amicable partnership. They did not have children, which resulted more from an unenthusiastic sexual relationship than from any definitive decision.

It was not long before Lloyd realized that his rapid advancement had come to a halt. The firm for which he worked merged with a larger conglomerate, and the higher positions were assigned to employees who had been with the conglomerate before the merger. Feeling that he was again the undeserving victim of unfortunate circumstances (and in this case, maybe he was), Lloyd resigned and took a position with a competitive firm. However, his domineering and critical behavior toward his supervisors had only been tolerated at the first firm because of his father's high position. Lloyd had no such protection in the second job, and he created so much resentment among his staff members that he was asked to resign.

Lloyd, who had not experienced a significant failure since first grade, brought suit against the firm, claiming that they had yielded to pressure from the competitive conglomerate to fire him. The suit was quickly dismissed. However, the litigation marked Lloyd as a troublemaker, and other local firms were now reluctant to hire him. His father was retired by this time and thus unable to use his influence to secure a position for Lloyd. In addition, he criticized Lloyd for not "playing the game" and accused him of ruining the family's good name.

Lloyd decided to start his own consulting firm and borrowed heavily to establish the business. He did well for a few months, then ran into conflicts with employees and customers. He continually complained of substandard performance and verbally berated clerks, staff members, and even customers on occasion. As a result, there were so many resignations and terminations that the firm became unstable and then folded.

Lloyd's usual externalizations were becoming unacceptable even to Ellen. She pronounced him a failure in life and filed for a separation (with the approval of her parents). Lloyd's parents agreed that he was a failure in life but saw a divorce in the family as an unacceptable social blight. They urged Lloyd to prevent a divorce and criticized him for being unsuccessful. The separation and business failure were financially draining for Lloyd. He declared bankruptcy, moved to another city, and enrolled in dental school, something he said he had always wanted to do.

His problems continued in dental school. First, his negative social tendencies did not change, and there were numerous conflicts with instructors, patients, and dental hygienists. Also, Lloyd's manual dexterity was poor. He performed well on written exams, but his practicum evaluations were barely passing. Lloyd, of course, blamed these low evaluations on prejudiced instructors, difficult patients, errors of timekeepers, and so forth. He did graduate from dental school and passed the written licensing exam with honors. However, he could not pass the practical exam in two tries, refused to attempt it again, and so was unable to practice dentistry as an independent professional. Opportunities arose to work under the supervision of a licensed dentist, but Lloyd regarded these positions as inferior and unacceptable. His reaction to this third failure was extreme rage reactions and sullen anger. He even made some threats of recriminations against several of his dental school professors whom he had especially disliked.

Treatment

Ellen, who had occasionally still visited Lloyd on weekends, became increasingly concerned about his condition. She insisted that he accompany her to see a family physician, which Lloyd agreed to do only after much arguing. The physician prescribed some tranquilizing medication and set Lloyd up for sessions with a clinical psychologist in their health maintenance organization.

The psychologist had several sessions with him, but Lloyd would never allow any trust to develop. After his anxiety subsided a bit, it became clear that he was only continuing in order to placate Ellen and his parents. The one positive change occurred as a result of the psychologist's referral of Lloyd to a physical therapist to work on his poor manual dexterity. The exercises, combined with some remedial practicum work at the dental school, improved Lloyd's dexterity and he was finally able to pass (albeit barely) the practical portion of the licensing exam.

He went into practice shortly thereafter. He was able to make an adequate living, although he never developed a good practice because of the unattractiveness of his personality. He eventually divorced Ellen and moved to a distant city, possibly in an attempt to distance himself as much as possible from his prior "failures." He became increasingly involved with an extreme right-wing political organization. He was once arrested for having an unregistered machine gun and paid a heavy fine. His personality never changed much; he lived out his life in his established way and died of a heart attack at age 49. There was no clear history of heart disease in his family; its appearance here may be support for the concept that chronic hostility can be a major generic factor in heart disease.

Etiology

Just as with Daniel Schreber (the prior case), the use of shaming techniques as a disciplinary technique was a factor in Lloyd's pathology. However, of far greater import here was the modeling for social isolation and elitism that Lloyd's parents provided, as well as the direct control over friendships that helped to further his isolation. Their own tendency to project failure onto others (again modeled by Lloyd) and their unwillingness to accept any failures or problems in Lloyd similarly made him unwilling to accept these in himself. There is little or no evidence for a genetic component as critical in paranoid personality disorders.

After Lloyd once started failing, the societal labeling as a "troublemaker" and "difficult person to get along with" combined with the increasing alienation from the few supportive interpersonal relationships he had left (Ellen, his parents) to make him even more vulnerable. He could not tolerate this status, which resulted in anxiety and even more inappropriate projections and expressions of his chronic anger (Meyer, 1998b).

The underlying beliefs (Beck, Freeman, and Associates, 1990) that paranoids often struggle with are: (1) I am unique and others are jealous; (2) others will exploit my mistakes; (3) it always pays to be wary, accusatory, and adversarial (some paranoids do make good trial lawyers); (4) people who are trusting or content are fools, so I can't be that way; and (5) negative events are generated purposefully by others.

Comment

It is rare for paranoids to come into therapy without significant coercion from others. In order to relate to, or even treat the paranoid personality, it is essential to gain the client's trust through empathy, but not through participation in the disorder patterns. It is especially necessary to empathize with and then articulate to the paranoid the consequences of such behavior, such as the sense of being isolated and not understood or the interpersonal rejection that appears unfair to the paranoid.

Ironically, paranoids will frequently be correct in assuming that other people are against them or, as some put it, "A paranoid is a person who has all the facts." Such groups as immigrants, the elderly, and the sensory-impaired are somewhat prone to paranoid thinking; thus, it may be more accurate to say that "A paranoid is a person who has all the facts he is able to obtain, given who he is."

7

The Affective (or Mood) Disorders and Suicide

The mood (or affect) disorders have always been a common problem, but they are especially prevalent in modern society (DeBattista, 1998; Alford and Beck, 1997). *Affect* refers to the subjective experience of emotion, whereas *mood* designates a consistent and pervasive emotion that influences our view of our world and ourselves. The affective disorders are broadly defined in the *DSM* as primary disturbances of mood and affect in contrast to disordered thinking, which characterizes the other two severe disturbances previously discussed, schizophrenia and the paranoid disorders. Included among the Affective Disorders classification in the *DSM* are symptom patterns that were formerly labeled as Depressive Neurosis and even on occasion as Cyclothymic Personality Disorder. Symptom patterns in this category range from mild to moderate depressive episodes to the psychotic affective reactions.

The major categories are those of Bipolar Disorder (I and II), Major Depression, and the specific affective disorders, which include Cyclothymic Disorder, Dysthymic Disorder, and Substance-Induced Mood Disorder. The Bipolar Disorder, which replaces the traditional term of Manic-Depressive Psychosis, is discussed here in the case of Virginia Woolf. Major Depressive Disorder categorizes severe, possibly chronic depression; it is discussed in the case of Joseph Westbecker.

Normal depression is characterized by a brief period of sadness, grief, or dejection in which disruption of normal functioning is minimal. Mild disturbances of mood and thought are manifested by apathy, impaired concentration, and increased guilt. These reactions are often responses to discrete environmental events, such as the loss of an important other (of high stimulus value, although not necessarily loved), or disappointments in career or finances. This depression may require no treatment and often lifts with the passage of time. Moderate episodes (as discussed in the case of Danielle in Chapter 2) are more disruptive to normal functioning and may be associated with distorted cognitions and/or skill deficits that require various psychological therapies. The more severe (and sometimes psychotic) depressive syndrome necessitates a multimodal therapeutic approach, usually including chemotherapy, psychotherapy, and cognitive behavior modification; some of these techniques were employed in the treatment of Joseph Westbecker.

Major Depressive Disorder Associated with a Suicide Attempt

The Case of Joseph Westbecker

Well, I think you got anhedonia. It affects maybe one out of a hundred. It means you can't have fun. No kind of fun. Just like you on a golf course. You look like Torquemada's got the hot pliers on your nuts instead of just enjoying the game.

—Joseph Wambaugh, *The Secrets of Harry Bright* (1985)

Depression is a disorder of mood and affect, with these primary symptoms: (1) dysphoria (feeling bad) and/or apathetic mood; (2) a loss or decrease in the potency of stimuli, for example, through the death of an important other (a condition referred to as a *stimulus void*); and (3) *anhedonia*, or a chronic inability to experience pleasure. These symptoms were well described by the noted existential philosopher and theologian Soren Kierkegaard in his 1844 book *The Concept of Anxiety* (Princeton University Press).

> I do not care for anything. I do not care to ride, for the exercise is too violent... I do not care to lie down, for I should either have to remain lying, and I do not care to do that, or I should have to get up again, and I do not care to do that either... I do not care at all." (p. 19)

These primary symptoms are often associated with a various admixture of the following secondary symptoms: (1) withdrawal from contact with others; (2) a sense of hopelessness; (3) rumination about suicide and/or death (4) sleep disturbance, especially early morning awakening; (5) psychomotor slowing or agitation; (6) decrease in and/or disruption of eating behaviors; (7) self-blame, a sense of worthlessness, irrational feelings of guilt; (8) lack of concentration; (9) lack of decisiveness; (10) increased alcohol or drug use; and (11) crying for no apparent reason.

Virtually everyone has been depressed at one time or another in their life. Indeed, it is a normal response to loss or disappointment. But when it persists and/or becomes so severe that it significantly disrupts a person's world, depression becomes pathological. At least 200,000 people each year are hospitalized for depression. It is also estimated that up to one-fourth of the office practice of physicians who focus on physical disorders is actually concerned with depression-based symptomatology. It is noteworthy that about 85% of the psychotropic medication dispensed for depression is prescribed by nonpsychiatrists, primarily internists, gynecologists, and family practitioners (Nathan et al., 1995).

Whereas manic disorders and depression with a manic component usually begin before age 30, depressive disorders can begin at any age. Peak occurrence is in the 20–45 age range; episodes in older people are likely to include more severe symptoms and a more precipitous onset. Predisposing factors include a family history of depression, a depressive episode in childhood (e.g., there is a 75% chance of recurrence in later life if a child has a first episode during the period of age 8–13), alcohol abuse, high negative stress, recent losses, chronic low self-esteem, and any history of chronic illness. Co-morbid anxiety or panic disorder predicts a more negative prognosis, as does melancholia (a syndrome including such symptoms as early morning awakening and more severe dysphoria in the morning, psychomotor agitation or retardation, loss of ability to experience pleasure, and, occasionally, anorexia). Melancholic features are associated with a family history of depression and also with a better response to ECT and tricyclic anti-depressants. One in seven with a major depression will make a suicide attempt, and one in three will develop some form of substance dependency (Strupp, Lambert, and Horowitz, 1997; Nathan et al., 1995).

It's sobering to realize that in nations as separate as the United States, Taiwan, Lebanon, and New Zealand there is evidence that recently each successive recent generation is growing more susceptible to depression. Of those Americans born before 1905, only 1% had experienced a major depression by age 75; of those born after 1955, 6% had suffered a significant depression by age 30. Certainly better recognition is a factor, but so is the stress of modern life. It is estimated in *DSM-IV* that approximately 3% of males and 6% of females have had a depressive episode sufficiently severe to require hospitalization. However, this "gender gap" is narrowing, especially for those under the age of 40. An important aspect of the greater incidence of depression in females compared to that in males is the accentuation of behavior prescribed by traditional sex role expectations. Also, abuse early in life, other patterns of victimization, unhappy marriages, and infertility or a large number of children (especially when the latter is combined with low economic resources) are factors that predispose women to depression. Several other factors predict depression: economic deprivation, low self-esteem, a preoccupation with failure, a sense of helplessness, a pessimistic attitude toward the world, and narcissistic vulnerability.

Dimensions of Depression

The normal–pathological continuum is one way of typing or conceptualizing depressions. Other continuums on which one can categorize different depressions are: acute–chronic, agitated–slow, neurotic–psychotic, primary–secondary, and of course the unipolar–bipolar dimension that would differentiate Joseph Westbecker's typical pattern of depression (unipolar) from that of Virginia Woolf (bipolar) in the cases in this chapter. Another particularly important continuum is the endogenous–exogenous one. This popular classification system attempts to categorize depressions by cause. Endogenous depressions are assumed to originate from internal psychic and physical causes (such as genetics and/or hormonal disruption), exogenous from external ones (such as personal loss). The four traditional behavioral indications of a significant endogenous depression are: (1) generally slowed response patterns, (2) early morning sleep disruption, (3) more severe mood problems, and (4) significant weight loss without dieting.

The Case of Joseph Westbecker

Joseph Westbecker is a classic example of an affect disorder, as well as an early and prototypical case of workplace violence. His case also became the first civil (rather than criminal) trial concerning the drug Prozac. Throughout his life, including the first time he checked himself into a hospital because of his disorder, Joseph consistently showed three themes central to the diagnosis of depression—suicidal ideation and anger. He also showed evidence of mania-agitation, but seldom if ever any mania-euphoria.

Ultimately his affect consumed him. On September 14, 1989, Joseph Westbecker walked unnoticed into the Standard Gravure printing plant, where he had worked for 17 years, and killed eight and wounded twelve of his former co-workers with copper-jacketed bullets from an AK-47 semi-automatic rifle. He then killed himself with a Sig Sauer 9-mm pistol.

While this appeared to be an insane outburst, his suicide prevented any close examination of his sanity. However, the consensus of the evidence does suggest that he (1) knew what he was doing at the time, (2) could control at least some of his behavior during the episode, and (3) had at least considered some form of a specific plan almost a year before he carried it out.

His long, downhill slide probably started even before his birth. There is sketchy but reasonable evidence from family history that his genetics at least predisposed him to a degree of mental disorder. His maternal grandmother was twice placed in a state mental hospital, reportedly showing depression, suicidal ideation, and delusions of persecution. But other factors certainly contributed mightily to Joseph's condition. His birth was normal, and nothing untoward was noticed in his first year of life. But just before his first birthday, his father fell while repairing the roof of a church, fractured his skull, and died. His widow, Joseph's mother, was 17. She moved back in with her parents, and her father was appointed Joseph's guardian. But, less than a year later, he was killed at his railroad job when he slipped beneath the wheels of a train engine. Then, only 2 years after that, Joseph's paternal grandfather, the only other adult male figure in his life, died of heart disease.

Although Joseph was raised by his apparently dedicated maternal grandmother, there were few financial or emotional resources, and Joseph spent almost a year in an orphanage when he was 12–13 years of age. The family also moved many times, and various family and friends occasionally took a parenting role. His schooling was equally disrupted, and he attained only an eighth-grade education. During that time he showed both dyslexia and delinquency but eventually did attain a general equivalency high school degree.

In 1960, he obtained a job at a printing company, and in July of that year he was married. While no one ever characterized Joseph as gregarious or joyful or even happy for any length of time, the better times of his life were in the years before and just after his first marriage.

He was competent in his job and consistently put in long hours of overtime. But this, along with his personality, took a toll on the marriage. He was also increasingly upset over his wife taking a job outside the home, and, in 1978, he moved out, reportedly in the hope that his wife would give up her job. She didn't. There is good reason to believe this was a catalyst for the emergence of clear psychiatric symptoms.

Joseph's mental disorder was first noticed in early 1980 by a physician treating him for bursitis in the right shoulder. He referred him to a psychiatric unit at a hospital, where he received 1 week's inpatient treatment for agitation and depression. The psychiatric summary reported: "He worked 16 hours a day, bar hopped at night, slept only 2 to 3 hours and drove himself mercilessly."

About this time, Joseph began another serious relationship. He eventually married Brenda in August 1981. His continuing bouts of depression, problems with stepchildren, and anger toward Brenda's ex-husband (whom he perceived as making money "too easily") kept this from being an especially happy interlude. Joseph's anger toward his wife's ex-husband was so severe that he followed him for about a month and later confided the "thought of blowing his brains out, but he always has a witness with him." During the next few years personal disputes led him to break off relations with both his oldest son and his mother. In 1984, he made the first of what were to be several suicide attempts. His wife told police that seeing him with a gun threatening suicide was the catalyst for her decision to divorce him. They separated in May 1984, a month after he was released from a psychiatric hospital. But they continued to have a relationship until his death and occasionally lived as man and wife.

It was about this time that pressures at work increased, and Joseph asked to be excused from working the "folder," a piece of machinery that required sustained concentration and decision making, a request supported by his psychiatrist. While there is evidence that he seldom, if ever, was asked to work the folder from that point on, management's refusal to state they would never ask him to work it fueled a growing anger toward the company and some of its management personnel. His depression and agitation increased, possibly abetted by a diet centered on cookies and ice cream (sometimes a gallon at a time) and often a dozen or more diet colas a day. Joseph was again hospitalized in March 1987, and in a reply on a sentence completion test to the sentence stem "How do you feel about yourself?" he wrote, "I don't like feeling weak. I feel I've been screwed. I'm angry." His concerns about working the folder continued, and he filed a complaint that he was being discriminated against because of a mental handicap. A human relations committee felt they had no jurisdiction over the case, and the union later was disinclined to support Joseph's case. He insisted he was still asked to work the folder (although again, it's doubtful this was so), and he also complained that co-workers teased him, calling him "Westbecker the whacko, . . . the sickie," etc. About this time, Joseph began buying guns, reading gun magazines, and occasionally bringing a gun with him into work.

In the summer of 1987, he began seeing Dr. Lee Coleman, the psychiatrist who would treat him for the duration of his life. Dr. Coleman first diagnosed Joseph with Bipolar Disorder, Atypical Type because of the paranoid overtones, and he prescribed various medications. Nothing worked well. His condition continued to deteriorate, and Coleman suggested he go on medical leave. Joseph worked his last day at Standard Gravure in August 1988. Shortly before that he had told Brenda he would like to go there and kill "a bunch of people." The Social Security Administration determined he was disabled, and they awarded him $892 a month. His behavior over the next year was relatively unremarkable, except that he occasionally divulged plans of revenge (to acquaintances, not his psychiatrist) and bought guns. However, his beloved grand-mother suffered a stroke on July 8, 1989, and died on August 5. Joseph had continued to see his psychiatrist about once a month. Coleman had by then diagnosed Joseph's condition as a schizoaffective disorder. Three days before the shootings, Joseph visited his psychiatrist, who noted Joseph's increased agitation and cognitive disruption. During this session, Joseph cried and related that he had been forced to have oral sex, in front of several employees, in order to be excused from working on the folder. There was never any later corroboration of this story, and his psychiatrist believes it was probably a delusion. He advised Joseph to voluntarily check himself into a mental hospital, which Joseph refused to do, and to discontinue the Prozac. The autopsy after the shootings revealed a moderately high level of Prozac and lithium in his blood, as well as small amounts of three other anti-depressants and a sleeping medication. His psychiatrist says Joseph was taking these on his own.

The morning of the shooting, Joseph left $1720 in cash on his dresser (a large amount for him) and left a *Time* magazine of February 6, 1989, which was devoted to "Armed America," on a kitchen table, open to a story on Patrick Purdy (see Etiology section).

He took his bag filled with guns and bullets to the plant, where he moved from floor to floor killing and shooting people he knew (even some he had apparently liked a bit) and some he didn't know. He did let a couple of people go that he reportedly knew and liked. Ironically, he never found and killed the people he viewed as his main enemies.

Case Etiology

Certainly Joseph Westbecker's ultimate, sad legacy was not a product of any single factor. As noted, genetics gave him a bad start. Also, the severe disruptions and losses in his early childhood not only robbed him of a chance to develop the cognitive and personality variables that most people use to effectively overcome emotional burdens, but also may have predisposed him to depression. Such early stressors may lead to a later hyperactivity of the hypothalamic-pituitary-adrenal axis, from overproduction of the hormone corticotropin-releasing factor (CRF), which in turn leads to an oversecretion of stimulating hormones under stress, facilitating any agitated depression. The lifelong, ambivalent, and often negative relationship with his mother also voided the chance to develop better coping patterns and no doubt increased his pain and distress.

As he became increasingly distanced even from those who cared about him, including his oldest son, Joseph's no-better-than-slim chances of turning his life around became virtually nil. This was especially so as he accumulated means of acting out his hurt (a variety of weaponry) and opened himself to influence from the many models of deviance and destruction provided by the media. For example, after the carnage, police found a *Soldier of Fortune* magazine (a magazine for mercenaries, the curious, and no doubt some gun and violence groupies) as well as the *Time* magazine, whose cover story focused on Patrick Purdy, who also used an AK-47, killing five children and wounding thirty children and adults in a Stockton, California, schoolyard in 1989. The data from researchers such as Phillips (1974) make it clear that violence toward others (and suicide) is in part attributable to the quantity and intensity of media portrayals of such acts.

Legal Aftermath: The First Major Civil Trial of Prozac

Joseph Westbecker's "fame" increased after his death when the survivors, along with the estates of those killed, joined to file a civil suit for damages. A number of people alleged to have committed crimes had already tried a "Prozac made me do it" defense in a criminal trial, with little success. Dr. Coleman was eliminated early on by the trial judge as an available target for suit. This left Eli Lilly, the manufacturer of Prozac, as the major target, and thus the suit became the first clear legal test in a civil action (liability for damages) of this drug's alleged propensity to facilitate violence in some patients.

After 2 ½ months of testimony the jury deliberated for hours and came back with a 9-3 decision that found Westbecker totally responsible for the action, thus exonerating Eli Lilly and Prozac. There will be other suits, and those juries may find differently, especially to the degree those cases may differ from West-becker's on points such as (1) his documented long history of mental illness; (2) his verbalizations of a desire to hurt someone up to a year before the episode; (3) his purchase of guns and ammunition long before taking Prozac; and (4) his psychiatrist's reported admonition to him 3 days before the event to stop taking his Prozac, with some evidence that Westbecker did not do so.

Etiology of Depression

A variety of theoretical perspectives on the etiology of depression were presented, along with their related treatments, in the case of Danielle in Chapter 2. In the present case of Joseph Westbecker, both biological and psychological factors are involved, as they are in most serious cases of depression (DeBattista, 1998; Nathan et al., 1995). These external and internal factors usually combine in varying degrees in an actual case of depression to produce a self-perpetuating sequence like the following:

> Negative environmental condition + biological predisposition → social withdrawal + lowered information processing → inadequate social behaviors + guilt and self-blame → further self-devaluation + social withdrawal → more biological change → depression

Treatment

The case of Danielle in Chapter 2 detailed the options available for the treatment of depression. As with many cases of major depression the primary treatments used were chemotherapy (see Table 7–1) and "supportive therapy," that is, relatively short office contacts that are not based on any particular theoretical orientation. When some form of formal psychotherapy is used with depressives, the most effective are usually interpersonal psychotherapy (IPT), which aims at promoting more effective interpersonal relationships, thus improving self-esteem as well; or cognitive behavior modification (CBM) (Alford and Beck, 1997; Chambless et al., 1996; Beck, 1976). CBM aims at determining the rules that govern the life of the depressed person. It makes the assumption that "what we do

TABLE 7–1 Anti-Depressant Drugs

Name (Generic/Trade)	
Tricyclic and tetracyclic anti-depressants amitriptyline (Elavil) imipramine (Tofranil) desipramine (Norpramin) nortriptyline (Pamelor) protriptyline (Vivactil) doxepine (Sinequan) maprotiline (Ludiomil) amoxapine (Asendin) clomipramine (Anafranil)	**MAO inhibitors** tranylcypromine (Parnate) phenelzine (Nardil) **Other anti-depressants** fluoxetine (Prozac) bupropion (Wellbutrin) trazodone (Desyrel) sertraline (Zoloft) paroxetine (Paxil) venlafaxine (Effexor) serzone (Mefazodone)

and how we think about it determines how we feel." Brief dynamic therapy can also be effective here (Chambless et al., 1996).

With anti-depressant medication, CBM, and/or IPT, depression is quite treatable. Nevertheless, no matter how much change is attained, relapse is common. Depressives who are most likely to relapse back into depression show (1) a greater number of previous episodes of depression; (2) a higher depression level at the entry point into treatment; (3) a family history of depression, especially with a history of depression in first-degree relatives; (4) poor physical health; (5) a higher level of dissatisfaction with their major life roles; and (6) a definite episode of clinical depression in late childhood or early adolescence.

The Prozac Controversies

The most controversial newer-generation anti-depressant is fluoxetine (Prozac). Like sertraline (Zoloft) and paroxetine (Paxil), it is a selective serotonin reuptake inhibitor (SSRI). This versatile compound was initially accepted with great hopes for the treatment of depressed patients and quickly became highly controversial. Despite Prozac's demonstrated lack of toxic physiologic side effects, the drug was accused of creating some of the very conditions it was supposed to treat. Reports surfaced of individuals on Prozac increasing their suicidal or homicidal ideation and sometimes going so far as to act on those impulses. In the mid-90s, many such controversies were continuing despite the fact that there were only a few hundred reported cases of this kind of behavior in a population of almost five million people worldwide who have taken the drug. It is clear, however, that Prozac must be administered with great care to someone who is agitated. A second controversy erupted with the data that Prozac actually seems no more effective than the traditional anti-depressants, data allegedly glossed over by the drug company. The controversy centered first on Prozac, but it is in reality the concern around the overprescription of all such drugs that are abused in the Orwellian sense of placating the everyday anxieties of life rather than treating true disorders (see Chapter 9's section on prescription drug abuse).

Seasonal Affective Disorder

Most of us on occasion have experienced a touch of "winter blues"; if the blues are persistent and significantly disruptive, the episode may earn a clinical label. Although it can take several forms, by far the most common seasonal affective disorder (SAD) pattern is winter depression (Oren et al., 1994), and that is what SAD will refer to herein. SAD is primarily marked by decreased energy with vegetative changes in appetite and sleep, with related (probably consequentially) negativism and lowered self-esteem. Women are affected three to five times as often as men, and a degree of Premenstrual Dysphoric Disorder may be a co-morbid symptom. Estimates are that as high as 5% of the population suffer SAD. Although referred to as "holiday blues," it is clear that SAD occurs in people in the southern hemisphere, where Christmas is a summer holiday. SAD does occur in children, but severity usually reaches clinical significance when SAD sufferers are in the twenties or thirties. A move to a higher latitude (e.g., moving north in North America) may set off SAD in vulnerable individuals.

The treatment of choice for SAD is exposure to light (DeBattista, 1998; Oren et al., 1994). Light therapy works best with clients whose symptoms include increased appetite, hypersomnia, craving for carbohydrates, and a worsening of symptoms in the evening. It is less effective when symptoms include melancholic symptoms, that is, anxiety, suicidal tendencies, insomnia, and a worsening of symptoms in the morning. Light therapy apparently acts by affecting melatonin productions and the circadian rhythm. Of course, anyone embarking on light treatment should be cleared by an ophthalmologist if there is any history or indication of eye disease.

Delivery of light can be adjusted on four parameters: intensity, wavelength, duration, and timing. Intensity has to be bright enough to suppress nighttime melatonin production; 2500 lux is suggested. A standard dosage is 2500 lux for about 2 hours, once a day at first, then tapered to once every other day if improvement is maintained.

Traditionally, timing of treatment was not held to be important. However, more recent findings suggest that the majority of SADs are "phase-delays" (referring to circadian rhythm delays), indicated by characteristic morning hypersomnia and clear vulnerability to shortened photoperiod exposure (Oren et al., 1994). For the phase-delays, whose circadian rhythms are cued by dawn rather than dusk, light therapy should be administered as soon as feasible upon awakening. For "phase-advance" types, cued by dusk, whose sleep disruption is usually more toward morning, light therapy should be administered at night, preferably between 7 and 9 P.M. To help orient the circadian rhythms, phase-delays should avoid bright light exposure at night (e.g., in bright malls); phase-advances should minimize it in early morning. Persons with characteristic early morning awakening and early evening fatigue, "advanced sleep-phase syndrome," should receive light therapy before bedtime. Occasionally people will shift from one pattern to another, requiring a timing change for the light therapy.

There is some indication that the oral administration of melatonin, a hormone produced by the pineal gland and available without a prescription, can produce results similar to light therapy. Melatonin production usually has a strong diurnal rhythm. It is released primarily and in most cases only at night, as its production shuts down when daylight reaches the eyes and is perceived by the brain; thus, it is seasonally patterned. Manipulation of serotonin levels can also help SAD sufferers, as the supra chiasmatic nuclei, thought to be a critical component in our "body clock," is heavily endowed with nerve cells rich in serotonin.

Suicide

Some severe depressions do not involve suicide, and some suicides do not involve depression. However, very often when there is significant depression, as with Joseph Westbecker, suicide is a concern. There is a long list of famous suicides, including Ernest Hemingway, Marilyn Monroe, Jack London, Amadeo Modigliani, Adolf Hitler, Samson, and Cleopatra. However, in general, the typical suicide attempter "profile" is: an unmarried white female, with a history of past and recent stressful events, who had an unstable childhood, and who now has few social supports and lacks a close friend to confide in. On the other hand, the typical suicide completer profile is: an unmarried or divorced or widowed white male who is over 45, lives alone, has a history of significant physical or emotional disorder, and probably abuses alcohol.

Suicide Types and Prediction. Emile Durkheim (1951) pioneered an emphasis on sociological factors contributing to suicide. Members of certain subgroups lose cohesiveness and feel alienated. His typology of suicidals (anomic—under conditions of normlessness; egoistic—lack of group ties; altruistic—suicide for the good of some cause) is still influential (Shneidman, 1985), as is evident in the following list of types of suicides:

- *Realistic:* These are suicides precipitated by such conditions as the prospect of great pain preceding a sure death.
- *Altruistic:* The person's behavior is subservient to a group ethic that mandates or at least approves suicidal behavior, like kamikaze pilots in World War II.
- *Inadvertent:* The person makes a suicide gesture in order to influence or manipulate someone else, but a misjudgment leads to an unexpected fatality.
- *Spite:* Like the inadvertent suicide, the focus is on someone else, but the intention to kill oneself is genuine, with the idea that the other person will suffer greatly from consequent guilt.

- *Bizarre*: The person commits suicide as a result of a hallucination (such as voices ordering the suicide) or delusion (such as a belief the suicide will change the world).
- *Anomic:* An abrupt instability in economic or social conditions (such as sudden financial loss in the Great Depression) markedly changes a person's life situation. Unable to cope, the person commits suicide.
- *Negative self:* Chronic depression and a sense of chronic failure or inadequacy combine to produce repetitive suicide attempts eventually leading to fatality.

Clues and Correlates to Suicide. Suicidal individuals tend to give clues to those around them, and these areas should be the focus of any evaluation. In addition to being depressed, suicidal people are likely to show feelings of hopelessness and helplessness, a loss of a sense of continuity with the past and/or present, and loss of pleasure in typical interests and pursuits. Conversely, a strong element of perfectionism is a risk factor for suicide, when mixed with depression and a crisis and/or ego insult. "Perfectionistic" suicidals show less response to medication or psychotherapy than do other depressed persons. For one thing, they tend to misinterpret small success, such as the typical process in treatment, as failure.

The basic risk factors for suicide have been consistent over the years: older, white male, live alone, active alcoholism, a loss experience, medical illness, schizophrenia, depression, and a sense of hopelessness. In recent years, add AIDS and a diagnosis of panic attacks or borderline personality disorder. In addition to these factors, suicidal persons are more likely to: (1) have a personal and/or family history of depression, especially a major endogenous depression, or of psychosis; (2) have had a parent or other important identity figure who attempted or committed suicide; (3) have a history of family instability and/or parental rejection; (4) be socially isolated; (5) have a chronic physical illness; (6) show a preoccupation with death and/or make statements of a wish to die, especially statements of a wish to commit suicide; (7) manifest consistent life patterns of leaving crises rather than facing them (in relationships: "You can't walk out on me, I'm leaving you"; or in jobs: "You can't fire me, because I quit"); (8) show a personal or family history of addiction patterns; (9) live alone, or are involved (married or similarly occupied) with a loved mate who is interpersonally competitive and/or is self-absorbed; (10) show sudden cheerfulness after a long depression; (11) are noted to be putting their affairs in order, for example, giving away favorite possessions, revising wills; (12) show some abrupt atypical behavior change, for example, withdrawal from family or friends; (13) show a family history of self-damaging acts; and (14) have a history of self-damaging acts, often previous suicide attempts (in this context the first axiom of psychology could well be "Behavior predicts behavior," and the second axiom could be "Behavior without intervention predicts behavior"). The initiation of the suicidal event is apt to be triggered by a major life stress, for example, the experience of a chronic debilitating illness or the loss of an important social support, such as a spouse, beloved relative, or a confidante. Violent impulsivity with high-risk mental disorders (e.g., depression, panic) suggests high risk for suicide.

The following factors increase the potential for attempted suicide and the probability of completion (there is about a 10–15% probability that a *serious* attempt will be successful):

- A cognitive state of constriction, that is, an inability to perceive any options or a way out of a situation that is generating intense psychological suffering
- The idea of death as a catalytic agent for the cessation of distress
- Acute perturbation—high distress/agitation/depression
- An increase in self-hatred or self-loathing, especially if the result of a recent shameful behavior
- Perception of the self as a source of shame to significant others
- Fantasies of death as escape, especially if there are concrete plans for one's own demise
- Easy access to a lethal means, e.g., as in physicians, who show high suicide rates
- Absence of an accessible support system (family and good friends)
- Life stresses that connote irrevocable loss (whether of status or of persons), such as the relatively recent death of a favored parent, or even something like retirement, which is particularly important if the person at risk is unable to overtly mourn the loss
- High psychophysiologic responsiveness: cyclical moods, a propensity toward violence, and a high need for stimulation seeking in spite of suicide thoughts (High rates of the serotonin receptor 5-HT$_{2a}$ in blood platelets of a potentially suicidal individual add to the prediction of serious intent.)
- Serious sleep disruption and/or abuse of alcohol or drugs
- Lack of a therapeutic alliance and/or constructively supportive friendship alliance
- Noncompliance with prescribed psychotropic medication
- Persistence of secondary depression after remission of primary disorder and/or recent discharge from a psychiatric hospital (in the last 3 months)
- A history of panic attacks and, even more importantly, recent panic attacks

Suicide Prevention

Several things can be done both on a societal and individual level to lower the incidence of suicide (Shneidman, 1985; Phillips, Lesyna, and Paight, 1993; Phillips, 1974). Educating the public on the myths and facts of suicide is an important first step. Second, there is evidence that suicide prevention telephone hotlines and centers can at least slightly decrease the suicide rate. Lastly, suicide prevention at the societal level requires restriction on media publicity about suicides (Phillips, 1974; Phillips et al., 1993).

In his initial research endeavor, Phillips (1974) compiled a list of suicide stories appearing on page 1 of the *New York Times* from 1946 to 1968 and then examined U.S. monthly suicide statistics from 1947 to 1967, with appropriate corrections for the effects of trends and seasons. He found U.S. suicides consistently rose significantly just after suicide stories. He termed this the "Werther effect," after the German author Goethe's fictional hero whose suicide was thought to have triggered imitative acts. He accepted the hypothesis that this effect is caused by imitation and suggestion, after considering and eventually rejecting any reasonable competing explanation (of which the four most plausible are:

1. The Coroner Explanations: In ambiguous cases, coroners may shift unclear suicides into the competing categories of homicide, accident, or undetermined death. If so, the numbers of deaths in these competing categories should decrease after a suicide story, but they don't.

2. The Precipitation Explanation: Suicide stories only hasten suicides that would have eventually occurred anyway. If so, the post-story peak in suicides should be followed by an equally larger drop in follow-up periods, but that doesn't happen.

3. The Prior Conditions Explanation: This argues that in actuality a prior social change, such as an economic depression, causes a rise in both publicized and unpublicized suicides, but this cannot explain the consistent correlation of a suicide story and a post-story rise in suicides.

4. The Bereavement Explanation: Grief rather than imitation is the reason for the post-story rise, but if so, nonsuicide celebrity deaths would generate a post-story rise in suicides as well, and they don't.

Other researchers have shown that television movies about fictional suicide can produce the same effect, especially multi-program portrayals. In fact, the most powerful evidence for the effect of a fictional suicide comes from a clever German study by Schmidtke and Hafner, cited in Phillips et al., 1993. In 1981 and also in 1982, West German television broadcast a fictional story about a 19-year-old student who killed himself by throwing himself in front of a train. There was a nationwide increase in railway suicides immediately after each broadcast. The increase was highest for young males, the closest in identity to the fictional role model. Here also, other competing explanations did not fit the data. Subsequent data indicated the Werther effect is weak or nonexistent for single-program fictional presentations, but does occur with multi-program presentations. In addition to the identity effect, it appears to trigger suicides in statistically predisposed groups, that is, males, white, unmarried, and people of retirement age.

Several precautions can also be taken for prevention of suicide at the individual level:

1. Attend seriously to people who voice a desire to kill themselves or "just go to sleep and forget it all." About two-thirds of people who kill themselves

have talked about it beforehand in some detail with family, friends, or others.

2. Take any complaint seriously. Attend especially to depressed individuals who speak of losing hope. For example, most terminally ill patients who are severely suicidal may give up such intent when they find out there are medications and techniques that will give them control over their pain.

3. To the degree possible, keep lethal means (guns, large prescriptions of sedatives) away from suicidal individuals.

4. Show a personal concern to a suicidal person. A suicide attempt is most often a cry for help; suicidal individuals need a temporary "champion" who can point them toward new resources, suggest new options—who at least in a small way can diminish the sense of hopelessness.

5. Try to get suicidal persons to perform some of the following behaviors: (a) engage in regular physical exercise, (b) start a diary, (c) follow a normal routine, (d) do something in which they have already demonstrated competence, (e) confide inner feelings to someone, (f) cry it out. Try to get them to avoid self-medication and other people inclined toward depression.

6. Make every effort to guarantee that a suicidal person reaches professional help. Making an appointment is a good first step; getting the person to the appointment is the crucial step.

Bipolar Disorder (Manic-Depressive Psychosis)

The Case of Virginia Woolf

Then Big Harry said to me, "You know, Bobby, I think old Suicides was crazy." He was right, too, because when his family sent for him the man who came explained to Commissioner old Suicides had suffered from a thing called Mechanic's Depressive. You never had that, did you, Roger?

—Ernest Hemingway, *Islands in the Stream* (1970)

That manic and depressive symptoms are components of a single disorder was suspected even by Hippocrates in the fourth century BC. Since that time, unipolar depression has been distinguished from bipolar disorder and is currently thought to result from different etiological factors (Whybrow, 1997; Ludwig, 1996; Nathan et al., 1995; Goodwin and Jamison, 1990).

The range of behaviors that typify mania is broad and most commonly includes (1) hyperactive motor behavior; (2) variable irritability and/or euphoria; and (3) a speeding up of thought processes, called a "flight of ideas." Manic speech is typically loud, rapid, and difficult to understand. When the mood is expansive, manics take on many tasks (seldom completing them), avoid sleep, and easily ramble into lengthy monologs about their personal plans, worth, and power. When the mood becomes more irritable, they are quick to complain and engage in hostile tirades.

Psychotic manic reactions involve grandiose delusions, bizarre and impulsive behavior, transient hallucinations, and explosiveness; these reactions may be confused with schizophrenic episodes. However, whereas schizophrenics (and schizoaffectives) are distracted by internal thoughts and ideas, manics are distracted by external stimuli that often go unnoticed by others. Also, whereas schizophrenics (and schizoaffectives) tend to avoid any true relationships with others during an active phase, manics are typically open to contact with other people.

As with the case of Virginia Woolf, suicide is a frequent complication of bipolar depression. It is estimated that about 15%, if untreated, commit suicide. This is thirty times the rate in the general population and is higher than for any other psychiatric or medical risk group. As many as 82% of bipolar patients have suicidal ideation (Goodwin and Jamison, 1990).

Although the onset of discrete manic episodes may be sudden, the disorder has a generally slow onset in many cases; as with Virginia Woolf, the person's life history may evidence preliminary symptoms in childhood or adolescence that at some point become more intense and debilitating. Lastly, the presence of a bipolar disorder is not always seen as totally negative, as it is with schizophrenia, and it may indeed be a spur to creativity.

Creativity, Poetry, and the Bipolar Disorder

"Why is it," Aristotle asked twenty-four hundred years ago, "that all men [i.e., people] who are outstanding in philosophy, poetry, or the arts are melancholic?" Three hundred years ago the English poet John Dryden wrote,

> Great wits are sure to madness near allied;
> And thin partitions do their bounds divide.

Dryden's sweet couplet has since degenerated into the cliché "There is a thin line between genius and madness."

As is evident, the concept that creativity may be a result of psychopathology is hardly new, and it is a persistent theme of certain authors like Arthur Koestler. Research (Ludwig, 1996; Goodwin and Jamison, 1990) offers impressive support for a creativity link in the particular instance of bipolar disorder (manic-depressive disorder), especially in relation to certain specific artistic endeavors. For example, Ludwig (1996) found that psychiatric disturbances were far more common among artists than among nonartists. For example, the rate of alcoholism was 60% among actors and 41% among novelists, but only 3% among those in the physical sciences and 10% among military officers. In the case of manic depression, 17% of the actors in the study and 13% of the poets were thought to have had the disorder, while those in the sciences were believed to have suffered from it at a rate of less than 1%, comparable to the incidence in the general population.

The list of first-rank artists who appear to have suffered a bipolar disorder is impressive. Painter Vincent Van Gogh, poet-painter Dante Gabriel Rosetti, playwright Eugene O'Neill; writers Herman Melville, William and Henry James, F. Scott Fitzgerald, Ernest Hemingway, Virginia Woolf (the next case), John Ruskin, Honore de Balzac; and composers Robert Schumann, Hector Berlioz, and George Frederick Handel. Indeed, Handel wrote *The Messiah* in a frenetic 24 days during a manic high. But it is poets who are most often bipolars. Byron, Coleridge, Shelley, Tennyson, Poe, and Gerald Manley Hopkins were all bipolars, as are many of the major American poets like Hart Crane, Robert Lowell, Anne Sexton, Theodore Roethke, Sylvia Plath, and John Berryman.

Some might argue that poets tend to be bipolars because poetry often celebrates the inner turbulence of one's psyche. But even in the eighteenth century, a time in which poetry did not really focus on such inner upset, a high proportion of accomplished poets also appear to have been bipolars, and many others at least experienced subclinical hypomanic states during creative moments. The relationship of poetry and bipolar disorder, then, may more directly result from the fact that frenetic but sporadic effort is more effectively productive in poetry than in other areas and because the imagery inherent in poetry is more like the primitive thought found in severe emotional disruption. Also, the depressions of the bipolar mood swing provide the fuel of emotional depth to the productivity of the manic high. As a result, some artists so afflicted avoid therapy, out of a fear that successful treatment would curb their creativity. It appears that in some cases they may be correct.

> *Time... a device to prevent everything*
> *from happening all at once.*
> —Paul William Roberts (1995)

The Case of Virginia Woolf

A Specific Instance of Bipolar Creativity

Virginia Woolf is regarded as one of the most talented prose writers of the twentieth century. In 1915, she published *The Voyage Out,* and in the next 30 years she wrote dozens of literary reviews, essays, stories, and fifteen more books, including classics such as *To the Lighthouse* and *The Waves.* The most famous, *A Room of One's Own,* established her as an early leader of the women's movement. In that book are reflected the extremes of her own life: "The beauty of the world ... has two edges, one of laughter, one of anguish, cutting the heart asunder" (Woolf, 1957). She was admired for fervently expressing all ranges of human emotion.

From childhood on, she was afflicted with bipolar disorder, which those around her described as lapses into insanity. The emotional highs and lows of that disorder contributed to her passion in writing novels, yet ultimately destroyed her (Bell, 1972; Lehmann, 1975).

Childhood

Virginia Stephen was born in 1882, the second of four children, in Cambridge, England. Her father was Sir Leslie Stephen, a distinguished editor. She had two half-sisters: one born to her father by his first wife, who was institutionalized most of her life for mental problems; and the other, Stella Duckworth, born to her mother and her mother's first husband. She also had two Duckworth half-brothers. Virginia was exceptionally attractive, and she lived in a home where aunts, uncles, and cousins circulated constantly. The family was in the upper-middle professional class and emphasized intellectual achievement.

Virginia read everything she could find. At first her father carefully chose what books she should read from their large library. However, by the time she was in her teens she had read so much that he permitted her to read whatever she desired. During these times this was a great amount of freedom for a girl. Virginia, who could not attend school because she was female, always envied her brother Thoby, who was educated at Cambridge. She taught herself English literature and received private lessons in Latin and Greek.

Virginia had been very close to her mother and described her mother's death, when Virginia was 13, as "the greatest disaster that could happen" (Lehmann, 1975, p. 13). Also, in reaction to her mother's death, Virginia's father became extremely demanding, unreasonable, and moody. Her stepsister Stella Duckworth took over their mother's role. This is when Virginia had her first breakdown. Her pulse raced and she felt uncontrollably excited (possibly a panic attack: see Chapter 3); later, she slipped into a deep depression. Her doctor prescribed outdoor exercise. Her lessons had been stopped, but she still read continuously.

Only 2 months after Virginia's mother died, her stepsister Stella, whom Virginia also loved deeply, died. Without Stella, Virginia's father became tyrannical and full of self-pity. The next-oldest sister, Vanessa, then took their mother's place. Mr. Stephen was so inconsiderate and selfish to Vanessa that Virginia found herself torn between loving her father and despising him for the way he was behaving. When her father died in 1904, Virginia had an even more extreme breakdown. It started slowly, with headaches and moments of intense irritation, and then escalated into a severe manic state in which she felt intense guilt about her father. Virginia saw her nurses as evil, refused to eat, and tried to kill herself by jumping out a window. When she was able to lie down, she believed the birds were chirping in Greek and that King Edward VII was swearing and hiding in the bushes. She lived in a time before effective treatment for this disorder had been discovered; therefore, the few doctors who examined her prescribed only rest.

Adult Years

Virginia's sexual development was deficient. Her two half-brothers had sexually abused her. Gerald examined her genitals when she was 5, and George would periodically come into her bedroom and paw and fondle her when she was a teenager. Also, during her adolescence, Virginia fell deeply in love with her cousin, a girl named Madge. Later an older woman friend who helped Virginia through her breakdowns became the object of Virginia's deepest love. Whether these women ever knew the extent of Virginia's affection is not clear.

With both parents deceased, Virginia and five of her siblings traveled to Greece. Vanessa, Violet, and Thoby contracted typhoid fever from impure milk, and from this disease Thoby died, another great blow to Virginia. Following this, Virginia's older sister married, leaving Virginia alone with her younger brother. Virginia and her brother took over a weekly social group that their older sister had started, and over many weeks Virginia became much more outgoing and willing to express her opinions, quickly becoming known for her sharp tongue. (Her fame in this regard, in concert with her pioneering role in the women's movement, inspired the title of the modern play by Edward Albee (later made into a movie), *Who's Afraid of Virginia Woolf.*

Virginia began her career by writing book reviews for several well- respected magazines. During this time, she was pursued by many men, and she finally accepted the marriage proposal of Lytton Strachey. Immediately after proposing, however, he changed his mind and admitted his homosexuality to her. Leonard Woolf, a friend of Lytton, soon began dating Virginia. They married in August 1912, despite the fact that he was Jewish and she was, at least at times, anti-Semetic.

Leonard Woolf passionately loved Virginia; however, she did not respond to him sexually at all, as her sexual preference was for females. Then in March 1913, she began another breakdown. Leonard described Virginia's episodes as lapses into insanity wherein she lost complete contact with reality. She experienced wild excitement, intense guilt and depression, and delusions that her nurses were evil. During one episode she talked rapidly for several days without stopping, after which she fell into a stupor. Virginia was able to remember most of what happened during her altered states.

Through the years, it seemed these episodes always occurred when Virginia was in the last stages of writing a novel. Through the 1920s, Virginia had no serious relapses, possibly because Leonard began enforcing total rest and quiet on Virginia when he detected another episode coming. Virginia was becoming famous, and, over the years, she was invited to the United States and Cambridge to give lectures and receive public honors, but she refused almost every invitation.

Finally, in the last stage of writing *Between the Acts* in 1941, she felt another attack coming. The fears and tormenting voices seemed real and endless. This time, she was convinced that the suffering would never stop. She wrote farewell letters to Leonard and her sister, filled her pockets with stones, and drowned herself in a nearby river. The letter to Leonard was as follows (Bell, 1972):

> Dearest,
> I feel certain I am going mad again. I feel we can't go through another of those terrible times. And I shan't recover this time. I begin to hear voices, and I can't concentrate. So I am doing what seems the best thing to do. You have given me the greatest possible happiness. You have been in every way all that anyone could be. I don't think two people could have been happier till this terrible disease came. I can't fight any longer. I know that I am spoiling your life, that without me you could work. And you will I know. You see I can't even write this properly. I can't read. What I want to say is I owe all the happiness of my life to you. You have been entirely patient with me and incredibly good. I want to say that—everybody knows it. If anybody could have saved me it would have been you. Everything has gone from me but the certainty of your goodness. I can't go on spoiling your life any longer. I don't think two people could have been happier than we have been.

> *My candle burns at both ends;*
> *It will not last the night;*
> *But ah, my foes, and oh, my friends*
> *It gives a lovely light.*
> —Edna St. Vincent Millay, "A Few Figs from Thistles"

Etiology and Diagnosis

The *DSM-IV* separates Bipolar Disorder into different categories depending on what the last episode was—Manic, Depressive, or Mixed. Bipolar I Disorder also is categorized according to (1) the long-term pattern of the illness, that is, if there is interepisodic recovery; (2) whether there is a seasonal pattern to the depressive episodes; and (3) whether it is accompanied by rapid cycling (at least four occurrences in the last 12 months). At her death, Virginia's diagnosis would have been Bipolar I Disorder, Most Recent Episode Depressed. Requirements for this include currently having a major depressive episode and having had at least one manic episode in the past. The diagnosis also requires that other disorders with some similar features have been ruled out, for example, Schizoaffective Disorder and Delusional Disorder. The *DSM-IV* also includes Bipolar II Disorder, which differs from Bipolar I by replacing the requirement for a manic episode with a hypomanic episode (milder than a full-blown manic state).

Another aspect of this illness is the propensity for psychosis. When the bipolar illness is severe, according to *DSM* requirements, the subject may be classified as (1) severe without psychotic features, (2) severe with mood-congruent psychotic features (i.e., the delusions or hallucinations are consistent with feelings of inflated worth), or (3) severe with mood-incongruent psychotic features (i.e., the delusions or hallucinations do not involve themes of inflated worth or power). Virginia's psychotic delusions and hallucinations were of the third type.

A series of manic and depressive episodes with decreased durations of well intervals in later years is common over the lifetime course of this illness. In rare cases, patients experience only manic episodes, without evidence of depression. In the overwhelming majority there is a bipolar pattern. Manic phases are characterized by elevated and expansive moods. The *DSM-IV* defines manic episodes as periods of unusual and persistent mood elevation, expansiveness, or irritability that last at least 1 week (or any length of time if hospitalization is required). Three of the following symptoms are required (or four, if the mood is irritable instead of expansive): a decreased need for sleep, talkativeness or pressured speech, racing thoughts, distractibility, increase in goal-directed activities or agitation, and extreme involvement in pleasurable activities that have a high potential for painful consequences. Virginia experienced both the expansive and irritable variations of this disorder. She also had the pressured speech, distractibility, racing thoughts, and agitation.

Some episodes of mania or depression continue for months or years, and others make a complete bipolar circuit in a matter of minutes (*micropsychosis*). Still others have *mixed mania,* in which one experiences mania and depression at the same time. These patients feel euphoric and despairing, tired and energized, at the same time (Ludwig, 1996; Goodwin and Jamison, 1990). *Rapid cycling* indicates a poorer prognosis.

In mania a bipolar patient's imagination seems to go into overdrive and great significance is found in ordinary events. Common sense seems to desert the patient. Examples of consequences of poor judgment during mania include imprudent marriages, extravagant purchases, drastic career changes, and self-destructive sexual engagements. There is also a heightened risk of violence toward self or others.

Mania eventually swings in the opposite direction. Ranging from sadness to despair, the pain of the depression is frequently nightmarish. Virginia described her depressions as extreme and unbearable; feelings during this phase often include hopelessness and exhaustion. Virginia's low self-esteem and self-deprecatory comments are also typical of this phase.

Predisposing Factors

Genetic transmission of bipolar disorder has been indicated by family studies, concordance in monozygotic and dizygotic twins, and correlations between adopted persons and their biological relatives (Nathan, 1995). The risk of having bipolar disorder increases with the proportion of genetic loading from either or both sides of one's family. Despite efforts to locate the genetic mode of transmission, no definitive conclusions have yet been drawn.

Treatment

Lithium is the standard treatment because of its ability to modify violent mood swings. It can be used prophylactically or during an active episode. Although there is tremendous support for lithium and its use, lithium may provide less protection to patients who already have had three or more episodes of the illness. Also, the benefits of lithium do not take effect immediately. Goodwin (1994) asserts that lithium should be taken for years before being evaluated for its effectiveness and concludes that, overall, lithium provides only minimal benefit. As much as 50% of the bipolar population does not respond to it. Lithium tends to be less effective if (1) a psychotic symptom (e.g., delusions) is the initial symptom, (2) there are problematic side effects or compliance problems, (3) there are co-morbid physical or psychological disorders (including substance abuse—relatively common in manics), (4) there is evidence of more rapid cycles of mania to depression and back, and (5) there is a depression-mania-well pattern of symptoms (rather than mania-depression-well). Even normal expectations of successful lithium treatment are limited. While taking lithium, there are still occasions when one experiences a manic or depressive relapse. Lithium generally offers an approximately 70% probability against a relapse after 1 year, a 50% probability against relapse at 3 years, and only a 35% probability against relapse at 5 years.

Side effects of lithium include tremors, tardive dyskinesia, weight gain (especially in the first 6 to 12 months), memory impairment, concentration problems, an altered sense of taste, a decrease in sexual interest or ability, acne, hypothyroidism, lethargy, and a subjective feeling of sensory dulling. Some claim it reduces their creativity. As a result of these limitations, other drug treatments, for example, divalproexsodium clozapine, neuroleptics, carbamazepine, or a benzodiazepine, are combined, alternated, or substituted.

Explanations for the decreasing effectiveness of lithium over time are related to the kindling or sensitivity model of bipolar disorder. Also related to this model is the fact that psychosocial stressors are involved primarily in early episodes of bipolar illness, and later episodes typically occur without an environmental stimulus. This theory is that after a certain number of episodes the bipolar illness gradually becomes more "well grooved" or autonomous. Post (1993) summarizes the model as follows: "As in the kindling model, a greater number of prior episodes may not only predispose to the phenomenon of spontaneity (where episodes emerge in the absence of psychosocial stressors or exogenous stimulation) but also to alter pharmacological responsiveness that appears to accompany this late-developing phase of the syndrome" (p. 88). This explanation makes early institution and long-term maintenance of lithium therapy critical. If the treatment is timely, the disorder is not as likely to take such a severe neuro-biological claim on the central nervous system (Post, 1993).

Also, systems that support compliance are critical. In addition to being educated about medications, their side effects, and the natural course of the illness, families should learn how to recognize early signs of the episodes.

Comment

Virginia was fortunate to have married Leonard, who remained dedicated to her until her death. More often this illness has a devastating impact on a marriage. The sense of trust, affection, and loyalty that accrues day by day may be trauma-tized by one bad day. Unpredictable behaviors create confusion and tend to elicit strong emotional reactions from spouses or children who do not understand why they are being treated so inconsistently (DeBattista, 1998). Additional problems stem from the propensity of bipolar subjects in a manic state to threaten divorce, make inappropriate sexual advances to others, and actually engage in affairs. Thus, education for family and society is important.

The evolution of lithium as an effective treatment is a good example of the driving force of the profit motive in pharmacological research. Lithium is a chemical element that was first isolated in 1817 by John Arfwedson, a young Swedish chemistry student. He named it lithium because he found it in stone (lithos in Greek). John Cade, an Australian psychiatrist, discovered the positive effect of lithium on mania by chance in the 1940s, while studying whether an excess of uric acid might be the cause of manic-depressive episodes. Cade injected urea from the urine of guinea pigs into human subjects (that is, they were sort of guinea pigs as well). Expecting to learn that uric acid (a compound containing urea) increased the toxicity of urea, he added the most soluble salt of uric acid, lithium urate, and was surprised to find instead that the urea was less toxic as a result. Further experiments isolating lithium eventually indicated its curative properties.

However, it was a long time between initial discovery and the recent wide-spread marketing and use of lithium. In general, there had been little research on lithium, while more exotic, less widely available compounds received much attention. Two explanations for this seem plausible. First, there was warranted concern about the significant side effects of lithium. Second, since lithium is a naturally occurring element, it cannot be patented. Drug companies are much more interested in researching new synthetic compounds that they can patent, so that they can control the market and gain substantial profits.

8

The Psychosexual Disorders

The variations in sexual behavior are limited only by an individual's imagination (Lo Piccolo, 1993). The psychosexual disorders are equally varied patterns in which psychological factors are assumed to be of major etiological significance in the development of disrupted or deviant sexual behaviors. They include the paraphilias, the gender disorders, and the psychosexual dysfunctions. The paraphilias are discussed first. The gender disorders, commonly referred to as transsexualism, are marked by felt incongruence between the actual physical sexual apparatus and gender identity. The essential feature of the psychosexual dysfunctions is inhibition in the appetitive or psychophysiological changes that accompany the complete sexual response cycle. Inhibitions in the response cycle may occur in one or more of the following phases: appetitive, excitement, orgasm, resolution.

Current thinking generally regards the psychosexual disorders as the result of faulty socialization and learning, affected in certain cases by genetic and temperament variables. Thus, they are considered responsive to a variety of treatment approaches, such as operant and classical conditioning, biofeedback, hypnosis, and/or sexual reassignment surgery. Outcome studies using these techniques have been generally encouraging, especially for the sexual dysfunctions, reasonably so for the gender disorders, but to a lesser degree for the paraphilias.

Paraphilias

Too much of a good thing is wonderful.

—Mae West

The Case of Jeffrey Dahmer

Paraphilia is the *DSM-IV* term for the sexual deviations, and both terms will be used interchangeably. The deviation (para) is in that to which the individual is attracted (*philia*). In the *DSM-IV,* all diagnoses of Paraphilia require fulfillment of (1) Criteria A—recurrent, intense, sexually arousing fantasies, sexual urges, or behaviors (with the specificity required by the particular disorder) over at least a 6-month period *and* (2) Criteria B—clinically significant distress or impairment in an important area of one's life caused by these fantasies, urges, or behaviors. The specific paraphilia categories included in *DSM-IV* are (1) Fetishism, (2) Transvestic Fetishism, (3) Pedophilia, (4) Exhibitionism, (5) Voyeurism, (6) Frotteurism, (7) Sexual Masochism, and (8) Sexual Sadism. Although the *DSM-IV* does not directly provide for a diagnosis of sexual compulsion, it is a factor in the case of Jeffrey Dahmer and in many of the following diagnoses.

The essential disorder in a paraphilia is an incapacity for mature, participating, affectionate sexual behavior with adult partners. Traditionally these disorders have been far more common in males, but this discrepancy has decreased slightly in recent years (Lo Piccolo, 1993). The following case presents an unusual manifestation of paraphilia.

The Case of Jeffrey Dahmer

Jeffrey Dahmer is one of the most infamous serial murderers in our history. Marked by his sexual obsession with dead and nearly dead bodies, Dahmer became proficient at drugging, murdering, dismembering, and consuming his victims.

Early Years
Jeffrey Dahmer was born on May 21, 1960, and during most of his childhood he lived on an estate in a wealthy suburb of Akron, Ohio. His father is a successful research chemist, and, consistent with that calling, now blames his son's aberrant behavior on the effects of medication Jeffrey's mother took during pregnancy. In the first grade, when his younger brother was born, Dahmer's teacher wrote a note to his parents saying Jeffrey acted as though he felt neglected. Although Dahmer was not physically or sexually abused, he remembered his home as constantly filled with tension because of his parents' continuous fighting. Ironically, after Jeffrey's death they fought bitterly over the custody of his remains. Dahmer reported feeling guilty for being born because his mother told him she had serious postpartum depression and a nervous breakdown after his birth.

There were reports of peculiar things Dahmer did as a child (as in many such cases, they were seen as more peculiar after his arrest than at the time). For example, his neighbors reported that Dahmer had a fascination with dead insects and animals, and his friends said he repeatedly listened to their hearts with his head on their chests. Dahmer collected animals that had been killed by cars, cut off their heads and placed them on sticks. He also removed and dried out their skin.

From early on, Dahmer demonstrated little regard for life and suffering. At age 5 Dahmer convinced a friend to put his hand in a wasp nest by telling him it was full of ladybugs. In grade school, Dahmer took some tadpoles to a teacher whom he liked.

When he found out that his teacher had given the tadpoles to Dahmer's best friend, he felt rejected by the teacher and decided to punish his friend. So he poured motor oil into the bowl where his friend kept the tadpoles, killing them. One of Dahmer's favorite activities as a teenager was seeking out dogs and killing them with his car.

Dahmer reported that in the eighth grade he masturbated daily and fantasized about sex with boys his own age. His first sexual experience was in the ninth grade. The boy who lived next door came over and lay naked with Dahmer, kissing and fondling him. They stopped after doing this two or three times because of the risk of being caught. After Dahmer dissected a pig in biology class, he took the head home, removed the skin, and kept the skull. At this time he began thinking about using corpses for his sexual pleasure. In high school, Dahmer began drinking alcohol frequently, even during school hours. Although he took part in a normal assortment of high school activities and earned average grades, he was essentially a loner.

The only evidence available of his involvement with a female was when Dahmer went to the prom. He neither danced with nor kissed his date. Halfway through the prom he left alone to get a hamburger.

Adult Years

When Dahmer was 18 years old, his parents were in a bitter divorce and fighting for custody of Dahmer's younger brother. It was at this time, in 1978, that Dahmer killed his first victim, Steven Hicks, age 19. Dahmer had his own car and lived alone. He had been drinking and was driving home when he picked up a hitchhiker. Hicks agreed to go to Dahmer's parents' luxurious house, where they talked, drank beer, and smoked marijuana. Reports vary as to whether Dahmer and Hicks had sex. When it came time for Steven to leave, Dahmer tried to stop him and the two wrestled. Dahmer hit and strangled Hicks with a barbell.

After knocking Hicks out, Dahmer took off his clothes and masturbated while standing over the body, ejaculating onto the body. At dusk Dahmer took the body to a crawlspace under his parents' house and cut it into pieces, placing the parts in plastic bags. At first he carried the pieces with him in his car, but later he returned and placed them in the woods behind his parents' house. Earlier that year, Dahmer had one day walked into the woods with a baseball bat while fantasizing about having sex with a teenage boy who Dahmer knew frequently walked through that area. Fortunately, the boy did not walk there that day, but the developing combination of aggression for control and sex is noted.

After this first murder, Dahmer spent the next several years drifting. He attended Ohio State University for a few months, spent a couple of years in the army, and lived briefly on a beach in Florida. In 1982, Dahmer went to live with his grandmother in Wisconsin, where he got a job at a blood plasma center. He was fired for poor performance after a year. Later he got a job in a chocolate factory. During the 9 years after the first murder, Dahmer continued to experience fantasies about capturing people but did not commit any homicidal acts.

When Dahmer returned from the army, he retrieved his first victim's body pieces and smashed them into fragments that he scattered in the woods. He began pursuing relationships in public places. He would go to a gay bathhouse or bar, meet a man, put drugs into his drink, and take the drugged man to a hotel room. When the man was in a sleep-like state, Jeffrey would have anal sex with him. He would then leave, and the man would awake the next morning with little recollection of what occurred. In what Dahmer described as an attempt to avoid killing, he once went to a funeral home to see the dead body of a young man whom he read had died. Dahmer tried to figure out how to dig up the body so that he could enjoy sex without killing. On another occasion, Dahmer stole a mannikin from a store and performed sexual acts on it. Dahmer's alcohol intake steadily increased.

In 1986, Dahmer was arrested for lewd and lascivious behavior when caught masturbating in front of two 12-year-old boys. Testimony at his trial suggests that Dahmer had a "reverse conversion" after killing his second victim; that is, he considered that there might not be a God and/or he was being influenced by the Devil or some evil force, and concluded that it was his destiny to kill. After that he no longer attempted to exert any strong conscious effort not to kill, as he reportedly had done up to that point, and the killings now came more easily and quickly. Placed in therapy for this offense, Dahmer was described as being cooperative and willing to change.

Dahmer did not commit any murders from 1978 to 1987. In 1989, just after having killed three men, Dahmer pleaded guilty to second-degree sexual assault and enticement of a child for immoral purposes. Dahmer had approached a 13-year-old boy walking home from school and offered him fifty dollars to come to his apartment to help Dahmer try his new camera. In the apartment Dahmer persuaded the boy to remove some of his clothes, and then Dahmer kissed the boy's stomach, unzipped his pants, and pulled out his penis. Dahmer touched the boy's penis, explaining this would make him appear sexier for the pictures. While this was occurring, the boy drank coffee in which Dahmer had placed alcohol and a tranquilizer. When the boy returned home, his parents noticed his peculiar behavior and filed charges when the boy described his experience with Dahmer. Despite his arrest and conviction for this offense, Dahmer's murders remained undiscovered.

At this time Dahmer again was briefly exposed to therapy. At the time a Department of Probation and Parole psychologist informed Dahmer's presiding judge that Dahmer was becoming more outgoing and relaxed, Dahmer was carrying the skull of his latest victim, which he had painted to resemble those bought in stores. He killed his fifth victim while waiting for sentencing. Another psychologist appointed by the court to examine Dahmer described him as uncooperative and unwilling to work on his problems. Therefore, the recommendation to cease treating Dahmer for alcohol and sex offenses, which was supported by two more psychologists, was accepted. Dahmer appealed directly to the judge and said emphatically that he wished to change his behavior. The judge responded by staying Dahmer's 5-year sentence and placing him on probation for 5 years. Even though Dahmer was directed to receive therapy, this was never carried out.

After he was released, Dahmer purchased a black table and made a temple on it of bleached and painted skulls. The temple, used to contain the skeletons of his victims, was to be an area of worship, to give him more energy and control in his life. In the summer of 1990, Dahmer was fired from his latest job for excessive absenteeism. His pace quickened as he killed twelve more men around that time and through the following summer.

Dahmer's Procedures with Victims
Dahmer was primarily interested in sex with unconscious men. He tried to make zombies out of his victims so they would forget their identity and stay with him. He did this in various ways, such as drugging them. He drilled holes in the heads of some men while they were alive and poured acid in the holes, hoping they would stay alive so that he could continue having sex with them. One victim walked around 3 days in this condition

before he died. Another way Dahmer tried to keep his victims was by storing and packaging their parts and eating the meat so that they would become a part of him. Dahmer had sex with every one of the seventeen victims after they were dead. With fourteen victims, Dahmer cut them open in the abdomen; then he placed his penis inside the cavity of the body, got an erection, and ejaculated while still inside the body. With five or six of the victims, Dahmer put his penis inside the mouth of the beheaded man, got an erection, and ejaculated. Dahmer also engaged in anal sex with five or six of the victims after they were dead. Dahmer talked about enjoying masturbating in front of and over the bodies.

Final Years

In May 1991, Dahmer gave his thirteenth victim a drugged drink, drilled holes in his skull, and filled them with acid. In the morning when the young man was sleeping, Dahmer went out to get a beer. As Dahmer was returning, he saw the man naked and sitting at the side of the road. Two women and the police and a firetruck were at the scene. Dahmer explained that the young man was a friend who had had too much to drink. The police then wrapped the man in a blanket, entered Dahmer's apartment, and laid him on the sofa. There was a body in Dahmer's bedroom that the police did not discover. When shown two pictures of Dahmer with the young man, a policeman said, "See, he is telling the truth." After the police left, Dahmer gave the man a final fatal injection. Dahmer proceeded to pose the victim, take pictures, perform anal sex with him, and masturbate on top of him. He acidified the flesh and skeleton and defleshed and saved the skull.

After killing four more men in less than 3 weeks, in July 1991, Dahmer approached Tracy Edwards, age 32. According to one account of what occurred that day, Dahmer offered Edwards the same opportunity he had presented to others: money in exchange for taking his picture. While Edwards was in Dahmer's bedroom watching *The Exorcist,* Dahmer handcuffed one of Edwards's hands and placed a knife at his chest. Dahmer began rubbing one of his skulls and said Edwards's skull would be staying with him, too. Edwards hit Dahmer, kicked him in the chest, and escaped. Edwards reported the incident to the police, who found the story so implausible that at first they were not inclined to investigate. Two police officers with extra time on their hands finally agreed to visit Dahmer. One entered Dahmer's bedroom, where several body parts were resting. The other opened the refrigerator and found human heads.

Dahmer readily confessed and supplied the police with detailed descriptions. He was charged with two counts of murder and thirteen counts of first-degree intentional homicide. Dahmer pled insanity, probably because there was no other option. Because his demeanor was that of a quiet, sensitive, and intelligent college student, the jury was not impressed. He was found sane and sentenced to 957 years via fifteen consecutive life sentences. After his capture, Dahmer repeatedly expressed remorse and was of the opinion that he did not deserve to live. In prison, he refused all efforts available to protect him from being attacked by other prisoners. On November 28, 1994, while washing a bathroom floor in prison, Dahmer and another inmate were beaten to death with a 20-inch bar from an exercise machine. Christopher Scarver was the third inmate on the bathroom detail. The motivation was first thought to have been racial. But Scarver, who once claimed to be the son of God, said, "God told me to do it." Given the horrendous nature of Dahmer's crimes, there are some who might argue that he wasn't delusional, that God probably did tell him to do it. According to the records released in March 1995 of the November 1994 autopsy of Dahmer, officials kept Dahmer's body shackled at the feet during the entire procedure, "such was the fear of this man," according to pathologist Robert Huntington.

Etiology

It is unusual for an individual to have just one diagnosis when the behavior involved is extreme like Dahmer's. For example, at one time or another, Dahmer has been described as having the following psychological diagnoses: pedophilia, borderline personality disorder, sadistic personality disorder, antisocial personality disorder, alcohol dependence, marijuana abuse, and mixed personality disorder. It does appear that Dahmer deteriorated over time, and may have experienced psychotic and/or dissociative episodes. For example, when, on July 22, 1991, his last victim escaped from him, Dahmer made no attempt to leave his apartment or otherwise avoid apprehension. In fact, according to that victim's report, Dahmer seemed disconnected from reality, and was shouting incantations as the victim left. When the police came, Dahmer did not ask about a search warrant or resist in any fashion, but simply let them in.

Ironically, the antisocial personality disorder diagnosis does not seem as singularly probable as the media descriptions of the crimes might suggest, and Dahmer does not appear to be a clear Factor 1 or primary psychopath (see Chapter 11). All indications are that Dahmer could experience a form of guilt-related anxiety, and in spite of his successful deception of the police in May 1991, Dahmer's tendency to lie was not so pronounced that it was regarded as pathological. Dahmer was always surprisingly open about his behavior and motives after being captured. Also, most sophisticated observers said his expressions of remorse and his move toward religion and spirituality in prison were believable. In any case, the diagnosis most pronounced with Dahmer is paraphilia, as he clearly fit the criteria for the residual category, Paraphilia Not Otherwise Specified (NOS).

Dr. Judith Becker, a psychologist who is an expert in sexual deviations, testified as a defense expert at Dahmer's trial. She could find no reference in the literature for Dahmer's unique variation of necrophilia, that is, his attraction to zombie-like humans—living bodies capable of little more than breathing.

Exclusivity, persistency, compulsivity, and pervasiveness like Dahmer exhibited are the hallmarks of paraphilia. It is typically a driven, focused pattern, often seen initially in fantasy or behavior in mid-adolescence (Lo Piccolo, 1993). Fantasies of sex with corpses first appeared in Dahmer's adolescence, with his pursuit of dead animals likely being a precursor to his full-blown variation of necrophilia.

Research does not support sex hormone or neurotransmitter abnormalities as the primary or major cause in the paraphilias. Rather, it appears that Dahmer aptly fits the description given by Lo Piccolo (1993),

> [P]araphilias are complex, multiple determined conditions, and . . . any single-element theory of etiology is oversimplified and incorrect. Rather, we should realize that paraphilias clearly involve a host of factors, including arousal conditioned to inappropriate objects, lack of internalized moral values, inability to weigh long-term

negative consequences against short-term sexual pleasure, distorted thinking about sexuality, lack of access to gratifying normal sexual outlets, lack of empathy for victim distress, disinhibition by alcohol or drugs, and, possibly, temporal lobe pathology. In individual cases, various combinations of these factors may be more or less important. (p. 340)

There is no evidence that one of these factors, temporal lobe pathology, applied to Dahmer, and nothing about Dahmer's past suggests there was any lack of access to normal sexual outlets. The rest of Lo Piccolo's descriptors bear a close resemblance to Dahmer. Dahmer's ability to weigh long-term negative consequences against short-term sexual pleasure seems to have deteriorated as both his alcoholism and his experiences with dead and almost dead bodies increased.

Treatment Options

Dahmer never pursued or received significant treatment for his disorder, which is not uncommon with paraphiliacs. The paraphilias range from disorders that involve passivity (sexual masochism) to those that involve coercive aggression and illegal actions (pedophilia), and treatments will differ as well. Indeed, anyone working in this area is constantly challenged by the creative diversity found in sexual preferences. For example, antisex crusader John Harvey Kellogg originated Kellogg's breakfast cereals to calm sexual lust and promote a generally healthy lifestyle in the general population. Kellogg avoided sex with his wife and obtained sexual gratification from enemas—a pattern known as klismaphilia. In general, all of the paraphilias are difficult to treat, success is often negligible and/or short-term, and relapse is common (Lo Piccolo, 1993).

Castration is a time-honored treatment, or to quote from James W. Hall's 1996 novel *Buzz Cut:*

> Testicles. The Greek word was *orchis orchid*, from the shape of the flower's tuber. *Orchidectomy* being the technical term for castration. Cutting away the orchid's roots. Or in the Latin, *castrare*, from *castus*, which meant pure. Castration being used on the eastern slaves to keep women pure. *Castus*, as in the caste system, to keep the races pure
>
> ... And there was the other Latin term, *testiculus*, which referred to the ancient practice of swearing an oath by putting a hand on the nuts." (p. 262)

However, even physical castration is not as effective as its admirers believe. Chemocastrators such as medroxyprogesterone acetate (Depo-Provera), which suppress *all* sexual arousal not just the undesired forms, can be effective. Neurosurgical castration via temporal lobe ablation has been used in some countries.

Most paraphiliacs are best treated in a formal treatment program, usually referred to as a sex offender program. Several factors can optimize such a program. It is helpful if the program can be delivered in the context of a psychotherapy or counseling relationship wherein a degree of trust has been generated.

However, the therapist must understand that, just as Dahmer did, these clients may well pretend sincerity, overstate gains, resist treatment, and prematurely terminate. One should be especially suspicious of a client's statements that he has spontaneously or quickly lost interest in deviant activities and/or has easily (or ever) become primarily interested in consensual sex with adult females. It almost never happens that way. The following are common components of a typical sex offender treatment program:

1. *Assessment of the offender.* For example, phallometric measurement of sexual responses to suggested imagery or to actual pictures of various stimuli is helpful in identifying the focus of the sexually deviant fantasies that are a key to treatment of the aberrant behavior. In a cooperative subject, direct measures of penile tumescence (usually via changes in a rubber tube encircling the penis, as in a pneumograph) are often used. In some cases, thermography has distinct advantages of ease of access and less embarrassment.

2. *Any necessary acute measures,* such as mandated residence changes, short-term chemocastration, etc. Other medications, such as anti-depressants, may be necessary in some cases.

3. *Group and individual therapy.* This is necessary to clarify the individual's range of deviancy, level of disorder, and level of commitment to change. This is an appropriate place to deal with cognitive distortions, such as "Women may act like they don't, but I can tell they secretly like it when I _____."

4. Covert sensitization is a behavioral technique, like items 5, 6, and 7 (Chambless et al., 1996). It is an imagery-based counter-conditioning procedure in which a client is instructed to imagine the relevant deviant sexual act or stimulus and then to imagine some negative reaction, usually severe anxiety, terror, or nausea, possibly assisted by a strongly noxious odor to develop a nausea response.

5. *Aversive conditioning* is when inappropriate sexual stimuli are presented to a client via slides, audiotapes, or videotapes, followed by the presentation of noxious stimuli such as electric shock or the inhalation of valeric acid or ammonia.

6. *Masturbatory satiation therapy* involves having the offender masturbate to an appropriate sexual fantasy while verbalizing it aloud. Following this, the offender is required to continue to masturbate for a period ranging from 45 minutes to 2 hours (or try, in some cases) while verbalizing deviant sexual fantasies. This should all be tape-recorded to check progress, possibility of malingering, etc.

7. *Aversive behavioral rehearsal* attempts to decrease sexually deviant behaviors and arousal by making the behavior publicly observable. The offender describes in detail the types of offense committed and then by use of mannequins, clothing, apparatus, etc., re-enacts the offense. This is narrated by the offender while discussing his plans, actions, feelings, and thoughts.

Having victims, friends, and/or family members as an audience heightens the aversive effect.

8. *Education programs* that focus on sexual education, social skills training, assertiveness training, and cognitive re-education.

9. A *support group* such as Sexaholics Anonymous, or specialized group therapy.

10. In many cases, it is critical to develop an ancillary surveillance and report group, specific to the individual client. This may involve family, friends, neighbors, etc., who are made aware of the situation on a need-to-know basis and who agree to report inappropriate or suspicious behaviors. A variety of other techniques that prevent relapse can be useful.

Social retraining toward an ability to attain mature heterosexual partners is often necessary. Unfortunately, recidivism is very high with the paraphilias.

Pedophilia

The Case of Jesse Timmendequas

Pedophilia literally—and ironically—means "love of children," and a pedophiliac is one who consistently seeks out sexual experiences with children. Pedophilia is rare in females, and although it is not a common behavior in any demographic group, it has traditionally been viewed as a disorder of middle-age males—"dirty old men." However, research indicates that a molestation pattern typically starts by age 15, and most early victims are known to the pedophile. Boys are more likely to be victims than girls, although girls are more likely to be victims of "hands-off" crimes like exhibitionism. Most pedophiles over time commit a wide range of crimes, including exhibitionism, voyeurism, and rape, and pedophiles who molest boys do so at a much higher rate than do those who molest girls.

The Case of Jesse Timmendequas

Jesse Timmendequas (pronounced tim-MEN-duh-qwas) first came to the clear attention of the authorities for his pedophilic interests in October 1979, at age 18, when he persuaded two 5-year-old girls in his neighborhood to go with him to hunt for ducks. He took their hands and walked down an embankment, but for an unknown reason one girl broke away and ran for help. Jesse took the other girl to the bottom of the hill, knocked her down, took her pants down, and apparently smelled her vagina, although he said he had only wanted to look at it. He was caught immediately. He pleaded guilty to attempted aggravated sexual assault, but the sentence was suspended on the condition he obtain counseling. He did not, but only served 9 months in the Middlesex County Adult Correction Center for his violation.

Shortly after his release in June 1981, he came up to two 7-year-old girls in the neighborhood and asked if they wanted fireworks for the Fourth of July. One girl panicked and went off screaming on her bike in search of her mother. Jesse describes what then happened, "We walked down the trail a little bit and I grabbed her by the throat and pulled her off to the side of the woods and when she started to turn blue I let her go and ran and that's it." Her mother later found her unconscious. There was no definite proof that he sexually assaulted her, although he left a black and blue handprint on her lower stomach where he had gripped her. He admitted that he had had sexual thoughts about these two girls for about a year, had waited for them about an hour on that particular day, and had been "a little bit" aroused by the attack.

Through plea bargaining, he pled guilty to attempted sexual contact and attempting to cause serious bodily injury. He spent only 6 years and 8 months (the standard length for a 10-year term, with time off for good behavior) at the Adult Diagnostic and Treatment Center in Avenel, New Jersey. People who worked at that center felt that he was never truly engaged in treatment, and one therapist there remembered Jesse as "a pouter, then he'd go hide. He spent a lot of time in bed." The staff consensus was that he would probably make someone his victim again, and yet they had to release him.

Upon release, he almost immediately associated with two sex offenders, Brian Jenin and Joseph Cifelli, whom he had met at Avenel, and eventually moved in with them into a two-story house owned by Mr. Cifelli's mother on Barbara Lee Drive in Trenton, New Jersey. Some of the neighbors knew of Mr. Cifelli's past, but not about the others. Jenin had in the past tried to join the Big Brother organization so that he could have access to young boys.

However, Maureen and Richard Kanka, who had lived across the street for 16 years, had never heard any of this, and thus had no reason to worry on the summer evening of July 29, 1994, when their 7-year-old daughter Megan went out to look for a friend who lived in the house next to the Cifelli's. Indeed, Mrs. Kanka reported that when she went to look for Megan, one of the first two people she saw on the street was Jesse, who said he saw the little girl earlier. Later he would tell police that he couldn't have done it because he "even looked for her and handed out flyers." For the next 23 hours, police and neighbors, including Jesse, searched for Megan, a bright and beautiful child who had already been named "Miss Congeniality" 2 years in a row in her baton class.

Jesse's housemates, Jenin and Cifelli, could account for their whereabouts, but Jesse seemed nervous and now admitted to being the last one to see her. Eventually, under questioning by Detective Sgt. Robert Schwarz, who had arrested Jesse in 1981, he admitted strangling her after he had touched her and tried to kiss her and was afraid she would tell her mother. Jesse had apparently lured her away by offering to let her pet his new puppy. Subsequent to his arrest, a substantial amount of pornography was found in his room.

Jesse's Early History
Jesse Timmendequas, apparently named for his father's hero, the outlaw Jesse James, was born in Somerville, New Jersey, in 1961 to Charles Hall and Doris Unangst. Testimony at trial by Carol Krych, who prepared Jesse's history for the state, is that Hall stole the name Timmendequas from a tombstone while fleeing the law. His version is that he was given the name by Indian friends, and he has since changed his name to Edward James Howard. Jesse's older brother, Paul, testified that his father, who was in and out of jail from age 12 to 35, was alcoholic, regularly beat Jesse, had forced both boys to stimulate him orally and then sodomized Jesse, and generally forced himself sexually on Jesse on numerous occasions from the time Jesse was 6 up to age 10. Their father allegedly tortured family pets as a warning to the boys not to report him and once killed Jesse's pet rabbit and forced the boys to eat it. He eventually fled the state to avoid being prosecuted for viciously stabbing someone in the stomach with a butcher knife in 1972. He now

lives in a small California town populated by isolationists and racists, and admits to being racist. The statute of limitations has run out to prosecute him on either the sexual assaults or the stabbing. He denies some of the allegations and points to his present marriage of many years as a counterargument.

Jesse's mother had a tested IQ of 73 at age 18, grew up in poverty, had been raped twice by her father when she was 5, and was a severe alcoholic. She eventually had ten children by seven different men and gave away or lost custody of seven of them. One of her partners would paint iodine on the penis of one of Jesse's half-brothers and threaten to cut it off, and another regularly raped one girl in the family. Only one of the seven partners, Edward Garmen, did not abuse Jesse, Paul, or their half-sister, and he was one of the few points of light in Jesse's life. Unfortunately, after only a year, he died of lung cancer, when Jesse was 12. Not surprisingly, school records indicate that was the one year Jesse was starting to handle school adequately, and a report the next year notes, "Jesse has taken this tragedy very hard . . . he is preoccupied with his own personal loss." There were no more points of light in his life.

Etiology

The etiology and the treatments discussed in the case of Jeffrey Dahmer are generally relevant here, as is the material in the cases of Charles and Abby in Chapter 13. In addition, as with physical abuse, having been a victim of sexual abuse makes one more susceptible to a broad spectrum of psychopathology, including sexual deviancy and/or dysfunction, and more specifically to becoming an abuser oneself. Other general factors that predispose one toward pedophilia (and many other forms of psychopathology) are a dysfunctional early or present family environment and general social or intellectual inadequacy. Factors that direct one more toward pedophilia are social-sexual inadequacy; fantasy activity involving pedophiliac patterns, which is often facilitated by the use of pornography; and easy and practiced access to victims. All of these factors are found in Jesse's history.

Treatment

Because of the disgust with which most people respond to this disorder, it is not surprising that the typical treatment approaches are somewhat coercive. As was the case with Jesse, pedophiles rarely bring themselves into treatment and are typically coerced by sociolegal pressure. The techniques described in the Treatment Options section of the Dahmer discussion are particularly relevant. It is also critical to correct such common cognitive distortions as (1) "My sexual contact with children is not really bad for them, and may even be good for them," (2) "children are able to reason, so if they consent to it, it is really not molesting," (3) "if they don't resist (or strongly resist), they actually want the sexual contact." It is unfortunate both that there is a high recidivism rate and there is no good way to differentiate those who will relapse from those who won't.

The Trial

Jesse Timmendequas went on trial for the death of Megan Kanka on May 5, 1997. On May 30, 1997, after only 4 hours of deliberations, Jesse was convicted of first-degree murder, that is, intentional murder "by his own conduct" as well as rape, sodomy, kidnapping, and felony murder—committing a murder in the course of another felony. It appeared that the defense attorneys knew they had little chance of avoiding a conviction and were directing many of their efforts to set the stage to spare him the death penalty. The second, "penalty phase" of the trial began on June 9, during which both aggravating and mitigating factors could be offered as arguments for and against the death penalty. In *Furman* v. *Georgia* 408 U.S. 238 (1972), the Supreme Court held that the death penalty was constitutional only if juries or judges were not given complete discretion in imposing death, that the death penalty could never be mandatory, that the defendant must be permitted to present any aspect of his or her character in mitigation (although not evidence from a polygraph), that states are permitted to allow judges rather than juries to impose death sentences after considering special mitigating and aggravating circumstances, and that imposing a death penalty for rape or kidnapping was disproportionately severe under the Eighth Amendment's "cruel and unusual" clause. Referring to that same clause, the Court later held, in *Stanford* v. *Kentucky* 492 U.S. 937 (1989), that states could execute children who were over the age of 16 at the time of the crime, arguing that the practice was at least not unusual as juveniles as young as 14 were regularly being executed at the time of the writing of the Constitution. An earlier decision, *Thompson* v. *Oklahoma* 487 U.S. 815 (1988), established that children under 16 at the time of the crime could not be executed.

Jesse's lawyers listed twenty-four potential mitigating circumstances, reflecting much of the history noted in the case study. These can probably best be summarized as five major original factors: severe and consistent sexual abuse, severe and consistent physical abuse, terrible parenting in all other dimensions, probable fetal alcohol syndrome effects from his mother's severe alcohol abuse while pregnant, and terrible genetics. Much of this was legally countered by the aggravating circumstances, such as the details of the crime, and the "victim impact statements," allowed since 1991 as a result of the Supreme Court decision of *Payne* v. *Tennessee* 501 U.S. 808 (1991). After 10 hours of deliberations over 2 days, the jury unanimously voted to impose the death penalty.

Megan's Law

Fortunately, the Kankas, including their two other children, did not have to view for long the house where Jesse lived. It was replaced by a park that was built in Megan's memory. However, an even more important memorial to her is "Megan's Law," which requires communities to be notified when convicted sex offenders move in. Several states have passed such laws or administrative requirements, and President Clinton signed a national "Megan's Law" on May 17, 1996, and in February, 1998, the Supreme Court rejected a challenge to the constitutionality of Megan's Law. Critics of these laws argue that such laws are an invasion of privacy and encourage the harassment of convicted offenders, and perhaps vigilantism. It is also argued that informing neighbors and schools unfairly punishes the offender, who has already paid his debt to society. The alternative position is that these crimes are already on the public record, such offenders have a high recidivism rate, and providing such information helps prevent these crimes. So far, the general thrust has been to uphold these laws if applied to persons convicted of such crimes after the law was passed. As a postscript, some released sex offenders who have been the recipients of neighborly attention such as signs and rallies in front of their houses, threatening phone calls, etc., have retaliated with civil suits asking for monetary compensation for the harassment.

Sexual Predator Legislation

Another critical socio-legal issue is whether or not we may constrain convicted pedophiles and other sexual predators once they have completed their prison sentence. Several states have passed legislation allowing these individuals to be institutionalized as dangerous, under some form of civil commitment. Civil commitment has traditionally required both (1) mental illness and (2) dangerousness to self or others, and the sexual deviations have never been construed as fulfilling the legal definition of mental illness. Hence, the legal challenge was whether legislation could be written to somehow allow a sexual predator pattern, absent another accompanying mental illness diagnosis, to be sufficient for commitment.

The Supreme Court addressed this issue in *Kansas* v. *Hendricks* (1997). Leroy Hendricks, who had a history of sexual misconduct with children, was scheduled to be released to a halfway house in 1994, having served 10 years in prison for molesting children. Instead of releasing him, Kansas sought to apply its then newly enacted "Sexually Violent Predator Act." That act established a civil commitment procedure for "any person who has been convicted or charged with a sexually violent offense and who suffers from a mental abnormality or personality disorder which makes the person likely to engage in the predatory acts of sexual violence," and the Supreme Court upheld the validity of this act. Because, as noted previously, the recidivism rate for crimes by sexual predators is very high, and because there is no clear way to discriminate those who will recidivate from those who will not, most decisions to release or not will present vexing dilemmas.

Transvestism

The Case of Randy	*Strange diseases, he thought, demand . strange remedies: he, her.* —John Updike, *Bech Is Back* (1982)

Transvestites, especially males who dress as females, receive much media attention. Transvestism, referred to as Transvestic Fetishism in the *DSM-IV*, is one of the paraphilias. Transvestic Fetishism is defined as recurrent and persistent cross-dressing that is initiated for the purpose of sexual arousal and which eventually becomes habitual. The transvestite experiences intense frustration when external circumstances interfere with cross-dressing.

The disorder is relatively rare and more predominant in males than females. Most individuals who have been involved in transvestism have cross-dressed by the age of 10, and usually much younger. Often the cross-dressing was significantly reinforced by parents, sometimes by "petticoat punishment," the humiliation of a boy by dressing him in girls' clothes. The cross-dressing behavior typically becomes paired with masturbation and eventuates in the classic transvestite pattern (Masters et al., 1991; Money, 1985).

Transvestism is commonly confused with transsexualism. The major difference is that transsexualism is considered to be a gender identity disorder whereas transvestism is a paraphilia. Transsexuals truly feel as if they should be the other sex. In fact, most transsexuals feel so strongly that they have been trapped in the wrong body that they actively pursue surgical alterations. The transvestite, however, does not have compelling desires to participate in sex-change surgery. Even though they seek sexual arousal through cross-dressing, they maintain identity with their biological gender.

The Case of Randy

Randy, a handsome 38-year-old man, came to his first appointment at the mental health center with his wife, clearly upon her insistence. With some prodding, Randy finally said that he was a transvestite and that he wished to change this, although with little evident enthusiasm for this change.

Even though he had been a transvestite throughout the 5 years of his second marriage, only recently had his wife become aware of it, when she found certain clothes and accessories that led her to conclude that Randy was having a standard extramarital affair. Randy felt he had no option except to explain his behavior. When he did so, it was clear that he had upset his wife much more than if he had told her he had been having an affair. She said she was shocked and embarrassed, and she insisted that he get help as soon as possible.

Social History

In many such cases it is not clear how the cross-dressing first started and became reinforced. In Randy's case, certain known variables make his inclination toward transvestism more understandable.

Until the age of 2, Randy's mother and father raised him normally. However, when Randy was 2, his mother contracted a rare respiratory disease and had to leave the area to go to a special hospital. Randy's father felt that his wife needed him near her and that he could not adequately care for Randy at the same time, so Randy moved to the home of his aunt. She was a 45-year-old woman who had lived alone ever since an early, short, and traumatic marriage. Since that time she had worked as a legal secretary and had lived a quiet, reclusive life. Although she was devoted to her younger brother, Randy's father, in general she was relatively hostile toward men.

As might be expected, she had little sense of what child rearing entailed. When Randy innocently put on a pair of her shoes, she thought it was humorous and cute. Randy responded to this reinforcement by trying on other articles of her clothing, and she accepted this behavior as long as he only did it in the house.

At times she would let Randy dress up and they would have tea parties. She even took pictures of Randy in his feminine dress to put in an album. The basic problem was that she had no idea of how to deal with a little boy and had no interest herself in the activities that are interesting to most young boys.

Randy's mother died when he was 4 years old. When Randy was 9, his father remarried and brought Randy to live with him and his new wife. The cross-dressing naturally ceased for a time as the usual stimuli that elicited it were now absent. However, his new stepmother once allowed Randy to put on one of her dresses, and she also thought it was cute. Some time after this she discovered Randy going through her lingerie drawer, and on another occasion she discovered him wearing a pair of her underpants. When she reported the incidents to Randy's father, he became very upset and whipped Randy. When they discovered him doing it again, Randy's father and stepmother attempted a homemade version of the therapeutic technique called "negative practice." That is, they forced Randy to dress entirely in women's clothing and wear the outfit all day. However, they did not realize that he went into a high state of sexual arousal and masturbated several times during that day. Randy did at least get the message that his parents disapproved of this behavior, and as a result he became secretive about it.

On the surface he showed a rather normal adolescence. He participated in many school activities in high school, and in particular became so skilled in tennis that he was elected team captain. He dated occasionally, and in all overt respects seemed to be relatively normal. However, in his secret life, he often stole women's clothes and wore them while by himself in a woods near their house, or at home when he knew his parents would not be around. He now consistently masturbated to orgasm when he wore the clothes. Randy continued to date fairly regularly. On those few occasions when he did become sexually involved, he would use fantasies of cross-dressing to initiate and maintain his arousal.

He first married when he was 23 years old; the marriage lasted about 2 years. He was only able to experience sexual arousal with his wife when he fantasized being in women's clothes. They rarely had sex. The divorce seemed inevitable and was not remarkably distressing for either party.

After the divorce there was a noticeable increase in Randy's transvestite behavior. Although he had a good job with an insurance firm, he would occasionally go off on vacation and spend most of the time dressing up in women's clothes and masturbating. Also, he found a club in a nearby metropolitan area that catered to transvestites. Randy managed to keep this aspect of his world separate enough so that it did not interfere with his work or other social behaviors. He met his second wife through his work. They had a number of mutual interests and both were somewhat lonely, so after a short courtship they married.

Etiology

Traditional theories have emphasized denial of masculinity and castration anxiety as critical in the development of transvestism, but the relevant social learning theory is somewhat more applicable to Randy's case. Very early in Randy's life, cross-dressing received much attention from the "significant other" in his world, who at that time was his aunt. She was also the major figure from whom Randy could model behaviors. Randy was involved almost exclusively in a traditionally feminine world with few other options to consider. Also, the attention and approval he received from his aunt for cross-dressing were particularly reinforcing (Money, 1985).

This attention continued when he returned to live with his father and new stepmother, at least for a short time. Their later attempt to frustrate this behavior by having him dress up totally as a female and keep the clothes on all day unfortunately backfired. Their idea was not that bad. Negative practice is effective in certain conditions, but it needs to be carefully monitored so that the experience is clearly aversive. Most parents are not psychologically sophisticated enough to carry this through. A professional consultation at this point could have turned things around. Randy went underground with his behavior, and his parents, of course, were relieved not to see any obvious evidence of it anymore, as it ended much upset and embarrassment for them.

Treatment

The clinician asked to treat a transsexual might consider a referral for transsexual surgery, but such an option would be irrelevant for the transvestite who does not really consider himself to be of the other sex. Actually, whether even a transsexual should undergo this surgery remains a controversial issue among professionals. Some argue that it is unnecessary, and that with counseling and the passage of time the transsexual individual can lose the compulsion to change sex. On the other hand, there is some evidence that transsexual surgery is effective in making a certain subgroup of individuals happier and more satisfied with their life situation (Masters et al., 1991; Money, 1985).

When Randy began to notice a change in his sexual preference, which occurred after four half-hour sessions of aversive conditioning and thought stopping (being trained to shout "stop" out loud whenever he felt the impulse to cross-dress), he was asked to participate in controlled masturbatory training. He was told that when he masturbated he was to force himself to imagine desired scenes, such as sex with his wife, at the time of orgasm. Also, he was to try to introduce these scenes in his mind as early as possible in the masturbation sequence. At first he needed transvestite scenes to obtain arousal. However, gradually he was able to replace these scenes earlier and earlier with imagined scenes of sexual behavior with his wife. In that way the reinforcement from his sexual arousal and orgasm increased the future arousal of these new images. Optimally this would generalize to his wife in actuality, which it did.

Naturally there had been some disruption of his marital situation. So Randy and his wife also participated in marital therapy and had several sessions in sexual instructions along the lines that Masters and Johnson (1970) and Masters et al. (1991) suggest. These sessions helped to enhance their relationship. All indications are that Randy's change was thorough and without regression to the transvestite pattern. It is true that in other such cases there might well be regression on occasion to the earlier behaviors, and booster treatments at that time would be necessary.

Sexual Dysfunctions (Impotence)

The Case
of Tim

*I was Romeo of the Roaches again, eating the
lamb patties of her hands, licking her yellow hair.
I grabbed her thigh ruthlessly, put my hand around
the ankle of the other leg. I need you, I said. Bored,
but having at it as the male of the species. I'd been
trained.*

—Barry Hannah, *Geronimo Rex* (1972)

As with the paraphilias, the sexual dysfunctions come in varied forms. It is generally estimated that most people have at least occasionally experienced some form of sexual dysfunction, and more enduring sexual dysfunction may affect as many as 50% of marriages (Masters et al., 1991). Over all, the determinants of any individual sexual dysfunction are often multiple—psychosocial, interpersonal, and/or neurophysiological.

In the *DSM-IV* the Sexual Dysfunctions are differentiated into four subcategories, based on phases of the sexual response cycle: (1) Desire—Hypoactive Sexual Desire Disorder (302.71), Sexual Aversion Disorder (302.79); (2) Arousal—Female Sexual Arousal Disorder (302.72), Male Erectile Disorder (302.72); (3) Orgasm—Female (302.73) and Male (302.74) Orgasmic Disorder, Premature Ejaculation (302.75); (4) Resolution—Dyspareunia (302.76), Vaginismus (306.51). To earn a formal diagnosis, "marked distress or interpersonal difficulty" has to occur as a result of the condition.

In practice, one has to be somewhat arbitrary in assigning a label of psychosexual dysfunction. Masters and Johnson in 1970 arbitrarily defined erectile dysfunction as a clinical problem if there are failures in 25% of the attempts at intercourse. Also, in most cases, total "erectile dysfunction" (the common term in the research literature) is fairly rare, and typically suggests a biological cause. Most often the dysfunction is partial. An erection occurs, but it does not persist long enough to provide satisfaction for the partner or for one's own orgasm to occur (Lo Piccolo, 1985).

Throughout this case history we will use the term *impotence*, but note that there is general pejorative connotation to this term. That is, *impotence* suggests general personality inadequacy and a weakness of character. The standard term for female psychosexual dysfunction, *frigidity*, in turn suggests a lack of emotional warmth. But there is no evidence that these implied traits occur more commonly in individuals who experience these problems (Doctor, 1998; Janus, 1994). It is interesting that the weakness in the male and the coldness in the female suggested by these terms are the exact opposites of the characteristics most clearly prescribed in the sex roles of our society—competence for males and sensitivity and warmth for females.

The Case of Tim

After suffering silently for some time, as is typical in this syndrome, Tim went to his personal physician asking for treatment of impotence. The physician referred him to a urologist, who through a careful medical examination ruled out the various physical and endocrinological factors that can affect impotence. So he referred Tim to a clinical psychologist who specialized in the treatment of the sexual dysfunctions. The clinical psychologist listened to Tim's story of his background as a preparation for initiating appropriate treatment.

Tim is 33 years old, college-educated, and makes a good first impression. He is handsome and in good shape physically, reflecting his prior occupation as a professional baseball player. He also dresses well, keeps himself well groomed, and relates to others with apparent warmth and interest.

Although he recently has been promoted to assistant vice-president in the bank where he works, the general impression he gives is that he is not strikingly successful or interested in his work. Also, in spite of his good first impression, it is quickly evident that he is moderately anxious most of the time. On several occasions, he had trouble articulating his concerns, and he sometimes needed to get up and move about during the interview.

From his description of his parents, his mother seems to be best described as passive and pious, and his father as authoritarian and perfectionistic. Tim describes his upbringing as "standard middle class Catholicism." Tim still attends church occasionally but is clearly not committed at any great depth to a religious orientation. The most important focus in his world still seems to be his relationship to sports. One of his most vivid early memories is of playing in a baseball game as a very young boy, possibly age 3 or 4, and hearing his parents' cheers as he ran from base to base. Yet his parents were extremely demanding in the area of sports, in particular his father, but also his mother more subtly.

His positive early images of his participation in sports are clouded by several other memories of his father's role in his early feelings about sports. His father coached his Little League team and harangued Tim if he made any errors. His father was also demanding of the other children on the team, but he certainly hollered more at his son when he made a mistake, possibly to avoid any accusations of favoritism. It was only when Tim performed competently that his father showed any positive response at all, and, of course, in the early years such moments were not common. Tim's father also demanded a great deal of off-the-field discipline and practice. Although these demands may have taken some fun out of growing up, Tim still refers to the discipline as "a necessary evil that allowed me to develop the skills I needed later."

The most disturbing aspect of his parents' attitudes in this area is that they still so highly value his life in sports, even though his professional career is over due to an injury from which Tim did not recover well. Both of his parents fixate on his role as a professional baseball player and often refer to his achievements in their discussions of him with family and friends, even though he makes his discomfort apparent when they do so. They seem to have stopped seeing him as a developing person, retaining their image of him as the successful and applauded athlete. Surprisingly, they allowed Jack, Tim's younger brother, to pursue an interest in music, possibly because they felt their needs in the sports area would be filled by Tim.

Tim himself was rather ambivalent about his inability to function any longer as a professional baseball player. His career was first curtailed when he injured his foot sliding into a base. He returned and played earlier than he probably should have, before the foot was fully healed. He favored it slightly, which caused a subtle change in his pitching motion, eventually leading to a chronically sore arm. The orthopedic surgeon he consulted told him that he had strained the arm such that it would never return to full functioning.

Several things made his demise as a baseball player particularly painful to him and his parents. First, he had not made it to the big leagues until he was 29 years old, having spent more years in the minor leagues than is typical. It also appeared that before the injuries he was on the edge of stardom. He had started to win consistently, and there was no reason to believe this would not continue. He also had the prospect of being on a team that could make it to a championship. His injury curtailed this not only for himself, but for the team as well. It was particularly galling to Tim when some sportswriters suggested that he did not have the courage to "stick with it" and make a success of his baseball career after the injury.

Tim married his first wife when he was a junior in college, just as he had moved into a star role on the college baseball team. She was a freshman at the university and obviously enjoyed the moderate degree of glamour that surrounded Tim at that time. They married after a short courtship and had a child almost immediately. Then it began to dawn on them that they had few mutual interests, as well as totally different views on child rearing. Although he indicated there were no episodes of impotence in the marriage, their sexual life was sporadic at best. She began an affair with an attorney at the office where she worked and eventually left Tim to marry him. When her new husband obtained a job with a prestigious firm in a distant city, she moved, taking the child with her. Tim still manages to see his son, now 11 years old, with some regularity. But the distance and the early separation have prohibited the development of a strong relationship. In recent years, Tim has dated Pam, a woman with whom he had initially enjoyed a satisfying sexual relationship. She moved in with him a year and a half ago, 6 months before he decided not to continue with his baseball career. It is clear that Pam never saw Tim's career in sports as something she valued highly.

Tim has never been very clear as to whether or not he "loves Pam." Sexual attraction was a major part of their early courtship, and they had a very active sex life in the first several months of dating. Although Pam did not seem to respond specifically to his baseball career, Tim's overall athletic appearance was a strong factor in her initial attraction to him. They have talked of marriage, but neither feels confident about making that type of commitment. In the meantime, Tim's parents are upset that Pam and Tim are living together without being married, and they never mention Pam to any of their friends.

Tim personally links the first occasions of impotence with worries generated by sportswriters' criticisms about his alleged lack of desire to make a comeback. He remembers the first incident as occurring on a night when he had been drinking heavily, largely because he had been upset by reading an article noting how his absence had probably cost his former team a shot at the championship. He had also been feeling uncertain at that time about the permanence of his relationship with Pam. These factors together resulted in a distracted and apprehensive mental set. When he became aware that he did not have a full erection, he became even more anxious, thus deflating what erection he had obtained. Although Pam was not overtly critical at the time, she also was not very supportive, possibly because she also had drunk quite a bit. In any case, Tim saw this as a humiliating experience and anticipated (at least unconsciously) a repeat. This expectation brought on anxiety, and Tim continued having problems obtaining or maintaining an erection.

Tim had been raised with prohibitions against virtually all types of sexual behavior, but he did not take his religious views seriously at a conscious level. He had been taught to masturbate by an older male friend. In high school he engaged in much fondling and petting with Barbara, the first girl he dated with any consistency. But he had his first experience of intercourse with Carolyn, a good friend of Barbara's. It had been enjoyable, although at first it had been very anxiety-provoking. It occurred in the living room of Carolyn's home, and just as they got started, Carolyn's father called down and asked if anyone was there, scaring Tim and temporarily deflating his erection. But his high drive level at that time came to his rescue, and they went on to finish.

Etiology

As noted, Tim had received a complete physical examination that ruled out physical causes of impotence. Also, he spent an evening at the university sleep lab. The tests indicated that he did show normal nocturnal penile tumescence (NPTs), or erections while sleeping. Although not an infallible indicator, it has generally been found that men with physically based impotence show fewer or no NPTs (Masters et al., 1991)

The following cues are suggestive of erectile dysfunction in which organic factors play a major part:

- Gradual onset
- Sequentially deteriorating erections
- Normal libido
- Ability to initiate but not maintain erection
- Loss of nocturnal and masturbatory erection

The following are generally indicative of psychogenic erectile dysfunction:

- Episodic
- Sudden onset
- Acute, brought on by life stresses
- Normal morning and nocturnal erections
- Loss of libido

Several factors emerged from Tim's psychological evaluation that apparently contributed to impotence. Like his father, Tim had a strong need to control his environment and he felt threatened by change he could not control. The divorce, the problems with his baseball career, and the ambivalence about his present girlfriend all suggested a loss of control to Tim and in turn generated anxiety. The impotence provided a physical focal point for the vague feelings of anxiety. But his focus on the sexual concerns created what Masters and Johnson

(1970) have termed "performance anxiety." Under performance anxiety, persons take on a spectator role in the sexual act rather than letting themselves fully enjoy the pleasures of the response.

In addition to Tim's obsessive features, which generate a high need to control events, other characteristics could predict the impotence. Tim revealed that he perceived Pam as moving more heavily into the women's liberation movement than he would like. She had openly begun to discuss her need to "find herself" and "fulfill her own needs." She had begun to flirt while in his general vicinity, a behavior he allowed himself but frowned on in Pam. She had also insinuated that Tim had not really worked hard to recover fully from his injury. As a result of all these developments, Tim began to perceive Pam as threatening his self-esteem. When he experienced the impotence with her, these developing beliefs were strongly reinforced.

Residual guilt from his rather strict Catholic upbringing was also a factor with Tim. He had verbalized some concern about being divorced and now living with another woman, as he was still attempting to maintain a standard role in a church that forbade such behavior. Also, as Welch and Kartub (1978) found, the incidence of impotence is highest in societies in which sexual restrictiveness is high. In particular, a higher rate of impotence is likely if the society has had a restrictive belief system and also if it is now rapidly moving toward a more liberal value system.

As far as the specific instance that set off the impotence, Tim had experienced fatigue that day and had also overindulged in alcohol, a common factor when individuals first experience impotence (Doctor, 1998). Also, it is important to note that even though his early sexual experiences usually had been successful, they were often associated with a significant level of anxiety.

Treatment

A number of effective physical, chemical, and psychological techniques have been developed to treat erectile and orgasmic dysfunctions (Meyer and Deitsch, 1996; Masters et al., 1994). The prescription drug sildenafil (Viagra) is the most effective of these treatments. Administration of the hormone testosterone is common (although of questionable effectiveness for most cases). Penile artery bypass surgery can be used, although this is seldom needed. Various forms of revascularization are more likely to be useful. Certain prosthetic devices can be used for organically based cases and occasionally for severe psychogenic cases as well. One is a semi-rigid rod that is implanted in the corpora cavernosa, the parts of the penis that engorge with blood in an erection. The consequent permanent erection can be an embarrassment, and it interferes with urological diagnostic procedures. An alternative is a hydraulic inflatable device. Clients are generally satisfied with these, although many report less frequent intercourse than expected; indeed, some seem content to just have the device and don't use it much.

It should be noted that the idea of a prosthesis is not a modern scientific invention, as is documented in this true anecdote reported by R. O'Hanlon in his book *Into the Heart of Borneo* (1984).

"But Leon, when do you have it done? When do you have the hole bored through your dick?"

"When you twenty-five. When you no good any more. When you too old. When your wife she feds up with you. Then you go down to the river very early in the mornings and you sit in it until your spear is smalls. The tattoo man he comes and pushes a nail through your spear, round and round. And then you put a pin there, a pin from the outboard motor. Sometimes you get a big spots, very painfuls, a boil. And then you die."

"Jesus!"

"My best friend—you must be very careful. You must go down to the river and sit in it once a month until your spear so cold you can't feel it; and then you loosen the pin and push it in and out; or it will stick in your spear and you never move it and it makes a pebble with your water and you die."

"But Leon," I said, holding my knees together and holding my cock with my right hand, "do you have one?"

"I far too young" said Leon, much annoyed; and then, grinning his broad Iban grin as a thought discharged itself: "But you need one Redmon. And Jams—he so old and serious, he need two!" (pp. 82–83)

Injections into the penis, at the time sex is desired, of a vasodilator such as papaverine (although the maker, Lilly, disavows such use) or prostaglandin E, along with the alpha-blocker phentolamine, is effective in providing erections in 65–80% of cases. Those who do not respond are usually the very old, the very ill, and those with vascular impairment (so these administrations can have a diagnostic function as well). Aside from the requirement of self-injection, other drawbacks are the high costs and, in some cases, accumulated scarring, decrease of effectiveness over time, even abnormal liver functioning and priapism (a constant erection—an example of the old adage "Be sure of what you ask for; you may get it").

The vacuum construction device (VCD) is a moderately effective, noninvasive technique. The VCD is a cylinder that is placed over the penis and pressed against the body to produce an airtight seal. A vacuum is created, which engorges the penis, and rubberbands are slipped off of the end of the device, retaining the erection for up to 30 minutes. VCD-produced erections are less rigid although slightly larger than normal ones and are especially helpful with erectile dysfunction where vascular insufficiency is a critical factor.

However, the safest and generally most effective treatments for both arousal and orgasmic disorders are the psychological "sensate focusing" techniques pioneered by Masters and Johnson (1970) and the more sophisticated cognitive therapies, which are both used to help the client stop spectatoring (becoming too distanced from the act). These are particularly effective if carried out with a stable partner from the client's natural world. Sensate focusing is not a totally modern development: Sir John Hunter, a physician practicing around 1750, advised his clients to go home and lie in bed "a fortnight and caress and fondle." His only reported difficulty was that "no one ever completed the treatment."

Tim's actual treatment began with sessions with the psychologist to clarify his feelings about the relationship with his girlfriend, the guilt about sex he experienced at a less-than-conscious level, and his perfectionistic needs. Tim gradually felt more confident of his relationship with Pam, and he asked her to participate in the latter part of the treatment program with him.

This phase of treatment proceeded along the lines suggested by Masters et al. (1991). The therapist emphasized to Tim and Pam that they were to focus on the pleasures of fondling and petting, and for a period of time they were admonished not to proceed into intercourse. When they were doing well with this and also were becoming strongly aroused, the therapist suggested that they proceed to intercourse, but not attempt to reach orgasm. Eventually, as their arousal continued to be very high, intercourse was allowed and was successful. Other areas of their relationship continued to improve as they clarified the meaning and impact of their communications, and a year after the treatment they got married. The marriage helped with Tim's relationship with his parents, but he needed to work on clarifying his dependence on their approval. During some follow-up therapy sessions he was able to distance himself from this need, while retaining a caring relationship for them.

Tim enrolled in some refresher courses related to his work and also took up painting. All of these changes helped his self-esteem, which in turn allowed him to initiate new behaviors, thus creating a positive cycle, the antitheseis of the negative cycle often seen in psychopathology.

Female Psychosexual Dysfunction

**The Case
of Virginia**

I have a coded list of 23 names and numbers in my billfold . . . each time is like the first time all over again, a strain. It's a job. I'll have to do well. I liked it better when they thought they were doing us a favor. I'm sorry they ever found out they could have orgasms too. I wonder who told them.

—Joseph Heller, *Something Happened* (1966)

Many of the same treatment issues, as well as most of the diagnostic considerations, noted about the male psychosexual dysfunctions apply equally to the problems of female psychosexual dysfunction (Masters et al., 1991), and the reader is referred to the immediately prior sections. There is usually less significant personality pathology correlated with most cases of female psychosexual dysfunction. As the case of Virginia developed, it became apparent that vaginismus had to be dealt with first. Vaginismus is a condition in which the vaginal musculature goes into intense involuntary spasms, primarily in the bulbocavernosus muscle and also in the leviator ani muscles. As a result, intercourse is impossible or is accompanied by extreme pain (dyspareunia). Vaginismus is not necessarily associated with sexual inhibition or orgastic problems, although it often is, as we see in Virginia's case.

The Case of Virginia

Virginia had suffered with her problems most of her adult life, and indeed had seldom had any satisfactory sexual experiences. Yet she waited until 3 years into her marriage to report her difficulties to her gynecologist. This lag in reporting such difficulties is not uncommon in the sexual disorders. Virginia's gynecologist gave her a thorough physical examination, which revealed severe vaginismus, but no physical cause was found, a not uncommon finding. The gynecologist referred Virginia to a clinic that specialized in the treatment of sexual disorders. Virginia's husband was also referred to the clinic as it was clear that he also had some disturbance in the sexual area.

Virginia, who is 23 years old, is reasonably attractive and pleasant interpersonally. She was initially interviewed alone, during which time she talked about her childhood and adolescence as well as her present concerns. Virginia's family had lived a middle class existence in a small northwestern town. Her early life would best be described as stable and quiet. At the same time there was a repressive atmosphere regarding sexuality in the home. Both her father and mother avoided discussing it, and Virginia learned most of what she knew about sexual matters from her friends in school. Her mother did attempt to discuss menstruation with her. But when she did, she generally communicated the feeling that it was an inherently painful event and something that she should not talk about. Virginia naturally assumed that the whole business was shameful; in part this attitude contributed to the substantial pain she experienced during her menarche.

Virginia's father, nominally a Roman Catholic, did not practice his religion. Her mother, however, was devoted to her fundamentalist Protestant faith, and the church's admonitions that the expression of sexuality outside of marriage was wrong caused Virginia to experience guilt and anxiety on occasion. She began to masturbate regularly when she was 16 years old, and for quite a while felt very guilty about it. She had little difficulty experiencing orgasm in masturbation.

Virginia was allowed to go on group dates when she was 15, and to date individually when she was 17. Yet, because she was rather quiet and unassuming and did not run in the more active groups in her school, she had few dates until she met David, her husband-to-be. She was primarily attracted to him because he seemed "older and wiser" than most of the other men she knew. David was mild-mannered and passive, and even after they had dated for several months, they were still only giving each other a good-night kiss. They married after about 1 year of dating. At this point they had not done much sexually except mild petting.

Three months before they were married Virginia developed a vaginal infection, and she virtually panicked, fearing that she may somehow have contracted a venereal disease. She went to a gynecologist who was competent medically but did not have much of a bedside manner. He was a bit rough in the examination. He was also slightly sarcastic in telling her that she had no venereal disease, or as he put it, "Not likely," given her sexual history. Virginia came away shaken and upset and vowed never to go back to him.

Virginia and David's wedding went happily except for an uncomfortable moment when her mother attempted to give her a last-minute lesson about sexuality. The most positive thing she could say was that although it would probably hurt the first several times, it "wouldn't be that bad."

As is common when both parties have had little sexual experience, the honeymoon was a disaster. David's apparent maturity and wisdom did not extend into the area of sexuality. Virginia adopted the strategy that if she just remained quiet and passive, he would know what to do. David's role by default propelled him into taking initiatives, even though he knew little about what to do. He attempted penetration after only minimal foreplay and before Virginia had any vaginal lubrication. Virginia's vaginal muscles spasmed almost immediately, causing her intense pain. She screamed and David withdrew right away, confused as to what he did to cause the pain. They were both so distraught that they did not attempt intercourse again until the third night of the honeymoon. Virginia again had intense pain. This time she attempted to endure the pain, but it was clear to David that it was distressing her and he withdrew, soon losing his erection. They were both upset and embarrassed about the situation and avoided any further attempt at intercourse during the honeymoon.

Over the years they have only attempted intercourse approximately once or twice a month, usually with the same accompanying problems. They never have been able to continue intercourse to the point that either of them experienced orgasm. They eventually began to engage in mutual masturbation, yet both felt this was "not real sex," and they both reported being dissatisfied.

Virginia did not seek help for several reasons. She did not want to return to the gynecologist who had been sarcastic and rough with her, and she feared repeating that experience with another gynecologist. Also, she was quite embarrassed and hoped that her mother's prophecy that it would gradually be all right would come true. After 3 years the couple began to experience other problems in their relationship, largely because of their inability to communicate. Also, it was hard for them to find a way to express affection without having to consider the possibility of intercourse, which by this time they avoided at all costs. Virginia went to the phonebook and simply sorted through to a name she somehow felt comfortable with and made an appointment. Fortunately, this random selection led her to a gynecologist who was understanding of and empathetic with her situation.

Etiology

Virginia's background is not unusual for a woman with vaginismus (Lo Piccolo, 1985). She is not significantly pathological psychologically, although her background induced a substantial amount of sexual guilt and repression. Not only was she made to feel that sexuality was sinful, but, even more importantly, she felt that it was shameful and dirty. In addition, she received little accurate sexual information. As she grew up, she had to seek information from her friends, most of whom were equally uninformed. As a result, many of her general beliefs about sexuality crystallized around inaccurate information.

Consequently, Virginia basically rejected her bodily experiences; she saw them as intrusive and as a cue for anxiety. Although she was able to masturbate to orgasm, she experienced much guilt in the process.

The traumatic gynecological examination that she experienced shortly before her marriage also contributed to her problem. Again, this is not uncommon. Many women with vaginismus fear gynecological examinations, and any insensitivity on the part of the gynecologist increases the potential for vaginismus.

A major contributing factor was her husband's inexperience in sexuality. Any normal woman would likely experience some pain if penetration was attempted before lubrication had begun. Their mutual inexperience led them to attempt this, which exaggerated the pain experience already initiated by her own expectancies and prior experiences. Her mother's admonition that her initial sexual experiences would cause her pain led her to believe that the severe pain she experienced was a normal response. As a result, she did not immediately seek treatment and unfortunately she and her husband then repeated the experience in trials that reinforced the vaginal spasm sequence. Spasms became conditioned responses to all attempts at intercourse. From that perspective, vaginismus can be seen as a phobic response, an irrational anxiety that occurs in response to anticipated vaginal penetration. Anxiety and muscular spasms then naturally occur. The spasms cause intense pain, which naturally furthers the strength of the phobic response.

Treatment

The treatment for vaginismus can be fairly straightforward. In addition to brief psychotherapy and possibly mild tranquilizers, as well as counseling on how to facilitate sexual functioning and cognitive-behavior modification to correct any distorted beliefs that contribute or have developed, treatment may involve the use of dilators, graduated in size, that are inserted into the vagina until the vagina relaxes, with larger catheters gradually inserted over sessions. Masters and Johnson (1970) recommend that the partner participate in the insertion of the catheters and also suggest that he witness any pelvic examinations that occur in an effort to dispel any irrational fears he may have developed. It particularly reassures the partner that the vaginismus is not a direct response to his efforts at intercourse. Masters and Johnson (1970) report a success rate of 100% (probably an overestimation) with simple vaginismus using this technique. However, as in most cases, Virginia's vaginismus is compounded by other sexual problems.

Virginia and her husband participated in some simple sex education sessions, were then taught the technique of sensate focusing, and then moved on to using the dilators. The use of dilators is analogous to systematic desensitization therapy, in that the phobic anxiety that caused the spasm is confronted with an in vivo stimulus—that is, with something inserted directly into the vagina. The therapeutic effect occurs because the person is kept relaxed and comfortable so that the spasms ultimately subside.

The first dilator is very small. Her husband handled the dilator during insertion while Virginia guided his hand. Larger dilators are used as the muscle spasms decrease each time, and ultimately the husband guides the dilator himself.

The largest dilators, which are about the size of the erect penis, are kept in place for several hours. It may take 5 to 6 weeks of treatment with the dilators before actual intercourse is attempted. Virginia and her husband proved responsive to this technique, and in 4 weeks they were able to have intercourse.

Along with the use of the dilators, Virginia was taught the use of the "squeeze technique" because her husband had been experiencing occasional premature ejaculation. The squeeze technique has been highly effective in helping the partner delay ejaculation, thus prolonging intercourse. Virginia was taught first to manipulate her husband's penis to a full erection and then to place her thumb on the frenulum (on the underside of the front of the penis) with her first two fingers on the opposite sides at the top of the penis, one on each side of the ridge that separates the shaft from the glans. Squeezing hard at this point for about 3 seconds causes the urge to ejaculate to substantially lessen, and some of the erection is also lost. At first this procedure may be repeated every half minute or so, with gradually greater time periods interspersed.

When they were first allowed to have intercourse, Virginia initially used the largest dilator long enough to let her vagina relax fully. Before David inserted his penis, she employed the squeeze technique a couple of times and then straddled him in the female superior coital position. This position allowed her more control plus the ability to pull away if she began to have spasms. If the spasms did recur, they returned to working with the dilators until she again felt comfortable. At first, both remained motionless for a long time as they became used to the penis being in the vagina. Then David was allowed to thrust enough to maintain his erection and obtain some sexual pleasure, but it was emphasized to him to keep his movement very slow. Gradually the speed of thrusting is increased, the time of insertion is increased, and different sexual positions are attempted. When they show control throughout these variations, progression to orgasm is allowed.

Virginia and David were highly motivated, not only reflecting their mutual desire to enjoy the sexual experience, but also because of their deep caring for each other and the desire to make a good marriage. The combination of therapies took approximately 3 months and was very successful. It is highly probable that the success will continue.

Comment

Like Virginia (and the prior case of Tim), most sexually dysfunctional individuals are physiologically capable of adequate sexual performance. Most sexual dysfunction occurs when psychological factors inhibit what is normally a series of reflexive responses. Most individuals (male or female, or couples) who have any of the psychosexual dysfunctions often need to be challenged on underlying, yet common, problematic cognitive assumptions, such as (1) sex should be "perfect," "special," "ecstatic," "novel," "routine," etc.; (2) sex should occur "in bed," "in the dark," "somewhere exciting," "after a show of romance," "with all our clothes off," etc.; (3) without intercourse, it's not "real" sex; (4) without both of us having an orgasm, it's not "real" sex.

While not the case with Virginia, relapse among people treated for sexual dysfunction or inhibited sexuality is commonly reported. Success rates are much better when specific coping strategies for relapse have been taught and monitored. Such skills include role playing a discussion with a partner about a dysfunction occurrence; articulating and then replaying specific behaviors learned in therapy; using specific cognitive "mantras" such as "I was told this would happen, but I know it will pass," etc. (e.g., recovering heart attack victims may need to add mantras such as "It's absurd to think I'd die because of intercourse—I'll feel better"); reading positive information books or pamphlets; generating a sensual, romantic, and/or erotic mind-set; and undergoing booster sessions.

9

The Substance Use Disorders

Although we relish our combination of "Puritan" and "pioneer" traditions, the evidence is clear that we have an early tradition of substance abuse in the United States. In fact, a staggering amount of alcohol was consumed in early colonial times, in part abetted by the widespread and possibly accurate belief that drinking water those days was hazardous to health. Hard apple cider was the accepted substitute. It is also noteworthy that in the 1770s, New York had almost four hundred taverns, at a ratio of about one for every twelve adult males (compared to only twenty-two churches).

Unfortunately, modern Americans must deal with an increasing number of substances that are abused (Garner and Garfinkel, 1997; Petraitis, Flay, and Miller, 1995; Prochaska et al., 1992), and this is reflected in the *DSM-IV* (also, see Table 9–1). The first matrix in the *DSM-IV* system refers to those drugs that are commonly abused, such as marijuana (cannabis), cocaine, amphetamine, and heroin (opioids), and are given separate subcategories. Caffeine and nicotine use disorders are also included, the latter being especially important as a precursor to other forms of chronic substance abuse. Other categories in the *DSM-IV* are hallucinogens; inhalants; phencyclidines; sedatives, hypnotics, and anxiolytics; polysubstance use, and "other."

The "three *E*'s"—effect, expense, and ease of access—are the critical determinants of drug use patterns. But other factors especially impact on certain subgroups. For example, methamphetamine, or "crank" (so nicknamed because it was often hidden in the crankcases of the bikers and truckers who first popularized it in the 1950s), has become a favored drug of white females (along with "ice," the smokable form of methamphetamine). In addition to methamphetamine's potency and low cost, it appears to be favored by this group because of its concomitant weight loss effect and its availability from sources other than the violent gangs who provide so much of the cocaine.

TABLE 9–1 Controlled Substances

DEA Class	Characteristics	Examples
I	High abuse potential; no accepted medical use	LSD, heroin, marijuana
II	High abuse potential with severe physical and psychological dependence	Amphetamines, opium, morphine, codeine, barbiturates, cocaine
III	High abuse potential with low to moderate physical dependence and high psychological dependence	Compounds containing codeine, or narcotic analgesics
IV	Low abuse potential with limited physical and psychological dependence	Benzodiazepines, certain barbiturates, other sedative-hypnotics
V	Lowest abuse potential	Preparations with low narcotic levels

The terms *dependence* and *abuse* are seen throughout the *DSM's* substance abuse matrix, and they are defined similarly across substances.

Substance dependence is a maladaptive pattern, signaled by impairment or distress, with three of the following occurring in a 12-month period: (1) tolerance—need for greater amounts to achieve similar results or diminishing effect with use of the same amount; (2) withdrawal—individual symptoms for each substance or the use of the substance to relieve or avoid withdrawal symptoms; (3) unintended use of larger amounts or for longer than intended; (4) inability to control use or persistent desire for the substance; (5) high time cost to obtain, use, or recover from the substance; (6) giving up of important life activities because of use; (7) continued use in the face of use-related psychological or physical problems.

A diagnosis of *substance abuse* presumes no prior diagnosis of dependence. It does require impairment or distress from a maladaptive pattern within a 12-month period as evidenced by at least one of the following: (1) failure in a major life role obligation in some recurrent pattern; (2) recurrent hazardous behavior such as driving impaired; (3) recurrent consequent legal problems; (4) persisting use despite use-related socio-interpersonal problems.

Before proceeding further in this area, let us clarify several other terms that are common in the substance abuse literature.

- *Synergy*. A compounded effect resulting from using a drug combination. The effect is *antagonistic* if the effects of one or more of the drugs are reduced or canceled out, *additive* when the effect is a sum of the effects of the separate drugs, or *supra-additive* when the effect of the combination is greater than a sum of the separate drugs. A good example of supra-additive synergy is the lethal potential that results when relatively small amounts of alcohol and barbiturates are taken together.

- *Physiological dependence.* This state occurs when a drug that has been used for some time alters the user's physiological functions in such a way as to necessitate continued use of the drug in order to prevent withdrawal symptoms, such as happens with heroin, nicotine, and even caffeine.

- *Habituation.* Dependence on a drug because of a strong desire to replicate the psychological state produced by the drug and/or from indirect reinforcement of psychological needs, such as oral needs and relief of depression.

The "danger signs" signaling possible abuse are disruption in job, marriage, or other significant relationships; deteriorating financial or physical health; frequent job changes; an arrest record; complaints of anxiety, depression, or insomnia; and direct signs of addictive personality and social patterns. Reports of significant others are very useful, as is knowledge of addictive patterns in blood relatives. For instance, young males who from early on showed a high tolerance to the effects of alcohol are much more likely to later become alcoholic, and having had an alcoholic father is a strong predictive factor for young males.

Alcohol Dependence and Abuse

**The Case of
Betty Ford**

*I swear, a certain amount of beer can make a man
feel like he could beat cancer. (p. 16)*

—Larry King, *Of Outlaws, Con Men, Whores,
Politicians, and Other Artists*

Alcohol has been used as long as any drug available today and is used and abused in most societies. As far back as 8000 BC, in the Paleolithic Age, mead, an alcoholic beverage derived from honey, was used. Beer and berry wine were imbibed as early as 6400 BC. Alcohol has almost certainly been abused for as long as it has been used, and the costs to the abuser, physiologically and psychologically, have always been high. Alcoholism is especially costly to society at large in our present era, as it exacts an enormous toll through alcohol-caused accidents (especially auto accidents), disruption of family life, facilitation of violence in certain individuals, and inefficiency and loss in the business realm.

Alcohol is still the preeminent drug of abuse, as approximately 10–14% of Americans have problems with alcohol, and well over ten million are alcohol-dependent. Approximately 35% (these estimates vary considerably) of people with an alcohol problem have a co-morbid mental disorder.

The psychological euphoria from alcohol is functionally a toxic response. Alcohol is not digested but absorbed through the stomach and intestinal walls and metabolized in the liver by the process of oxidation. In this process, alcohol fuses with oxygen, and the resulting pure grain alcohol, or ethanol, is converted by enzymes to acetaldehyde, which is further broken down to acetic acid (vinegar).

The vinegar is then broken down by enzymes into water and carbon dioxide, which are passed out of the body. The liver can only break down approximately 1 ounce of one-hundred-proof whiskey per hour, assuming the person is of average weight. Any excess that cannot be broken down directly affects the brain, causing intoxication. Interestingly, even when males and females are of equal weight, this process is slower in females, making them more vulnerable to intoxication, for several reasons. Females have (1) more body fat, (2) less body water, and (3) a slower rate of alcohol metabolism. Also, given equal amounts of alcohol intake, females will develop liver cirrhosis faster. Whereas male alcoholics are more likely to carry a second diagnosis of antisocial personality disorder, female alcoholics are more likely to carry a second diagnosis of anxiety or depression. Women are more likely to drink in private and to show guilt about the behavior. A curious finding: On the average, nonalcoholic women report taking their first drink at an earlier age than alcoholic women.

Pharmacologically, alcohol acts as a depressant that first inhibits the higher brain centers and only later depresses the lower brain centers. The resultant decrease in control of overt behavior has led to the mistaken belief that alcohol is a stimulant. With continued alcohol intake there is a loss of the more complex cognitive and perceptual abilities and eventually a loss in simple memory and motor coordination.

It is interesting that part of the strength of the effect depends on whether people are getting drunk or sobering up. Because of a short-term tolerance effect, those who are sobering up generally appear less drunk and actually perform a bit better on short-term memory and perception tasks than those who have the same blood level of alcohol but who are getting high.

Long-term alcohol abuse is likely to result in central nervous system dysfunction or organicity, especially in older alcoholics (see Chapter 15 for relevant diagnostic considerations). This dysfunction is not simply a result of B-vitamin deficiencies from the poor diet that often accompanies chronic alcoholism, but is at least in part caused by the toxic effects of alcohol per se.

The Case of Betty Ford

Betty Ford is the wife of the thirty-eighth president of the United States, Gerald R. Ford. During her time as First Lady, she was a very influential positive force in America, speaking out about breast cancer and championing the women's movement. But it was not until Gerald Ford's defeat in the 1976 presidential election that Betty Ford's primary influence was manifest. On April 1, 1978, Betty Ford reluctantly admitted to her family that she was addicted to prescription drugs and alcohol. One week later she was in a local hospital to begin a month-long treatment program. Inspired by this treatment program and with a desire to help others and put a positive note on her disorder, she made plans to open a clinic for people with similar addictions (Ford and Chase, 1978, 1988; Weidenfeld, 1979). On October 3, 1982, the Betty Ford Clinic for drug and alcohol addiction was dedicated.

The Betty Ford Clinic is modeled after Betty's own treatment program. It has an intensive treatment program and there are few luxuries, beyond a beautiful environment and a large, caring staff. It is based on each individual's desire to recover. All those admitted, whether busboy or movie star, share rooms with three other roommates. The patients are required to work for their recovery and attend classes, lectures, and therapy sessions nearly every day. Although the clinic has often been in the media's eye due to the famous clientele that it serves, Betty has been quick to let everyone know that there is no special preference given to the rich and famous, and that financial aid is often offered to those who cannot pay for treatment. The Betty Ford Clinic is one of the most widely recognized names associated with the treatment of alcoholism and drug addiction.

Betty was born in 1918 and grew up in Grand Rapids, Michigan. Her father, a traveling salesman, was gone from the family home quite often. Her adored mother was a strong and principled woman who was a perfectionist and demanded the same standards in each of her children. Betty viewed her mother as a strong role model in handling adverse situations with strength and courage, never asking for help or letting the children know of problems. Betty's childhood was positive, pleasant, and "normal," the only dark shadow over her youth being her father's death when she was 16 years old, in 1934. Despite the Depression, insurance helped Betty and her mother and two older brothers to survive comfortably. Betty learned after her father's death that he had been an alcoholic; she had never known because he only drank while traveling on business and never at home. Betty's brother Robert was also an alcoholic.

Betty's first experience with alcohol was when she was a young child and her mother would put a teaspoon of bourbon in hot tea to ease an ailment; however, she remembers being a prude about drinking up until she was about 18 years old. Betty developed into a socializer, enjoying late nights of dancing and partying with friends. She worked as a model for a while at a local department store, but her dream was to go to New York and become a famous dancer. She went to New York when she was 20 years old, but like the great majority with that same dream, did not succeed. Under peer pressure, she began to drink more at social gatherings in New York. At her mother's urging, she returned home to Grand Rapids for a trial period of 6 months that ended with her staying in her hometown permanently. A while after her return to Grand Rapids, at age 24, Betty met and married a young man she had known in her youth. Betty claimed that what had made their courtship so much fun (partying at the local bars) was the very thing that ruined their marriage. She was ready for settling down and he was not. They divorced after 5 years.

Not long after, Betty met her current husband, Gerald Ford. Jerry (as Betty calls him) was a lawyer with a good reputation in Grand Rapids who was just beginning his political career. Betty describes him as "the most eligible bachelor in Grand Rapids . . . good-looking, smart, and from a good family." Their wedding plans were often dominated by Jerry's campaign for a seat in Congress—he was late for their wedding—and Betty received her first taste of what her life with Jerry Ford would be like. Jerry was an inexhaustible man who often put his work ahead of everything.

During the next several years, Betty became the mother of three boys and a daughter. Betty and her husband had and still do have a strong and loving relationship, and the couple shares an equally loving and strong relationship with the children. Betty often took the role of mother and father because Jerry was always busy with his job in Washington. It was during this time that Betty had the first of many medical problems. In 1964, she developed a pinched nerve in her neck that caused her excruciating pain. A hospital stay was needed and multiple treatments were applied—physical therapy, hot packs, and medications. Betty worried about her pain reoccurring after she went home from the hospital. When she voiced her fears to one of her doctors, she was told not to allow the pain to even begin and was given strict orders to keep her medications close at hand. This was the beginning of a vicious cycle: Betty would develop a tolerance of one drug and the doctors would simply prescribe a new one. Her pills became an avenue of escaping physical pain and made her more vulnerable to increased alcohol usage.

All of this had occurred just as her husband was beginning to gain a strong position in Washington. Betty began to feel lonely and unimportant. She tells of feeling like a doormat for her children and her husband and of her dreams of being someone important in the world being overridden by her role as her husband's behind-the-scenes support system. Her personal role models were always strong, independent women, like her mother, and when she compared herself to these "faultless" women, she felt like a failure. She often second-guessed herself, assuming that people could not like her or appreciate her for who she was. She was self-conscious that she had not made the grade as a dancer or obtained a college degree. She developed the attitude that "if I act smart and look smart, maybe people will think I'm smart." This attitude of "acting the part" helped her conceal her growing problem of addiction and alcoholism.

Over the years, Betty gave a few warning signals to many people that she had a problem. The first occurred in 1965, about a year after she began to drink alcohol while on her medication. She took her daughter to the beach and spent the whole day away from home, hoping that the rest of her family would become worried about her. As a plea for attention the stunt worked enough to get her an appointment with a psychiatrist. However, this physician said nothing about her alcohol use and chose to look at her self-esteem problems instead. Another warning signal was a diagnosis of pancreatitis. The treating specialist told Betty to stay away from liquor for a while. Jerry asked this physician specifically if Betty's pancreatitis was caused by alcohol. The physician responded that it was a possibility, even though it was known that alcohol is one of the prime causes of pancreatitis. Like most alcoholics, Betty was surrounded by enablers, including her physicians, friends, and family.

When Jerry Ford became President of the United States on August 9, 1974, Betty realized that, as First Lady, she had a renewed opportunity to be that person she felt was lost years ago. She became happier than she had been in a long time. Her schedule was busy with public engagements defending important causes. During her stay in the White House, Betty was diagnosed with breast cancer and subsequently had to have a breast removed. This, surprisingly, seemed to cause Betty little emotional turmoil (as she was happy to be alive), and she used it as another vehicle to become a positive force to the public, to become an advocate of all cancer victims. The experience did not, however, help Betty's dependence on drugs. She was now at a point that any physical pain was associated with the temporary comfort medications or alcohol gave her.

Although Betty enjoyed her time in the White House, she admits it was filled with pressure and that the pace kept was grueling. She describes nights when pills were the only thing able to bring on sleep and mornings when pills would get her started. During the "White House years," Betty often showed signs of the effects the pills and alcohol had on her. As her husband campaigned for re-election in 1976, Betty was constantly on the move, suffering from extreme pain caused by the pinched nerve in her neck and the emotional drain the campaign trail inflicted. Her medication and cocktails were the tenuous thread that kept her together during those final weeks.

After her husband's defeat and the move from the White House and the limelight in 1977, Betty's condition grew much worse. The couple had moved to California, into a new house they had built, and Jerry continued with his hectic schedule of public speaking engagements and meetings all across the nation. Betty's youngest child had moved out on her own, and the other children had long been living out of the home. This was a time when Betty was truly alone. Further isolation occurred as she declined social invitations. Eventually she had fewer close friends than she had in the past. She was on multiple medications and combined the pills with alcoholic beverages throughout the day. Her daughter Susan was distressed by her mother's illness and initiated a small "intervention" in which no other family members participated. This first intervention angered Betty and was a failure for the most part, but it gave the attending physician an idea of the magnitude of her illness.

The second intervention occurred just a few weeks after Betty's 60th birthday. This time all family members were present. During this intervention, which took Betty completely off guard, each family member relayed with love an incident in which her addiction had caused them pain. This was desperately needed because Betty felt that she did not have a problem because for so long everyone around her had covered up for her. Betty completely denied she had a drinking problem and justified her drinking by telling of the many cocktail parties she had been required to attend as First Lady. She argued she wasn't an alcoholic because she kept herself neat and tidy, was not a falling-down drunk, didn't drink in the morning, and didn't drink too much at the cocktail parties. She did admit a problem with the prescription drugs but resisted admitting to abusing alcohol. Each took a turn talking to her. For example, Betty's middle son, Jack, told of how he did not like to bring friends home for fear of what kind of state she might be in on that particular day. Her husband talked about a recent fall in which Betty had cracked some ribs and chipped her tooth.

The physicians on hand at the intervention later brought out a blackboard and listed every drug Betty took each day, how many times she took it per day, how much the dosage was, etc.; the amount was staggering. There was some fear that the detoxification process would be brutal, if not fatal. Faced with all of this, Betty still agreed that after a week-long detoxification (to be completed at the Ford home) she would check herself into a local naval hospital and begin a month-long treatment program.

Etiology

A review of information Betty has given in her autobiographies makes it evident that the substance abuse, especially her alcoholism, may have been caused by two key factors. First, there was a probable genetic predisposition for alcoholism, as Betty's father and brother were both alcoholics. Second, there were many psychological factors that may have been responsible for Betty's addictions. She lived many lonely years without a strong support system, due to her husband's absences, while raising four children. She endured time in the media spotlight for years, with her every move and word monitored, analyzed, and criticized. The stress was overwhelming.

Genetics play a part in alcoholism, although few researchers believe there is one single gene involved or that genetics alone *compel* one into alcoholism. More likely, many genes together *predispose* a person toward abusing or depending on alcohol. For example, young men who have a low response to alcohol (which is apparently genetically determined)—in other words, they have to drink more than other people in order to feel any effect—are at a substantially increased risk of becoming alcoholic years later.

It is also known that peer pressure and exposure to dysfunctional models for drinking behavior, as well as any societal acceptance and affirmation of dysfunctional drinking, play a major part in facilitating an alcoholic pattern. Behavioral scientists have identified many traits that seem to affect a person's propensity to drink, but alcoholics may have countless combinations of these traits. Alcoholics tend to have different sensitivity to alcohol than nonalcoholics: They may eventually develop tolerance for large amounts of alcohol and dependence on its effects; they may feel rewarded when they drink and suffer withdrawal when they don't. Temperament may also play a role in drinking. Alcoholics tend to be more aggressive, hyperactive, and prone to risky behaviors. Any or all of these traits may be inherited.

The general progression into alcohol dependence is as follows:

1. *Prealcoholic phase:* Social drinking and an occasional weekend drink are the major symptoms. Both tolerance and frequency of drinking increase, usually slowly. Alcohol use serves primarily as an escape from anxiety, mild depression, or boredom.

2. *Initial alcoholism:* Tolerance, frequency, and abuse increase. More is drunk per swallow; often there is a shift to more potent drinks. Disruptive-dysfunctional behaviors and/or depression often increase, along with loss of self-esteem over drinking patterns. Occasional blackouts occur.

3. *Chronic stage:* True loss-of-control patterns (such as drinking throughout the day and using any source of alcohol) predominate. Inadequate nutrition affects functioning and physical health. Signs of impaired thinking, hallucinations, and tremors emerge.

The disease model that is dominant today generally assumes that: (1) substance abuse disorders, particularly alcoholism, reflect a physiological disorder, possibly genetically determined; (2) abusers have virtually no control over their intake of the substance because of this dysfunction; and (3) with some substances, especially alcohol, they permanently retain their status, even when they are able to abstain.

The assumptions in the disease model of substance abuse have been shown to be not entirely true in their implications. For example, some alcoholics are able to return to a pattern of social drinking even after many years of chronic alcohol abuse. In the 1960s, D. L. Davies, a British physician and alcohol researcher, published data to show that a few people who were treated for alcoholism eventually returned to a pattern of normal or moderate drinking and did not relapse into alcoholism. Since that time, others have noted similar data, leading to an alternative goal to abstinence, but one that works with only a relatively small subset of "problem drinkers" (as opposed to true alcoholics). Those who are younger, are regularly employed, show only modest symptoms of problem drinking, and have a relatively unremarkable family history for drinking are candidates for a "reduction" rather than an abstinence approach. There is also clear evidence that many alcoholics, even while in the status of chronic alcoholism, can refrain from the first drink (a bedrock assumption in Alcoholics Anonymous).

Treatment Options

As with Betty Ford, most alcoholics who have been chronically imbibing will need an initial period of detoxification, especially in light of the mild confusion and memory and concentration problems commonly found as acute withdrawal symptoms in the 1 to 3 weeks following the cessation of drinking. In addition, a period of hospitalization or other controlled living environment may be necessary to keep them from giving in to strong immediate habits that would return them to drinking.

The first critical steps in the treatment of alcoholics are simply getting them to admit they have a problem and then getting them involved in any ongoing treatment program. Hence, some form of "motivational enhancement therapy," typically involving confrontation techniques, may be necessary. During consensual data gathering, it is good to write down critical agreements and pieces of data, for the alcoholics to refer to later if short-term memory is temporarily impaired. Another helpful approach was first pioneered by Craigie and Ross (1980), who used videotape to model self-disclosing behaviors and treatment-seeking behaviors with a group of alcoholics in a detox unit because, as with many disorders, people have to learn what it takes to be an effective "patient."

From a general treatment perspective (Garner and Garfinkel, 1997; Perkinson, 1997), several techniques can be employed:

- *Detoxification.* Many alcoholics need an initial period of detoxification to "dry out." This stay in a hospital or other controlled living situation also keeps them from giving in to compelling habits that would return them to drinking.

- *Medication.* Naltrexone, actually an opiate receptor antagonist, has proven to be effective in reducing the need for alcohol. Buspirone, a nonbenzodiazepine anti-anxiety drug, is useful for alcoholics in long-term recovery, particularly if they have a propensity toward anxiety symptoms. When depression is an issue, the SSRIs (selective serotonin reuptake inhibitors) appear to be most useful (Schuckit, 1996).

- *Antabuse.* Antabuse, which causes severe nausea if alcohol is consumed, can be helpful in controlling the immediate impulse to drink, although the effects of the medication can be easily bypassed by simply not taking it (this bypass could be eliminated by a time-release, implanted form). Antabuse helps adequately functioning alcoholics who want to change, but even with them it is generally accepted that the drug is of little use as the sole or pre-dominant intervention technique (Schuckit, 1996).

- *Self-help group.* Some form of a self-help facilitation process, such as provided by AA or a similar group, is often highly beneficial. The benefits of AA are discussed right after this list.
- *Family therapy.* Because alcoholism is extremely disruptive to family life, family and/or marital therapy is often necessary to repair damaged relationships, as well as to help maintain abstinence.
- *Aversion therapy.* Aversion therapy can help control specific problem behaviors unique to the client.
- *Relapse-prevention coping skills.* Cognitive-behavior approaches teach techniques for achieving and maintaining sobriety, such as coping with potential drinking situations, managing thoughts and urges about alcohol, and learning ways to refuse a drink. The critical first step is learning to recognize and prepare active coping strategies for high-risk situations. Most relapse occurs as a result of a negative emotional state, peer pressure, or a distressing interpersonal conflict.
- *Psychotherapy.* Alcoholics commonly experience conflicts, anxiety, and self-esteem problems. A variety of psychotherapy techniques can be of help with these problems.

In recent decades the consensus opinion on the appropriate primary psychotherapy treatment thrust was as follows: (1) People with greater alcohol dependency, greater desire to seek meaning in life, and a social environment that promotes drinking should do best with a twelve-step facilitation such as AA because it provides spiritual support and a new social network that encourages abstinence. (2) People with high cognitive impairment and people with severe psychological problems should improve most with cognitive-behavioral therapy because it directly addresses these co-occurring problems. Because women experience these problems more than men, research indicates that they should also benefit best from this type of therapy. (3) People with low motivation to recover but without severe psychological problems or social pressures to drink should have the most success with motivational-enhancement therapy.

However, this consensus has been called into question. The largest clinical study of psychotherapies for alcoholism, Project MATCH, completed in 1996, an 8-year, multisite study funded by the National Institute on Alcohol Abuse and Alcoholism (NIAAA), randomly assigned 1726 alcohol-dependent people to one of these three psychosocial treatments and concluded that all three of these treatments worked, but they all worked equally well with different types of alcoholics. The only significant effect of matching was for patients with few psychological problems, who did better in twelve-step facilitation therapy than in cognitive-behavioral therapy. (The NIAAA published three treatment manuals that detail the treatment protocols. For information on obtaining the manuals, contact NIAAA's Scientific Communications Branch at (301) 443-3860 or access its web page at http://www.niaaa.nih.gov.)

There is no question that Alcoholics Anonymous (AA) is still a predominant treatment. Continued contact and long-term cognitive retraining are just two of the advantages of AA, founded in 1935 by New York stockbroker Bill Wilson and Ohio surgeon Bob Smith. A favorite AA saying is "Stinkin' thinkin' leads to drinkin'." In addition, AA forces alcoholics to openly acknowledge they are in need of help, and it gives them a new social network composed of nondrinkers, as well as a strong support system they can call on when they are tempted to drink. Although AA's data supporting the claim of high rates of success are at times flawed methodologically, AA has clearly been helpful to persons who have trouble with impulse drinking, who need a new social network, and who are able to work within the somewhat rigid demands of the AA belief system.

Once alcoholism has developed, 9 to 15 months are usually needed to adjust to an alcohol-free lifestyle. But many alcoholics can achieve a relapse-resistant recovery within 2 to 3 years. For many alcoholics the ability to have fun and enjoy life (and, as a result, to be more pleasant to have around) is a state-learned behavior (rather than a trait)—that is, it has become associated with the use of alcohol. Total abstinence means the loss of conditioned cues for enjoyment of life behaviors. Without relearning the "skills" to have fun and enjoy life, some recovered alcoholics become tedious to be around, further fraying relationships with friends and significant others. Helping recovered alcoholics develop these lost skills is an area ignored by most therapists.

Prevention of Alcoholism

The following should be included in any program for prevention of alcoholism at the family and community level.

1. Recognize that alcohol abuse patterns start to consolidate in the 11- to 15-year age range, much earlier than most people imagine. Recognize that genetic and modeling factors are both important.

2. If children are to be allowed to drink alcohol at all in later life, introduce it to them relatively early and only in moderation.

3. Associate the use of alcohol with food and initially allow its use only on special occasions; de-emphasize its value in controlling feeling states.

4. Provide a consistent model of low to moderate drinking; use beverages such as beer and wine that have a low-alcohol content, rather than hard liquor.

5. Make sure there is a thorough understanding of and agreement on the family rules for what is and is not allowed about drinking.

6. Never associate drinking behavior with evidence of attainment of adulthood or other identity accomplishments.

7. Label excess drinking behaviors as stupid and in bad taste rather than as "cool" or stylish.

8. Label help-seeking behaviors in people who have an alcohol problem as evidence of strength rather than weakness.

9. Encourage alcoholism education in community and public health programs and, even more effectively, support restrictions on both the availability and use of alcohol in certain settings and age groups.

Before turning to the issue of prescription drug abuse, consider the specific and relevant pattern of the student alcoholic.

The SA—Student Alcoholic

Alcohol is like love. The first kiss is magic,
the second is intimate, the third is routine.
—Raymond Chandler, *The Long Good-bye*

College people love to refer to people and phenomena by initials—GPA, RA, SATs, GREs, etc.—hence the "SA" for the student alcoholic. College is a time when much learning takes place. Unfortunately, not all of it is positive.

A preeminent expert in this area is Dr. Alan Marlatt, a professor of psychology and a researcher at the Addictive Behaviors Research Center at the University of Washington. Recognized as an expert on alcoholism in general, for many years Marlatt has specifically studied drinking behavior in student populations.

Marlatt has found that for many students, college is a place where drinking increases, for some students markedly so. He found that peer pressure and expectancies (often inaccurate) about sexual arousal and social acceptance increased the amount students drank and that, in addition to formal treatments, such practices as exercise, meditation, and involvement in community activities could decrease drinking. Also, even more than adults, young adults are most likely to relapse in the presence of nonabstinent peers.

One preventive intervention developed by Marlatt is a 6-week cognitive-behavioral program that challenges common beliefs about the "magical" effects of drinking, such as increasing confidence and sexual responsiveness; teaches students how to drink more safely by being aware of their drinking habits, such as how much they drink, where they drink, and what they do when they drink; and suggests alternatives to drinking, such as exercise, nonalcoholic parties, and community work. The program significantly reduced binge drinking among small groups of college students.

Such programs are especially useful with students identified early on as "at risk," that is, those who have a family member(s) who is alcoholic or have shown predictive patterns like consistent binge drinking, a high tolerance for alcohol, drinking when alone and/or depressed, or having had a DUI or other alcohol-related offense or problem.

Several antidrinking measures at the student-community level can also be helpful:

- Responsible beverage service policies that include no pitchers, minimal "happy hour" promotions, and waiters trained to be sensitive to excess drinking
- Programs to discourage liquor stores and parents from providing alcohol to people under 21
- Beefed up enforcement of drinking and driving laws
- Zoning to regulate the number of drinking establishments and their hours of operation

Prescription Drug Abuse

The *DSM-IV* differentiates a number of substance abuse patterns but does not specifically discuss a pattern called "prescription drug abuse." However, I feel that this is an important pattern because it is defined by a focus on the common characteristics of clients rather than on the specific drug that is abused, an approach that often cuts across personality patterns. Drug companies and physicians should openly acknowledge at least some degree of responsibility for the high level of prescription drug abuse in our society.

The common signs of prescription drug abuse are: (a) efforts to make sure prescriptions are quickly filled; (b) efforts to develop back-up prescriptions and/ or physician contacts; (c) resistance-avoidance toward any health care professional who begins to confront the pattern; (d) increased contacts with sympathetic health care workers; (e) depression and anxiety increase, especially if prescriptions-refills are delayed or renewals are threatened; (f) withdrawal from standard interests, friends, activities; (g) increased use of alcohol to supplement the effects of the pills.

Polysubstance Dependence

The Case of Elvis Presley   The term "polysubstance abuse" is also not included in *DSM-IV,* nor was it in prior versions of the *DSM.* However, there is in *DSM-IV* the category Polysubstance Dependence, in which a person has used at least three different substances (not including caffeine or nicotine) for at least 6 months, with no substance predominating. The polysubstance abuse of nicotine, alcohol, and marijuana is often the "gateway" from adolescent drug abuse to dependence. The relative neglect of polysubstance abuse reflects an essential feature of our society: the belief that there is a particular remedy for virtually any physical or psychological disorder that occurs (Garner and Garfinkel, 1997). The polysubstance abuser usually combines the expectancy that an external agent will take care of all problems with a high need for new experiences or sensation seeking.

The Case of Elvis Presley

Elvis Aaron Presley is one of the most well-known and popular entertainers of our time. His music and charisma changed the music industry and left such an impression that he was later called "The King" of rock and roll. From his first hit recording in 1956 to his untimely death in 1977 at the age of 42, Elvis Presley lived under heavy public scrutiny. It was not until just before his death that his public began to realize how he was deteriorating. As a result of many destructive personal habits, the most devastating being the abuse of prescription drugs, Elvis's health had begun to fail at an alarming rate. On August 16, 1977, he fell dead off of the toilet. The book he was reading at the time of his death was *The Scientific Search for the Face of Jesus.* Both an autopsy and toxicology test were administered; from the toxicology test it was determined that the key cause of death was an overdose of several prescription drugs. It is interesting to note that, even in the face of the evidence and personal history of Elvis's prescription drug use, several doctors testified in court that Elvis did not die of an overdose and, almost absurdly, that his drug usage was not out of the ordinary. The exact cause of and circumstances surrounding the death of Elvis Presley continue to be subjects of debate; however, the fact that The King severely abused prescription drugs is, without a doubt, fact.

Elvis Aaron (misspelled "Aron" on his birth certificate) Presley was born on January 8, 1935, in the small, rural town of East Tupelo, Mississippi. His family was poor and moved quite often. His father, Vernon Presley, was a friendly, vivacious man; his mother, Gladys, was considered a good mother and wife. When Elvis was about 4 years old, his father had some trouble with the law and spent 3 years in prison. As a result, Elvis's relationship with his father was distant. On the other hand, his relationship with his mother was extremely close. She was known to be obsessively protective of her only child. Many family members felt Gladys bonded so closely with Elvis because she had been pregnant with twins. Elvis had a twin brother who was stillborn. As a result of the difficult birth, Gladys could not have any more children. Elvis became the center of her world, and she devoted all her love and energy to protecting and raising him. Family members remember Elvis's mother being very tense and anxious after the birth of Elvis and reported that she would often take medicine for her "bad nerves" and to help her sleep.

Elvis had a reasonably happy childhood, aside from the problems already noted. In 1949, the Presley family moved to Memphis, Tennessee, in hopes of finding steady work. Elvis remained in Memphis until his music career took off. He graduated from high school, and his first recording, a 45-rpm recording of "Blue Moon of Kentucky" and "That's all right (Mama)," was published on July 14, 1954. In 1954, he debuted at the Grand Ole Opry and by 1956, under the controlling hand of Col. Tom Parker, Elvis Presley burst into the media and music scene. His first actual television appearance was on March 5, 1955, on the "Louisiana Hayride," and his first national television appearance was on January 28, 1956, on Tommy and Jimmy Dorsey's "Stage Show." From 1956 to 1958, Elvis had numerous hit records and made a few movies. His stardom reached unbelievable heights; he eventually had 142 gold records worldwide. However, in March 1958, he was drafted into the U.S. Army, and this marked a turning point—not in his career, as was first feared, but in his personal life. Before Elvis left for the army, he phoned his mother to tell her the news. She refused to speak with him. For the first time in his life, he was alone, without the support of his mother. After Elvis left for the army, his mother's physical and emotional health deteriorated. Over the next several months she was noted to be in a constant state of depression, broken only by fits of anger. She began drinking alcohol heavily, was eventually diagnosed with hepatitis, and died in August 1958.

The death of Gladys Presley marked a period of isolation for Elvis. After his release from the army in 1960, he made several unimpressive records and movies. He felt he had lost his creativity and consequently began to distance himself from fans and the world. In 1968, at age 33, he married Priscilla Beaulieu. Priscilla asserts (and is believed by many who knew both her and Elvis) that she slept with him in his bed for 6 years before they were married and that she was a virgin when she married. Nine months later they had a daughter, Lisa Marie. Elvis had his first number-one hit in 7 years, "Suspicious Minds," in 1969. But by this time he was an emotionally drained man whose living habits had become destructive. He began to be promiscuous sexually, and his sleeping schedule was out of sync. He would sleep from 8 A.M. until 4 P.M. and party from 4 P.M. until the early morning hours. His eating habits were poor, with meals consisting of high-fat, fried foods in excess. Perhaps most destructive of all was his increasing dependence on and abuse of prescription drugs.

From the time Priscilla sued for divorce in 1973 until his death, Elvis's weight and drug use markedly increased. Many close friends felt that after Priscilla left, he simply gave up. Elvis had little privacy. He felt his life and destiny were out of control; amid the love and admiration he received he grew more and more alienated and alone. He experienced numerous physical disorders and drug-induced incidents, often collapsing or behaving inappropriately on stage or canceling tour shows. In 1973, after discovering that Priscilla was involved with another man, he had to be heavily sedated for several days. In the same year he experienced problems with his throat that affected his singing. In 1974, he almost collapsed on stage due to a high fever and thereafter began to spend days in his room at Graceland in complete isolation. In 1975, he was admitted to a hospital for a liver problem, but it was rumored that it was for detoxification. For a while after this trip to the hospital, Elvis seemed to be content. However, in 1976, his drug use again increased. During the years after his divorce from Priscilla, Elvis's behavior fluctuated from highly irrational to severely depressed. In 1974, he began going on wild spending sprees, often visiting car dealerships and buying every car on the lot, giving the cars away soon after. Gross amounts of money were also given to charities, with the amounts increasing over time. He began to have "giggle fits" on stage, not being able to control himself and often breaking into hysterical laughter for no reason at all. When a gun was thrown onto the stage at one of his concerts, he played with the gun for a while, much to the confusion and apprehension of the crowd. He often seemed confused, and he sweated profusely. He almost encountered a lawsuit when, at a late-night party, he was wrestling with a woman and "accidentally" broke her ankle. The crew at his shows reported that he was very irritable and always looking for a fight. All of these instances were offset by periods of seclusion and depression, and his drug abuse continued to increase.

In the 32 months prior to Elvis's death on August 16, 1977, his personal physician, Dr. George Nichopoulos, allegedly prescribed nineteen thousand doses of drugs for Elvis. He asserted that many of the pills given to his patient were placebos and was acquitted of drug charges. Elvis relied on sympathetic doctors and pharmacists and friends in cities all over the United States to fulfill his demand for prescription drugs, such as codeine, morphine, Valium, Quaaludes, and Demerol. His common excuse for getting the prescriptions filled was "tooth problems," and he often explained late arrivals at concerts by telling the crowd he had a dentist appointment. One of his pastimes toward the end of his life was to study medical and prescription drug reference books; he did this to avoid deadly combinations of the pills he was taking. The day before his death he had a dentist fill a prescription for Dilaudid, a painkiller.

Although the exact cause of Presley's death is still debated, there is no denying his extensive use of prescription drugs. Not surprisingly, Dr. Nichopoulos vehemently denies that his patient's death was caused by polypharmacy, but he will admit that Elvis's health was "controlled." He explains that Elvis took pills for sleep, a colon problem, and for high blood pressure and that these were not "happy pills." He may be accurate in the literal sense; there is little evidence that Elvis was very happy at this time. David Stanley, who worked closely with Elvis, feels that his death was most likely a suicide caused by drug overdose, because in the bathroom where Elvis had just died David saw three empty pill packets (called "attacks") lying near Elvis's body (Stanley and Loffey, 1994). Three of these pill packets contained a total of thirty-three pills and nine shots of Demerol. This is an enormous amount of medicine, even when taken at 3- to 4-hour intervals, yet it appeared that Elvis had taken the medicine in a shorter-than-normal period on this occasion. The coroner ruled, in a decision supported by several physicians, that Presley had died of a cardiac arrhythmia and not of a drug overdose, as the amounts of drugs in his body were alleged to be too low to point toward death by overdose. The autopsy report reads that he had heart disease, clogged arteries, and a distended liver. However, it is important to note that the toxicology report from the Bio-Science Laboratories in Van Nuys, California, states that Presley died of polypharmacy, a report strongly attacked by the autopsy physicians. But the evidence from the report is staggering. The report lists the following drugs as present in Elvis's body tissues: codeine, steroids/ACTH (used for colitis/bowel problems), Valium, ethchlorvynol (a sedative/hypnotic), Demerol, Amobarbital (a short-acting barbiturate used to help bring on sleep—sedative/hypnotic), phenobarbital, and Methaqualone (Quaaludes—there was a very high amount of this drug found in the tissue).

Comment

There may be evidence of some predisposition for addiction from the accounts of Elvis's mother's drinking and dependency on pills to help her relax and sleep. His mother also showed signs of depression and anxiety—signs that Elvis showed as he became famous. And his father showed at least some antisocial patterns. No doubt the immense pressure Elvis felt from his occupation and the consequent alienation and seclusion that accompanied his fame were also factors, as was the willingness of his physicians and dentists to provide medications.

As can be seen in this case, abusers could be described as psychotics without the loss of reality contact: They show deterioration of behavior in a wide variety of arenas (work, school performance, interpersonal relationships, and motivation), especially if they have been abusing drugs for a substantial length of time. Affect is generally flat, or, when emotion is manifest, it is quite labile. As with the alcoholic, there are often many protestations of future positive change, and, also like the alcoholic, the promises are seldom fulfilled (Perkinson, 1997). These protestations do not appear to be a manipulative deception, as the person seems intellectually committed to changing, yet the motivation and behavior necessary to actuate that change cannot be generated. Such protestations did not occur with Elvis, as no one had enough influence or leverage to obtain such promises from him.

Nicotine Dependence

**The Case of
Dr. S.**

He fought a hard battle. Some of his last words were: "Take care of the children. Tobacco will kill you, and I am living proof of it."

—Louise McLaren, talking about her son Wayne McLaren, the "Marlboro Man" of cigarette ads, when he died in July 1992 of lung cancer

In 1492, Luis de Torres and Rodrigo de Jerez, two of Columbus's crew, observed natives of Cuba drying and then smoking some plant leaves. De Jerez tried it himself, apparently becoming the first confirmed European smoker. When he tried it back in Spain, his countrymen were alarmed at the smoke coming out of his mouth, assumed him to be possessed by the devil, and imprisoned him via the Inquisition. Unfortunately, this did not prevent his legacy from being returned to North America. The first English settlement, at Jamestown, floundered economically until John Rolfe, the future husband of Pocahantas, planted some tobacco seeds. The plants flourished, and tobacco became the critical cash crop.

Smokers in general are about 50% more likely than nonsmokers to require health care each year, and the smoke they disperse is harmful to those around them. Historically, efforts to deter people from smoking, such as warnings from the Surgeon General's office, have had only limited effects, and those who do quit are extremely vulnerable to relapse. In the seventeenth century even Turkish sultan Murad IV's campaign of torturing and executing those addicted to tobacco was not overwhelmingly effective, nor was a 1683 Chinese law that authorized beheading simply for possessing tobacco.

Seven major factors are usually considered to be crucial in initiating and maintaining tobacco addiction. The primary factor is the physiological addiction component, although researchers such as Saul Shiffman have found a small subgroup of smokers who can regularly and moderately smoke without becoming addicted. The addiction apparently stems from nicotine's role in speeding up and intensifying the flow of glutamate, a neurotransmitter that causes a sharp increase in the firing rate of synaptic signals flashing through the brain. Much of this intensification occurs in the limbic system, whose physiological activation acts as a reward system for the brain. Other factors are: (1) modeling and ease of access to tobacco, promoted by significant peers, authority figures, and media idols; (2) peer pressure, especially for early adolescents; (3) genetic predisposition; (4) habit and ritual; (5) the paradoxical tranquilizing effect of nicotine on the chronic smoker (pharmacologically it is a stimulant); and (6) the fulfillment of personalty needs (such as oral eroticism) (Petraitis et al., 1995).

It is difficult to set out clear diagnostic-test correlates for nicotine abuse or dependence given (1) its legal acceptance by society, (2) widespread patterns of accepted daily usage, (3) society's traditional tolerance of smoking by adolescents, and (4) society's failure to clearly discriminate use from abuse. The *DSM-IV* does offer a diagnosis of Nicotine Dependence, defined by the same criteria as other substance dependencies. Of those people who continue to smoke regularly through age 20, 95% will become nicotine-dependent.

The Case of Dr. S.

As a result of a severe flu attack at age 38, Dr. S. experienced an irregular heartbeat. His personal physician and colleague, Dr. F., told him that his habit of smoking cigars had caused it and advised him to stop smoking. When Dr. S. tried to do so, he became depressed and occasionally suffered an even worse pulse rate. After several attempts at stopping, he returned to smoking about twenty cigars a day. He developed cancer of the jaw at age 67. Despite thirty-three operations and the removal of his entire jaw because of various cancerous and precancerous conditions, Dr. S continued to smoke. At age 73 he developed angina pectoris (chest pains from heart disease), which was relieved whenever he stopped smoking. Yet, although he continued to try to stop smoking, he could not. He died from cancer at age 83 after many years of severe suffering from operations, cancer, and heart disorder.

Comment

Unlike most of the cases in this book, this is not a recent case, as Dr. S. was born on May 6, 1856, in Freiberg, Moravia (now part of Germany). And the fact that Dr. S. is Sigmund Freud offers strong testimony to the difficulty of changing this behavior. Every tactic imaginable has been used. Most of these efforts have had either no or limited success; none has shown complete success. Even in an intensive resident (inpatient) program that combines all the techniques and medications that seem to help, for example, at the Mayo Clinic, the success rate is no better than 40%. In many cases, individuals are able to control their smoking significantly during the treatment phase, only to remit gradually afterward. The relapse rate is very high. A single "lapse" that consists of smoking more than one or two cigarettes leads to a resumption of smoking almost 50% of the time, and virtually all who relapse twice eventually resume smoking. Heavy smokers are most prone to relapse.

Treatment Options

There is some consensus on what techniques (best delivered in the context of a psychotherapy) seem to help (Meyer and Deitsch, 1996; Petraitis et al., 1995):

- Increasing delay strategies—gradually but increasingly delaying smoking the first cigarette of the day up to the point of quitting—and/or the use of a planned "quit day"
- Use of drugs like naltrexone or buproprion to mute craving and/or obsessive focus components

- Use of nicotine, via patch or gum, to fade the addiction component
- Use of a short-term and/or "as needed" prescription for psychotropic medication to mute anxiety, depression, and apprehension, especially during the first few weeks or months
- Use of hypnosis and/or relaxation training to develop long-term methods of coping with stress and situational anxiety and to enhance motivation
- Counseling, along with follow-up queries on progress, from the primary care physician, with a continued emphasis on the need to quit
- Use of rapid smoking techniques to create aversion-extinction responses
- Attention to diet and exercise to enhance self-esteem and physiological health
- Direct treatment of any concomitant disorders such as depression or anxiety
- Participation in a support group
- Work with significant others to facilitate their support of attempts to change

A successful quit typically proceeds in the following stages:

1. *Consideration of change:* The individual talks and thinks about the possibility of quitting and the personal ramifications.
2. *Crystallization:* A goal to actually quit is accepted. Cost–benefit analyses (e.g., health reasons) are explored. Lists should be prepared to concretize expectancies about annoyances, personal costs, relapse traps.
3. *Concrete preparation:* The commitment to quit is finalized and a time to quit is picked, preferably a relatively stress-free period. Anti-stress mechanisms (e.g., hypnosis, yoga, prescription for benzodiazaprenes, contracts with significant others) can be put in place.
4. *The "just do it" phase:* The move is made, with preparations put into action. New behaviors to fill "smoking time" are put in place. Smokers are avoided. Some coping strategies are activated to deal with the actual experience of the addiction, which continues for 3–6 months, and the change in metabolism, which can lead to weight gain.
5. *Maintenance:* A more healthful lifestyle (physically, emotionally, and spiritually) must be put in place.
6. *Anti-relapse:* The possibility of some relapse is expected (approximately 45% do remit within 1 month), and coping for that is planned ahead of time. Enhanced mechanisms to avoid relapse are put in place (e.g., a public commitment to anti-smoking campaigns, allowing family members to destroy any tobacco products).

Continued success usually requires that the significant persons around the smoker be supportive of a change to nonsmoking. Friends and family (particularly if they are also smokers) often give lip service to the smoker's pledge to quit, only to subvert—consciously or unconsciously—such efforts. As with many other substance abuse patterns, prevention is more efficient and effective than cure. The combined efforts at prevention and treatment have caused the smoking rate in U.S. adults to drop from 42.2% in 1966 to approximately 15% in 1998, and the rate continues to fall. The smoking habit persists most strongly in lower socio-economic classes.

10

The Eating Disorders

Eating disorders have become epidemic in the United States—indeed, in most affluent cultures (Garner and Garfinkel, 1977; Agras, 1995; Friedman and Brounell, 1995). The first case, of Karen Carpenter, examines anorexia nervosa. The second case, of Princess Diana, focuses on bulimia nervosa.

> *Ask your child what he wants for dinner only if he's buying.*
>
> —Fran Lebowitz, *Social Studies*

Anorexia Nervosa

The Case of Karen Carpenter

> *We're still generally a hideously fat people with immense bubble butts.*
>
> —Julia Child, TV chef and cookbook author

Anorexia nervosa is literally translated as "not eating because of nervous causes." The essential requirements for a diagnosis of Anorexia Nervosa, according to *DSM-IV,* are refusal to maintain body weight at or above 85% of expected minimum normal weight for age and height or failure to meet that 85% minimum during periods of growth; intense fear of gaining weight or being fat, even though underweight; and related body image distortion or denial of seriousness of current low body weight.

Anorexia nervosa was traditionally seen primarily in middle and upper socio-economic classes of women. However, in recent years, anorexia as well as bulimia is increasingly observed in preadolescent girls, adolescent and young adult males, and older women. It typically occurs first during puberty as a young woman becomes more conscious of her self-image (Wolman, 1998). Over 75%

of cases originate between age 13 and 18; about 1 in 200–250 females in this age range can be expected to develop the disorder, and follow-up studies estimate long-term mortality rates at between 5% and 15%. Sexuality may be channeled into the eating area, as these women usually avoid sexual acting-out. After the "sin" of eating, they may resort to self-induced vomiting and laxatives to "cleanse" the body of food. Anorexia nervosa is less common in males. When it does occur, there are systematic differences from female anorectics. Males are less likely to diet or to use laxatives, are often less conscientious about school, are less likely to have had large appetites premorbidly, are more likely to over-exercise and to report enjoyable sexual experiences, and are less likely to die from the condition. Anorectics who also show episodes of bulimia (binge eating) in general are more disturbed than anorectics who do not (Garner and Garfinkel, 1997; Agras, 1995).

The parents of anorectic are typically very controlling, yet caring, individuals. The anorectic appears to use the disorder as a statement of independence from the family in the narrow area that she can control. The salient personality characteristics are excessive dependency and sensitivity, introversion, perfectionism, and subtle but persistent selfishness and stubbornness (Bruch, Czyzewski, and Suhr, 1988).

Anorectics without bulimic characteristics are typically shy, passively controlling, perfectionistic, confused about sexuality, and stubborn. Bulimics who are also anorectic are more likely to be extroverted, industrious perfectionists who attempt to control their peers in direct ways. Many bulimics weigh in at normal levels, while others are obese; anorectics are almost always cadaverously thin. Both groups come from families in which food is a focus, as in socialization or recognition. Anorectics will often cook exotic meals for others, although they may eat only a small portion themselves. Bulimics do not usually like to cook because they are afraid they will eat all the food before the guests arrive.

The Case of Karen Carpenter

Karen Carpenter is known best for her velvety smooth voice that charmed the country from the late 1960s through the 1970s. Songs of Karen and her brother John, such as "We've Only Just Begun" and "Close to You," are still heard on the radio. Charming and gregarious, Karen idolized her brother and loved music. Karen's life appeared idyllic, which made her battle with anorexia nervosa difficult for many, including her family, to comprehend.

The Early Years
Karen Carpenter was born on March 2, 1950, into a family of her parents, a brother 3 years old, and a 13-year-old cousin. At age 4, Karen was taking lessons in ballet, tap, and acrobatics. She frequently sang with her adored older brother. Karen was often teased for being overweight as a child; her family referred to her weight as "baby fat."

When Karen was in grade school, she was known as a tomboy, playing ball games in the street and her front yard. While she played outside, her brother practiced the piano. Karen always acted cheerful, even when others knew she was down. Karen's teachers remember her as energetic, motivated, and sincere (Coleman, 1994).

The Teens

When Karen was 13 and her brother 16, the family moved to California to provide opportunities for John in music. Karen was still cheerful and bursting with energy, as well as willing to eat any sweets that came her way. In high school she was known as a good basketball player. While Karen was very friendly and outgoing, her brother was not well liked. He did not do well in school or in sports, and Karen often protected him at school (Coleman, 1994). Despite this, Karen idolized him. When Karen was 14, she started playing drums in duets with her brother. By her late teens and early twenties, Karen had joined John in public musical performances. Strong-willed, uncompromising, ambitious, and intense, her brother was in charge of the band, the music, and Karen. He was known as a genius and Karen was depicted as a singer who played the drums. Karen let her brother run their careers, while she kept meticulous track of appointments.

When she was 17, Karen, whom her brother called "Fatso," weighed 145 pounds. Big hips were "in the family," and Karen's mother said there was no getting rid of them. Karen lost 25 pounds and stayed around 120 pounds from age 17 to 23.

When Karen was 19, Herb Alpert (of "Tijuana Brass" fame in the 1960s), signed Karen and her brother to produce albums for A & M Records. At this point in her career, Karen was urged to come out from behind the drums and sing center stage. Extremely reluctant, Karen ultimately agreed. With no drums to protect her, Karen became more self-conscious about her appearance. At age 20, Karen's recording of "Close to You" was a best-seller. Karen regarded her brother as the reason for their success.

The Family

Karen never seemed to stand up to her mother, who always showed a preference for Karen's brother. While Karen's father was passive and conflict-avoidant, her domineering mother functioned at a high anxiety level. She was the family disciplinarian and kept a spotless home. She wanted Karen to stay near home so she could keep control over her. Karen felt this control keenly when, as an adult, she tried for more than a year to tell her mother that she wanted to move into her own place. If Karen received a compliment, her mother would point out how her brother was even better. The message was that Karen should never be placed higher than her brother. Karen felt unattractive, overweight, and inferior to her older brother.

Physical affection was not displayed in Karen's home because her mother felt it was not necessary. A friend of 23 years reported she never saw Karen's mother show Karen any type of physical affection—never a farewell hug or kiss from her parents when Karen left on tour. The Carpenter family structure was like a straitjacket. Friends described Karen as starving for love and recognition from her parents. The whole family, including Karen, was devoted to her brother and his career.

Karen's brother followed in their mother's footsteps. When he and Karen performed, he would set everything up and Karen would simply come in and sing. Known as a tyrant in the studio, John kept Karen constantly under his thumb. Karen saw herself as inadequate and her work as never quite good enough.

The Celebrity

As Karen's career soared, she became more obsessed and perfectionistic. Her home was spotless like her mother's, everything organized to the extreme. Karen was still obsessed with her weight. When she was 23, she saw herself on television and criticized her fleshy arms and thick butt. Her brother agreed. After reading reviews critical of her weight, Karen began dieting.

It is hard to tell when her anorexia started because Karen had always been concerned with her weight. Her family first noticed Karen was not eating at a family dinner when she was 24. She had lost weight to the point that her rib cage showed through her clothes. She thought she looked wonderful while those around her gasped at her appearance. Adept at hiding her disorder, Karen repeatedly said that she was almost through dieting and denied any problem. When eating out, she would order something different from the others and then avoid eating by offering everyone a portion of her dish. She spent hours each day trying to burn off calories by exercising excessively.

At age 26, Karen took 2 months of bed rest at home to recover from exhaustion. She started missing rehearsals and shows because she was continuously sick with one virus after another, as her immune system began to fail. She became addicted to laxatives, and, in order to burn up more calories, she took ten times as many thyroid pills as were prescribed.

The Final Years

At age 30, Karen married a man after knowing him only a few months. The wedding ceremony was extravagant, reflecting her dreams for a happy marriage and family. Within a year the marriage fell apart. Karen's husband openly admitted he was a dictator when it came to ruling over her.

Karen saw several therapists in California for her anorexia and then moved to New York, where she was hospitalized and then treated as an outpatient. Her therapist said Karen never felt cared for and was intensely lonely. The family showed little interest in Karen while she was in New York. Her brother disapproved of her for getting outpatient treatment.

Karen's therapist developed the impression that her family just wanted him to fix her, like a machine. Despite this lack of support, while she was in the hospital, Karen went from 83 to 108 pounds and overcame her addiction to laxatives. Unfortunately, she insisted on leaving New York after 6 months of treatment.

It is believed that, after returning home, Karen started swallowing ipecac, an over-the-counter drug that induces vomiting, every night, eventually increasing her intake to an entire bottle. This drug was found in her system after death and could have facilitated her final heart failure (Diliberto, 1985).

Etiology

Like Karen Carpenter, anorectics are usually talented, ambitious, young, white, and female. Karen was one of the older victims of this disorder; it typically appears during puberty as a young woman becomes more conscious of her appearance. Karen's anxiety over her appearance increased with public exposure. Karen had the "Binge-Eating/Purging Type" of anorexia nervosa, evidenced by her use of laxatives in the early years and her self-induced vomiting in the later years. The other *DSM-IV* category, the "Restrictive" type, is defined as an absence of bingeing and purging. To give the reader an idea of what a full *DSM-IV* diagnosis would look like, here is Karen's probable diagnosis:

Axis I	307.1 Anorexia Nervosa, Binge-Eating/Purging Type, Severe
Axis II	Dependent Personality Disorder (Provisional)
Axis III	Hypothyroidism, acquired; malnutrition, protein-caloric, severe
Axis IV	Severity of psychosocial stressors: moderate
Axis V	GAF = 80 (a general estimate of her level of functioning for the prior year, in this case, the year before death)

Karen, like others who have anorexia nervosa, believed that she was too fat even when she was emaciated. Typically the anoretic sets an ideal weight goal; when that is reached, the goal shifts downward. Also typical of this illness is the anorectic's continuous fear of gaining weight. Even when audiences gasped at Karen's bony structure when she came on the stage, she continued to lose weight, yet kept her eating behavior a secret. She consistently denied she was ill and minimized the effects of her illness. Deception is central to maintaining this disorder.

Perfectionism, in both the anorectic and her family, is common. Like her mother's house, Karen's home was spotless and orderly down to the finest detail. Karen was never satisfied with her performance on stage. Perfectionism often goes with low self-esteem, the theory being that a person tries to make up for perceived inadequacies by doing everything perfectly.

One theory on how the cycle of self-starvation continues is that the person experiences a hurt, such as rejection, disapproval, or lack of control. Feelings of anger are turned inward and masked by an increased attempt to be perfect. Irrational thinking convinces the person that if he or she does more or better, things will improve. Perfectionistic living creates more stress, which further drives the person to escape through extreme eating behaviors (Agras, 1995; Bruch et al., 1988). Karen's living and working arrangements fit this hypothesis.

While growing up, Karen was teased for being fat, and her mother told her that being overweight ran in the family and it was unlikely Karen would be any different. As an adult, Karen continued seeing herself as fat even though she was severely underweight. Such a distorted body image is a prevalent characteristic of those who have anorexia nervosa.

A common theory of the origins of this illness focuses on the person's ability to control his or her life. Typically, anorectics feel powerless and overwhelmed by life and turn inward to exercise control over their bodies. Like Karen's mother and brother, the parents of anorectics are typically very controlling individuals. The anorectic uses the disorder to establish independence in one area over which she can keep control.

Treatment Options

General goals include weight restoration, treatment of physical complications, and a change in the relentless pursuit of thinness. Because anorexia nervosa often results in very severe—even life-threatening—weight loss, hospitalization combined with forced and/or intravenous feeding may be necessary. Nutritional counseling may be helpful, but one has to be careful to avoid moving into the anorectic's favorite battleground—food. At this stage a behavior modification program to develop feeding behaviors may be helpful, although the critical issue is deriving the reinforcements that can build up the feeding behavior (Agras, 1995).

A more psychodynamic approach has been found to be useful as a person moves into more normal functioning, with a focus on the ambivalence over dependency, the high need for perfectionism, and, as trust develops, the subtle selfishness and narcissism that emerge (Bruch et al., 1988). Family therapy is also likely to be necessary because so much of this pattern is related to interactions over dependency and control in the family.

Relapse prevention is critical with both anorexia nervosa and bulimia nervosa. Clients should receive exposure training for high-risk situations, as well as cognitive training to eliminate negative self-talk and to discriminate lapses from relapse.

Any person with an eating problem needs counseling about diet facts and simple control of eating behaviors, counseling of the type used with the more common problems of binge eating without purging, general obesity, and persistent-eating disorders. These facts can be modified to the specific eating disorder involved.

- Changing exercise amounts and energy-burning patterns in general is more critical in generating weight loss than changing diet amounts and patterns. But don't use this as an excuse to ignore the quality and quantity of your diet.
- There is a biological drive toward high-fat and very sweet foods, so control should be directed toward "what" as much as "when" and "how much."
- Weight loss is not hard to attain; maintenance of weight lost is.
- It is more difficult to lose weight during the second diet than the first.
- Most diets are broken in the late afternoon.
- Persons trying to lose weight must keep fluid intakes high. The body needs much more water and other fluids when undergoing weight loss.
- If activity level remains the same and there is a cessation of smoking, there will be a weight gain.
- For women, food cravings often increase in the days before their menstrual periods, so they are more vulnerable to lapses during these times.

Also, it is highly recommended that any person with an overeating or binge-eating disorder of any significance implement and monitor, via a diary, a day-to-day program based on general diet tips such as the following:

- Drink six to eight glasses of water each day, *at least*. This may be the single most effective technique.
- Eat a high-carbohydrate breakfast and avoid eating anything at least 2 hours before going to bed.
- Eat a salad or have a low-calorie beverage or a cup of soup before a meal, then delay eating any main meal for an extra 5 minutes. Hot tea is effective for many people.
- Slow down while you eat, chew longer, and savor flavors.
- Don't eat standing up, in front of the TV, while talking on the phone, in the car, or on the run. Try not to eat alone.
- Try to eat two or three main (but not large) meals and two smaller snacks every day at predetermined times so you develop a feasible routine. Don't wait until you are extremely hungry to eat.
- Avoid drinks with alcohol or sugar.
- Be creative. For example, visualize yourself eating slowly before you even sit down for dinner.
- Use thought control. About to binge? Yell "Stop!" or at least whisper it if you are in a public place.
- Avoid keeping food around, other than planned food.
- Brush your teeth after every meal; you'll be less likely to snack.
- Identify times when you are prone to binge or overeat and plan alternative activities that are not compatible with eating.
- Avoid weighing yourself unless it is specifically prescribed.
- Develop an exercise program that is effective and which you can comfortably integrate into your life. Make a decision to walk rather than drive whenever possible.
- If you find yourself thinking too much about food or body image, this may be because you have a conflict you haven't dealt with and/or you are anxious or depressed. Try to identify what's going on and take some positive, coping measures.
- Plan ahead as to how you will handle "tough" situations like being in a supermarket, at a party, etc. Drink a lot of water and a high-fiber snack a half-hour or so before you go.
- Set aside some time each day to reflect on how you are doing in this area and in life in general. Decide what you are doing well, affirm yourself for that, and visualize how you can improve in areas where you are not doing as well.

- Recruit help from family and friends and any other source of help that has meaning or usefulness to you. Be open about your decision to lose weight, ask them to help you, and then spell out how they can help.

Bulimia Nervosa

**The Case of
Princess
Diana**

*I drink too much beer and eat too much ice cream,
and if I don't swim, I will look like a little round
bowling ball, and it will be disgusting...*

—House Speaker Newt Gingrich

Bulimia nervosa is a chronic pattern of binge eating. Bulimia (from the Greek words for "hunger of an ox") is known as the gorge-purge syndrome. The essential features, according to *DSM-IV,* are recurrent binge eating, denoted by a sense of lack of control of eating, *and* eating in a discrete time period much more than others would normally eat; a minimum of two binge episodes a week for at least 3 months; recurrent, inappropriate compensatory attempts to control weight, for example, by diets, laxatives, or vomiting; and body and/or self-image distortion.

Blouin et al. (1992) found significant seasonal variations in bulimia. They found a high correlation of binge behaviors, but not purging behaviors or severity of depression, with number and occurrence of dark hours within the month, and a much higher overall rate of binging and purging in the winter months.

Bulimia nervosa affects individuals physically as well as emotionally (Agras, 1995). This is especially true when vomiting is the chosen method of purging. Essential nutrients are removed from the system during frequent vomiting, which increases the tendency to feel tired and depressed. Vomiting is reinforced because it alleviates both the pain of having too much food in the stomach and the guilt of having consumed too much food. In addition, the pain of vomiting causes the release of endorphins, which are chemicals that create a mild "high." Thus, the frequency of vomiting usually increases. After vomiting the system attempts to return its PH balance back to normal, but it is interrupted by the next bout of vomiting. All of this causes chaos in the system, which provides a basis for physical and emotional instability. Frequently the bulimic will often suffer from some related physical disorder.

Between bingeing episodes the sufferer usually diets, fasts, or vomits. Typically, bingeing and purging are kept secret, and as with Diana, the secret is well kept and the individual usually has a cheerful disposition and a demonstrated interest in helping others. Inside, however, there is often a great deal of unexpressed anger, as well as guilt and depression, both of which are apt to occur after bingeing. Also, as with other eating disorders, bulimics often have a distorted view of their body, seeing themselves as fat and ugly when in fact they are of normal weight.

The Case of Princess Diana

Princess Diana was a celebrity member of the royal family of Great Britain. From the outside, her life initially at least appeared to be the ideal story of a fairy princess. However, while facing tremendous turmoil in her private and public life, Diana struggled with bulimia nervosa and depression for years following her marriage to Prince Charles, the heir-apparent to the throne. The following description is based on Diana's own perceptions along with related accounts (Morton, 1992, 1994; Campbell, 1993).

The Formative Years

On July 1, 1961, in Sandringham, Norfolk, Honorable Diana Spencer, the third of four children, was born to Edward John ("Johnnie") and Frances Ruth Burke Spencer. Johnnie was not a kind husband. Frances, who married at age 18, stayed with him at least in part to give birth to a boy, who, unlike a girl, would be able to inherit the vast Spencer fortune. Before Diana was born, Frances had given birth to a boy who lived only 10 hours. The parents were shattered at the baby's death. They convinced themselves Diana would be the boy they wanted so much, and they were bitterly disappointed that she was a girl. Diana sensed, then learned of her parents' disappointment, and she felt guilty for letting them down.

Diana grew up in an atmosphere of privilege and noble heritage. Despite this, she was not snobbish. She occasionally socialized with the Queen and family, who lived nearby. Diana received a traditional upbringing including christenings, godparents, and discipline. During Diana's early years her family was very social. There were many birthday parties for the children and a yearly fireworks party. Despite these and other occasions that made Diana and her family appear ideal, at home Frances and Johnnie fought constantly. Diana remembers her mother weeping, her father not speaking, and her younger brother crying himself to sleep at night. With a tendency toward violence, Johnnie was known to have monumental rages as well as a drinking problem.

In 1967, when Diana was 6, two major events changed her life. First, her two older sisters were sent off to boarding school. Second, Frances left her family to begin a trial separation from Johnnie. This devastated the family and was a shock to British society, where divorce was considered embarrassing and extraordinary. Diana remembers having many nannies and many unanswered questions after her mother's departure.

Frances was branded as selfish for this move, but her children always cared a great deal for her. Her reason for leaving was that Johnnie was never good to her. Although he was a gentleman to outsiders and a kind father, he was emotionally abusive toward his wife. In addition, Frances had fallen in love with Peter Shand Kydd, a kind, witty, and wealthy man who was already married with children.

Frances was sensitive in explaining her departure, but she did not realize that except for a few occasional months with Diana and her 3-year-old brother Charles, this was to be a permanent separation. At that time, unless the mother was extremely incompetent, fathers were not usually given custody of the children. However, just by asserting her adultery, Johnnie was awarded custody. Frances then married Peter, who himself had just divorced. In part because of gossip in London, Frances and Peter moved to a distant part of England.

This parting and the subsequent divorce are topics that Diana would not discuss with others, even her close friends, until her adult years. Diana later reported that she felt rejected and alone, and her trust was violated. The sense of isolation may have been exacerbated by the formal atmosphere in the family, and neither Diana nor her parents were physically demonstrative.

Diana's distress was manifested in various ways, such as her tendency toward neatness, washing both herself and her clothes compulsively. She even offered to wash clothes for others. She dressed meticulously. She was constantly moving about, not staying with one activity for long. She began to be a compulsive talker and socializer.

Fortunately Diana adored her school, which was small, private, traditional, and disciplined. She impressed her teachers as well behaved, cheerful, yet playfully mischievous. Diana did not excel academically, and she panicked when taking exams, sometimes failing them because her mind "went blank." She liked to take care of the younger children and mothered her younger brother. Diana always had a large assortment of activities such as horseback riding and swimming available to her. She was an excellent athlete and talented dancer. Those who knew her were impressed with her positive, bubbly personality and her ability to get along with others.

Although some girls at her school were anorectic, Diana never seemed to have this problem and loved to eat. She did notice that she could gain weight easily, and when she did, she simply cut back a bit on eating. Avoiding such temptations as smoking or drinking alcohol, Diana was not as successful at resisting sweets.

Diana was upset when her grandmother died in August 1972. In 1975, her grandfather died, which meant that Johnnie was given the official title of "Earl" and Diana became a "Lady." Her father was in the process of moving to the home he had inherited, a famous landmark with an art collection considered one of the finest in Europe. Because she had a difficult time saying goodbye to her home of many years, Diane escaped during the packing and went to a beach house, where she gorged on food with a friend.

Another major change, which horrified Diana, was her father's affair and subsequent marriage to Raine, Countess of Dartmouth, a charming and dominating woman. Raine succeeded at controlling Johnnie, but she could not control Diana. As a result of her feelings toward Raine, Diana began avoiding visiting her father, yet was generally respectful to her stepmother.

The Prince Arrives

Prince Charles had dated Diana's older sister Sarah, who was struggling through anorexia nervosa. In 1979, Sarah introduced Charles to Diana, then age 16. Despite her sophisticated background, the teenage Diana was shy in unfamiliar settings, wore no makeup, and dressed in clothes purchased by her mother. Diana decided to drop out before completing finishing school.

After a frustrating attempt to teach dancing to groups of children, Diana decided to work at a kindergarten. She enjoyed this work. She also did cleaning or baby sitting occasionally. By September 1980, however, the press had identified Diana as Charles's new love.

Diana found Charles well settled (later, this would be seen as "rigid") in his daily routine. Charles seemed to enjoy his bachelor lifestyle, but many believed that the demands of his title compelled him to wed and produce an heir to the throne. Diana was excited by the attention he and others gave her when they were courting. Diana went wherever he directed. He called her "Diana"; she called him "Sir." She was certainly infatuated and probably in love; he probably never was in love with her. He proposed to her when she was 19.

Before their wedding, on July 29, 1981, Diana moved into Buckingham Palace for 3 months. Her first night at the Queen Mother's London residence was spent alone, not welcomed by any of the members of the royal family. Although she had a brief lesson from the Queen Mother in royal protocol, Diana felt unprepared to take on the duties of a royal family member. Up to the wedding, Diana felt isolated and cried frequently in the face of demands of the public, the press, and the royal family. This is when Diana first began purging food from her body after eating, usually by vomiting. Her waistline dropped from 29 to 23 inches.

Things unraveled rapidly. Diana asserted that she learned 2 days before the wedding that Charles intended to give Camilla Parker Bowles, his former girlfriend and wife of a member of the Queen's household, a bracelet with their nicknames, "Fred" and "Gladys," inscribed. The night before their wedding, Charles told Diana she should make the most of their last night of freedom. On their honeymoon, Diana saw pictures of Camilla fall out of his diary and later she noticed that he was wearing cufflinks with her initials. She reported vomiting four or five times a day during her honeymoon.

While Diana and Charles were gregarious in public, in private they argued continuously, frequently about Camilla. This, in addition to pressures from the press, caused Diana to continue vomiting. She sought counseling and refused recommended medication when she discovered she was pregnant. Allegedly, she sought Charles's assistance; however, she found him unresponsive. Finally, on New Year's Day in 1982, 3 months pregnant, she tearfully threatened to commit suicide. Charles did not take her seriously and began preparing to go riding. Diana then threw herself down to the foot of a wooden staircase, where she was discovered by a very shaken Queen Mother. Charles continued getting ready to go riding. Except for a few bruises, Diana and her unborn child were fine.

Diana's bulimic rituals became more frequent. Those around Diana continuously noticed her large appetite in stark contrast to her petite size. Examples include an evening when she ate a whole steak and kidney pie, and another evening when she consumed a pound of candy and later had a large bowl of custard. On one occasion, Charles commented on Diana being chubby, which triggered her to induce vomiting to rid her of her food. She later realized this helped her gain a sense of control and gave her a chance to express her anger.

Throughout the years of their marriage, Diana continued to feel threatened by Camilla. She reacted with more suicide attempts, which she considered to be cries for help. One time she hurled herself against a glass cabinet, and on a different occasion she slashed her wrists. Another time, while in an intense argument with Charles, she picked up a knife and cut her chest and thighs. Watching Diana bleed profusely, Charles only chided her. At the time, Diana explained these attempts as the result of having trouble adjusting to her new position. Actually, the trouble was the culmination of the bulimia, her problems with Charles, and the stress of consistent morning sickness. Although Diana was able to present herself well in public, she learned not to expect any praise from Charles or any other member of his family.

A major stressor involved dealing with the press. Diana consistently received more public attention than any other member of the royal family. At first the press nicknamed her "Shy Di." To regain privacy, she did things such as fleeing out of a fire exit of a store and climbing over garbage containers to avoid the press. Despite her fear of and frustrations with the press, Diana remained courteous to them. At first, when there were no devastating surprises, Diana was able to treat the media attention as a joke. However, soon it made her feel panicky. One of Diana's early experiences was agreeing to be photographed while with a couple of children from her kindergarten. What the photographers did not tell Diana was that the light behind her shone through her skirt, exposing a clear outline of her torso and legs. Diana, horrified, was reduced to tears when she saw the photographs.

Diana carefully monitored her appearance, keeping herself photo-ready at all times. Her taste in clothes and personal grooming was impeccable, and she sought guidance in responding to crowds. However, on a face-to-face basis, she needed no help dealing with people.

Diana gave birth to William, her first son and next heir to the throne after his father, in June 1982, and her bulimia temporarily ceased. Soon, however, some postpartum depression set in and the bulimia returned. She also believed Charles was becoming jealous of the attention she was getting from others and the press.

Diana's turmoil about Camilla increased. She panicked whenever Charles was absent unexpectedly. Once she heard him on the telephone saying, "I will always love you." Diana began to keep personal friends and family at a distance, and the royal family, already distant, began seeing Diana as a threat because of changes in Charles, such as his decisions to become a vegetarian and to quit shooting.

Diana was now chronically depressed. Her original infatuation with Balmoral, the Queen's highland retreat, waned. When she left Balmoral for Kensington, it was to seek psychiatric help, although the press accused her of returning so she could shop.

First Diana tried therapy with a Jungian therapist who primarily analyzed her dreams. This was not especially helpful for her, so she tried other therapists, who also did not seem to help. Her thoughts again turned to suicide, and she felt the press was persecuting her.

Despite her depression and bulimia, Diana slowly gained confidence as she toured the world and received abundant media attention. The media's focus on Diana seemed to increase the couple's already serious problems, and Diana was often physically ill. When Diana was pregnant with their second child, Charles made it clear he wanted a girl. When he saw the baby boy, Harry, he merely said a few words and then went off to play polo, which had a lasting impact on her feelings toward him.

Diana was visibly more confident in public. Once, while attending the ballet with Charles, she slipped away toward the end, put on a silk dress, and performed on stage, dancing to an arrangement of Billy Joel's song "Uptown Girl." The audience went wild, and in public Charles seemed amazed and pleased. In private he angrily told her she was undignified and too demonstrative. Her bulimia continued, and her self-esteem plummeted.

Charles left for extended periods of time, often spending time with Camilla, which was never mentioned by the press. Yet any social encounter, no matter how innocent, that Diana had with members of the opposite sex was front-page news. At one point, after Charles had returned from a long trip, Diana voiced complaints about the pressures from the press. This time his indifferent response caused her to decide that any hope of a loving relationship with him was gone. It no doubt also spurred her own involvement in a secret love affair.

When Diana heard from a friend that depression can result from mineral deprivation that occurs with bulimia, she again sought treatment. This time, therapy was somewhat successful. Consulting with a therapist specializing in eating disorders on a weekly basis, she began a slow recovery. At her therapist's recommendation, Diana read about her condition; she was reassured to learn that there were others like her. After 6 months Diana's former ritual of vomiting four or five times a day changed to once every 3 weeks. Relapses occurred when she was exposed to increased stresses within the royal family.

Diana's slow recovery took many turns. Over time, she turned for help to a hypnotherapist, an astrological counselor, a deep-tissue masseuse, an aroma therapist, an acupuncturist, a cranial masseuse, a practitioner of osteopathy, a clinician who gives regular colonic irrigations (a water treatment that cleanses the bowels), and a new-age therapist (similar to Primal Scream Therapy) who encouraged her to shout, scream, and hit a punching bag. Her bulimia remained under control, probably aided by all these procedures.

The relationship between Charles and Diana continued to deteriorate. Despite her troubles, Diana always respected the way the Queen handled herself over the years. A degree of peace came in 1992, when Diana and Charles finally agreed to separate, allowing Diana to continue her activities.

On February 9, 1996, Princess Diana agreed to a divorce, and the divorce became official on August 28, 1996. She received an estimated lump-sum settlement of 22.5 million dollars, the right to keep her jewelry and to continue living in Kensington Palace, and approximately $800,000 a year to maintain her private office. Her most important loss in the divorce settlement was losing the right to be called "Her Royal Highness."

Then, almost a year after the divorce, a fairy tale life paradoxically full of conflict ended tragically. Attempting to elude paparazzi (photographers of celebrities for the tabloids), she died early in the morning of August 31, 1997, at age 36, after the 600 series Mercedes she was riding in went out of control and crashed in a tunnel near the Eiffel Tower, the speedometer stuck at 120 mph. Her latest boyfriend, wealthy Egyptian playboy and film producer (e.g., the 1981 Oscar-winning *Chariots of Fire*) Emad "Dodi" Fayed, and the chauffeur were also killed; a bodyguard survived. One of the paparazzi, who immediately started taking photographs of the accident, was beaten by horrified bystanders. There is evidence that the driver was legally drunk, with a blood alcohol level of .23, and there was evidence of two psychotropic medications in his blood.

Etiology

In addition to pressure from society to be thin, it is believed that the most immediate triggers for the onset of bulimia include unusual or extreme stressors and feelings of loss of control (Agras, 1995). Diana's initial symptoms coincided with sudden demands from the press, the public, and the royal family to present her best appearance and be on her best behavior while at the same time harboring fears about Charles's commitment to her.

Striegel-Moore, Silberstein, and Rodin (1986) found that, although about 20% of bulimic women do not show any specific personality pattern, the other 80% are divided between those who show an obsessive-compulsive pattern and those who show more of a classic addictive pattern. Diana, with her constant cleaning and organizing, in addition to her continuously perfect appearance, fits into the obsessive-compulsive pattern.

In addition, several researchers (Striegel-Moore et al., 1986) note a number of other specific factors that increase the tendency to develop a bulimic pattern: (1) acceptance of a traditional feminine role, (2) middle to upper class social status, (3) attendance away at college or a boarding school, (4) early physical maturation, (5) a lower metabolic rate, (6) higher stress, (7) tendencies toward depression, (8) a prolonged history of dieting attempts, (9) family isolation, (10) a high valuing of appearance and thinness, and (11) a high belief in the ability to use one's will to control the self and the world. Diana's history includes most of these factors.

Another explanation is that bulimia may be related to continuous dietary restriction. The "natural weight" of many women is higher than what is required to match society's ideal image. While the body naturally seeks one weight, the woman struggles with long-term dieting to maintain a different one. Bingeing may occur when food intake is constantly restricted over a long period of time. The binge brings satisfaction, but guilt soon follows. Purging then relieves the guilt. This becomes a self-perpetuating cycle that allows the bulimic to satisfy food cravings without suffering the consequences.

Diana especially seemed to fit Hilde Bruch's pioneering descriptions and Agras's (1995) later explanation of predisposing variables of eating disorders and specifically of bulimia. Families of bulimics usually have upper socio-economic status and make a good impression. Privately, problems are either not dealt with or are handled poorly. Bulimics and anorectics tend to be model children. They grow up believing they must live up to their parents' expectations and prove to their parents they were good role models. When circumstances require giving up control, the girl dutifully complies and then uses bulimia to regain personal autonomy. Just as during the early years Diana's family gave the impression of being ideal, Diana herself consistently exhibited perfect social skills and the appearance of happiness and showed no evidence of having any problems.

Treatment

Cognitive-behavioral psychotherapy, even in group settings, has shown positive results in treating bulimia (Garner and Garfield, 1997; Chambless et al., 1996; Beck, 1976; Agras, 1995). This involves assessing dysfunctional beliefs that perpetuate bingeing and purging. Examples of beliefs frequently found in those with bulimia are "Pleasing others is more important than my own needs"; "I must do this to maintain my weight so I will appear attractive to the opposite sex"; "In order to be attractive I must look like the models on television"; "My body is fat and ugly"; and "If I do not purge my food, I will gain weight and people will not like me." When the client learns the sources of these beliefs and their inaccuracy, an underlying force for this behavior is removed.

Behaviorists have not spent much effort trying to formulate the etiology of bulimia. Rather, they have focused on devising token economy, aversion therapy, and contracting programs that have been useful in an overall treatment package (Bongar and Beutler, 1995). Family therapy, which includes an acknowledgment that this disorder at least in part reflects a disturbed family system, is usually necessary if the bulimic is to recover. A particularly difficult task here is to get family members to see that they are not doing this for the bulimic; rather, that the bulimic's disorder is in large part the natural evolutionary result of a specific system of family expectations, values, and controls (Agras, 1995). For adolescent bulimics, group therapy is particularly effective (Chambless et al., 1996). This provides a sense of control as well as a source of feedback.

Another treatment model for bulimia focuses on the anxiety that occurs after bingeing due to the client's fear of gaining weight. Vomiting is reinforced by relieving the anxiety. The client brings food to a therapy session that is used to binge and then eats it to the point at which he or she would normally vomit. Then, instead of vomiting, the client deals with the anxiety and is able to observe that the anxiety declines over time. This treatment is thought to break the connection between vomiting and the relief of anxiety.

Although it is known that Diana's problem with bulimia substantially subsided after 6 months of therapy, it is not known exactly what type of therapy was used. One thing that her therapist recommended that Diana reported as being very helpful, however, was reading books about her condition. This alone has been shown to be effective in the healing process for those motivated to recover from bulimia.

Diana refused to take medication for her condition. The medication that is sometimes prescribed for those with bulimia is anti-depressants. Serotonin reuptake inhibitors such as Prozac have been shown to be particularly effective because in addition to alleviating symptoms of depression they also reduce feelings of hunger.

It is difficult to determine which therapy is most effective because there are different ways to define improvement. Some believe that a higher self-esteem through more functional cognitions is the goal, while others believe the actual number of binge-purge cycles is the only way to determine improvement. Most likely a successful recovery will involve elements of all the different conceptualizations of this disorder.

Bulimia is difficult to treat effectively. Because of its secretive nature the disorder is usually well entrenched before help is sought. Thus, a major problem with treatment is the drop-out rate. Characteristics of bulimics that are associated with successful outcome include late-age onset, lack of prior hospitalization, shorter duration of the illness, less serious nature of the illness, fewer social stressors, and a good social or work history.

Conclusion

Because bulimia can be life-threatening, it is important to be aware of how a focus on dieting and physical attractiveness, and conflict over self-expression can meld into this disorder, particularly in middle and upper class women.

11

The Personality Disorders

The personality disorders are chronic, pervasive, and inflexible patterns of perceiving and responding to the environment that are sufficiently maladaptive to cause disruption in functioning and environmentally generated subjective distress. They are common patterns. People with a personality disorder are not typically as disturbed or as concerned by their behavior as are friends and relatives. People with a personality disorder view their own particular personality traits as ego-syntonic, that is, as consistent with their self-perception. Thus, persons with personality disorders are more likely to be brought to the attention of professionals by other people than by themselves, such as by spouses, relatives, or the criminal justice system.

The personality disorders are listed here in the "appearance clusters" suggested by the *DSM*:

Disorders That Appear Odd or Eccentric
Paranoid: hyperalert, suspicious, litigious, and authoritarian

Schizoid: asocial "loners," not "schizophrenic-like"

Schizotypal: "schizophrenic-like" but no consistent hallucinations or delusions

Disorders That Appear Dramatic, Emotional, or Erratic
Histrionic: emotionally flamboyant and dramatic, though shallow

Narcissistic: chronically inflated sense of self-worth

Antisocial: chronic antisocial patterns, does not learn from experience

Borderline: irritable, anxious, sporadically aggressive, and emotionally unstable

Disorders That Appear Anxious or Fearful

Avoidant: shy and inhibited, afraid to "risk" relationships

Dependent: seeks dependent relationships; naive, yet suspicious

Obsessive-Compulsive: controlled, formal, perfectionistic; "workaholics without warmth"

Passive-Aggressive: passively resistant through stubbornness, inefficiency, or threatened aggression (not included in *DSM-IV* as an official diagnosis, but only as an optional, secondary descriptive category)

The personality disorders are coded on Axis II in *DSM-IV*, which unfortunately can allow the implication that the personality disorders are not "clinical" syndromes, but rather are behavioral and psychosocial conditions, and thus are "less important." Although *DSM-IV* does not always disallow these diagnoses in children, the diagnosis of a personality disorder in a person under 18 is traditionally discouraged.

Personality Types and Their Potential Disorders

Although genetic and other biological factors may sometimes play a part in predisposing an individual to a personality disorder, the specific disorder patterns are learned and refined because they are effective, at least in the short run, in coping with that person's individual environment, and, most important of all, the environment they grew up in. Of course, the more distorted or disturbed that environment is, the more likely it is that a distorted coping pattern will emerge and become reinforced (Meyer, 1998b; Strupp et al., 1997). Yet the behavior pattern is seen as within the normal range of adjustment. Within this perspective, a personality type is a waystation on the developmental road toward a full-blown personality disorder. It is important to realize that we all fit reasonably well with one or more of these personality types. Table 11–1 describes the common personality types, along with the personality disorder they are most likely to become if they are exaggerated and crystallized.

The cases in this section were chosen to demonstrate the most important personality disorders, and the reader is also referred to the case of Perry, in Chapter 6. The histrionic personality disorder, described in the case of Hilde, is a common pattern, and often critical to the development of marital and family distress, as well as to eventual personal unhappiness because of negative social feedback. The antisocial personality disorder, the case of Theodore Bundy, exemplifies what is arguably the most common personality disorder and certainly the most socially destructive pattern. The case of Theodore Kaczynski is a good example of the schizoid personality disorder.

TABLE 11–1 Personality Types and Correlated Traits and Disorders

Personality Types	Typical Behaviors	Interpersonal Patterns	Thinking Styles	Mood-Affect Expression	View of Self	Probable Personality Disorders
Controlling	Manipulative, demanding	Authoritarian	Calculating	Disappointment, resentment	Unappreciated	Passive-aggressive, sadistic, paranoid
Aggressive	Bold, initiating	Intimidating	Dogmatic	Anger, distrust	Assertive	Antisocial, sadistic, paranoid
Confident	Poised, distant	Unempathic	Imaginative	Calm, unconcerned	Self-assured	Nacissistic, paranoid, antisocial
Sociable	Animated, engaging	Demonstrative	Superficial	Dramatic, labile	Charming	Histrionic, borderline, narcissistic
Cooperative	Docile, submissive	Compliant	Open	Tender, fearful	Weak	Dependent, compulsive, avoidant
Sensitive	Erratic, responsive	Unpredictable	Divergent	Pessimistic, hurt	Misunderstood	Passive-aggressive, borderline, avoidant
Respectful	Organized, formal	Polite	Respectful	Restrained, content	Reliable	Compulsive, paranoid, passive-aggressive
Inhibited	Watchful, preoccupied	Shy	Repressed	Uneasy, wary	Lonely	Avoidant, schizotypal, self-defeating
Introverted	Passive, quiet	Withdrawn	Vague	Bland, cool	Placid	Schizoid, schizotypal, compulsive, avoidant
Emotional	Energetic, engaging	Provocative	Distracted	Intense, frenetic	Interesting	Borderline, schizotypal histrionic, narcissistic

Source: Adapted in part from T. Millon and G. Everly, *Personality and Its Disorders* (New York: Wiley, 1985).

◢ *Histrionic Personality Disorder*

The Case of Hilde

It ain't bragging if you really done it.
—Dizzy Dean, All-Star pitcher, St. Louis Cardinals

The specific criteria that mark the histrionic personality disorder include dramatic and intense emotional expressions; efforts to gain the center of attention; and shallow, insincere, and disrupted interpersonal relationships (Kernberg, 1984). Such people are likely to overreact emotionally, even in everyday situations, and they are inclined toward suicide gestures as a manipulation of others. Somatic complaints such as "spells of weakness" and headaches are typical. Vanity and self-absorption are common traits.

Histrionic personalities appear to be emphatic and socially perceptive, so that they easily elicit new relationships. As they then turn out to be emotionally insensitive and with little depth of insight into their own role in relationships, they are likely to avoid any blame for the inevitable problems in the relationships. In this way, they are closer to the defense mechanism of paranoid patterns. Histrionic individuals are often flirtatious and seductive sexually, although there is little payoff if one follows these cues. The behavior of the histrionic personality resembles the traditional concepts of ultrafemininity, so for that reason it is more common in females than in males. Indeed, the Greek root of the term is *hustera*, meaning uterus.

Denial is a common approach to conflict in this pattern, often limiting intellectual accomplishment relative to potential, and there is a de-emphasis on analytic thought. As a result, histrionic individuals tend to be dramatic, yet gullible and impressionable.

> *Left to their own devices, the three networks*
> *would televise live executions. Except Fox—*
> *they'd televise live naked executions.*
>
> —Garry David Goldberg, Television producer

The Case of Hilde

Hilde is a 42-year-old homemaker who sought help from her family physician for a combination of complaints, including headaches, mild depression, and marital difficulties. The family physician had attempted to treat her with quick reassurance and Valium. When these proved ineffective, he referred her to a private psychiatrist. In the initial interview, she appeared to be motivated, although at times she rambled so much that he had to bring her back to the subject at hand. As one listened to her, it became apparent that she had not really reflected in any depth on the issues that she discussed and was only pumping out information much as a computer would. She delighted in giving extensive historical descriptions of her past, again without much insight (or even interest) as to how these had any causal role in her present distress. When confronted with any irrelevancies in her stories, she first adopted a cute and charming manner, and if this proved ineffective in persuading her psychiatrist to change topics, she became petulant and irritated.

When she described her present difficulties, she was always inclined to ascribe the responsibility to some person or situation other than herself. She stated that her husband was indifferent to her and added that she suspected he had been seduced by one of the secretaries in his office. This situation, along with a "lot of stress in my life," was given as the reason for the headaches and depression. When pressed for more details, she found it hard to describe interactions with her husband in any meaningful detail.

A parallel interview with her husband revealed that he felt he "had simply become tired of dealing with her." He admitted that his original attraction to Hilde was for her social status, her "liveliness," and her physical attractiveness. Over the years, it became clear that her liveliness was not the exuberance and love of life of an integrated personality, but simply a chronic flamboyance and an intensity that was often misplaced. Her physical attractiveness was naturally declining, and she was spending inordinate amounts of time and money attempting to keep it up. Her husband admitted that, when he had married her, he had been reserved and inhibited. He was a competent and hardworking individual but had had little experience with the more enjoyable aspects of life. He viewed Hilde as his ticket to a new life. Now that he had established himself on his own, and had both matured and loosened up emotionally, he had simply grown tired of her childish and superficial manner. As he put it, "I still care for her and I don't want to hurt her, but I'm just not interested in putting up with all of this stuff too much longer."

It is interesting that when Hilde was asked about her children, she immediately responded that they were both "wonderful." They were now 14 and 16 years old, and Hilde's description of them suggested that they were exceptionally bright and happy children. She was adamant about this, saying, "They are doing fine, and it's my problems that I want to deal with here." Unfortunately, her husband's description of the situation suggested that both children showed patterns analogous to Hilde's. They were both spoiled, and the oldest boy in particular had some difficulties keeping up with his schoolwork.

Hilde was raised as a prized child of a moderately wealthy family. Her father owned a successful grain and feed operation. Her mother was active socially, joining virtually every socially prominent activity in the city. She did not have much time for Hilde, yet delighted in showing her off to guests. Hilde was one of those individuals who is born with many gifts. She had potential for high intellectual achievement, easily adapted to all the social graces, and was almost stunningly beautiful. The sad part is that the family provided few if any rewards for achievements in the intellectual area. Hilde was expected to get decent grades, but there was no incentive for high grades, and the family often made fun of others in the town who were "intellectual snobs."

Her beauty was prized, and the response it received from friends in her parents' social circle also provided her with more than simple attention. Her mother delighted in having her stay up and greet guests at their parties, something she never consistently allowed Hilde's sisters to do. Also, Hilde soon discovered that if she misbehaved, a charmingly presented "I'm sorry" to her father usually voided any punishment.

As Hilde moved into adolescence, she developed a wide circle of friends, but she never attained much depth in any one relationship. Her beauty, social grace, and high status in the community made it easy for her to flit about like a princess among her court. Males came to her as bees come to a flower. She had a reputation for being loose sexually, but it is clear this was based on hopes and rumor rather than on actual behavior. As Hilde put it, "They like the promise—you don't really have to pay off."

Throughout high school, she was active as a cheerleader and as an organizer of class dances and parties. She was usually elected to be class secretary and once was the class vice president. No one ever considered her as a candidate for class president, and she herself would not have cared for the position. She had little trouble with her coursework. Although she seldom spent much time preparing, she usually obtained B's and C's, with an occasional A. Hilde remembers her junior high and high school years as "the happiest time of my life," an assessment that is probably accurate.

Hilde's college years were not unlike her high school years, except that some notes of discord began to creep in. She had to work harder to obtain the moderate grades she had always been pleased with, and she was not always able to carry through with the required effort, particularly as she was wrapped up in sorority activities and cheerleading. She dated many people but rarely allowed dating to get to the point of a sexual experience. When it did happen, it was more to try it out than as a result of any strong desires on her part.

After college, she took a job in a woman's clothing store whose clientele were primarily the rich and fashionable. One of her customers subtly introduced Hilde to her son, Steve, a young attorney with one of the most prestigious firms in the region. He courted Hilde in whirlwind fashion. They went out almost every night, usually attending the many parties to which they were both invited. Each was enraptured by the other, and they were married 5 months after they met. Both families had mild reservations about the short courtship. However, since each was from "a good family," no strong objections were lodged.

Over the years, Steve's practice developed rapidly. He not only had the advantage of being with an excellent firm, but was in addition both intelligent and hard working. Hilde meanwhile moved into many social activities, although she sometimes abruptly found that they demanded more than charm and attractiveness. In spite of her best efforts, her beauty is naturally fading, and the bloom has worn off the romance that impelled them into marriage. She and Steve seldom do anything together that involves a meaningful interaction. Most of the time he is absorbed in his work, and they only go out together on ritual social occasions. They seldom have sex, and usually only after Steve has drunk a bit too much at a party. There is not much conflict in the marriage; there is not much of anything else, either.

Etiology

The Greek physician-philosopher Hippocrates provided one of the original explanations for this pattern, holding that the unfruitful womb becomes angry and wanders about the body, causing hysteria. As is obvious, Hippocrates thought the disorder only occurred in women, a conception that has since proven to be inaccurate. Freud saw conflict over the expression of sexual impulses as critical. Interestingly enough, both Hippocrates and Freud prescribed marriage as the cure. As marriage would provide a legitimate outlet for sexual desires, in some cases this medicine might be effective although, as with all medicines, there are side effects, some not so desirable). In Hilde's case, marriage exaggerated the problem instead of curing it.

Her background has a number of factors that facilitate the development of a histrionic personality disorder. Hilde's mother showed little interest in her, except when she wished to show Hilde off, in essence responding to her as an object. A lack of consistent maternal attention can commonly produce intense strivings for paternal attention as a replacement, and this appears to have been the case with Hilde. Although her father obviously cared for her, he had little time available to attend to her. As a result, he, too, responded primarily to the superficial aspects of her being. Indeed, histrionics have often been raised in households where "showy love" and "act as if we love each other" ethics were primary and appearance was reinforced—and indeed may have been the only means effective in eliciting attention from and/or controlling the caregiver. Sickness or weakness, as long as it was not too repulsive, often was similarly effective.

In addition, both parents allowed Hilde to use her charm and physical attractiveness as an excuse for not fulfilling the responsibilities that are expected of most children. Hilde learned to deflect punishments with charm. So she never came to see her personality and decisions as the responsible agents in the problems she naturally encountered. As she grew up, other people often gave her the same allowance, although not to the degree her parents did. The inability to examine and respond effectively to the long-term consequences of her behavior was never reinforced and developed in Hilde.

As a result, Hilde made a wide range of friendships, but none with any real depth. They were oriented around social activities but involved little self-disclosure or sharing of personal vulnerabilities. Similarly, her parents never openly manifested their own personal vulnerability. They always put forth an optimistic and cheerful facade, even when it was apparent that they were having problems in their own lives.

It is most unfortunate that Hilde's potential for intellectual competence and analytic thinking withered in the face of the type of reinforcement she received from her family. The high level of attention to her physical attractiveness and social skills stood her in good stead during her adolescence. Physical attractiveness naturally decreases with age and does not carry one through the intricacies of any long-term relationship. Analogously, she had long ago learned to see her sexuality as a means of interpersonal manipulation and was never able to focus on the achievement of mutual intimacy and pleasure. It is as if she saw her responsibility ending at the point a male showed initiative behaviors toward her.

Her husband Steve came from a family that emphasized status, hard work, and vocational achievement. Hilde appeared to him as a guide to a new world, one in which pleasure, intimacy, and social activity were paramount. It was only when their whirlwind courtship, extravagant wedding, and expensive honeymoon were well behind them that the bloom went off the relationship. He gradually recognized the lack of depth in their relationship, and when he attempted to talk this out with Hilde, she became upset. She accused him of not loving her and of having another woman. She also responded by trying to make herself even more attractive. She did not age gracefully, and Steve even began to think of her as "pathetic" in this regard. Their meager sexual life dissipated even further. He eventually did start to see other women. Because he still cared for Hilde in a platonic way, he attempted to keep these affairs from her, and did so rather successfully.

By this time Hilde's father had become a kind of patriarch in the area. He was a man of great wealth who still enjoyed indulging his favorite and most beautiful daughter. Hilde emotionally moved back toward her family, although, like Steve, she kept up the facade of the marriage. She also became depressed on occasion and periodically drank too much. The cycle spiraled, as if at some level of consciousness she realized her own role in her problems, as well as her inadequacy to deal with them.

Treatment

Over time the following guidelines for intervention with a histrionic personality disorder (HPD) are indicated:

- Reward their product, not their presentation—the opposite of their behavioral history.
- Reward any attention to reflective thoughts or efforts toward systematization or routine behaviors—again, a real change.

- Emphasize appropriate assertiveness and mastery behaviors.
- Avoid the role of rescuer, understanding that you will be guided toward that role and toward feeling frustrated and/or responsible for any of the HPD's failures.
- Avoid the demands that the HPD be treated as "special."
- Writing assignments help develop analytic and problem-solving thought patterns (usually sorely lacking) and attention to detail.

The histrionic personality needs to challenge such common underlying beliefs as: (1) Unless my emotions at least appear intense, they won't mean anything to others (and eventually, even to me). (2) Being responsible or attending to details means the loss of "zest for life." (3) Rejection is disastrous. (4) People won't love me for what I do but what I pretend to be, or what I present to entertain/entice them. (5) Being "special" means never having to say "I'm sorry" (or at least I don't have to feel it or mean it).

In Hilde's case the first and most difficult task is to gain her trust. To that end several sessions were held in which the therapist adopted a posture not unlike that employed with the paranoid individual. He listened to Hilde's discussion with empathy, yet at the same time bemusedly offered alternative explanations for her behavior. He did not confront her directly, as it had been her life-long pattern, probably both as a result of temperament and parent training, to run away from any confrontation.

As trust developed, other therapeutic modes were tried in order to help her defenses gradually lessen. Bibliotherapy, or the reading of certain prescribed books, was used. She was asked to read various novels and plays that portrayed individuals who had grown up feeling as if they were appreciated for external rather than any ongoing essential personality factors. Of course, some of these individuals had developed coping strategies that were not unlike Hilde's. The works of Tennessee Williams, Edward Albee, and Jean Genet convey these concepts quite well. She was then asked to write her own poetry or short stories that focused on characters who developed similar defenses. This led eventually to the use of role playing. Her therapist would take the role of Hilde's mother, for example, and Hilde would play herself in some typical childhood interaction. It is also effective to role play the opposite roles, so Hilde would play her mother and the therapist would play Hilde as a child. This role playing was expanded to include interactions with her father, her husband, and some of her friends.

Unfortunately, at approximately this time, Hilde's husband told her that he had fallen in love with another woman and wanted a divorce. He refused to consider marital therapy, said that his decision had functionally been made long ago, and that he had only waited to find a woman with whom he could really become involved. Hilde made a mild suicide gesture, overdosing on a small bottle of aspirin, obviously hoping to manipulate her husband's decision. She was unsuccessful.

At this time, it was recommended to Hilde that she also enter group therapy. Her first reactions were that "those people won't understand me," and "I don't have really bad problems like they do." After the therapist was able to work through her defensiveness in this regard, she asked Hilde to commit to go to at least three sessions. It was agreed that if Hilde felt as if she could not continue after that, she could leave the group. Hilde made the contract and went for the three sessions. Fortunately, the group was supportive of her, something she needed at this point, particularly because of the divorce. It is also ironically probable that Hilde enjoyed this forum, in which she could dramatically replay many of the events in her life. She started to attend the group regularly and began to improve her ability to confront the responsibility she had for the events that happened in her life. She felt she could stop seeing her individual therapist, although at her last contact with her, Hilde was still struggling substantially with the problems of her world.

Antisocial Personality Disorder

The Case of Theodore Bundy

All universal moral principles are idle fancies.
—Marquis De Sade, *The 120 Days of Sodom* (1785)

The essential characteristic of the antisocial personality disorder (ASP) is the chronic manifestation of antisocial behavior patterns in amoral and impulsive persons. Persons with ASP are usually unable to delay gratification or to deal effectively with authority, and they show narcissism in interpersonal relationships. The pattern is apparent by mid-adolescence (usually earlier) and continues into adult life with consistency across a wide performance spectrum, including school, vocational, and interpersonal behaviors (Meyer, 1998a; Lykken, 1995; Hare, Hart, and Harpur, 1991).

The *DSM-IV* term "Antisocial Personality Disorder" has evolved through a variety of terms and now supersedes the terms "psychopathic" and "sociopathic," at least in formal diagnostic labeling. Pritchard's introduction of the term "moral insanity" in 1835 is considered by many to be the first clear forerunner to the present APD label. "Psychopath" first emerged in the label "psychopathic inferiority," introduced by Koch late in the nineteenth century (Cleckley, 1964).

Terms incorporating "psychopath" were common until the *DSM-I,* published in 1952, used "Sociopathic Personality." The *DSM-II,* in 1968, introduced the term "Antisocial Personality," which is used in the *DSM-IV.*

To apply the ASP diagnosis, the *DSM-IV* requires that the individual be 18 years old, there is a pervasive pattern of disregard or violation of others, and there is evidence of Conduct Disorder with onset before the age of 15, as supported by evidence of at least three of the following: (1) failure to conform to socio-legal norms as denoted by repeated acts that are grounds for arrest; (2) irritability and aggressiveness, as seen in repeated fights or assaults; (3) consistent irresponsibility in work or financial obligations; (4) impulsivity or failure to plan ahead; (5)

deceitfulness, as indicated in lying or conning; (6) reckless disregard for one's own or other's safety; or (7) lack of remorse. This category as it is formulated in *DSM-IV* is probably best conceptualized as "a deviant child grown up." APD apparently accounts for no more than about 30% of the overall prison population.

> When a man says he approves of something in
> principle, he means he hasn't the slightest
> intention of putting it into practice.
>
> —Prince Bismarck of Germany

The Case of Theodore Bundy

Theodore (Ted) Bundy was born on November 24, 1946, in Burlington, Vermont. Bundy was illegitimate. He never knew his father, nor does he remember ever wondering about him. Bundy spent his first 3 years in Philadelphia, where he remembers his grandfather with adoration. At age 4 he moved to Tacoma, Washington, to live with his uncle's family. Bundy was extremely upset when he and his mother moved away, leaving his grandfather behind. His mother met Johnnie Bundy, who worked at a local military base as a cook, at a church activity. His quiet, southern style attracted her to him. Like any child, Bundy reacted to his mother's romance with jealousy. In 1952, after Bundy's mother and Johnnie Bundy were married, they had their first child. Later they had three more children. All Bundy knew about babies was that his mother's pregnancy had something to do with Johnnie Bundy and that his mother suffered extremely while giving birth.

Bundy idolized his first-grade teacher, and she wrote superlative evaluations of Bundy and his academic skills. When this teacher left to have a baby, Bundy was very upset. His second-grade teacher, however, was a different story. He despised her, and remembers her breaking a ruler over his hand because he had punched a schoolmate in the face during lunch. The peculiar sense of unease that Bundy later identified as growing into the "entity" that murders, was already felt then, at age 7. He described it as simply a disturbing uneasiness.

Bundy recalls fondly his mother helping him with his homework. Throughout his school years, Bundy did well in school, and always receiving A's in major projects. He attributes his scholastic success to his mother's diligent efforts. There was never any discussion between Bundy and his mother about personal matters such as sex. He felt that his mother just couldn't be open with him. He described his mother as someone who didn't enjoy socializing or gossiping with others. She never discussed her childhood, either. However, right after high school, Bundy's mother had become pregnant by a man who came and left. Bundy's status as illegitimate haunted him throughout his life, abetted by his mother's evident resentment.

Bundy went to Sunday school every week through high school. He studied the Bible extensively, but felt he retained none of it. Bundy was politically oriented and remembers telling his mother about the hypocrisy of Christianity. His parents neither smoked nor drank. Johnnie Bundy, despite his quiet nature, had a violent temper when provoked. Ted never really interacted with his stepfather.

Although Bundy felt different as a child, nobody noticed. He felt haunted by a vague disquiet that later grew into murderous rage. When he was 15, Bundy had two friends in his neighborhood. The two friends enjoyed Bundy's company, except when he became angry. He became known as having a short fuse.

From the very beginning, Bundy chose to be alone. He was enthralled with his radio and spent his spare time listening to it. In later years, Bundy found it difficult to integrate socially. When he was a child, Bundy would investigate neighborhood trash cans to find pictures of naked women. He took part in few organized sports activities because he felt they were too serious and that he was too small. His stepfather never attended Bundy's games and his mother disliked the sports because they cost money. Bundy found it traumatic when he could not get on the baseball and basketball teams. As a result, he became proficient at skiing. It is suspected that his expensive ski outfit was stolen. Bundy established a ticket forgery system that allowed him to ski free of charge. He was never caught.

Obsessed with material possessions, Bundy fantasized about being adopted by Roy Rogers and Dale Evans, who would give him his own pony. He felt humiliated to be seen in his family's economy car. Instead of any physical or emotional abuse, Bundy depicted his childhood home life as empty. He felt overlooked and forgotten.

In junior high, he had some friends and went to some parties, but he failed to acquire good social skills. Unlike his experience in junior high, Bundy became shy and introverted in high school. He saw himself as a serious student who did not enjoy drinking. Others saw him as arrogant. In high school, Bundy never got in trouble, nor did he desire to do anything wrong. He felt inept with girls and only had one date during high school. Because his family had limited income, he always felt inferior to others who had more material possessions.

As a senior, Bundy volunteered to work in a local political race. A few years later he drove the Republican candidate for lieutenant governor, and later he worked to help elect a candidate for governor. Through his political efforts, Bundy found friends with whom he could socialize.

Bundy described himself as having an entity in him that was not separate, which he sometimes referred to as "the malignant being," which compelled him to kill. He asserts that his desire during the killings was not the violence itself (not entirely believable), but that he wanted to have full possession of the victim. The sex was not extreme, and he claims to have spared the victims as much pain as he could. The "entity" grew slowly within him, becoming stronger and more powerful after every deviant act.

Bundy's first documented murder occurred in Seattle in January 1974, where he smashed Sharon Clarke's head with a rod while she slept in her bed. After a lengthy coma she survived, with no memory of the event. Sharon was a stranger to Bundy and no explanation was ever given for the attack. Within weeks a college student living a few blocks from Sharon, Lynda Ann Healy, disappeared. Thereafter, over a period of 7 months, young women disappeared with appalling regularity. From March through June 1974, four more female college students disappeared while either attending a concert or a movie, leaving a bar, or simply walking across campus.

On July 14, 1974, Bundy approached several young women with his arm in a sling, asking them to help him put a sailboat on top of his car. One woman went with him to his car, but when he said she needed to go with him in his car to get the boat, she refused. Others also refused. But Janice Ott agreed to help him, and she was never seen again. The same day another young woman who was in the public washroom at the same lake disappeared. The remains of these and other unidentified women were later found in a forest near the lake. The killing spree continued in full force through October 1974. His victims tended to be college-age, white, attractive, with long hair parted in the middle.

In November 1974, a young woman who believed Bundy was a police detective agreed to get into his car. After Bundy placed one handcuff on her, she screamed and fought her way out of the car. She caught a crowbar mid-air with which he tried to smash her skull, and she leapt in front of an oncoming car, which stopped and picked her up, and she escaped. The very same day, Bundy abducted and killed another victim and approached a third woman, who turned him down.

In January 1975, Bundy began killing in Colorado. One woman was taken from her bed while sleeping; another disappeared on her way to meet a girlfriend in a bar. A third victim was found fully clothed except for her jeans being pulled down. More women disappeared—one from a gas station, another from a mine shaft. Finally, on August 16, 1975, Bundy was arrested for driving suspiciously slowly down a street and refusing to stop when ordered by a patrolman. The police found a hair in his car matching one of the victims, and a witness said he saw Bundy the night another victim disappeared. Bundy was tried for murder in Aspen, Colorado.

Bundy's charm, intelligence, sense of humor, and good looks soon convinced those in charge of him that he was special. Bundy was exceptionally cooperative, and his captors showed him every courtesy such as special health foods and no physical restraints when he attended court. Because he insisted on defending himself, he was provided law books as requested. During pretrial hearings, Bundy was allowed to wander through the Aspen law library as he pleased. It should have come as no surprise when he jumped out of a library window and escaped. Eight days later he was recaptured and kept under heavy guard.

Bundy testified that he was a victim of circumstances and there was no clear proof that he committed any of the murders. He also contended that many men had his same physical description. His legal skills helped him delay the case as he filed numerous motions. During this time he lost weight, and with a hacksaw carved a hole around the light fixture in his prison cell. He squeezed through a 12-inch opening and escaped again. From Aspen, Bundy went to Chicago, Michigan, and Atlanta, and then decided to stay when he reached Tallahassee, Florida, a few blocks from Florida State University sorority houses.

On January 15, 1978, five young women in a sorority house were severely beaten. Two of them died. They were bludgeoned and at least two were raped. One month later a 12-year-old girl disappeared after leaving her school. She was found strangled to death, with her sexual organs mutilated. Bundy had been living under the pseudonym Chris Hagen and survived by stealing a car and using stolen credit cards. On February 15, 1978, a police officer, suspicious of the slow prowling manner that Bundy was driving at 1:30 A.M., began following him. As the officer was checking on his radio to learn if Bundy's vehicle was stolen, he turned on the car's blue pursuit light. Instead of stopping, Bundy accelerated, and then finally stopped. The officer ordered him to lie on the ground, and, just as one handcuff had been secured, Bundy knocked down the officer and ran. Eventually the officer again had Bundy restrained. Bundy was arrested for driving a stolen vehicle and possessing stolen goods. He identified himself as Kenneth Raymond Misner, the name on one of his stolen credit cards. It did not take long to discover that Kenneth Misner was the Ted Bundy wanted for murder in Colorado.

Bundy adamantly claimed he was innocent of all wrongdoing. One severely incriminating piece of evidence was matching his teeth with the teeth marks on the buttocks of one of his victims. At trial in Florida for two of the murders, Bundy again displayed his charm and intelligence before the jury. When he was found guilty and twice sentenced to death, the judge told him he would have made a good lawyer. When asked about Bundy as a child, his closest friends could think of nothing showing him to be anything other than quiet, bright, witty, wholesome, handsome, and serious-minded. Bundy was flooded with attention from those wishing to interview him to find out what he was like. Using his legal skills, Bundy was able to keep himself alive for 10 years while his appeals worked through the system. Finally, after the efforts had expired, he admitted to twenty-three of his murders. He died in the electric chair on January 24, 1989, in Florida. When those standing outside of the prison heard of his death, the crowd cheered, setting off firecrackers in celebration.

Bundy appears to be a classic case of a high Factor 1 psychopath (see following discussion), that is, high on the indices of true psychopathy, rather than on the social deviance Factor 2 indices. The major ways in which his case is atypical for psychopaths are his higher level of intelligence (despite the myth of the bright psychopath, most are less intelligent than comparable normals), and the few indices of psychopathy early in life. This lack of early evidence may be explained by the fact that he was not under enough scrutiny, his mother probably covered for some of his deviance, and/or his intelligence allowed him to hide some of it.

Related Diagnostic-Etiological Considerations

In the nineteenth century, Caesare Lombroso advanced the theory that criminals manifest distinct physical markers, such as a low forehead. Although the theory has been discredited, much modern research (Strupp et al., 1997; Lykken, 1995) supports the idea that biological factors, especially those that are derived genetically, influence the production of criminality, of the antisocial personality disorder, and especially psychopathy. But it is unclear how these biological factors translate into specific behaviors. Possibilities include deficits in specific types of intelligence or learning skills, brain dysfunctions, neurohormonal disorders, etc. For example, Robert Hare (Hare et. al, 1991) views psychopaths as language-disordered at a neurological level and weak at processing the emotional meaning of words. Others point to psychological factors, for example, patterns of parenting, as primary, arguing that harsh or abusive parenting, or even permissive parenting can facilitate psychopathy, especially in predisposed individuals.

One major difference theoretically is between those like Hare who view psychopathy as stemming from some "defect" causing one to be "born bad" or "defective" and those, namely Lykken (1995), who view psychopaths as "born difficult." In the latter theory a particular constellation of "normal" characteristics are inherited that predispose to psychopathy, and the degree and direction of disorder are then determined by how often and how intensely the factors occur and/or the type of parenting received. The FUMES acronym can be used to describe the difficult characteristics that a parent reacts to with such a child:

Fearless

Unresponsive to pain

Mesomorphic (muscular)

<u>E</u>mpathy-deficient

<u>S</u>timulation-seeking

While these are "normal" characteristics, they require skill, indeed great skill, in parenting in order to develop a conscience, prosocial habits, success in a standard classroom, avoidance of using power to manipulate others, etc. In an environment with models for aggression, sexual or physical abuse, dishonesty, substance abuse, deviant sexual patterns, etc., the flavor of the psychopathic "stew" is set into a particular direction.

An influential modern conceptualization views psychopathy as composed of two main factors: (1) affective-cognitive instability, and (2) behavioral-social deviance (Hare et al., 1991). This view has helped generate and, in turn, has been facilitated by Hare's Psychopathy Checklist—Revised (PCL-R), a twenty-item assessment technique that uses self-report and interview observation data, which are then cross-checked with collateral information. The following components contribute to affective-cognitive instability (Factor 1), the part of the overall ASP category that is closest to the term "psychopath": glibness, a grandiose sense of self, pathological lying, conning-manipulative behaviors, lack of remorse, shallow affect, callousness and lack of empathy, and failure to accept responsibility. Components of behavioral-social deviance (Factor 2) are a higher need for stimulation, a parasitic lifestyle, poor behavioral controls, early behavior problems, lack of realistic goals, impulsivity, irresponsibility, having been adjudicated delinquent, and a history of violating supervision or probation.

In general, research (Lykken, 1995; Hare et al., 1991) on the psychopath (much of which includes use of the PCL) indicates:

1. While there is a drop-off in criminal activity for psychopaths at about age 40–45, this effect holds primarily for nonviolent crimes. There is only a slight drop-off for violent crimes.

2. Concomitantly, while the behavioral-social deviance factor starts to drop off at age 40–45, the affective-cognitive instability factor (the "psychopathy") only lessens slightly with age.

3. Similarly, while the behavioral-social deviance factor is a good predictor of general criminality and recidivism; is highly correlated with criminality; and is negatively correlated with socio-economic status and, to a lesser degree, IQ, Factor 1 is a better predictor of violence but is virtually uncorrelated with socio-economic status and IQ.

4. While treatment may effect a positive change in the average criminal, it seldom does so with psychopaths, especially to the degree they are strong on Factor 1, as was Ted Bundy. Indeed, there is evidence that psychopaths who are high on Factor 1 may get worse with treatment. Group and individual psychotherapy can be a "finishing school" for psychopaths (Rice, Harris, and Cormier). True to their nature, they seem to learn little about themselves in therapy, but learn more about others, and then more boldly use such information. At least in part this is because they are language-disordered in the

sense that the emotional components of language are weak or missing, voiding the likelihood of empathy or remorse.

5. In general, while socio-economic and family background variables are good predictors of general criminal behavior, they are relatively nonpredictive for psychopathy, especially where it is loaded on Factor 1.

6. Expect such clients to be deceptive about virtually anything they report. To the degree feasible, independent corroboration of any critical questions about history or present behaviors is necessary.

> *Identifying criminals is up to each of us. Usually they can be recognized by their large cufflinks and their failure to stop eating when the man next to them is hit by a falling anvil.*
>
> —Woody Allen, comedian and filmmaker

Proposed "Common Path" for the Development of Psychopathy

As described by Meyer (1998a), the following is an outline of the evolution of the psychopath–antisocial personality disorder.

Pre-Existing Risk Factors

1. Biological (genetic, prenatal, birth, or early childhood) disruption
2. Low socio-economic status
3. Family history of vocational-social-interpersonal dysfunction
4. Family history of psychopathy
5. Characteristics of a FUMES child (see prior text)

From Birth to School Age

1. Child temperament factors
   a. Child's lack of emotional responsiveness and lack of social interest fosters rejecting responses from parents.
   b. Child's high activity levels may cause parental annoyance and elicit punitive responses.
   c. Lack of responsiveness to physical punishment, emotional "numbness," and deficit in associating emotion in language learning result in failing to learn behavioral contingencies.

2. Parental factors
   a. Inconsistent parenting results in child's failing to learn behavioral contingencies.
   b. Aggressive, punitive parenting and/or family interaction results in child's modeling aggression, experiencing hostility, becoming enured to punishing consequences, and developing a repressive defensive style (emotional "hardness").

3. Parent–child interaction

  a. Unreliable parenting results in, along with defective "expressed emotion," insecure attachment (i.e., interpersonally "avoidant" attachment style); child "goes it alone" rather than risk rejection and disappointment associated with unreliable and/or abusive parents.

4. Environmental factors (can occur anytime during lifespan)

  a. Toxic levels of heavy metals, especially lead, facilitate antisocial-aggressive patterns.

  b. Trauma and/or disease that results in some forms of brain disorder, especially frontal lobe damage, can facilitate a loss of inhibitory behaviors.

School Age to Adolescence

1. Predisposing personality factors

  a. Low baseline level of brain stem arousal (i.e., Eysenck's biological extraversion) contributes to impulsive, undercontrolled, and stimulation-seeking behavior.

  b. A combination of distorted physiological arousal, repressive psychodynamics, and habitual "numbness" to social contingencies results in child being insensitive to and unable to "condition" to environmental events; therefore, the child does not learn or "profit" from experience.

  c. Mesomorphic (muscular) and energetic components lead to increased physical manipulation-control of others and along with stimulation seeking lead to increased risk taking.

  d. Commonly correlated attention-deficit hyperactivity disorder and/or "soft" neurological disorder may exacerbate behavior problems.

2. Personality development

  a. Peer/teacher labeling may result in self-fulfilling prophecy effects.

  b. School and social failure result in sense of inferiority and increased interpersonal hostility; child develops "moving against" interpersonal style.

  c. Initial forays into antisociality (e.g., theft, fire setting, interpersonal violence) occur, with some "success"; evidence for diagnosis of conduct disorder mounts.

Adolescence

1. The young psychopath hones exploitative style in order to express hostility and "rise above" feelings of inferiority; "proves superiority" by hoodwinking and humiliating teachers, parents, peers.

2. Continued antisocial behavior results in initial scrapes with the law.

3. Increased use of physical and psychological aggression to control others.

4. Physiological impulsivity, inability to profit from experience (exacerbated by a disordered cognitive-attentional style), and interpersonal hostility and antagonism combine to make repeated legal offenses highly probable.

5. Contact with other antisocials in the context of juvenile criminal camps or prison results in "criminal education"; increased criminality results, along with a loss of the "time in place" that eventually brings accrued benefits to those who stay in the "mainstream" of life; criminal and antisocial behavior become a lifestyle in which the psychopath can "excel."

Adulthood

1. Antisocial behavior escalates through the psychopath's late twenties; increasingly frequent failure, rejection by others, and/or incarceration result in increased hostility and hardened feelings.

2. Unable to profit from experience, lacking in insight, and unable to form therapeutic bonds, the psychopath becomes a poor therapy-rehab risk and bad news for society.

3. There is a crystallization of these underlying cognitive beliefs:

   a. Rationalization: "My desiring something justifies whatever actions I need to take."

   b. Devaluing of others: "The attitudes and needs of others don't affect me, unless responding to them will provide me an advantage, and if they are hurt by me, I need not feel responsible for what happens to them."

   c. Low-impact consequences: "My choices are inherently good. As such, I won't experience undesirable consequences, or if they occur, they won't really matter to me."

   d. Entitlement: "I have to think of myself first; I'm entitled to what I want or feel I need, and if necessary, can use force or deception to obtain those goals."

   e. Rule avoidance: "Rules constrict me from fulfilling my needs."

4. Antisocial behavior decreases or "burns out" unevenly beginning in the early thirties (although less so with violent offenses); this may be due to lengthier incarcerations, to changes in age-related metabolic factors that formerly contributed to sensation-seeking and impulsive behavior, or perhaps to decrements in the strength and stamina required to engage in persistent criminal endeavors.

Treatment Options

The treatment problem with all the personality disorders—getting the client into therapy and meaningfully involved—is acute with the ASP, and success is rare. As British prime minister William Gladstone (1809–1898) put it, "The disease of an evil conscience is beyond the practice of all the physicians of all the countries in the world," and this seems to include psychologists and psychiatrists as well.

A variety of treatment possibilities have been suggested as appropriate for the ASP. However, like Bundy, most have no interest in changing their behavior and are only in a treatment program because they have been forced by circumstances (Rice et al., 1992). Some antisocial personalities, usually those with less

Factor 1 psychopathy, are changed as a result of treatment, and as noted, there are some changes as a result of aging. The great majority, however, are not changed markedly by either their environment or by treatment techniques. Indeed, a classic, well-designed study found that primary psychopaths who were in treatment actually did worse in the long run than did the untreated group. That is, they ignored the efforts to change them but used what they learned in therapy about human behavior to better manipulate others (Rice et al., 1992).

The Schizoid Personality Disorder

**The Case of
Theodore
Kaczynski**

I think of him as a misguided very quixotic romantic figure of another era.

. . . It's not that I'm sympathetic. I just feel I understand him.

—Author Joyce Carol Oates, commenting on
Theodore Kaczynski, in *The New York Observer*

Schizoid personalities (SPD) are asocial, shy, introverted, and significantly defective in their ability to form social relationships and are usually described as loners. The essential feature of this disorder is impairment in the ability to form adequate social relationships; as author Joan Didion states in *The White Album,* they are "only marginally engaged in the dailiness of Life" (p. 121). They typically have difficulty directly expressing hostility and have withdrawn from most social contacts. But, unlike that of agoraphobia (see Chapter 3), the behavior is ego-syntonic; that is, the person is essentially accepting of it.

SPDs usually show shyness, although the concept of introversion may be more applicable. There is at least an element of avoidance of people because of fear-anxiety embedded in the concept of shyness, whereas introversion is more clearly a preference for avoidance of others. As a result of this introversion, SPDs gravitate into jobs that require solitude, such as work as a night guard. As they age or become vocationally dysfunctional, they are likely to move into a hermit-like existence or a "skid row," particularly if they are males. Even though they excessively fantasize and communicate in peculiar ways, they show no loss of contact with reality.

The Case of Theodore Kaczynski

Theodore John Kaczynski was apprehended by the FBI on April 3, 1996, and charged with being the "Unabomber," so named because many of the bomb attacks were directed to university-related persons or places. His 17-year endeavor, including sixteen incidents resulting in three deaths and twenty-three wounded and maimed, first came to public notice on May 25, 1978, when a package found in a parking lot at the University of Illinois in Chicago was taken to Northwestern University because of the return address. It exploded the next day, injuring one person. The last known attack occurred on April 24, 1995, when a mail bomb was delivered to the Sacramento headquarters of the California Forestry Association, killing the president of the association, Gilbert Murray, when he attempted to open it.

Despite an elaborate intensive manhunt over 17 years, including the storing of at least twelve million bytes of information in computer databases, the efforts of a special eighty-person task force of FBI, ATF, and Postal Service agents, extensive psychological profiling, and a sighting by an eyewitness, the apprehension only came about when his sister-in-law Linda began to suspect Ted might be the Unabomber and then her husband, Ted's brother David, recognized parts of the 35,000-word "manifesto" published by *The New York Times* and *The Washington Post* as similar to writings of his brother that he came across at their mother's house.

They had already developed concerns about Ted's mental health. In a *60 Minutes* interview on September 15, 1996, David and Linda said that in 1991 they had taken two of Ted's letters to a psychiatrist, who said Ted was disturbed and could be violent. Civil commitment was considered, but they thought it would not be feasible. Later they did contact a physician in Montana, presumably Ted's, and asked him to get Ted into psychotherapy, but nothing came of that.

Theodore Kaczynski was born on May 22, 1942. Even as a young child, Kaczynski was quiet and reclusive, but his early childhood was unremarkable, with apparently loving parents. His mother is said to have spent long hours reading passages from *Scientific American* to him when he was very young. He and his family were withdrawn socially. A neighbor commented, "They didn't mingle with the people on our street." He added that Kaczynski didn't play with the other kids and would never respond to a hello. His only sibling, David, was born in 1950.

Kaczynski graduated from Evergreen Park High School in a white, middle class suburb, finishing high school in 3 years. He was hardly remembered by most of his classmates; what perceptions do exist view him as quiet and reclusive, although he had been a member of the German, math, and biology clubs. He was remembered as a teenager for having a high interest in pyrotechnics and explosives. Yet, while he liked blowing things up, he never directly hurt anyone, and was not remembered as angry or sullen, but rather as shy and very immature.

Kaczynski was a National Merit Scholarship finalist and at age 16 went on scholarship to Harvard University, where he graduated just after he turned 20. He earned only average grades and participated in no activities. For 3 years he lived in a seven-man suite in Eliot House, a Harvard dorm. One suitemate commented, "I don't recall ten words being spoken to him in the 3 years." He apparently took some graduate courses at both Northwestern University and the University of Chicago and then received a master's in mathematics in 1964 and a Ph.D. in 1967 from the University of Michigan. Somewhat ironically, his dissertation topic was "Boundary Functions." His professors generally remembered him as very bright, serious, and quiet. He published several outstanding journal articles before graduating. His potentially brilliant future continued with his acceptance of an assistant professorship of mathematics at the University of California at Berkeley for the 1967–68 school year. But two factors melded to seemingly produce a major life change.

First, he was apparently unsuccessful in his role as a professor. He was reportedly a poor teacher and received some terrible evaluations, including the comment "He absolutely refuses to answer questions by completely ignoring the students." He continued to be a loner; so again most people's recollection of him are vague. The second factor was the high level of radicalism in the 1960s. He had probably been exposed to much political activism in his student years. At Berkeley, a particular hotbed of radicalism, he had to have witnessed a wide variety of protests and riots, including the infamous People's Park riot of May 1969, which occured 1 month before he resigned from his post at Berkeley, on June 30, 1969. Kaczynski lived only a few blocks from the People's Park, and that conflict was related to a number of environmental-social concerns. There was little evidence of radical concerns and ideas in Kaczynski prior to Berkeley. It was not unusual for disenchanted Berkeley activists to give up on society and "move back to the land," which is what Kaczynski eventually did in Montana. However, he strongly opposed leftist political views, and the focus in his attacks was on genetic engineering, airplanes, and computers.

Kaczynski never gave anyone clear reasons for his resignation. As usual, information is sketchy. It is known that he lived in Utah and Montana in the 1970s and 1980s. His Harvard class's twentieth-anniversary report in 1982 listed his address as 788 Bauchat Pass, Khadar Khel, Afghanistan. No such place exists. He subsisted by way of odd jobs, menial labor, and a simple lifestyle. In 1990, his father, Theodore R. Kaczynski, who managed a small business, committed suicide after being diagnosed with cancer. This appears to have had no significant effect on his son Ted one way or another.

He eventually settled into a spartan, mountainside cabin near the tiny town of Lincoln, Montana, on 1.4 acres purchased by him and his brother in 1971. The 10- by 12-foot cabin had a table, two chairs, a narrow bunk, and a woodburning stove, but no electricity, indoor plumbing, or phone. He grew some of his own food; hunted rabbits, squirrels, and porcupines for food; and about once a week spent approximately $5 for provisions at the Blackfoot Market in Lincoln. He traveled on a dilapidated, one-speed bicycle, pieced together from mismatched parts, even occasionally riding 50 miles into Helena, Montana. He didn't drink or smoke, and his only leisure activity was reading, as he frequented discount book stores and the Lincoln library. He rarely spoke more than a few polite words to anyone. He was in part supported by periodic checks from his mother and received some money from his brother.

Shortly before he was apprehended, his life appeared to be fragmenting. His clothing was even more dirty and disheveled than before, if that was possible, and he looked depressed. Although he usually paid his property taxes on his land and cabin on time, he missed the November 30, 1995, deadline, and probably still owes $114.27. He even asked the owner of the Blackfoot Market for a job but was turned down. As far as anyone can remember, his last formal employment was in 1981. He eventually was found competent to stand trial, in January 1998. Almost immediately thereafter, on January 22, 1998, he pled guilty to all federal charges stemming from the bombings, accepting the conditions that he would never be released, and that he could not profit from his crimes. His attorneys stated that their client could not endure a trial that would portray him as—in Kaczynski's words—a "sickie."

Etiology and Diagnosis

While other diagnoses might apply to Kaczynski, especially toward the end of his Unabomber career, the schizoid pattern was apparently lifelong. It is generally accepted that, of all the personality disorders, the SPD is one wherein substantial determination of behavior by genetic factors is clearest. The parallel research on introversion and shyness similarly points to a high genetic component. There are indications of at least mild schizoid tendencies in other Kaczynski family members. For example, David enjoyed spending long periods of time living in a tent outdoors and for a period of time lived in a more remote part of Montana than did his brother.

In addition to the genetic predisposition toward shyness and introversion, his mother's general parental strategy to allow and even strongly facilitate intellectual, academic, and/or isolating behaviors turned out to be a factor. In Ted's Unabomber manifesto, he wrote, "It isn't natural for an adolescent human being to spend the bulk of his time sitting at a desk absorbed in study." Also, three specific situations may have contributed. When Ted was 9 months old, a severe allergy resulting in hives required that he be hospitalized for a week, and as was customary in those days, he was allowed virtually no contact with any of his family. His family reports that he became much more unresponsive and withdrawn after that experience. Second, when Ted was 7, his brother was born, and all reports are that he reacted very strongly to the consequent loss of attention. Their aunt commented that whereas Ted used to snuggle up and talk to her, he stopped doing that after David's birth. Thirdly, when he was allowed to skip the sixth grade, an already emotionally immature boy was now even further distanced from potentially interacting with a peer group. A few years later he skipped another grade, furthering the process.

Similarly, in the area of heterosexual relationships, Ted never developed emotionally. He never dated or even socialized with girls in grade school or high school. Just after his high school graduation, Ted had one or two dates with a girl, but he ended the relationship by expressing exasperation with her Catholic beliefs. There is no indication of any other heterosexual socializing of any sort until 1974, when he made an overture to a 19-year-old waitress he worked with at the Kibbey Corner Truck Stop in Lincoln, Montana. She had no idea he had an interest in her until after she left the job and returned to school. Ted's first letter-overture invited her to move with him to Canada and be his squaw. A second letter contained a résumé, almost as if he were making a date application.

His next romantic foray, and in some ways his most successful, was in 1978, at age 36, about 4 months after the first Unabomber attack. He approached his work supervisor, Ellen Tormichael, when he happened to see her pumping gas at a store. He went with her to her apartment and played cards with her and her sister and her boyfriend. They had two dates, but she then told him she didn't want to see him again. Ted's brother, David, reported that Ted became very depressed, and, just as an emotionally immature adolescent might react, he wrote an insulting limerick about her and anonymously posted copies in lavatories and walls around the factory where they worked and in which his brother and father had managerial positions. Ironically, and possibly prophetically, he forced his brother to fire him by coming up to David at a water cooler and as he watched, Ted posted a copy on the wall in front of David. David told him to go home, and he was not allowed to return to work there. That's about it for this area of his social life.

As is characteristic of SPDs, Kaczynski never showed any evidence of directly confrontative aggression. Actually, most SPDs don't even show high levels of passive aggression, in part because they usually show such low levels of overall interpersonal contact. In addition to the Unabomber activities, Kaczynski showed other patterns of "distant" and impersonal aggression, for example, in the following letter reportedly sent on October 1, 1974, to Joe Visocan, retired owner of the Kibbey Corner Truck Stop.

Dear, sweet Joe:

You fat con-man. You probably think I treated you badly by quitting without notice, but it's your own fault. You gave me this big cock-and-bull story about how much money I could make selling tires and all that crap. "The sky's the limit" and so forth. If you had been honest with me I would not have taken the job in the first place; but if I hadn't taken it, I wouldn't have quit without giving you a couple of weeks notice. Anyhow, I have a check coming. I am enclosing a stamped, self-addressed envelope in which you can send it. I had better get that check, because I know what authorities to complain to if I don't get it. If I have to complain about the check, then while I'm at it, I might as well complain about the fact that you don't have a proper cage for putting air in split-rim tires, which, if I am not mistaken, is illegal.

Love and Kisses,

Ted Kaczynski

From a cognitive perspective, the following are characteristic underlying assumptions that affect behavior of SPDs:

1. Any disruption of my emotional routine (however minimal the emotions are) is scary and messy. In this sense the SPD's experience is analogous to the obsessive-compulsive's fear of disruption of external routines.
2. People don't really mean anything to me.
3. I can survive alone (maybe not optimally, but at least predictably) and need space to do that.
4. It's necessary to be free and independent. Other people are like Brer Rabbit's "Tar Baby"—if you relate to them, you get stuck to them.

It is possible that at various points in his life Kaczynski might have earned more than one *DSM-IV* diagnosis, for example, paranoid personality disorder; antisocial personality disorder; or, if his ideas are construed as clearly delusional, psychotic paranoid disorder (see Chapter 6). He was apparently depressed enough to make a suicide attempt at some point in early January 1998, using his own underwear. Also, Dr. Sally Johnson, a federal prison psychiatrist, who found Kaczynski competent to stand trial, diagnosed him at approximately that same point in time as a paranoid schizophrenic (see Chapter 6). However, as I believe is evident from the following *DSM-IV* criteria for Schizoid Personality Disorder (SPD), this latter diagnosis fits Kaczynski over most if not all of his late adolescent and adult life.

According to the *DSM-IV,* although SPDs have few if any friends, they show no communication disturbance, which is true of Kaczynski. It is required that SPD—which is marked by social-relationship detachment, introverted behavior, and constriction of expression or emotion in social settings—causes vocational or social disruption by at least four or the following: (1) does not desire or enjoy close relationships, including with family; (2) almost always seeks solitary pursuits; (3) has little or no interest in sexual experiences with another; (4) takes pleasure in only a few activities at most; (5) lacks close friends-confidants other than first-degree relatives; (6) appears indifferent to praise or criticism; (7) is detached, cold, or flat emotionally. Although no one could make a definitive diagnosis without a formal, in-person contact evaluation, Kaczynski could easily be construed as fitting all seven.

Literary Obsessions and Violence

In Joseph Conrad's novel *The Secret Agent* a brilliant but deranged professor abandons academia in disgust for the isolation of a tiny room, his "hermitage." There, clad in ragged, soiled clothes, he fashions a bomb to destroy an observatory derisively referred to as "that idol of science," a symbol of "the sacrosanct fetish of today." Describing a similar character, also nicknamed the Professor, in his short story "The Informer," the Polish-born author wrote: "Explosives were his faith, his hope, his weapon and his shield."

The parallels fall neatly into place. Kaczynski, a brilliant man who was troubled most of his life, fled academia for a hermit-life existence in a Montana shanty. There, grossly unkempt, he lived for a time off turnips he grew behind his cabin. One of the anarchists in Conrad's novel lived on a diet of raw carrots. Further, the main character in Conrad's best-known work, "Heart of Darkness," abandons European civilization for the jungle of the Congo. Ironically, in 1995, investigators sent *The Secret Agent* and other Conrad works to scholars, hoping for insights into the mind of a killer who had eluded them for 18 years.

Investigators say they believe that Kaczynski used "Conrad" or "Konrad" as an alias on at least three occasions while staying at a hotel in Sacramento, California, where he went to mail bombs. By coincidence, literature reference books listed Joseph Conrad's birth-given name as either Teodore Jozef Konrad Korzeniowski or Jozef Teodore. Kaczynski's full name is Theodore John Kaczynski. Kaczynski's use of the initials "FC" on a number of bombs and in letters to news organizations is another similarity. The Unabomber's letters said the initials stood for "Freedom Club." In *The Secret Agent,* anarchists used the initials "FP," or "Future of the Proletariat," in their leaflets.

Kaczynski grew up with Conrad's complete works in his family's suburban Chicago home. During his 26 years in the Montana wilderness, he pored over Conrad's writings. In a 1984 letter to his family, "Ted said he was reading Conrad's novels for about the dozenth time," reported Washington attorney Anthony Bisceglie, counsel to Kaczynski's brother and mother.

If Kaczynski did indeed draw from Conrad's characters in plotting bombings, he would not be the first killer to find inspiration in literature or film. Mark

David Chapman, who killed Beatles singer John Lennon, was obsessed with the novel *Catcher in the Rye*. Timothy McVeigh, who committed the Oklahoma City bombing, was fascinated by *The Turner Diaries*. John Hinckley Jr., who shot President Ronald Reagan, was consumed by the film *Taxi Driver*.

Treatment

The Kaczynskis were concerned enough about Ted's social development to consult school counselors, but apparently there was never any more sophisticated examination, and there is no indication he received formal treatment. If he did, it was unsuccessful. SPDs are not likely even to enter into therapy because such a relationship is the magnification of what is usually avoided. If for some reason they do become involved in therapy, the therapist must help them develop trust in that relationship and not overwhelm them with initial confrontations.

Like psychopathy, SPD is a disorder in which efforts at early prevention will likely bring a greater payoff than will later treatment (Strupp et al., 1997). Shyness and/or introversion disrupt socialization and often requires better than average parenting to avoid later dysfunctional patterns. The following are some of the ways a parent can help a shy/introverted child. Ted Kaczynski's parents were clearly well intentioned but apparently violated a number of these guidelines:

- Use gentle encouragement rather than being too demanding or pushy. Consider whether a family ethic of perfectionism could be a factor.
- Openly discuss the situation. Make your child aware of your own struggles with shyness.
- Do role playing with your child to suggest ways to cope with difficult situations. Encourage the child to act out the positive patterns even if he or she denies being able to do it that way in real life.
- Ask your child what his or her "self-talk" is when feeling shy. Usually it's a negative self-statement like "I can't do it" or "If I go over there, they'll laugh at me." Try to get the child to say more positive things out loud about potential behavior. Reward the child for doing so.
- Help your child develop friendships. Provide rides or a pleasant place for children to gather and play.
- Avoid criticism as well as any negative comparisons with siblings or playmates. Don't use shaming as a consistent disciplinary technique.
- Teach your child to reflect and empathize with how other people feel. This serves to blunt some of the self-centeredness that is often part of introversion.
- Look for positive ways to deal with the shyness. Instead of telling a teacher that your child is shy, use words like "reflective" or "sensitive." It may well be that your child is a good listener and not just shy. If so, play up that quality as a strength, not a weakness.

- Avoid making comparisons between your child and others who may be more extroverted, athletic, and/or intelligent. This is usually done to get a child to try harder. But this usually backfires and makes a child even less certain that extra effort will pay off. Also the child, now intimidated, is inhibited around other children because of having been convinced of their superior abilities.

- Make sure that your child isn't lacking in basic social skills. These often are taken for granted. However, not every child is equally adept at skills like making eye contact, asking questions, talking clearly, appearing interested in others, and the like. Check these skills out by talking with your child and watching how he or she interacts with others.

- Be on the lookout for circumstances that are likely to increase a child's feeling of shyness. Few children are shy with everyone, but certain situations seem to bring out shyness. Among these are encounters with strangers, being the center of attention (for good or bad), being with peers and members of the opposite sex, and less obvious things like group singing or being in a classroom play. Again, role playing ahead of time how to handle these situations can do a lot to lessen any problems.

12

Disorders of Impulse Control

The extent to which an individual is in command of and can control urges to violate social rules is always an important consideration when evaluating emotional development. It is expected that young children will often find behavioral control difficult, but one is expected to achieve increasing mastery as socialization proceeds. Inadequate impulse control is symptomatic of a wide range of disorders, including alcoholism, obsessive-compulsive disorder, exhibitionism, and pyromania. Thus, the category of impulse control disorders could be so extensive and inclusive as to be meaningless. As a result, disorders in which an absence of impulse control is only a component are classified in accordance with other symptoms (eating disorders, substance abuse, and paraphilias, for example). However, there are at least five disorders for which poor impulse control is the primary feature and that are not elsewhere classified: pathological gambling (the case of Greg), kleptomania (the case of Clare), pyromania, intermittent explosive disorder (marked by incidents of inability to control aggression, resulting in serious attacks on others or destruction of property) and trichotillomania (the recurrent pulling out of one's own hair).

In all of the disorders of impulse control, a compelling impulse accompanied by a rising sense of tension is experienced. It may or may not be premeditated and/or consciously resisted. Then, when the act is committed, there is a sense of release, which may even be so intense as to be described as pleasurable or euphoric.

Pathological Gambling

**The Case
of Greg**

Money is a vile intermediary.

—Fidel Castro

Gambling may be one of civilization's oldest recreational activities. Historical documents of the ancients are replete with examples of people's interest in wagering with friends and others. Although a commonsense view of the gambling phenomenon would easily lead to recognition of at least its potential for pathological abuse, pathological gambling as a clinical phenomenon was not formally recognized until the third edition of the *DSM,* published in 1980. The *DSM-IV* categorizes pathological gambling as a disorder of impulse control, with the primary features being: (1) persistent and recurrent failure to resist an impulse to gamble or think about gambling, (2) an increasing sense of tension before committing the act, (3) an experience of either pleasure or release at the time of committing the act. As more states have moved toward various forms of legalized gambling, the prevalence of the disorder in the United States is constantly increasing.

Many compulsive gamblers report that they only feel alive when they are gambling and may refer to the rest of their life experience as boring. They are generally nonconformists and are narcissistic and aggressive (Kaplan, 1995). A number of compulsive gamblers work only to make enough money to gamble heavily when they get to a spot like Las Vegas. Others have a more normal outward appearance, especially those who gamble in more legitimate outlets such as commodities and stock markets. Statistically, most gamblers are male, married, extroverted, somewhat flamboyant, and competitive. They are brighter than average; yet they surprisingly often experienced learning difficulties as they grew up. Most had placed their first bet by the age of 15. They are more likely than nongamblers to be in debt and to have some form of legal trouble.

Little formal research has been done on compulsive gamblers, but it appears that the following factors can predispose a person to pathological gambling (Kaplan, 1995): family values that emphasize material symbols rather than savings and financial planning, an absent parent before age 16, an extroverted and competitive personality, and a gambling model in the family. Tacit cultural acceptance of gambling also increases the number of abusers. For example, traditional Chinese cultural values strongly disapprove of alcoholism but approve of gambling as an acceptable channel for stimulation seeking. As a result, the number of pathological gamblers is relatively high in Chinese cultures (Marsella, DeVos, and Hsu, 1985).

Pathological gambling behavior can be confused with and be seen as another form of thrill-seeking behavior for the individual with the antisocial personality disorder. In contrast, as seen in the case of Greg, antisocial behavior that occurs as the result of the pathological gambling disorder invariably results out of desperation when no other avenues to obtain economic funds remain open to the gambler. Also, in contrast to the antisocial personality disorder, the pathological gambler usually has at least a reasonably stable work history until work also becomes disrupted by his or her gambling behavior.

> *For though this exercise may be absorbing, it is not*
> *[harmful] in the hands of a man [who can] give it*
> *up when chance comes along*
>
> —Fernando Basurto, *Dialogue Between a Hunter and a*
>   *Fisher* (1539), speaking on the pleasures of fishing

The Case History of Greg

Greg was born in the early 1940s, and his childhood could be generally described as pleasant and essentially free from extreme pathological influences. He was the only son of an upper middle class family that strove to provide Greg and his sister with every emotional and material advantage. Until approximately the age of 16, Greg attended public school. Then his parents decided it would be in his best interest to attend a local private school, to receive a better education and consequently be better prepared for college. In addition, some thought was also given to Greg's exposure to a "better class" of people. It was felt that such friendships made in this moderate-size northeastern town would be enduring and of value to Greg later in life.

With these and undoubtedly other considerations in mind, Greg began to attend a private college preparatory school. He found the increased academic rigors to be stimulating but not overwhelming. His academic abilities were challenged and a growing sense of self-esteem or pride began to develop. Greg graduated from high school without academic difficulties, but also without any formal academic distinction. Generally, he was well liked by both his peers and his teachers. Despite a certain degree of interpersonal or social charm, few individuals anticipated that Greg would distinguish himself in any way in later life. Regrettably, Greg may have also begun to entertain this hypothesis regarding his future or lack thereof.

Aside from the rather obvious academic benefits obtained by attending the private high school, Greg was also exposed to a way of life of which he previously had no knowledge. Although a wide variety of economic incomes were represented among the families who sent their children to this prep school, many individuals came from extremely wealthy families. They wore the most expensive clothes, had seemingly inexhaustible allowances to spend on their recreational needs, and frequently drove the most expensive automobiles. Although Greg's family was solidly upper class and he enjoyed all the benefits consistent with that station in American economic life, Greg's family could not compete with many of the other families who sent their children to this school. Greg grew to realize that perhaps he could not "compete" with the individuals who were his dearest friends.

Upon graduation, Greg entered the state university. His choice of universities was not based on academic reputation but on reduced tuition. In contrast, many of his friends attended private colleges with varying reputations for academic excellence; all were very expensive.

Greg's time in college was essentially unremarkable. He received only passing grades. Generally, he divided his psychic energy between preparation for classes and socialization with his friends, both old and new. Typically, all of Greg's friends belonged to the same social circle. Most of them were extremely wealthy or at least had direct access to large amounts of money. Second, and perhaps just as importantly, a significant majority of them were bored with life and depressed over its seeming emptiness and futility. A large number of Greg's friends would receive access to very large trust funds at designated points in their life or upon graduation from college would assume important roles in their families' companies. To some extent the passage of high school and college were seen as periods to be endured or even perversely enjoyed, as contrasted to periods of intellectual and emotional growth.

As a result of this prevailing group dynamic, a variety of behaviors were practiced in an effort to avoid the boredom and simultaneously instill some semblance of meaning into their lives. Gambling or wagering in a variety of forms was frequently practiced. Greg was first exposed to gambling in the latter years of high school. His attraction to the practice of wagering was almost immediate and escalated quickly throughout his college years. Gambling in all forms was enjoyed, for example, card playing, betting on the horses, betting on a variety of sporting events, etc., but greatest joy was extracted from "the sport of kings," horse racing.

After nearly 3 years of college, Greg dropped out to get a job. His reasoning was that he needed more income than his parents could provide or that he could supplement with a part-time job. Although a variety of excuses were offered, Greg was totally blind to the increasing role that gambling was playing in his life and the economic toll it was extracting. As Greg was a likable and naturally engaging individual, his vocational pursuits naturally turned to the area of sales. He began selling jewelry and was an overnight success. His social charm and honesty with his customers were a unique combination that quickly earned him a positive reputation among other dealers and his repeat customers.

Two independent events occurred that had a profound influence. His best and closest friend married an extremely wealthy young woman, rumored to be one of the richest heiresses in the United States. Whether the rumor was true or not, Greg began to be exposed to an economic lifestyle that was most enjoyable to him and that he would never have the means to replicate. At about the same time, Greg's sister became engaged to a wealthy individual who had generated his own fortune. In both situations, Greg had first-hand exposure to the benefits of extreme wealth, including the most expensive personal acquisitions, gifts, homes, boats, airplanes, etc. Although Greg envied his sister's and best friend's good fortune, he never became jealous. Their good luck only further increased his desire to obtain more money himself.

As a result of the discontent with his own life, Greg began to significantly increase the frequency and intensity of his gambling behavior, with a number of rather obvious benefits. In addition to the occasional "big win," Greg was able to continue to associate with his wealthy friends on a somewhat more frequent basis, as they also enjoyed a certain amount of wagering. Second, it allowed him to maintain a perhaps less than conscious dream of one day becoming extremely wealthy. At a more psychological level the gambling allowed Greg to avoid a sense of emptiness, depression, and futility. Simultaneously it gave him a rather unique sense of identity; he was known within his circle of friends as being a gambler. Such an identity allowed Greg to repress his perception of being a faceless man in a world of celebrities.

As might be expected, Greg's compulsive gambling behavior only further escalated his own psychological conflicts, in addition to creating a wide variety of problems within his environment. The compulsivity that he effectively utilized in his job was rechanneled over time into his gambling behavior. He worked long hours in order to obtain extra money so that he might gamble more intensely. Unfortunately for Greg, he generally lost more money than he won. Lack of betting savvy frequently necessitated obtaining small loans from his friends. The loans were generally repaid. Over time, as he began to incur larger losses, more sizeable loans were acquired from local banks. Finally, he took out a rather large consolidation loan as the number of loans became beyond his ability to pay.

Greg began to consume increasingly larger amounts of alcohol in order to deal with the growing pressure, anxiety, and depression. As the level of alcohol consumption increased, his judgment about his everyday life decreased. Finally he resorted to "borrowing" the down payments for recent jewelry sales without anyone's knowledge or permission. The strategy helped at first, but his losses continued to escalate. Finally, out of desperation, Greg decided to rob a savings and loan company. As might be anticipated, his plan was poorly formulated and his capture was almost immediate. This was the first antisocial behavior in what was to be a very short criminal career. Although Greg had no real belief in the probability of succeeding as a bank robber, it may be speculated that unconsciously he wanted some external force to take control of his life. To this extent, Greg's plan was totally successful.

Greg was tried in federal court approximately 18 months after his arrest. Much of that time had been spent in obtaining a series of lengthy psychological evaluations of most aspects of Greg's life. All forensic experts concluded that Greg suffered from an impulse disorder known as pathological gambling. Fortunately, Greg received strong support from a variety of individuals at his trial. He was sentenced to 25 years in prison. With credit being given for the previous 1½ years, the remaining 23½ years of the sentence was probated. Without question this was the greatest payoff for a long shot in Greg's life.

Not surprisingly, the presiding judge was adamant in requiring that Greg receive all appropriate forms of psychological treatment so as to decrease or eliminate the possibility of any recidivistic acts. The problem then became one of effective treatment for the pathological gambler.

Stages of Compulsive Gambling

Most compulsive gamblers go through some variation of the following stages:

1. *Winning phase.* Occasional gambling is marked by heightened excitement when winning and a heightened ability to forget or ignore losses. "Big win" and "big shot" fantasies increase, and the occasional actual big win takes on an increased psychological focus.

2. *Losing phase.* Fantasizing, actual gambling time, and losses increase, as do gambling alone, disruption of work and personal life, and debt and/or borrowing.

3. *Desperation phase.* Monetary, vocational, and interpersonal difficulties become disruptive at a critical and/or clinical level. Allied patterns such as

depression, anxiety, and/or substance abuse intensify. The addictive component is evident and controlling.

Therapeutic Intervention with Pathological Gambling

Therapeutic interventions favor treating compulsive gambling similarly to any other type of addictive disorder, typically including the following phases of intervention:

1. Elimination of immediate opportunity to gamble by way of inpatient hospitalization for a variable number of weeks, depending upon individual needs
2. Immediate initiation of an educational process about pathological gambling and the insidious role it takes on in every individual's life
3. Individual and group psychotherapy to help the individual explore the attitudes and beliefs that have supported the gambling behavior over a period of years
4. Economic counseling for living within a set income
5. Continued outpatient treatment in the form of weekly sessions that specifically deal with the issue of gambling
6. Periodic inpatient hospitalizations as a preventive measure once every 6 to 18 months
7. Regular attendance at Gamblers Anonymous
8. Utilization of family and/or couples therapy when indicated

Comment

Five years after his initial probation, Greg continues to do well in his new life. His motivation for gambling remains under control, and there have been no regressions to antisocial or criminal behavior. His need for vocational achievement has remained high, and, as a result, Greg has continued to experience success in this area. The treatment for his pathological gambling will likely continue for the indefinite future.

Kleptomania

The Case of Clare

If I make a set of rules, then a guy goes out and steals an airplane. He comes back and says, "It wasn't on the list of rules."

—Abe Lemons, college basketball coach

Kleptomania refers to a recurrent inability to resist the impulse to steal. It is important to note that the motivation for stealing in kleptomania is not the value of or the need for the article. The *DSM-IV* emphasizes that the stealing is done to gain the strong feelings of gratification that occur with the release of tension that the act brings in such an individual. These acts are seldom accompanied by significant preplanning, are primarily impulsive, and are usually carried out alone.

Although kleptomaniacs (the use of the subterm *mania* is unfortunate) may have problems in interpersonal relationships, their general personality functioning is likely to be within the normal range. Kleptomania can begin as early as the first school years, and it is likely to be chronic without some kind of direct intervention. Anxiety and depression, as well as guilt over the fear of being apprehended, may accompany this condition.

Stealing is a common behavior in our society. About one out of every twelve shoppers is a shoplifter, but less than 5% of shoplifters are kleptomaniacs. Most shoplifters steal to get something they want for free. Also, a substantial proportion of shoplifting occurs in isolated acts and the person does not repeat the behavior very often. Some thieves, particularly adolescents, shoplift in a group to gain peer acceptance, which can act as a precursor for later kleptomania.

Because this disorder is not necessarily accompanied by significant pathology or by clear-cut childhood syndromes, we will not analyze this case history as much as we do with others in this book. But it is worthwhile to examine this pattern, particularly as it can be compared to the antisocial personality disorder case.

All my possessions for a moment of time.
—Queen Elizabeth I, (1533–1603), on her deathbed

The Case of Clare

Clare is a bright and attractive young woman of 28 who has an interesting and responsible position in an advertising firm in the large western city in which she grew up. She first talked about her problem with a minister whom she met at a book club she attended monthly, and he referred her to a private psychologist.

Clare reports that she has been compulsively stealing off and on since she was 13 years old. She had never sought treatment before, but several recent events had heightened her fear of being apprehended. On these occasions, Clare was sure that she had been seen stealing by other customers and began to realize that she had been very lucky never to have been caught. Also, one day when she was out browsing in a department store on her lunch hour with one of her co-workers, she compulsively stole a pair of stockings and she is afraid that the co-worker saw her take them. She knows that if she is ever caught and prosecuted, it will mean losing her job, and most certainly the blemish on her record would hurt her in any number of ways.

Clare's description of her emotional responses during the stealing behavior fits the classic kleptomania pattern. She first experiences an intense state of nervousness and general tension, which gradually crystallizes into an irresistible impulse to take some specific object. She tries to resist the impulse but generally stays within the immediate range of the object, almost as if she enjoys a further tension buildup. Eventually, she steals the object, at which time she experiences a release of tension and a feeling of satisfaction. Her telling about these events sounds like a description of the buildup and release of tension in orgasm, on a milder scale.

Although Clare does use some of the items she steals, many others that she takes go unused. For example, she had accumulated more cosmetics than she could ever hope to use in the next 10 years. Also, for some reason, possibly the ease with which she has been able to steal them, she has accumulated a boxful of men's jewelry—cuff links, etc. Clare reports that she is not really limited to any subgroup of items in her stealing but primarily reponds to her impulses by going into the nearest store and meandering about until the act takes place.

Clare had a basically normal childhood and says that she was happy at this time in her life. She did very well in school and received much attention for this. Her parents both loved their children (Clare is the second oldest of four), although they did not show much physical affection. Many family activities occurred, such as picnics and fishing trips. But seldom did either parent attend for long to any one individual child, with the possible exception of her older sister, who had been for a time the only child.

When Clare was about 9 years old, she began to steal money occasionally from her mother's purse. She used the money to buy candy and other small items at a local small grocery store. When her parents found out about this, they were very distressed and sat down with Clare and had a long talk about the moral issues involved and how people would not trust her any longer. But they did not really punish her, nor did they have her make any meaningful restitution for the acts she committed. As she reflects on this, Clare feels that her parents' concern came mostly from the potential embarrassment that could occur if she began to steal outside the home. She continued to steal occasionally and became more sophisticated about it, so that her parents rarely caught her. When they did, they only repeated the same moral prohibitions, without forcing any means of restitution on her. When she was 10, Clare attempted to steal candy from the local grocery store and was apprehended. The woman who ran the store reported to Clare's parents. This time, they severely spanked her and followed the spanking with a repeat of the discussion of the moral issues involved.

From this point, Clare only stole occasionally until she was 13 years old. She then began associating with four other girls who would occasionally take "stealing trips" to downtown stores. This was not an everyday occurrence, but it was common enough to become a ritual behavior in their social interactions together. They would go downtown, and each of them would try to steal a specific object that was predetermined before they went into the store. They did this off and on for several years, and, amazingly, only one girl was ever caught. She feigned great distress, stating that she had never done anything like this before, and carried off a very emotional scene. The storekeeper responded sympathetically and did not report the event either to the police or the parents.

Clare did exceptionally well in high school academically and enrolled in a premed program at the university. She did reasonably well during her first year. The stealing behavior ceased when she came to college. In her sophomore year, she had trouble with two courses and received low grades. She realized that she was not likely to be accepted into medical school. Coincidentally, she had the first disappointing love affair of her life.

During high school, she had dated regularly, yet never developed any long-term, meaningful romance. However, in her first year at the university she dated another student seriously for almost a year, but then he became bored with the relationship and dropped her for another girl. She had sexual intercourse with him, the first time for her, and she rationalized it by saying that she thought they would some day get married.

When they broke up, she at first had a great deal of guilt about this, to add to her general disappointment.

It was at this point that Clare began occasionally stealing again, and now she was doing it alone. She would experience a buildup of apprehension and then would find relief when she shoplifted an item successfully. During this time, she was very careful as to how she went about it. She usually chose small stores that had only one proprietor, so the risk was low.

After graduation from the university, she took a glorified secretarial job in an advertising firm. Through her job she met a man whom she dated for about 4 months, after which time they somewhat impulsively married. The marriage lasted for 2 years. It was clear from the start that her choice had been a bad one, as her husband was sexually inadequate most of the time and also had a drug problem. Clare ended up supporting him, and when it became apparent that he was not going to change his behavior, she left him. But she had always believed that "marriage is forever," and so the divorce caused her a great deal of hurt. She threw herself more forcefully into her job, and her intelligence and hard work won her a promotion to a position that was a steppingstone to executive rank.

After the divorce, Clare had a series of intense romantic involvements, but she was fearful of making any new commitments. When she was not involved in a relationship, she was prone to anxiety and depression, and it was at these times that she was drawn to the stealing behavior. As she quipped, "I'm still looking for Mr. Goodbar," but as she also noted later, "at times I'm pretty scared that I'll find him."

Etiology

Clare is typical of most kleptomaniacs in that there is no remarkable history of pathology in childhood nor any significant problems as regards thought disorder, consistent neurotic behavior, or psychopathy. However, as with many other anti-social or criminal patterns (Lykken, 1995), the evolution of her kleptomania occurred in several gradual phases.

Phase one occurred when she was 9 years old. Like many children this age, she stole money that she found easily available, and, like most of these children, she was caught. But in her case this originally utilitarian pattern was reinforced by the paternal interest and lack of effective punishment. As noted, there was much caring in her family, yet little individualized attention to any one child. Stealing gained her individual attention. Although it did have negative costs, these were not strong enough to void the reinforcement of her pattern.

She moved into phase two when the stealing not only reflected the reinforcement but, in addition, became a channel for hostility toward her parents. She saw their hypocrisy, and she was developing clearer anger feelings over not getting any individual attention from them. Her stealing behavior was a lashing out at them that forced them to attend more individually to her.

The next phase in this evolution is a common one in the background of kleptomaniacs. She became involved in a peer group that integrated stealing into their social rituals. Clare was happy with these girls, got along well with them, and enjoyed many activities with them, only one of which was the stealing behavior. At this point she only stole while she was with her friends.

The fourth and final phase in the evolution of her pattern occurred when she moved from her peer stealing back to individual stealing. The stealing alleviated some of the anxiety and boredom she was experiencing as she went through the trials and tribulations that occur in most people's lives. The disappointment in the failure of her first true romantic attachment came close on the heels of her realization that she would not be able to fulfill her goal of entering medical school. So she had a lot of self-evaluation to do, which generated anxiety and depression. There is also evidence that these feelings combined with her ambivalent resolution of her sexual needs. Sometimes she would behave rather promiscuously, and at other times she would return to a more restrained pattern. In any case, when she felt any buildup of general tension, the stealing behavior would distract her and in that sense also give her a thrill and a feeling of satisfaction. Although Clare saw the behavior as ego-alien, she usually could no longer restrain herself.

The realization eventually hit home that this behavior put her at risk for endangering other areas of her life. One could even speculate that she became more careless in her recent stealing behavior from an unconscious motivation to shock herself with the realization of the risks that she was taking. In the last incident before referral the presence of her co-worker was a concrete reminder that her job, which was her one positive source of self-esteem, could be lost if she were apprehended. As a result, she then sought treatment.

Treatment

As with most of the habit disorders, the treatment must first focus on the specific behavior itself and then later attend to any ancillary issues, such as accompanying anxiety, depression, and/or interpersonal difficulties. Eliminating the problematic habit behavior is particularly crucial in Clare's case, in which there is a potential legal difficulty if she continues in it. There has not been much research attention to the elimination of kleptomania; the treatment rendered Clare reflects most of the work that has been done.

The first phase of Clare's treatment used an aversive conditioning procedure similar to that pioneered by Kellam (1969) to cure another chronic kleptomaniac. Clare was asked to simulate her entire shoplifting sequence in a room that was made up as much as possible to look like a store. The procedure was videotaped, and Clare was asked to amplify this in her imagination as strongly as she could while the videotape was being replayed. At critical decision points, she was administered a painful electric shock, which acts to suppress the behavior. To strengthen this effect, Clare was asked occasionally to imagine herself in a shoplifting sequence at various times outside the treatment hour and to hold her breath until discomfort occurred. This discomfort, like the electric shock, acts as an aversive cue to help suppress the behavior. A small portable electric shock unit could have been used as an alternative to holding her breath.

Once Clare felt she was gaining control over the stealing impulse, she was asked to go to various stores in which she had stolen. She was asked first to respond to any stealing impulses with the holding the breath technique. If the impulse could not be suppressed by this approach, she was to slowly pick up a fragile item, such as a vase, and then deliberately drop it on the floor near a number of customers. The idea was to paradoxically generate as much disturbance and embarrassment as possible (Seltzer, 1986). She was to stay around as long as possible while the item was being cleaned up, and insist on paying for the item. This action interrupts the compulsive sequence and also pairs the impulse with actual unpleasant and embarrassing consequences of an in vivo situation. Over a period of 6 weeks, the intense application of this three-stage aversive procedure (shock with the simulated videotape, the discomfort of breath holding while imagining the sequence, and generating the embarrassment while in the actual store) suppressed Clare's desire to go through a shoplifting sequence. She could comfortably go into stores, and although she occasionally felt a twinge of the old impulse, she was able to avoid ruminating about it or feeling compelled to carry it out.

Along with the aversive approach, she was taught a relaxation technique to dissipate some of her ongoing anxiety. It was hypothesized that anxiety and other emotions were channeled into the impulse to steal; hence, it is worthwhile not only to suppress the specific problem behavior itself, but also to lessen the anxiety that generated it. Clare responded well to the relaxation training and reported a gradual lessening of anxiety. She was also seen in psychotherapy weekly for six sessions, during which she clarified some of her interpersonal conflicts and corrected cognitive distortions (Alford and Beck, 1997).

Clare did shoplift three different times during the first 2 weeks of this combined treatment approach. But, as she gained control of the relaxation response and as the aversive technique took effect, she was able to avoid the stealing behavior altogether. The changes were then solidified by her gaining more awareness of how she mishandled certain areas and also by dissipating some of the feelings that had accumulated around past events in her life. Clare was followed up by her therapist for 2 years, and there was no recurrence up to that time.

Comment

Clare's case is one in which compulsive stealing became a conditioned emotional response to depression and distress. Her initial stealing from her parents could have remained one of those isolated episodes of misbehavior that characterize the development of most people. The reaction of Clare's parents was only mildly negative, and she was subsequently strongly influenced by the pressures of her peers. More attention early in the pattern may have curtailed it.

13

Disorders with Violence

Violence in America has become rampant and seems to be increasing. Many experts believe violence will continue increasing because of gangs, drugs, availability of powerful weapons, and a growing tolerance of violence in society. Understanding the cause of violence is an ongoing challenge among mental health professionals. The classic debate is whether personality traits or social stressors predict violence (Hillebrand and Pallone, 1995). There is evidence supporting both theories. Several other cases in this book also discuss patterns of violence, that is, the cases of O. J. Simpson in Chapter 1, Joseph Westbecker in Chapter 7, Jeffrey Dahmer in Chapter 8, Ted Bundy in Chapter 11, John Hinckley in Chapter 16, and to a lesser degree some of the other cases. Here the focus is on the causes of violence. The first case of Jack Ruby looks at violence in general; the second looks at patterns of violence and abuse in the family.

Causes of Violence

The Case of Jack Ruby On Friday, November 22, 1963, while in a motorcade with his wife Jacqueline and others going through the streets of Dallas, Texas, President John F. Kennedy was assassinated. The individual captured for this murder was Lee Harvey Oswald, who was imprisoned in a local Dallas jail.

Two days later, on November 24, Jack Ruby entered the basement of the jail where Oswald was in the process of being transferred to a different facility. Somehow Ruby was able to penetrate a legion of police to fatally shoot Oswald. Great controversy still surrounds Jack Ruby because his connections with crime created grave questions about possible motives for Kennedy's assassination. There are several approaches that can be taken in diagnosing Ruby's mental status. The early years of Ruby's life will first be presented, followed by alternative theories that focus on different facts from Ruby's adult life (Kantor, 1978; Scott, 1994; Summers, 1980).

The Case of Jack Ruby

Jacob Rubenstein was born in Chicago in 1911, the fifth of eight children. Jacob's parents' marriage had been arranged through a traditional Jewish Polish marriage broker. His mother, Fanny Rubenstein, who came with a dowry, was uneducated, emotionally unstable, and, like Jacob, an incessant talker. His father, Joseph Rubenstein, was short, stocky, and mean. He had no trade and was known for cursing, drinking, and beating women. Joseph beat Fanny regularly. The couple had come from Poland to America and settled in Chicago in 1905.

Jacob's home was poor and unhappy. His parents had violent fights that frequently resulted in Fanny filing assault and battery charges against Joseph. Joseph also regularly slapped his children hard, and he insisted they end their education after grade school.

When Jacob was 10, his parents separated. He and his siblings were placed in foster homes. Occasionally he stayed with his mother, who abused him physically and emotionally. She was demanding, ate compulsively, was lazy, threw temper tantrums when things didn't go her way, and often announced that she did not like any of her children. Finally, in 1937, at age 61, she was committed to a mental hospital and diagnosed as having deteriorating paranoia, a term that probably reflected some degree of organic deterioration.

At age 11 Jacob became noticeably defiant and depressed. He constantly skipped school and was disobedient to anyone in authority. The welfare department described him then as having an adequate IQ and being impulsive, unable to pay attention, and self-centered. Jacob quit school in the eighth grade at age 16 and began spending all of his time in the streets. He was unsuccessful at his attempts to hold a regular job because of tardiness and his violent disposition. Some of his ventures included selling race track tip sheets, novelties from a pushcart, peanuts at athletic games, and chocolates in strip shows. He also scalped tickets, and ran errands for Al Capone. Later he was a nightclub bouncer and waiter. He worked out regularly, wore expensive clothes, and saw himself as a ladies' man.

Jacob soon gained a reputation for engaging in senseless violence. It appeared he was determined to prove to the world he was a man and a Jew. Jacob frequently got into fights with those who expressed anti-Semitic feelings. Before he was a teenager, Jacob had already fought in a gang against others who taunted Jews.

As is often the case, the facts in a case may support more than one theory. The following sections present several theories that might explain Jacob Rubenstein's (who later changed his name to Jack Ruby) murder of Oswald, along with the facts of the case relevant to each theory.

Social Psychology Theories

Social psychology views behavior as resulting from interactions between the person and his or her environment. One explanation for Ruby's tendency toward crime and violence is that he learned this behavior from his parents when he was a child. He also probably learned that his parents did not love him. Cognitive dissonance theory maintains that a person with two conflicting beliefs feels tension or stress and is motivated to find ways to remove the conflict. As a child, Ruby may have had conflicting ideas along the line of "I love my parents and they love me" and "Both of my parents are cruel to me and say they do not like me." One way to resolve this conflict is to conclude, "I don't really need my parents so it doesn't matter what I think of them or they think of me." Perhaps Ruby learned not to care about society's values, leaving him more apt to resort to criminal activities.

At age 26 he became a union organizer for scrap iron workers. This position evolved into working with Jimmy Hoffa, an underworld leader and head of the Teamsters Union, who was known to have threatened the life of John F. Kennedy. By age 28 Ruby was entrenched with the most notorious criminal leaders of Chicago.

The influence of stress on behavior is a related theory. The diathesis/stress theory of behavior is that everybody has weaknesses and strengths, and when stress increases, a person's weak area is more likely to surface. For example, in his twenties, Ruby was in another gang that attacked anti-Semites, and in his thirties, he beat up a sergeant who called him a "Jew bastard." Here, the diathesis is being a Jew while knowing there are people who hate Jews. Another diathesis was a predisposition to violence, triggered when the stress of being taunted or hated as a Jew becomes too great.

Organic/Biological/Genetic Theories

The condition of deteriorating paranoia in Ruby's mother indicates that Ruby may have inherited some genetic predisposition to a form of organic dysfunction that resulted in delusions. For example, in his mid-fifties, while in jail, Ruby believed Jews would be tortured as a result of his shooting Oswald. This became most apparent after Ruby was found guilty of first-degree murder and during his subsequent time in jail. Similarly, Ruby's mother's delusions increased as she became older.

An organic explanation for Ruby's actions offered at trial (possibly because the attorneys had no other option) that he used in trying to prove he was innocent by reason of temporary insanity was psychomotor epilepsy. Epileptic seizures are subdivided into two major groups: partial or generalized. Partial epilepsy, also called focal epilepsy, is a type of seizure that begins in a limited area of the brain and either stays in that area or spreads adjacently. It may or may not be associated with loss of consciousness. Generalized epileptic seizures involve large areas of the brain from the beginning, and invariably involve loss of consciousness.

Psychomotor epileptic seizures are complex partial seizures. These involve experiences of illusions and behavioral responses to the illusions. Applying this diagnosis to Ruby would construe his behavior immediately before and during the shooting of Oswald as outside of his normal consciousness. He may have experienced visions that he thought were real and to which his shooting responded. Testimony at his trial described the shooting as occurring during an epileptic blackout.

However, there were problems with this diagnosis—for example, evidence suggesting that he planned this act. In addition, psychomotor epilepsy has a particular physical course that was not exhibited by Ruby. Even if it could be persuasively argued that this was the very first seizure he had ever had, which would be unusual, there was no evidence that he experienced any subsequent seizures. Psychomotor epilepsy takes a kindling course, which means that after one seizure occurs, it takes less stimulation to produce future seizures. Finally, there is no evidence that Ruby was ever prescribed anticonvulsant drug therapy for this condition. However, there was some evidence at autopsy of a brain tumor, which could support the diagnosis.

If testimony in support of psychomotor epilepsy was along the lines of there being a disruption in Ruby's consciousness, a more appropriate diagnosis may have been a dissociative disorder (see Chapter 4), a condition in which the predominant feature would be an interruption in the usually integrated mechanisms of consciousness. However, this diagnosis would also be difficult to prove in light of there being no prior or subsequent events similar to the alleged dissociative experience. Thus, with psychomotor epilepsy as Ruby's main defense, it is not a great surprise that Jack Ruby was found guilty of first-degree murder and sentenced to death.

There is another interesting and alternative biological perspective on violence. For centuries many theorists have held to the hypothesis that only humans deliberately kill others of their own species without survival reasons. However, Richard Wrangham and Dale Peterson (1996) reported a lethal chimpanzee raid in Gombe National Park in Tanzania. Eight chimpanzees purposefully traveled to the border of their range, entered a neighboring chimpanzee territory, attacked and mortally wounded a young male from another community, and then returned home. The event was significant not only as an example of another species that killed its own deliberately, but also because the species happened to be the one most closely related to humans.

Affective Disorder Theory

An intriguing possibility is that Ruby suffered from an affective disorder such as atypical depression, bipolar disorder (major mood swings), or cyclothymia (less intense mood swings) (see Chapter 7). Information is insufficient to determine if he was prone to have periods of time when he was uncharacteristically active (manic). There were times, however, when he was depressed; the welfare department described him as being depressed as a child. Ruby admitted that as an adult he overate in order to ward off depression. He then took medication to depress his appetite and give him energy. Later Ruby stopped taking his weight-loss medication when he worried that it was making his hair thinner.

Unlike some diagnoses such as ASP that are manifest throughout a person's life, the diagnosis of depression or a related affect disorder leaves open the opportunity for remission. Something like this occurred in 1944, the same year that Ruby's mother died, when he joined the U.S. Army Air Force. Ruby's experience in the Army Air Force was in contradiction to his previous behavior patterns: He was an aircraft mechanic who seldom got into fights and earned a good conduct medal. When he was discharged in 1946, he was a private first class.

Ruby did not necessarily seek out the life of a criminal. When he returned to civilian life he struggled for 8 years in a business distributing punch boards, key chains, and other miscellaneous items with his brothers, with whom he fought constantly. This experience may have caused Ruby's mood swings to return. It was after this that Ruby allegedly responded to instructions from organized crime to go to Dallas.

Depression can be accompanied by psychosis (DeBattista, 1998). When Ruby heard the verdict of electrocution, he likely lost all hope. His delusions about all Jews being killed took control, and he realized he would never see his dogs again, whom he considered to be his wife and children. Expecting electrocution at any time, he tried several times to kill himself first in different ways, such as by crashing his head against the wall, hoping to split his skull. At this point in his life, all would agree Ruby was very depressed.

Psychopathy–Antisocial Personality Disorder (ASP) Theory

Ruby's life of crime that began as a child supports the diagnosis of psychopathy and/or antisocial personality disorder (see Chapter 11). His connections with Cuba linked him with the U.S. government and the underworld. Six years before the assassination he began smuggling guns and ammunition to Cuba in support of Fidel Castro. Organized crime supported Castro to ensure good relations when the revolution ended. However, later the same group turned against Castro because he would not endorse their activities. It may not have been a coincidence that the head of the underworld wished Kennedy dead.

Examples of additional activities characteristic of the antisocial personality disorder abound. For example, Ruby's name became associated with the expansion of organized crime into Dallas. He became involved with smuggling narcotics and operating bootleg whiskey. In addition, he opened nightclubs where underworld figures attended regularly. He beat up those who crossed him, but he never was punished. Once Ruby had an argument with his sister while he was driving. He slapped her, stopped the car, and shoved her out. Throughout the nightclub years, Ruby was arrested nine times for various acts of violence, but the only thing he ever received a punishment for was a traffic violation. This probably reflects his manipulativeness as well as the extent of his contacts among local law enforcement officials and judges.

The antisocial personality would be willing to kill for money, and that is what many believe caused Ruby to kill Oswald. In 1963, before Kennedy's assassination, Ruby was in financial trouble. Debts and unpaid taxes forced him to sell one of his nightclubs. He agonized over finances, and then suddenly, immediately before the assassination, he behaved entirely differently, confident his financial troubles would soon end. Three days before Kennedy's assassination, Ruby told his tax lawyer he was going to be able to pay his debts as a result of a connection. There is some evidence that he received large sums of cash payments immediately after Kennedy's assassination.

Another characteristic of the ASP disorder is deceitfulness. Immediately following the assassination, Ruby showed up at a variety of public places and displayed an exaggerated amount of grief about Kennedy's death (although this could reflect a dissociative process as well). The possible deceit continued, as, after killing Oswald, Ruby denied any connections with the underworld or Cuba. His verbalized motive for killing Oswald was allegedly to save Mrs. Kennedy from the pain of attending Oswald's trial.

However, there were facts that contradict the psychopathy–antisocial personality disorder theory. The most striking is the way Ruby killed Oswald. He was certain to get caught and be punished, something a psychopath would certainly try to avoid (Meyer, 1998a).

Conclusion

Despite the appropriateness of any of these theories to his case, Jack Ruby was found guilty of the first-degree murder of Lee Harvey Oswald on March 14, 1964, and was sentenced to death. Ruby died in 1967 of cancer while awaiting a new trial after his death sentence conviction was overturned.

Interventions

As noted, there are numerous potential causes of violent behavior. The following gives an overview of the common causes, along with consensus intervention strategies.

1. *Violence as an inherent part of human nature:* (a) individual psychotherapy to modify basic personality patterns; (b) medications to diminish anxiety

and minimize inappropriate reactions; (c) psychosurgery to change or interrupt patterns of brain functioning.

2. *Violence as a consequence of social learning:* (a) family therapy to change home environment or facilitate coping in the family setting; (b) group therapy to enhance appropriate coping in social situation; (c) assertiveness training and social skills training to give concrete training in self-assertion without violence; (d) systematic desensitization (SDT) to desensitize client to the precipitating stimuli, so as to diminish inappropriate or excessive reactions; (e) token economy, time-out, social isolation to extinguish violent behavior through removal of environmental reinforcers, as well as to strengthen appropriate responses; (f) classical conditioning to extinguish violent behavior, as in aversive conditioning; (g) parent effectiveness training, Parents Anonymous to enhance adequate coping skills and provide a supportive peer group.

3. *Violence as a consequence of frustration and other situational factors:* (a) traditional psychotherapy to release frustrations and to change coping patterns; (b) family therapy—see 1a; (c) group therapy—see 2b; (d) assertiveness training, social skills training—see 2c; (e) token economy to provide opportunities for positively reinforcing experiences while extinguishing the violent behavior; (f) parent effectiveness training, etc.—see 2g.

4. *Violence as a means of communication:* (a) expressive therapies to substitute alternate means of expression of feelings underlying violent acting-out; (b) assertiveness training, etc.—see 2c; (c) SDT—see 2d; (d) parent effectiveness training—see 2g.

5. *Violence and aggression as protection of territorial integrity and body space:* (a) SDT—see 2d; (b) assertiveness training—see 2c; (c) individual psychotherapy to improve the sense of self and self-esteem.

Prediction of Violent Behavior

The prediction of violent behavior is perhaps one of the most formidable tasks asked of any psychologist. At a personal level it may be viewed as an unpleasant and anxiety-producing situation that brings the psychologist too close to the darkest side of the human condition. On a professional level, Monahan (1981) was one of the first to thoroughly describe many of the problems inherent in making such judgments. The difficulties for the professional were heightened even more when in 1976, a major precedent was set by the California Supreme Court in *Tarasoff* v. *Regents of the University of California* (551 P.2d 334 (Cal. 1976)). Tatianen Tarasoff had become the romantic obsession of Prosejit Poddar after she gave him a ritual New Year's Eve kiss. In therapy at the counseling center, Poddar told the therapist that he felt like killing Tarasoff. The campus police were sent to pick Tarasoff up, but he convinced them he would not be a problem, so they left. He later killed Tarasoff. Her estate sued, and the California Supreme Court held that the therapist had a "duty to warn" Tarasoff (later amended to a "duty to protect"). Unfortunately, given the low base rates of severe aggressive behaviors (and suicide, as well), making an accurate prediction of specific actual behavior is virtually impossible, and overprediction is common.

The Problem of Overprediction

Four factors primarily contribute to overprediction. First, predicting rare events is an inherently difficult task, and violence (and suicide) is something of a rare phenomenon. Any attempt at predicting a low base rate event will guarantee a significant number of false positives. A second bias toward overprediction stems from the relative costs of mistaken predictions. Mistakenly labeling an individual dangerous—a false positive—may result in continued confinement to a hospital or treatment program, with little potential for adverse consequences for the therapist. By comparison, incorrectly labeling someone safe who later commits a violent act—a false negative—exposes the predictor to public outcry and civil liability. The high costs of false negatives create a bias to overpredict out of self-defense.

Third, most studies on the prediction of dangerousness to self or others are based on long-term follow-up, usually for many years and seldom less than 1 year. Yet, in the real world, the requested predictions are usually for "imminent" predictions, that is, for that day or a few days. Fourth, "dangerousness" is not a simple trait or predisposition. People vary along many dimensions. So they may be dangerous or violent at some point, but no one is invariably and constantly dangerous. Under the right conditions nearly any individual may become assaultive, while even very impulsive, hostile individuals are not violent most of the time. Unlike other characteristics that are viewed as highly stable, dangerousness fluctuates over time in accordance with a variety of environmental factors, maturation, changes in level of adjustment, and so forth. Violence and dangerousness may be viewed most parsimoniously as an interaction of personality and environmental factors. It is the second group, environmental factors, that greatly confounds the prediction problem due to their constant variation.

Specific Indicators of Aggression

Monahan (1981) has pinpointed eight most critical demographic predictor variables for aggression. Violence is more common if the potential perpetrator (1) is young (this variable correlates strongly up until the 30 to 35 age range, after which the correlation is close to random), (2) is male, (3) is of a lower socio-economic class, (4) is from a disadvantaged minority, (5) is less educated, (6) has a lower intellectual level, (7) has an unstable school and/or vocational history, and (8) has a history of juvenile violence and/or alcohol and/or drug abuse.

Other demographic indicators of a potential for violence that have been noted throughout the literature are (1) a prior history of violent behaviors; (2) a prior history of suicide attempts; (3) a history of family violence; (4) soft neurological signs; (5) command hallucinations; (6) fascination with weapons; (7) histrionic personality traits; (8) a pattern of cruelty to animals as a child or adolescent; (9) a rejecting or depressed father; and (10) recent stress, especially if associated with low levels of serotonin.

Family Violence—Physical and Sexual Abuse of Children and Spouse

The Cases of Charles and Abby Throughout history, as well as across cultures, the abuse of children has been clearly documented (Melton et al., 1997; Finkelhor and Dzuiba-Leatherman, 1994). Although it is frequently abhorred, few actual preventive steps have been taken, and it is ironic that the first formal legal intervention in a child abuse case, that of Mary Ellen in New York in 1875, had to be prosecuted through animal protection laws and primarily as a result of the efforts of the Society for the Prevention of Cruelty to Animals. However, all fifty U.S. states have now established legislative routes to identification of abusive families and to intervention. As a result, the number of identified cases has grown enormously. Because of the private nature of abuse and the reluctance of both perpetrators and victims to reveal it, clearly identified cases of child abuse are still generally believed to represent only a portion of actual cases. Estimates vary widely, and debate over incidence of child abuse will doubtless continue. However, whatever the true incidence rates, the problem is obviously substantial.

The consequences of abuse to children are usually extensive and debilitating (Finkelhor and Dzuiba-Leatherman, 1994), and the effect goes beyond consequences to the child to encompass consequences to others with whom the child later interacts; for example, abused children are prone to grow up to be abusers, as will be seen in the following case of Abby. The problem is of massive proportion.

Spouse Abuse

As the data indicate, there's no place like home, for either happiness or violence. As a marriage breaks down, the potential for violence soars. The violence may be directed toward a child or toward the spouse. Estimates of the percentage of couples who experience physical violence at some time in the course of a marriage range from 30% to 60%, and it is clear that the amount of reported violence is far less than the amount of actual violence. In most cases the wife is the victim, although there are a few reports of husbands being abused. Family therapy can sometimes be helpful, although often by the time the abuse pattern has been made public, the bonding between the two parties has been so violated that reconciliation is highly improbable. As is noted in the subsequent case of Abby, many spouse abusers were themselves abused as a child by one or both of their parents.

Recognizing a Potentially Abusive Adult Relationship

Cases such as O. J. Simpson's (see Chapter 1) and recognition of such patterns as "date rape" bring home the need to be aware of the cues that help one recognize a potential abusive adult relationship and/or a potential batterer, especially when entering a relationship. The following patterns may suggest potential abuse behavior:

- Having been a participant in, a victim of, or witness to (in that order of predictive power) abusive patterns, or to a lesser degree, one abusive or violent episode
- Violence toward pets, other animals, or even inanimate objects
- General problems with anger control or evidence of a "temper"
- Problems in impulse control
- "Playful" use of force during sex
- Threats of violence and/or use of force or threats to manipulate arguments
- Evidence of control issues, especially when there are problems of relinquishing control in relationships, and especially when this is combined with tendencies to avoid responsibility for behaviors or project blame on others
- Evidence of possessiveness toward persons, or jealousy
- An increasing dependency on the relationship
- Substance abuse in either party
- Verbalizations of strong adherence to traditional male-female roles in relationships
- Evidence of psychopathy or sadistic personality patterns
- Feelings of being possessively controlled, jealousy, or anger easily elicited by the person potentially abused
- Indicators of emotional or physical isolation, or vulnerability, or being prone to masochism or excessive dependency in the person potentially abused

Child Abuse

I was coming home from Kindergarten—well, they told me it was Kindergarten. I found out later that I had been working in a factory for ten years. It's good for a kid to know how to make gloves.
—Ellen DeGeneres, star of the TV show "Ellen"

We'll first present a classic pattern of child sexual abuse, the case of Charles, followed by one of physical abuse, the case of Abby.

The Case of Charles

Charles is a 39-year-old civil engineer who lives in a medium-size city in Kentucky. He works for a large construction business, makes a good salary, and would certainly be characterized as a model citizen by most who know him. He is a long-time member of a church (although he doesn't profess or practice any strong religious beliefs) and belongs to a number of civic organizations. All indications are that he had a normal childhood. He has never sought help for any psychological disorder.

Charles married at age 25. The marriage was certainly a good one at the outset, and both he and his wife were delighted when she had a baby girl, Vicki, when Charles was 30. Unfortunately, the marriage started to deteriorate shortly thereafter. Charles's wife enjoyed the status of being a mother, but not the functions. She returned to her job as a secretary as soon as she could after Vicki's birth and often hired babysitters to escape the routine demands of child care. She had always been a regular social drinker, but she now began to drink more secretively and more often, probably to dissolve both guilt and anxiety. Within several years she had developed a true alcoholic pattern. She was just barely able to hold on to her job and was almost nonfunctional as a wife and mother.

Charles, on the other hand, enjoyed fathering and developed a strong bond with Vicki. He had few friends or interests away from home. He and his wife now simply tolerated each other, with only rare sexual or emotional encounters. He satisfied his sexual needs in several ways: an occasional affair, a visit to a prostitute, or by masturbation to stimulation from pornographic magazines and videotapes.

Charles had always allowed Vicki to lie down next to him or put her head in his lap for 15 minutes or so before she went off to bed. One night, when Vicki was 8, he let her lie next to him on the couch for almost an hour, enjoying the closeness to her, a closeness that seemingly was not available to him elsewhere. He became aroused sexually and responded by sending Vicki off to bed. Several nights later he was again lying with Vicki and again became aroused. This time, he just lay there. After a while, as Vicki moved around a bit, he suddenly had a strong orgasm. He felt some upset at this time, but allowed a repetition on a couple of subsequent occasions.

Then, a week later, the situation escalated further. When Charles had become very aroused, he raised the back of Vicki's nightgown and gently rubbed his penis against her buttocks, again having a strong orgasm. He told Vicki everything was all right and not to be upset, and she wasn't. This, however, was the first time that he had acted to directly cause a sexual act, and this seemed to break down any remaining inhibitions. He would now sometimes have Vicki reach behind her and rub his penis. Also, he would touch her occasionally on her genitals and would bring on his orgasm by rubbing his penis between her legs. He eventually asked her to "lick it" at a point of high arousal and would ejaculate on her face, all the time presenting all of this to Vicki as a sort of game, although always emphasizing her need to keep secret about it. He tried to penetrate her vagina a couple of times, but quickly backed off when Vicki complained that it hurt.

This pattern went on for about 6 months. There was some reason to believe that Charles's wife may have been at least vaguely aware of what was happening. But she did nothing, and in fact had been using alcohol even more heavily over the last year or so. Then, one day while Vicki was playing with a neighbor girl, the word "penis" came up, and Vicki blurted out, "Well, Daddy lets me lick his." The friend's mother overheard this, asked Vicki what she meant, and Vicki described it all in vivid detail. The neighbor called her husband, who as a physician knew it had to be reported, and where, and did so.

When confronted by a worker with the child protective services division, Charles broke down and confessed. He was later convicted. But based on his history and the recommendations of a psychologist and social worker, his sentence was probated, with a stipulated requirement for community service and treatment.

Treatment was successful in the sense that Charles never sexually abused Vicki again. But, he and his wife could never reconcile their feelings about this, and were divorced within the year. It's not yet clear how much psychological damage Vicki has incurred. However, it was probably quite a bit; indeed, it is very likely that over time she will pay the highest price of all.

> *Then spare the rod and spoil the child.*
> —Samuel Butler, *Hudibras* (1663)

The Case of Abby

Abby was born to a poor family in the mountains of West Virginia. When she was 4, the family moved to Akron, Ohio, in hopes of her father getting work in a tire factory, where her uncle already had a job. Unfortunately, this was at the time such jobs were drying up. After struggling for several years, often surviving only on welfare, the family moved to Tennessee to try to find work at a new General Motors plant being built there.

There were no dramatic problems or incidents in Abby's childhood. However, child care was minimal and there was little value placed on education or achievement. She seldom had any interaction with her father, who spent his time away from home when he could. When he was home, he spent his time eating, sleeping, drinking, or beating Abby's mother or one of the five children if they gained too much of his attention. Abby's mother loved the children, but her emotional, intellectual, and physical resources were overwhelmed to the point that she could do little more than meet their basic needs.

Abby made it through high school, albeit with close to failing grades. She had become pregnant in her junior year but aborted without letting her parents know. One month after getting out of high school, she discovered she was again pregnant, but this time she maneuvered the father into marrying her. They moved to a nearby city and she delivered a healthy girl, and almost immediately became pregnant again. This pregnancy and labor were difficult and the child, a boy, soon showed some signs that he had incurred brain damage.

Abby's husband soon had enough of fatherhood and left town, to be seldom heard from again. Abby was not especially attractive, and was neither very bright nor had any marketable skills. With two young children and no money, she did not attract the most eligible of men. She had a string of live-in boyfriends, and several of them would beat whichever child bothered them in some way, and it was usually the youngest child.

Abby herself was confused and overwhelmed by the tasks of child care. Her daughter was quiet and docile, almost to the point of being withdrawn, so she caused Abby few problems. However, as her youngest became more mobile, he became more difficult to control. Abby had few skills or resources to bring to the task, and more and more she quickly resorted to beating this child. A week after yet another boyfriend had abruptly walked out on her, her son broke a small vase that Abby had received years ago from a much loved grandmother. Abby started shrieking at her son, grabbed him roughly, dragged him by the arm into the kitchen, and started hitting him and beating him. When she finally stopped, he was bleeding and bruised, and it became evident he could hardly move his arm. He was still not moving the arm the next day, and Abby took him to a hospital emergency room, where they quickly recognized the probability of child abuse. Abby at first tried to deny it, but eventually admitted what had happened. She was diverted into treatment and a parents' training group and began to make some progress in handling her children. But there were repeat incidents, and then Abby left town with a new boyfriend. No follow-up information is available, but it is probable the abuse occurred again, becoming a legacy her children would carry into their own world as parents.

Etiology

Many overall factors contribute to the ultimate emergence of an episode of physical and/or sexual child abuse (Melton et al., 1997; Hillebrand and Pallone, 1995; Finkelhor and Dzuiba-Leatherman, 1994). These factors are found within three contributing systems, socio-cultural, familial, and individual. To the degree these factors are present, the probability of an occurrence of child abuse is increased. At the most basic level are the following *socio-cultural* factors that facilitate an increase in episodes of child abuse:

- Lack of affirmation and support of the family unit
- Lack of emphasis on parent training skills as a prerequisite to parenting
- Acceptance of and high media visibility of violence
- Acceptance of corporal punishment as a central child rearing technique
- Emphasis on competitiveness rather than cooperation
- Unequal status for women
- Low economic support for schools and day care facilities

Socio-cultural factors heighten the probability of abuse in conjunction with the following *familial* factors:

- Low socio-economic and educational level
- Little availability of friends and extended family for support
- A single parent or merged parent family structure
- Marital instability
- Family violence as common and traditionally accepted
- Low rate of family contact and information exchange
- Significant periods of mother absence
- High acceptance of family nudity
- Low affirmation of family member privacy
- "Vulnerable" children, that is, to the degree they are young, sick, disturbed, retarded, or emotionally isolated

The probability of abuse in a specific instance is then in turn increased by the following *individual* factors:

- History of abuse as a child
- Low emotional stability and/or self-esteem
- Low ability to tolerate frustration and inhibit anger
- High impulsiveness
- Lack of parenting skills
- High emotional and interpersonal isolation
- Problems in handling dependency needs of self or others
- Low ability to express physical affection
- Unrealistic expectancies for child's performance
- Acceptance of corporal punishment as a primary child rearing technique
- Presence of drug or alcohol abuse

As with most cases, many but not all of these factors are found in the cases of Charles and of Abby. Some predict more to physical abuse and some to sexual abuse, but most factors predict to either type of abuse. However, from an overall perspective, the following general factors were evident in the cases of Charles and of Abby:

- *Impulsivity:* The actual incident often occurs in persons in whom either training or temperament (or both) has predisposed to immediately act on impulse, not bring inhibitory belief systems to bear on impulse or delay gratification. In a similar vein, the demands of child rearing are too much for an immature personality, who lashes out in retaliation at the cause for these demands. Remorse may follow, but the damage is done.

- *Incompetence:* As with Abby, far too many parents come to this crucial task with little preparation or support (e.g., poverty markedly increases the potential for child abuse). When the task overwhelms them, they react with harsh punishments in an attempt to regain control.

- *Disturbance:* Psychological and physical disturbances (not in the child) such as schizophrenia, drug and alcohol abuse, mental retardation, or (as in the case of Charles) a disrupted marriage generates problems that facilitate child abuse.

- *Modeling:* The child who has been abused or who has witnessed a pattern of spouse abuse is much more likely to become an abuser than the average child.

- *Characteristics of the child:* As was the case with Abby's younger child, children who have characteristics that make frustration or disappointment more likely (e.g., ADHD, physical or psychological handicaps) are more likely to be abused. The amount of parental bonding and the vulnerability of the child are also relevant; thus, stepchildren and younger children are more often the victims. Indeed, live-in boyfriends are a common source of child abuse.

Physical Abuse

Mothers physically abuse more in absolute terms; fathers more in abuse events per contact hours. Predictors of physical abuse of children (with the greatest applicability to mothers) are: (1) single parent, (2) younger, (3) less educated, (4) lower SES, and (5) having a history of abuse. These are the best predictors; but demographic predictors are not usually responsive to intervention. Mediating-causative variables, which offer more potential for intervention, are: (1) higher physiological reactivity to a crying child, to children in general, and probably just in general; (2) a higher proclivity to label negative child behaviors with internal and stable attributions and positive events with external and transient attributions; (3) acceptance of fewer mitigating factors for problematic behavior (thus facilitating judgments of "badness" and subsequent punishment); (4) unrealistic expectations before and after birth for a child's performance, especially as regards more complex behavior sequences; (5) more rigid attitudes; (6) higher than normal rates of physical illness, stress, and depression; (7) lower self-esteem; and (8) lack of empathy. Surprisingly, they show only slightly higher levels of precipitating substance abuse. They generally like their children less (there is some research to indicate this is not usually based on objective fact), and they attend to and track their children's behavior less often (Milner, 1998).

Sexual Abuse

The factors that generate physical child abuse are also often relevant to cases of sexual child abuse. However, a number of specifically relevant factors are also critical. For example, psychodynamic features here include the interaction of such parental factors as marital discord, personality disorder, loss of an important relationship or fear of disintegration of the family, and emotional deprivation. Other factors include the equating of sexuality and affection, the importance of heterosexual success to self-identity, a focus on sexual acts rather than on relationships, and any acceptance of younger and smaller sexual partners.

The seriousness of consequent disorder in the child resulting from sexual abuse appears to depend on several factors. More serious problems are likely if (1) the offender is in a close relationship to the child, such as the father; (2) the sexual activity included genital contact, and especially if this includes penetration; (3) the child is older, for example, adolescent, at the time of abuse; (4) the abuse is frequent and/or of long duration; (5) the child has strong negative feelings about the abuse and/or is somehow aware of its wrongness; and (6) much upset and/or distress occurs around the event, for example, via court testimony.

Diagnostic Problems in Sexual Abuse

The following, adapted in part from the review of research and clinical data, by Michael P. Maloney, the lead defense psychologist in the McMartin trial, presents the levels of confidence or quality of inference allowed by various types of evidence often employed in assessing allegations of child sexual abuse.

1. Personal involvement/personal observation	Typically conclusive
2. Pregnancy	Typically conclusive
3. Photographic documentation	Minimal inference
4. Sexually transmitted disease	Minimal inference
5. Confession by offender in context of child accusation	Minimal inference
6. Physical/medical findings with disclosure	Minimal/moderate inference
7. Physical/medical findings without disclosure	Moderate inference
8. Inappropriate sexual behavior or knowledge with disclosure	Moderate inference
9. Sexualized responses to anatomical dolls with no contextual behavior	High inference
10. Nonsexual inappropriate behavior with disclosure	High inference
11. Sexualized drawings with no contextual behavior	High to extreme inference
12. Inappriate behavior with no disclosure	High to extreme inference
13. Verbal report with no contextual behavior	Extreme inference
14. Examiner/therapist "Hunches"	Extreme inference

Note that a determination of moderate to extreme inference does not suggest that abuse did not occur, but rather that such a conclusion is based on limited critical data. These cases necessitate a careful analysis of a variety of contextual factors. Any conclusions must be carefully weighed and documented.

Treatment

The interventions noted in these two classic patterns, that is, of Charles and Abby, are those typically employed. The emphasis is obviously going to differ depending upon issues in an individual case. However, in addition to individual psychotherapy, there are three core approaches that are potentially useful in almost all such cases:

1. *Family Therapy:* Because the family is virtually always disrupted, family therapy is necessary. Even when the family system eventually changes, as in the case of Charles, family therapy can help to mute the damage to all concerned.

2. *Parent training:* When the abuse comes from a parent, parent training is necessary to deal not only with the problems that led to the abuse, but to those generated by the abuse as well.

3. *Support systems:* As in the cases of both Charles and Abby, abuse often comes when there has been a sense of having been emotionally isolated. In

this vein, a community-based counseling and support group is helpful to both victims and abusing parents.

These three approaches can be supplemented by other interventions, such as attempts to change the person's employment possibilities or social skills (both would be important for Abby). When there is a couple involved, marital therapy is likely to be necessary if the marriage is to continue. Lastly, and from a moral perspective, it is emphasized that the most deserving of specific treatment attention is the child victim, or other siblings who may be vicarious victims.

Comment

Treatment may help in a specific case. But the greatest changes will come with efforts at prevention (e.g., parent training before becoming parents, the reduction of the percentage of very young and/or single parents without enough skills or resources, educational programs in the schools) or cultural change (e.g., efforts to reduce the acceptance of the common use of physical discipline).

14

Disorders of Childhood and Adolescence

This section documents cases that are characteristic of the earlier years of life. As in all the sections of this book, representative cases have been chosen to sample the relevant range of disorders and age ranges. Symptoms of the first three cases, developmental language disorder, attention-deficit hyperactivity disorder, and early infantile autism, are usually evident in early childhood. As with many of the childhood disorders, however, they may not cause a major disruption in the child's and/or family's world until the child moves into the structured social demands of day care and formal schooling. The first case, Delano, a child with the development language disorder, is a particularly good example of this phenomenon. Although the disorder did not emerge until he went to school, there was hard evidence of disorder as early as 18 months of age. Even though all three of these disorders may take a severe toll on a child's later adjustment, Delano's symptomatology is subtle when compared to that seen in the autistic disorder case.

The next two disorders discussed, the separation disorder and the oppositional defiant disorder, are more characteristic of middle childhood, particularly the early school years, although again the initial symptoms may appear much earlier. These disorders present contrasting styles of coping with a major developmental task—the establishment of a new and separate sense of identity. In the separation disorder a too fearful coping style makes adequate separation very difficult and results in a school phobia, whereas in the oppositional defiant disorder uncontrolled assertiveness blocks an adequate adjustment. The final case, that of Mr. E., demonstrates the potential complexities of identity development in adolescence and adulthood.

Developmental Language Disorder

The Case of
Delano

We spend the first 12 months of our child's lives teaching them to walk and talk, and the next 12 years telling them to sit down and shut up.

—Phyllis Diller, comic

Children with language and other skill achievement problems are likely to show signs of the disorders from early on. However, it is when these become manifest in school-related problems that there is often a referral for psychological assessment. In such cases the psychologist's role often focuses on evaluating the child's level of cognitive and intellectual skills and on making recommendations for intervention within the school system (Wolman, 1998). Such intervention often requires the integration of a great deal of history from a variety of sources, with the consequent problem of organizing a small mountain of information into a diagnostic impression of the child.

The term *learning disabled* is often used to describe children who encounter more than the usual degree of difficulty in mastering basic school subjects. Any implication that such children have central nervous system impairment is not accurate. A 1980 federal law, Education for All Handicapped Children (P.L. 94-142), incorporates a definition of the learning-disabled child that is useful here, as it is broad enough to encompass many of the types of school-related problems that clinical psychologists are called on to deal with. Implicit in such a definition is that a child with a learning disability possesses skills in other areas and is not simply deficient in performance abilities across the board.

"Specific learning disability" means a disorder in one or more of the basic psychological processes involved in understanding or in using languages, spoken or written, which may manifest itself in an imperfect ability to listen, think, speak, read, write, spell, or to do mathematical calculations. The term includes such conditions as perceptual handicaps, brain injury, minimal brain disfunction, dyslexia, and developmental aphasia. The term does not include children who have learning problems which are primarily the result of visual, hearing, or motor handicaps, or mental retardation, or of environmental, cultural, or economic disadvantage. (P.L. 94-142, sect. 121a. 5 (9))

In a general way the *DSM-IV* aids in the identification of school-related disorders owing to its expanded treatment of childhood disorders, including the common problems of the disorders of reading and language. The former condition is diagnosed when there is a significant discrepancy between a child's IQ score and a standardized assessment of reading proficiency. Reading disorders are generally first identified after a child has been in school for some time—long enough for a discrepancy between reading and intellectual skills to develop. In many instances, however, reading disorders may be preceded by disorders of language, which are included in the *DSM-IV* under the Communication Disorders.

The following case, Delano, illustrates a situation in which both a receptive language disorder and a reading disorder were concurrently diagnosed. In this case a comprehensive psychological evaluation revealed evidence of specific developmental disorders affecting both receptive (and some expressive) language and reading ability. Although the child's problems became most obvious once he had started school, their origin could be traced to evidence of central nervous system impairment evident at a very early age, when epileptic seizures first occurred.

The Case of Delano

Delano ("Del") was referred to a local psychology clinic for a series of tests to determine his overall ability level. Although 7½ years old, he was still in first grade, having failed the first time. Del's parents could not understand his poor school performance and had been of the impression that he possessed at least average intelligence. They described him as a quiet, well-mannered child who was well liked by his classmates and his teacher.

According to the developmental history supplied by the parents, Del, one of three children, was the product of a planned pregnancy and normal delivery. He was described as a "good baby" but manifested a series of medical problems, including allergies, ear infections, pneumonia, and psychomotor seizures—the latter first diagnosed when Del was about 18 months old. At this time, both parents had noticed that Del would occasionally become preoccupied with the movement of his hands and also seemed to withdraw from social contact and take on a glassy-eyed stare. These episodes were reported as occurring before sleep or on first waking, then later began to occur during the day as well. According to the parents, these trance-like states could usually be interrupted by calling Del's name.

Shortly after these episodes began, Del was taken to the family pediatrician, who recommended a neurological examination. As part of the exam an electroencephalogram (EEG) recording was made. In this technique small electrodes placed on various parts of the head are used to monitor electrical activity in brain tissue immediately underneath. Because certain characteristic brainwave patterns emanate from various locations, any abnormalities are readily evident.

In Del's case the EEG report indicated "mild dysrhythmia," with evidence of a "focal discharge" in the posterior region of the temporal lobe of the left hemisphere. That is, electrical activity in Del's brain was mildly irregular and also was comparatively uncontrolled in one specific location. Numerous studies have demonstrated that this region of the brain plays a significant role in understanding speech and language. The presence of irregular electrical activity in this portion of Del's brain suggested some disruption of brain structures involved in the ability to understand language. The seizure activity and the underlying irregular brain wave activity were subsequently controlled with a medication called phenobarbitol, and at the time of the assessment, Del had not had a seizure in years. Nevertheless, it was apparent that the early brain trauma associated with the seizures somewhat curtailed his development of certain skills during the critical early formative years.

Thus, it was not surprising to discover that Del's speech and language skills were slow to develop. He did not speak clearly until he was almost 3, and his parents reported that it was often necessary to repeat instructions endlessly, after which time there was still no guarantee that he would do what he had been told. At the age of 3, he was enrolled in a nursery school, where he displayed a behavior pattern characterized by a short attention span, low frustration tolerance, and social immaturity. This pattern continued into first grade. Despite attending a summer tutoring program before entering school, he did not do well in first grade, which he was repeating when the psychological assessment was made.

One of the most obvious things about Del was that he was a likable child. During the psychological testing, he proved easy to get along with and worked industriously if given clear structure. He was attentive to task instructions but occasionally misunderstood the examiner, especially when asked to define words. For example, he confused the word *donkey* with *doggie* and repeated the word *diamond* several times, as if trying to form the memory of a word that he had never heard, yet he knew what a diamond was. It seemed that tasks such as word definitions gave Del the most problem; he did best on test items that provided contextual cues that aided comprehension. Del adopted a rather passive stance toward testing—almost timid at times. He was reluctant to ask for repetitions of test questions, even when it was evident that he did not clearly understand them.

In addition, he created the general impression of a somewhat shy child, less talkative than many children of similar age. As it turned out, Del had developed this style as a result of feeling sensitive about having to ask people to repeat things that he did not understand the first time; he felt that others thought him stupid. Indeed, several of the kids at school, with their unerring ability to focus on other children's weaknesses, had taken to calling him "Spaceman" because he seemed to be "out of it" much of the time. Nonetheless, despite the reserve apparent in Del's behavior, he was an appealing child.

The results of the psychological assessment revealed that Del did possess average intellectual skills, or the overall mental ability necessary to handle normal academic demands. Even this level was felt to be an underestimate of his actual potential, due to the language disturbance, which inhibited the expression of intelligent behavior. Not surprisingly, a standardized test of intellectual abilities, the Wechsler Intelligence Scale for Children (WISC-R)-Revised, revealed that Del's verbal skills were less highly developed than abilities that made use of nonverbal activity, such as visual-motor coordination. The examiner had access to Del's scores on the same test when it had been administered about a year earlier; it was notable that Del's language skills were not keeping pace with his development in other areas. One of the most significant revelations of the assessment was that Del's performance improved markedly whenever he was able to process test information visually. For example, he performed rather poorly on a vocabulary test in which the examiner read words for Del to define. His performance improved dramatically when vocabulary was assessed by having the examiner show Del pictures of objects or events and ask him to select those that corresponded to words read.

Performance on a number of the tests revealed that Del was adept at using contextual cues to obtain meaning from what was going on around him. In this regard, it was fascinating to find that, despite markedly subaverage performance on measures that evaluate basic reading skills—for example, word and letter identification and word comprehension—Del was able to read and comprehend passages in grade school readers at nearly a second-grade level. It appeared that Del had developed a reading strategy in which he used contextual cues to understand much of what he read. For example, he appeared to search for familiar words in a passage and then try to fit them together with words whose meaning he was unable to decipher. In the absence of such contextual cues, as when word comprehension was tested, he was at a considerable disadvantage because he was not able to sound words out effectively. (Word sounding is an invaluable skill that helps many readers trigger acoustic memories that are associated with the visual images of words.) Del, in contrast, relied almost solely on visual cues to make sense out of what he read and was thereby clearly handicapped in his efforts to read all except materials that were familiar to him.

The overall results of the psychological assessment indicated that, despite possessing visual comprehension skills and reasoning abilities well in excess of his current grade level, Del manifested a significant deficit in auditory processing—specifically, in comprehension. It was found that Del required frequent repetitions of task instructions and items and that his ability to remember auditorially presented information for immediate recall was markedly below average.

The results of the assessment helped tie together a number of observations that had been made about Del. It became evident that his difficulty in comprehending spoken language went back a long way—to the early stages of language development—and may have reduced the amount of information about his surroundings that Del was able to assimilate. His difficulty in understanding others led him to become somewhat shy and withdrawn in social situations. He preferred to appear as if he understood what was going on rather than to risk peer censure (comments such as "Earth to Del, Earth to Del . . ."), which inevitably followed his attempts to have people repeat things. The language impairment became a real handicap when he entered school, where he was forced to repeat first grade despite possessing average intelligence. He appeared to have developed moderately effective compensatory strategies in school-related areas, including the use of visual and other contextual cues. However, the numerous indications that receptive language development had not kept up with relatively normal development in other cognitive skills made this a prime target for remediation recommendations. Using *DSM-IV* terminology, primary diagnoses of Mixed Expressive-Receptive Language Disorder and Reading Disorder were made.

Treatment

A number of specific recommendations were made to help Del overcome the effects of his language disability. First, it was recommended that he receive intensive training in basic auditory encoding skills necessary for reading. For children who need work in this area, a format such as that provided by the television program *Sesame Street,* in which sounds are accompanied by visual representations in animated form, is often quite effective. This format permitted Del to apply his visualization skills to aid him in auditory encoding skills like word attack and comprehension. As he became more familiar with the basic sound combinations, the use of visual prompts was gradually phased out.

Second, it was felt that Del should participate in second-grade reading classes because his overall comprehension level was considerably in advance of his first-grade placement. Much of the second-grade reading material used extensive pictorial cues, so Del would be able to use these in understanding what he read. Moreover, as the additional training in auditory encoding began to have an effect, it was thought that his reading skills would increase even more. Efforts were also made to develop rewards for reading, including giving Del access to appropriate comic books and other texts that employed a lot of visual cues. Del's parents were encouraged to spend time with him going through magazines and other such materials, giving Del additional reading experience as well as access to the modeling of adult reading behavior.

An issue related to developmental language delays concerns Del's difficulty in organizing his approach to various tasks. Children with this sort of problem profit from several strategies. First, they learn from exposure to role models who provide visual cues about task performance and also talk their way through tasks, explaining each step in turn, with frequent repetitions. Second, it is often helpful to sit down with such children before beginning a new task and have them verbally rehearse the steps to be followed, while perhaps jotting them down either in written or pictorial form. Many situations existed both at school and at home in which it was possible to build such routines into Del's daily activities. For example, his father began to work with Del in building plastic models and adopted an approach in which he would explain, rehearse, and demonstrate the sequences of necessary steps for Del as a means of helping him develop a more organized, less impulsive approach. Model building soon became a favored activity and provided the basis for more emotional closeness between father and son.

If the list of recommendations seems extensive, it is because deficits in language skills have so many far-reaching implications that must be addressed in planning intervention. In Del's case every effort was made to keep him in a regular classroom, in order to avoid further stigmatizing him. Both school officials and parents responded positively to the recommendations and were able to implement most of them without significantly altering Del's daily activities. Within 6 months, Del showed marked improvement in basic reading skills and continued to do well in his second-grade reading class. His parents reported that he was becoming socially more responsive around other children and less defensive about his difficulties in understanding. At last report, he was doing well in school, and the administrators were considering a phased promotion plan that would permit Del to move gradually into more advanced classes as his abilities permitted.

Comment

Children who manifest early indications of biological vulnerability and developmental delays are often slow to develop socially and interpersonally. They frequently feel themselves to be somehow different from other children, although they are often unable to articulate their concerns. Prompt recognition and treatment of conditions that compromise a child's development and contribute to the child's sense of psychological vulnerability ensure the greatest potential for subsequent adequate adjustment.

Attention-Deficit Hyperactivity Disorder

**The Case
of Matt**

*Children nowadays are tyrants. They contradict
their parents, gobble their food, and tyrannize
their teachers.*

—Socrates, 425 BC

The term attention-deficit hyperactivity disorder (ADHD) is used to describe a condition that involves (1) the persisting inability to keep one's attention focused in a sustained manner and (2) an impulsive, hyperactive-motoric factor. Children with ADHD are presumed to possess adequate basic cognitive capabilities, but they are typically unable to focus themselves effectively enough to get things done.

The current recognition of ADHD in the *DSM-IV* reflects the belief of physicians, teachers, and psychologists over the years that persisting problems in regulating both attentional processes and motor behavior make up a distinct syndrome frequently seen in clinical settings (Kronenberger and Meyer, 1996; Wender, 1995). Originally, terms such as *hyperactivity, hyperkinesis,* and *minimal brain dysfunction* were used to characterize the condition, which was believed to involve various forms of mild central nervous system (CNS) impairment. So strong was the assumed association between excessive activity and underlying brain impairment that the corresponding diagnostic terms were used interchangeably for years. In practice the nature of this deficit was seldom clearly specified, owing to the wide range of disorders and conditions that may have hyperactivity as an associated symptom. This caused endless confusion among professionals and considerable anxiety on the parts of parents whose children were labeled as having "minimal brain damage" or the "hyperkinetic syndrome."

Modern research, however, strongly suggests that neither attentional problems nor hyperactivity should *necessarily* be assumed to involve CNS damage, although maturation and integration of CNS components are involved. Current research has amply documented the fact that genetic, physiological, nutritional, motivational, social, and environmental factors all may play important roles in the regulation and allocation of attentional capabilities (Kronenberger and Meyer, 1996; Barkley, 1998).

The *DSM-IV* recognizes a pattern of ADHD in which attentional problems are primary, a pattern in which hyperactive-impulsive patterns are primary, and a mixed pattern. Findings of field trials confirmed differences among the subtypes: (1) The predominantly hyperactive-impulsive youth was significantly younger (by 3–4 years) than the predominantly inattentive and combined types; (2) The greater occurrence of ADHD in males than females was most characteristic of the combined type and least characteristic of the predominantly inattentive types; (3) scores on a global rating of impairment demonstrated the worst impairment for the combined type and least impairment for the inattentive type; (4) on the basis of teachers' and parents' ratings, the inattentive and combined types had significantly greater academic impairment than the hyperactive-impulsive type; and (5) social impairment was greater among the hyperactive-impulsive type than the inattentive and combined types. By *DSM-IV* estimates, some 3–5% of children show ADHD. Note that ADHD often continues, in varying degrees, into adulthood (Wender, 1995). There is a 5:1 ratio of males to females, with an even higher ratio of the more active and aggressive forms. Approximately 25% of first-degree relatives of children of ADHD show some clear indices of this disorder. ADHD is prognostic of a heightened chance for a variety of psychological dysfunction patterns later in life, as well as criminality and nicotine and cocaine abuse.

It is ironic that stimulant medications are effective with children who already appear to be overstimulated. These chemical agents, of which Ritalin is perhaps best known, appear to stimulate brain systems to a level at which they can exert normal influence on the regulation of attention and behavior. However, not all children with ADHD respond favorably to stimulants (Duncan et al., 1995). For this reason, it is important to carry out a detailed assessment of any children referred for this problem.

Assessments of children with ADHD in school and clinical settings have often been somewhat imprecise, due in part to the difficulty of specifying the criteria for attention and of determining just how active a child should be before being considered hyperactive. In recent years, however, a number of advances have been made in diagnostic procedures, resulting in more clearly defined and more stringent criteria for assessing the presence of ADHD (Barkely, 1998).

Appropriate assessment practices go beyond simple behavioral ratings. A thorough assessment (Mash and Terdal, 1997; Kronenberger and Meyer, 1996; Lezak, 1995) includes an evaluation of the following factors: (1) the child's overall behavioral repertoire and patterns of interactions with the environment, (2) patterns of motor activity, and (3) how the child typically approaches and works through tasks. Frequently, by the time an evaluation has been completed, a child with attentional problems may have been assessed by pediatricians, teachers, psychologists, and parents. Each of these individuals has a specific perspective on the child's behavior that often must be taken into account in designing appropriate intervention strategies.

The Case of Matt

It was not until Matt was nearing the end of first grade that his inattention and poor concentration became apparent. He was a bright child, according to the results of school-readiness testing, who began the year with predictions of great accomplishments. At first he seemed to live up to his promise, but as the months passed, he seemed to have persisting difficulty absorbing new information and finishing his daily lessons. His teacher felt that from the outset he had been considerably more active than his classmates but attributed this to a high level of curiosity that constantly led him into new undertakings.

At home, Matt had never been considered to be a problem child. The second of five children, he had grown up in a family that encouraged independence and imposed minimal constraints on the children's behavior. He was not watched especially closely by his parents but was instead encouraged to develop his own interests and keep himself occupied. With four other children around the house the level of ongoing activity was rather high, and Matt's behavior did not seem markedly atypical by his parents' standards.

The problem that emerged at school involved the fact that Matt found it extremely difficult to focus his attention effectively on his work. Moreover, he seemed to be restless and physically agitated much of the time. Accustomed as he was to working on things that interested him and at a pace that suited his somewhat high-strung temperament,

Matt found it difficult to work under the constraints imposed by his teacher at school. He constantly fidgeted in his seat, was easily distracted by things going on around him, and seldom completed his assignments on time. Because his behavior was not especially disruptive to others, it initially received little attention. But after the first few months of school his teacher had become aware that the quality of his work consistently failed to measure up to the standards she felt were reasonable based on his aptitude test scores.

By the end of the first grading period, Matt was passing in all his academic subjects, but he received several "Unsatisfactory" ratings in such areas as "Paying Attention," "Completing Work on Time," "General Work Habits," and "Ability to Work Independently," which surprised his parents. A meeting with Matt's teacher achieved no particular resolution, mostly because it was difficult to specify precisely just what Matt needed to do in order to work more effectively. His teacher did suggest that he have a physical examination, however, as she felt that his restlessness might have a physical basis.

Matt's physical health had been generally good throughout his early development. His mother's pregnancy was free of major complications, and, although the labor had been difficult, he was born without incident. He was sometimes colicky as an infant and seemed more demanding than her other children had been. She viewed him as more active than the other children right from the start and recalled that his attention was constantly being diverted from one thing to another. But this did not create any particular problems at home, and prior routine physical examinations had uncovered no major health problems. Thus, the first real suggestion that anything might be amiss did not occur until after Matt had started school.

The physical exam done at his teacher's suggestion once again found Matt to be basically in good health, although on the basis of the teacher's report and his own observations, Matt's pediatrician felt that the boy's behavior might warrant a consideration of "hyperactivity." Until Matt's behavior was evaluated more precisely, however, the pediatrician was reluctant to prescribe any medication. He recommended that Matt be evaluated by a clinical psychologist in private practice and that a decision regarding medication be postponed until the assessment was completed.

Matt's parents were perplexed and somewhat upset by the lack of clear definition of Matt's problems. They were also distressed by the apparent insinuation that Matt's problems might have a psychological rather than physical basis. Despite these reservations, they proceeded with the recommendation and had the evaluation performed. Matt and his parents were seen by the clinical psychologist, who saw the entire family together as a unit after an initial interview with the parents. She also carried out basic psychological testing on Matt, using tests designed to assess general mental abilities, school achievement levels, work habits, and basic personality dimensions. Finally, she visited Matt's school to observe his reported problems firsthand. The results of the assessment indeed suggested that Matt had greater difficulty than most children with respect to sustained concentration and attention. In addition, his typical activity level at school appeared markedly higher than that of the other children.

Evidence came from several sources. First, Matt's performance on the WISC-R was marked by an overall above-average level of performance but relatively poor performance on a group of component measures that collectively form a "Freedom from Distractibility" factor. Each of these tests demands sustained, careful attention to a fairly complex task, an undertaking that was beyond Matt's powers of concentration. On some portions of the Wechsler IQ scale, Matt's performance was at a level indicative of above-average general abilities. Further testing revealed that, although he possessed sufficient basic academic skills to master the demands of his schoolwork, Matt seemed at a loss in controlling the process of analyzing the various parts of any complex task and working systematically toward a solution.

Classroom observations by the psychologist tended to corroborate the test data. Matt seemed unable to work out and stick to a plan for getting his work done. He dawdled, played with objects in his desk, looked around the room, and accomplished little during the study time allotted. Some part of his body seemed to be perpetually in motion, even during rest periods when many of the other children were napping.

The available information suggested that Matt's inattentive behavior fit the *DSM-IV* criteria for ADHD. It was stressed to Matt's parents that he was a child of above-average abilities whose problems involved chiefly his method of approaching tasks and an excessively high level of activity. The psychologist developed a program for Matt's teacher and parents designed to help him focus his attention on tasks more effectively. She also referred the parents to the pediatrician for a trial of Ritalin, which was to be used in conjunction with an activity rating form completed daily by the teacher.

Treatment
The intervention program for Matt involved elements of both behavioral and cognitive approaches. Biofeedback training was helpful, as was a technique of teaching Matt to "talk to himself" as a means of keeping his attention focused on a particular task. This involved modeling of on-task behavior in which the therapist performed an activity while describing exactly what she needed to do each step of the way. At first his tendency was to ignore the instructions and to work inconsistently as he had habitually done. But gradually, through a combination of judiciously selected activities and an animated, often humorous style of verbal modeling, the therapist succeeded in capturing Matt's attention and engaging his participation.

One activity that he particularly enjoyed involved assembling model autos and trucks. Normally he worked so quickly and haphazardly that the finished product bore little resemblance to its namesake. With the therapist's assistance, Matt learned to slow his pace down, plan each step of the assembly in advance, gather the necessary materials before starting, and work at a slow but steady pace. At the outset the therapist had him talk himself through each step before actually doing anything. Often at first she either had to prompt him directly or else remind him to prompt himself. But gradually the use of language as a task mediator became more habitual, to the point that eventually Matt was able to work systematically without having to say anything audible at all.

This procedure was combined with a behavioral program at school in which Matt was issued periodic rewards for staying in his seat and working on his assignments. The combination of these techniques achieved the basic goal of engaging Matt's attention more consistently than had been the case before. More importantly, his added powers of concentration contributed to a demonstrable improvement in the quality of his work. As this occurred, the satisfaction derived from good schoolwork provided a source of intrinsic motivation that further engaged his interest.

In a matter of weeks he had made considerable gains in three important areas. First, he became much more effective at planning and monitoring his work. Second, his ability to work both productively and independently improved markedly. Third, his overall grades improved to the point where his performance was beginning to approach the potential his parents and teachers had known he possessed all along. In addition to these gains, Matt's motor activity diminished somewhat as a result of the Ritalin. He was described by his teacher as somewhat calmer, but fortunately seemed to have lost none of the curiosity and alertness that characterized his previous behavior.

Comment

Matt's situation is in part one that is commonly experienced by young schoolchildren. "Paying attention" is a skill that is generally taken for granted, but one that is much too important to go unevaluated. Matt had no lack of basic intelligence; rather, he was unable to harness it effectively to get things done at school. Having been raised without many rules and regulations, he had perhaps never really learned effective work habits. In terms of the underlying etiology, no single specific factor came to light, although in many similar cases genetic or birth defects appear to be causal (Wender, 1995; Duncan et al., 1995). Yet it did appear that, in their effort to let their children be independent of adult authority, Matt's parents may have erred somewhat by not providing effective role models.

This case illustrates the effective application of a multimodal intervention program (also see the case of Roger in Chapter 2). A combination of psychological and medical procedures was employed to treat a problem that, years ago, would probably have been diagnosed and treated exclusively from a medical standpoint. Unfortunately, treatment using only medication, especially Ritalin, is still common. In fact, the production of Ritalin for use in the United States increased five-fold between 1975 and 1995. Viewing problems such as ADHD from a broader perspective that encompasses both psychological and physical factors makes it feasible to consider a wide range of intervention techniques, each of which makes a unique contribution to the problem's solution.

Autistic Disorder

The Case of Audrey

If the child really isn't lovable, you simply have to fake it.

—B. F. Skinner

Autistic disorder is a pervasive, debilitating disorder having its onset prior to 3 years of age. The term *autistic* connotes a failure to relate effectively to one's environment. People described as autistic are viewed as being absorbed in a private world of their own that is inaccessible to others. Historically the term *autism* was used by Bleuler to describe one of the cardinal symptoms of schizophrenia. However, it has since been associated with other forms of psychopathology, most notably with the pattern of disturbed behavior in childhood first described by Leo Kanner in the 1940s and named "Early infantile autism" (Kanner, 1943). The children studied by Kanner manifested a pattern of detachment and severe communication impairment.

Detailed studies of these children have revealed a number of additional symptoms as well, including restricted, repetitive, and stereotyped behaviors; emotional withdrawal; cognitive impairments; and unusual behavioral mannerisms. Among the latter, echolalia and self-stimulation are especially notable. Children with echolalia continuously repeat words and phrases uttered by another person, making effective communication all but impossible. Self-stimulation may take any of several forms. A child may sit for hours waving a hand in front of his or her face, transfixed by the constant movement. Other children engage in more destructive behaviors, such as head banging or pinching or biting themselves. Observations of such behaviors have led to the suggestion that autistic children are especially sensitive to what is termed *proximal* stimulation, which is very tangible and immediate. In contrast, these children are less responsive to *distal* stimulation, emanating from sources that are physically more remote (such as the sound of someone speaking from a distance of several feet).

In terms of cognitive functioning, some autistic children are frequently found to possess "splinter skills" within a broader context of impaired mental functioning. Splinter skills are isolated capabilities possessed by autistic children that in some instances are developed to exceptionally high levels (dramatically portrayed by Dustin Hoffman in the movie *Rainman*). Mathematical, artistic, and various other skills have all been found in autistic children whose behavior is otherwise globally impaired.

Kanner's work with autism led him to believe that the disorder was essentially the result of severe emotional deprivation. He noted that the parents of these children seemed in general to be intellectually and analytically oriented, while lacking in emotional warmth. The term "icebox parent" resulted from characterizations such as this and fostered the impression that autism was essentially an acquired condition. According to this theory, unremitting exposure to nonnurturing parents brought about progressive withdrawal from the world and increasing self-absorption.

In retrospect, it is clear that this conclusion was erroneous, being the result of biased sampling procedures (Kronenberger and Meyer, 1996). The most telling criticism of this theory comes from the increasing evidence that symptoms of autism are in fact present at birth, in the form of neurological and related abnormalities. This in turn suggests that parental aloofness, when present, reflects essentially a defensive reaction to a child whose behavior is atypical and frequently characterized by unresponsiveness.

Mental Retardation

Autistic disorder and mental retardation have occasionally been confused diagnostically. However, a comparison reveals several points of contrast. A fundamental difference concerns the scope of the two terms. Whereas *autism* involves a very specific behavioral syndrome, the term *mental retardation* encompasses a descriptive classification system with many variations. Mental retardation, characterized by impaired intellectual and social skills, is a condition that may be associated with a variety of psychological disorders and which may stem from a wide range of psychological, physiological, and genetic causes.

Let us now turn to the case of Audrey, in which issues related to both autistic disorder and mental retardation are featured.

The Case of Audrey

Audrey was born a full-term infant, her parents' third child. She was a beautiful baby whose exquisitely delicate features were cause for endless comment by her family, relatives, and the hospital staff. However, shortly after Audrey's birth her mother began to worry that her daughter was not as responsive as her previous children. Audrey did not respond to being held like most children; rather than "molding" herself when cradled in her mother's arms, she was stiff and rigid. This made nursing a significant problem, and it was not long before she was weaned to a bottle because of the tension and inconvenience involved in feeding her.

Audrey's physical development appeared to advance at a somewhat accelerated pace, at least in terms of basic motor skills. However, she did not seem to vocalize as consistently as most children, and it was difficult to engage her in the sort of make-believe baby talk that is so much a part of early parent–child interactions. Despite reassurances from the pediatrician that Audrey's language was merely delayed, her parents felt that the problem went deeper.

As the months passed, their concerns increased. It proved extremely difficult to toilet train Audrey, largely because she seemed unwilling or unable to follow even simple instructions. She would frequently parrot instructions or phrases verbatim, repeating them continuously in a sing-song rhythm. Even getting her attention proved difficult, because she tended to either avoid eye contact or direct her gaze in such a way that anyone holding a conversation with her would feel that she was looking through them.

One afternoon Audrey's mother found her three year old sitting on the nursery floor staring at her left hand, which she dangled before her eyes and shook at a rapid pace. When the mother tried to intervene, Audrey resisted her attempts and cried loudly. Nothing her mother did succeeded in appeasing the child, who eventually returned to her place on the floor and continued to play with her hands.

Audrey made no friends during this time. She seemed frightened by nearly any changes in her customary routine, including the presence of strange people. She either shrank from contact with other children or avoided them altogether, seemingly content to play by herself for hours at a time.

She scrupulously maintained her toys and other possessions in precise arrangements. She initially shared a room with an older sister, but she was so particular about the placement of various objects that it was not long before she was given a small room of her own right next to her parents. Here she spent literally hours each day arranging and rearranging things; staring at her hands; gesturing and making incoherent sounds; and occasionally running around the room, whirling herself in circles. Increasingly upset, her parents obtained a thorough physical and psychological evaluation. Although somewhat prepared for the results, it still came as a shock when they were told that Audrey's condition was diagnosed as autistic disorder.

They were put in touch with a nearby school for children with serious psychological handicaps, administered by the local school board. During their initial visit, they were surprised to see a number of children very much like Audrey. Virtually all of the children manifested significant communication difficulties, and there was little, if any, contact between them. The staff members worked both individually and in small groups with the children, using techniques reflecting a behavioral approach, far and away the treatment of choice for this disorder. Token reinforcers were everywhere. They were used as rewards to painstakingly shape verbal responses to questions, to reward socially appropriate behavior, and to acknowledge the children's efforts in doing seatwork. Yet, whenever possible, naturalistic reinforcers were used, for example, giving Audrey a model car to play with instead of candy when she said "car." Also, picturebook stimulus guides were used to introduce new skills, for example, a picturebook illustrating the proper sequence of getting dressed. To Audrey's parents the school appeared to tolerate a great deal of noise, confusion, and disorder. But they soon realized that the needs of each child were so diversified that highly individualized treatment plans were needed.

Audrey was enrolled in the school, which prepared a detailed treatment plan. Initial emphasis was placed on helping her develop some basic self-care and rudimentary communication skills. Her parents were instructed in the use of techniques employed by the staff and were also invited to participate in a parenting group run by the staff for parents of severely disabled children. Great care was taken to make them feel as though they were an integral part of the treatment program, and a staff psychologist spoke with them on occasion to help alleviate their unfounded fears that they were directly responsible for their daughter's condition.

Audrey made slow but perceptible progress in the program. Language development was targeted as a primary treatment goal, and she was immediately assigned to a staff member who held several daily sessions with her, working on basic skills like naming and identifying people and common objects. At first a great deal of effort was required simply to capture her attention for a few seconds at a time. Eventually a combination of simple directives (such as "Audrey, look at me now") and both primary and verbal reinforcers achieved the desired effect. Once this was achieved, it was possible to draw Audrey's attention to other features of the environment and help her begin to identify them.

Audrey's treatment involved other activities as well. Toilet training and personal hygiene were stressed from the beginning, and Audrey's parents were enlisted to help with a behaviorally based program that was employed both at school and at home to train these skills. Social skills training was another aspect of the program. Once she had begun to establish something of a relationship with the staff member who was teaching her language skills, another child was introduced into their interactions for a brief period each day. Initially the children ignored each other or became irritated if one was deprived of attention in favor of the other. Gradually, however, transactions began to take place between the two, initially in response to highly specific prompting by the staff worker.

Audrey's stay in the program was characterized both by periods of significant progress and regression. By the end of the first year, at age 4 she had a working vocabulary of between 80 and 100 words, largely nouns, that she was beginning to use spontaneously. She did not speak in sentences but rather gestured and used individual words on occasion to make her intentions known. Her use of language was characteristically that of a younger child.

In other areas, Audrey made somewhat more limited progress. Toilet training proceeded quite slowly, in part because of minor neuromuscular abnormalities, which were detected on a neuropediatric examination. Social skills training eventually made it possible for Audrey to greet and attend to several very familiar members of the staff and her family. However, her lack of effective communication skills coupled with an ability to entertain herself alone for hours at a time made it difficult to engage her in interactions with others in any but a highly routinized manner.

Audrey was at her best when making drawings. Quite by accident, she was discovered to have surprising artistic talent, and a number of her scribbled drawings suggested a level of maturation several years in advance of her age. Her favorite subject was cats, which she drew in a variety of shapes, sizes, and poses. She seemed fascinated with small animals and would attempt to keep the family cat captive during her long periods of solitary play. She did not really play with the animal, but held and petted it mechanically while it tried to escape. It was after one of these exchanges that she had picked up a pencil and drawn the head of a cat in amazing detail.

By the time she was 5, Audrey had made a significant number of advances, although she was never able to enter a regular school program. Her working vocabulary continued to increase somewhat, although she retained a telegraphic style of communication characteristic of her.

Comment

Audrey's case is not unusual as far as the syndrome of autistic disorder is concerned. As is often the case, despite making reasonable progress, she was permanently left with problematic language and social skills that made it hard for her to participate in regular classroom settings. This is consistent with a significant shift in attitudes about the causes of autism. The preponderance of recent research data points to either prenatal or genetic factors as likely explanations for the condition. Because of this, parents with autistic children are now less likely to develop guilt about their child's condition and are more likely to become involved in a collaborative treatment effort.

Separation Anxiety Disorder Associated With School Refusal

The Case of Julie

To be adult is to be alone.
—Jean Rostand, French biologist

The term "separation anxiety" was first coined by Johnson and his associates in 1941 to describe the acute distress and attachment behavior exhibited by some children when separating from their mothers to go to school, and related to pioneering work on attachment of John Bowlby (1973). In more current use the term refers to a more general disorder of childhood in which excessive anxiety occurs when a child is separated from major attachment figures or from home. Anxiety reactions may range from displays of anger and protest to symptoms of panic. Discussions in the clinical literature suggest that the disorder is fairly common— about 4% (American Psychiatric Association, 1994)—with approximately equal prevalence among boys and girls. When separated from parents or other attachment figures, the children often become obsessed with fears of accidents or illnesses befalling themselves or significant others. These fears may be expressed openly and verbally or may be manifested in nightmares and fantasy. Sometimes fears are displaced onto animals, strangers, or surroundings. Sleep disorders, including nightmares and sleep terror, are common, and children may experience great difficulty falling asleep alone and require that someone, usually a parent, be with them when they fall asleep. Somatic complaints are also common in response to the threat of separation.

The relationship between separation anxiety and school first described by Johnson et al. (1941) is still important, although the term "school phobia" to describe the disorder is frequently misapplied. It is usually not the stimulus of school from which the child retreats that is of clinical significance, but the attachment to parents or others that he or she seeks. Thus, the term "school phobia" is a bit of a misnomer; the term "school refusal" is generally more appropriate.

The clinical literature is in substantial agreement regarding the personalities and behaviors of children with separation anxiety and their parents (Kronenberger and Meyer, 1996; Bowlby, 1973; Johnson et al., 1941). With the exception of the symptoms associated with the disorder, these children are generally well behaved, although they often appear shy, overly anxious, and socially inhibited. Families are often intact, with close relationships between parent(s) and children, and family members have often not experienced long or frequent separations from home. A clear distinction can be drawn between these children and children with conduct disorder, who may also refuse to attend school or other activities but typically come from highly unstable families with a long history of separations. Whereas children with conduct disorder characteristically do not stay home when truant and engage in a variety of antisocial behaviors, the school refuser is generally quiet and cooperative once in school.

The problem of school refusal may appear to be clear and straightforward when first addressed in treatment. However, the dynamics of separation anxiety are often deeply enmeshed in a larger family context and may involve a variety of issues of clinical significance, as in the case of Julie, described here.

> *Your mother can't be with you anymore.*
> —The Great Prince, speaking to Bambi,
> in *Bambi* by Felix Seton

The Case of Julie

Julie P., an 8-year-old second-grader, was court-referred for outpatient treatment because of school truancy. During her first year in school, Julie had refused to enter her classroom without her mother and would scream and throw herself on the floor if her mother tried to leave her at school. As a result, Mrs. P. accompanied Julie to her classroom each day and stayed with her for the remainder of the morning. If Mrs. P. tried to leave the classroom, Julie would again throw her "mad fits," and only Mrs. P. was able to calm her. Because Mrs. P. held a job during the afternoon, she devised a plan in which she would accompany Julie to the lunch room and leave her while she was eating her lunch. Although Julie resisted at first, she gradually became accustomed to it, and this pattern was maintained for the remainder of the school year. In her mother's absence during the afternoons, Julie was generally well behaved, although she was extremely shy and interacted little with the other children. She also consistently refused to complete any schoolwork without her mother.

In second grade Julie's teacher would not allow Mrs. P. to remain with Julie in the classroom. Julie began to miss an excessive number of days in school for a variety of somatic complaints, including headaches, nausea, and stomachaches. The school insisted that the child be seen by a physician, who reported no apparent physical basis for Julie's problems. The school then insisted that Julie take the school bus to school each day and maintain regular attendance. Although Mrs. P. reported that she tried to force Julie to take the school bus, Julie refused to do so for fear that it would crash, and her attendance did not improve.

After numerous attempts were unsuccessful to encourage Mrs. P. to force Julie to go to school, the school filed a truancy petition with the court. In accordance with an alternative-to-court program a caseworker was assigned to the family. When Julie's attendance did not improve, the case was brought to court. On the recommendation of the caseworker, Julie was ordered to attend school and Mrs. P. was ordered to seek treatment for her.

During intake a number of clinical symptoms were reported along with school refusal that suggested a diagnosis of separation anxiety. Julie was plagued with obsessive ruminations of catastrophe befalling her mother, her grandmother, or herself, and she frequently personalized news stories, fearing that whatever disaster or tragedy was reported on the television news would soon befall the P. family. She also reported ongoing fears of being kidnapped or killed in a motor vehicle accident, such as a school bus crash.

In addition to these conscious fears, Julie experienced terrifying nightmares in which she or another family member would mysteriously disappear, become lost, or be killed. She usually awoke from these dreams in a panic state, and as a consequence, she reported a great fear of sleeping and insisted that sleep was not very important anyway.

Julie also experienced a variety of somatic complaints, always on the mornings of school days. Samples of her somatic complaints, as well as her "mad fits" in which she shrieked, cried, and banged her hands on the floor and table, were observed on several occasions at the clinic where she was seen when her mother was encouraged to leave her for brief periods of time. Once separated, Julie would regain her composure, sometimes dramatically, although she generally remained withdrawn and unable to concentrate on tasks for more than a few moments.

A series of family interviews revealed a number of significant events in the history of the P. family, although only Julie's brother, Gary, was willing to discuss these in any detail. Julie and Mrs. P. were more likely to argue about issues such as Julie's clothes or Mrs. P.'s mother, who had been living with the P. family for the past 3 years.

Mr. and Mrs. P. were divorced when Julie was 4 and Gary 7, with Mrs. P. retaining custody of both children. Shortly after the divorce, when Julie was in the care of her father one weekend, she was allegedly sexually abused by a friend of her cousin's, who reportedly took her clothes off and had her "play games" with him. Mrs. P. reported that Julie had told her of this the following week while she was taking a bath. Mrs. P. would not discuss this in the presence of the children and reported that it had never been mentioned since the bath. Following this incident, which Mr. P.'s family insisted could not have happened, Mrs. P. refused to allow Julie's father or anyone else in his family to see the children. A heated family argument was carried on regarding Mrs. P.'s decision.

Some three weeks after the incident, Mr. P. was killed in a motor vehicle accident. Mrs. P. reported that she did not bring the children to the funeral or cemetery because she believed that they would not understand, and she stated that they seemed to cope with their father's death very well, particularly Julie. Gary, on the other hand, began to steal things for no apparent reason. Not long after, Gary's stealing behavior stopped of its own accord, and he did not exhibit any behavior problems in school or at home thereafter. Julie, like her brother, rarely mentioned her father during the year following his death, but recently she had begun to insist that she be taken to visit him in the cemetery.

When Julie was 5 years old, her maternal grandmother moved in with the family. Mrs. P. described her mother as a demanding, helpless woman who always complained of her health and rarely got out of bed. She also reported that her mother was an extremely anxious and fearful woman who had not left her apartment for 15 years following her husband's death, suggesting the possibility of an agoraphobic condition.

As Julie reached school age, Mrs. P. became involved in a protracted dispute with the local board of education over the correct school district for Julie, and as a result Julie's entrance into first grade was delayed for a year. Once Julie started school, the problems began to surface. When Mrs. P. brought Julie to the outpatient clinic for intake, she described herself as a "nervous wreck," fearing on the one hand that the court might take Julie away from her and on the other hand that Julie "might be crazy." Mrs. P. reported that she had had a "nervous breakdown" herself when Julie was 2 years old and Mr. P. had started a new job that required extensive travel away from home.

Etiology

The history and symptoms of this case suggest several issues of etiological significance. First, as Bowlby (1973) has suggested, fears of separation and loss are generally traceable to real loss events in the history of the individual. In Julie's case, it is certainly important to note the loss of her father, the alleged sexual abuse, and the subsequent cutoff of her father's family in the development of her presenting symptoms, including her nightmares, her fears of catastrophe befalling her mother, and her fears that she herself would be kidnapped or killed in an automobile accident. All of these symptoms involved themes of separation and loss of attachment figures, which reflected unresolved issues of grief and an underlying feeling of insecurity regarding the stability of the world around her. The development of anxious attachment behaviors, such as a reluctance to sleep alone, school refusal, and agitation at times of separation, reflected Julie's fear that she might suddenly be left alone. In this sense, they were adaptive responses in that they served to promote attachment to significant others and to prevent further loss.

It is generally believed that a child's model of self is a function of stable parent–child or other attachment bonds. Thus, a child who experiences severe instability in her relationships with major attachment figures is likely to develop feelings of personal inadequacy and interpersonal insecurity. Thus, Julie's difficulties in establishing peer relationships, participating in play, and concentrating on purposive behaviors such as schoolwork likely reflected a poor self-image that was based in the losses and family instability she had experienced.

It is also clear that Julie's refusal to attend school was as much a function of her mother's unwillingness to let her go as it was a function of her own fears. Despite her insistence that she had tried to force Julie to attend school, Mrs. P. had implicitly condoned and reinforced Julie's "problem" behaviors from the start. On a typical day, Julie would wake up, complain of feeling ill, and then refuse to meet the school bus for fear that it might crash. If her mother tried to insist, Julie would become extremely agitated, scream, and throw things about the house. Once the school bus had come and gone, she would quiet down, Mrs. P. would fix her a nice breakfast, and they would watch the soap operas and game shows on television for the rest of the day while taking care of Julie's grandmother.

In one sense, both Julie and her grandmother provided a means for Mrs. P. to meet her own needs for adequacy and self-worth by playing the roles of underadequate persons who required Mrs. P.'s attention. Thus, despite Mrs. P.'s verbal protests about Julie's school refusal, it is clear that Julie's symptoms resulted in secondary gain for both parties, and that Julie's behaviors reflected a well-established family pattern of separation and dependency issues, as well as her own fears and anxieties.

Finally, the history of anxiety-related problems in Julie's mother and grandmother suggest both a role model for her symptomatology as well as a possible biochemical or neurological predisposition for an anxiety disorder. Certainly the overall level of anxiety and overt tension was high among all members of the P. family, supporting the possibility that genetically weighted variables may have increased the overall risk.

Treatment Options

Cases of separation anxiety like Julie's offer an opportunity for treatment from a variety of theoretical perspectives, largely due to the range of clinical symptoms that arise and the nature of etiological factors (Kronenberger and Meyer, 1996; Duncan et al., 1995). From a behavioral perspective, treatments involving contingency management programs and systematic desensitization (SDT) have been found to be successful in reducing symptoms of anxiety and improving school attendance. In these treatments, emphasis is placed on developing a relaxation response in association with a feared stimulus like school, separation from mother, or riding a school bus in an attempt to reduce and eventually eliminate fear responses, while at the same time assessing the system of overt and covert reinforcers that is maintaining the target behaviors. In Julie's case, school refusal was clearly being reinforced by her mother when she fixed Julie a nice breakfast and allowed her to watch television following her school refusal. In a contingency management program, reinforcers such as these would be used to reward school approach behaviors rather than school avoidance behaviors, and school refusal would result in punishments such as time-out, loss of privileges, or extra household chores.

From a psychodynamic or developmental perspective, symptoms of separation anxiety may be seen as mechanisms of defense that function to reduce the anxiety generated from intrapsychic conflict. In Julie's case unconscious conflicts involving object loss and individuation would need to be worked through using the therapeutic relationship as a mechanism of change, and perhaps involving techniques such as psychodynamic play therapy, fantasy storytelling, and art therapy to express unconscious material indirectly.

A family systems model would attempt to restructure family boundaries and communication patterns. In Julie's case, attempts might be made to strengthen the parental boundary between Mrs. P. and Julie and to more clearly establish family roles for all family members, including the grandmother.

Julie's Treatment

In the case of Julie, family treatment was recommended and accepted by Mrs. P. The P. family was subsequently seen weekly for approximately 2 months. Despite the therapist's early efforts, the grandmother never joined the family for sessions, which thus consisted of Julie, Gary, and Mrs. P.

During the first sessions great effort was expended by the therapist to side with Mrs. P. on all issues in an effort to support her role as executive of the family. To this end the seating arrangement placed the children together on one side of the room, Mrs. P. on the other, and the therapist in the middle, frequently moving over to physically side with Mrs. P.

Interventions initially included encouraging Mrs. P. to view Julie's school refusal and other behaviors as misbehaviors rather than problems or signs that she was "crazy." In keeping with this, a system of punishments was devised to make staying at home less favorable for Julie. While this met with early success in improving Julie's attendance, she soon began to fear the school bus again, and Mrs. P. did not enforce the punishment system out of sympathy for Julie's fears.

At this point, Julie was paradoxically praised by the therapist for not going to school and in so doing keeping the family together. Mrs. P. was praised at the same time for recognizing Julie's authority to do this out of respect for Julie's role as the holder of all family problems. These paradoxical approaches were designed to generate sufficient anger in Mrs. P. so that she would begin to more forcefully govern the family. This began to have a dramatic effect on family dynamics when Mrs. P. refused to feed her mother one evening, insisting that she feed herself. Not long after this, Julie's attendance began to improve significantly.

However, as family boundaries began to change and Julie's school attendance continued to improve, Mrs. P. began to cancel sessions. While Mrs. P.'s resistance to changing the family system was predictable and could potentially have provided valuable material for future sessions, the school and court again intervened, as the school year was drawing to a close and Julie would not have completed the requisite number of days of attendance to be passed on to third grade. Although Julie's attendance had improved, the improvement was not great enough to keep the P. family out of court, where removal from the home was threatened before Mrs. P. agreed to voluntarily sign Julie into an inpatient treatment facility.

After 2 weeks of inpatient treatment and near perfect school attendance, Julie convinced her mother to sign her out of the treatment facility against the strong recommendations of the treatment staff by promising her that she would never miss school again. When she returned home, Julie again refused to go to school and, sobbing and frightened, begged her mother never to let anyone take her away again.

At this time, the P. family's caseworker became so angry with Mrs. P. that she dropped the case, and it was returned to court, where removal from the home was to be considered.

Comment

Along with the diagnostic and treatment issues raised here, this case also highlights the need for carefully planned, well-organized intervention programs when several social systems are involved. In Julie's case commendable clinical progress was being made in both an outpatient and an inpatient treatment program, only to have this progress undermined by legal proceedings that threatened to permanently remove Julie from her home, which in the context of her previous traumas of separation and loss would likely be devastating. Yet, the P. family might likely have never sought treatment had it not been for the insistence of the school system and the courts. Thus, while it would appear on the one hand that the courts, the school system, and the mental health system were working at cross purposes in this case, the goals of each were reasonably equivalent. The observation that similar goals can at times result in conflicting intervention attempts is an important factor to remember when dealing with cases that involve a number of social systems in a community mental health setting.

Oppositional Defiant Disorder

The Case of Phyllis

Give to a pig when it grunts and a child when it cries, and you will have a fine pig and a bad child.

—Old Danish proverb

The oppositional defiant disorder (ODD) is marked by negativistic, hostile, and defiant behaviors, often elicited by attempts by parents or other authority figures to control the behavior of the child or adolescent. Stubborn and/or hostile resistance is manifested in a variety of behavior patterns, including consistent violation of minor rules and pouting, with an occasional temper flare-up. When it emerges most strongly in adolescence, as it often does, similar behaviors usually have been evident in the child's earlier behavioral history.

Adolescence is commonly a stressful period for teenagers, their families, and school officials. Pubertal changes, the task of identity formation, the renegotiation of relationships with parents, and rapid changes in the social environment can precipitate a variety of problematic behaviors (Wolman, 1998; Petraitis et al., 1995). Certain adolescents are unable to effect a logical or objective break from their earlier emotional bonds with parents, and thus teenagers' struggles for an autonomous relationship with parents may be a significant source of problems. Teenagers may become rebellious, emotional, or hypercritical in order to convince parents that they are no longer "children," and so must be accorded greater independence.

Oppositional teenagers, while emotionally unpredictable and argumentative, may elicit a generally positive response from others and may evidence stubbornness and emotionality rather than an antisocial value system or deliberate disregard for the feelings of others. Also, oppositional behavior usually has a compulsive component, which maintains the problematic behavior despite detrimental (and undesired) consequences. Oppositional behavior is consistent with the traditional concept of the neurotic paradox; that is, the behavior is goal-directed (aimed toward emotional autonomy and independent thinking), but not goal-attaining (usually resulting in descriptors such as "immature" or "irresponsible"). As in the case of Phyllis, compulsive violations and seemingly reflexive negative responses elicit mistrust and anxiety, resulting in criticism and further restrictions of freedom, to which the oppositional person responds with intensified negativism. Consequently, relationships with authority figures deteriorate and become increasingly conflict-ridden.

The Case of Phyllis

Throughout Phyllis's childhood her parents were U.S. embassy officials in several South American countries. When Phyllis entered high school, her parents moved back to the States and joined the political science department of a small private college. Phyllis attended public high school for 2 years and was suspended four times. Her parents enrolled her in a private girls' academy, hoping the structured atmosphere would "settle her down." However, Phyllis was suspended from the academy twice in the first semester, and the principal threatened permanent expulsion if her school behavior did not improve. The school had a weekly "detention hall" for students who had broken rules. Phyllis's suspensions resulted primarily from noncompliance with detention hall and the sheer number of outstanding detentions. The infractions for which she received detention were generally minor, such as talking during class, violations of dress code, and tardiness for detention hall.

Phyllis, the youngest of five girls, was the only daughter who still lived with her parents at the time she was referred by her school's guidance counselor to a clinical psychologist. There were 4 years separating Phyllis and the next youngest sister. Phyllis's parents described the family as close and loving. They said that the older girls had gone through brief periods of rebellion during adolescence but that they all grew out of it. The family was very achievement-oriented, and everyone except Phyllis had distinguished academic records.

Phyllis had been normal behaviorally through childhood, although she had been very stubborn and difficult as a preschooler and had often been prone to temper tantrums, causing her father to semi-affectionately dub her "the little witch." Phyllis had always produced an inconsistent academic performance. Throughout grammar school, she often earned above-average grades, yet her teachers consistently concluded that her potential was higher. Junior high school was characterized by a particularly erratic performance.

Similar inconsistencies were observed in Phyllis's social relationships. She had several "personality conflicts" with teachers, on whom she blamed her low grades, and her parents described her as "moody and difficult to get along with" as she neared adolescence. Frequent arguments erupted at home. When the tension in the home became intolerable, Phyllis would visit one of her sisters. However, these visits were often prematurely terminated by some disagreement with her sister concerning Phyllis's curfew.

In grade school, Phyllis apparently got along fairly well with her classmates. The family moved every 2 or 3 years, however, and Phyllis had not continued any of her childhood friendships. In high school, she moved from one close girlfriend to another, often within a few weeks. These friendships seemed to die from lack of interest on the other girls' parts and seldom resulted in an actual argument. Phyllis dated frequently but did not have a steady boyfriend. This was an additional source of conflict in the family because her mother suspected, without any hard evidence, that Phyllis was sexually active.

Etiology

Eric Erikson (1959) describes adolescence as a period in which one must resolve the crisis of self-definition by committing oneself to a role and adopting an ideology (attitudes, beliefs, moral values). The apparent ideology and role adopted by Phyllis are ones of counterdependence. That is, although her behavior is directed toward demonstrating autonomy, she remains defined by the external environment because her coping strategy is generally limited to acting in the opposite direction of perceived external forces. These dynamics are generally frustrating for everyone involved, including Phyllis. In addition to provoking predictable negative reactions from parents, peers, and teachers, the oppositional adolescent's behavior does not result in feelings of autonomy or independence. Rather, the adolescents are likely to feel that emotionally charged situations escalate too quickly and that they are unable to control their behavior. Phyllis said, "Sometimes I just get mad because someone's ordering me around. So I just don't do it, and then I get in trouble I'm sorry for later."

How adolescents arrive at maladaptive ideologies and roles is a process about which there is considerable speculation and scant empirical data. Generally, behavior problems in adolescents are attributed to predisposing family dynamics and/or deficient coping skills on the part of the teenager. In Phyllis's case, both groups of variables contributed to her poor adjustment. She was the youngest in her family and was no doubt accustomed to relatively unconditional affection, despite implicit expectations of high achievement. In addition to the typical problems experienced by adolescents with successful older siblings, Phyllis's process of self-definition was hampered by her family's indulgence and overprotection, which resulted in her lack of experience with problem solving. Phyllis was able to meet the social and educational demands of grammar school with minimal effort, but her level of effort and coping ability did not step up to the increased demands of adolescence.

Moreover, because of the family's many moves and the age gap between her and her sisters, Phyllis's only stable relationships were with her parents (who had become part of the problem). Harry Stack Sullivan (1953) was a pioneer in noting that an important predictor of problematic interpersonal relationships is the absence of an intimate same-sex relationship in preadolescence, as these friendships provide experiences with intimacy, essential reality testing, and a broader perspective from the combined experiences. Phyllis had missed this significant experience in childhood, and the constantly changing environments and associated behavioral norms (complicated by cultural differences among her numerous schools) had interfered with her development of a consistent set of attitudes and behaviors. It is not surprising that she adopted a rigid approach to the environment that was defined by being against the expectations of her parents and teachers.

Treatment

The most useful technique for oppositional children, as well as for conduct-disordered children, is parent management training (PMT). In PMT the therapist provides a brief overview of underlying social learning concepts, models, and techniques and then coaches parents in implementing the procedures.

> Procedures and interaction patterns practiced in the sessions are then used in the home. Parents usually are taught how to define, observe, and record behavior at the beginning of treatment because once behaviors (e.g., fighting, engaging in tantrums) are defined concretely, reinforcement and punishment techniques can be applied. The PMT therapist details the concepts and procedures derived from positive reinforcement (e.g., contingent delivery of attention, praise, points) and punishment (e.g., time out from reinforcement, loss of privileges, and reprimands). Reinforcement for prosocial and nondeviant behavior is central to treatment. Parents are taught how to use reinforcement and punishment techniques contingent on the child's behavior, to provide consequences consistently, to attend to appropriate behaviors and to ignore inappropriate behaviors, to apply skills in prompting, shaping, and fading, and to use these techniques to manage future problems. There is an extensive amount of practice and shaping of parent behavior within the sessions to develop skills in carrying out the procedures. (Feldman and Kazdin, 1995, p. 3)

The therapist maintains close telephone contact with the parents between sessions. These contacts encourage parents to ask questions about the home programs and give an opportunity for the therapist to prompt compliance with the behavior change program, to reinforce parents' use of the skills, to strengthen the therapeutic alliance, and to help the parents immediately confront and solve problems.

Because persons with an oppositional disorder often avoid accepting responsibility for the difficulties they encounter in their world, the classic Reality Therapy techniques that William Glasser (1980) developed while working with delinquent adolescent girls, who are especially inclined to avoid responsibility, can be appropriate here. Adlerian therapy, which melds some analogous approaches into a traditional psychodynamic therapy, is also successfully applied.

Once some of the oppositional tendencies are muted, either client-centered or nondirective therapies (variations of the original explorations by Carl Rogers, 1961) can be used to explore the conflicts over defining one's identity while adjusting to parental constraints. Similarly, Gestalt therapy techniques (Perls, Hefferline, and Goodman, 1958) can help the adolescent with oppositional disorder confront the underlying feelings toward parental figures, often via the "empty chair technique." Here the adolescent pretends the parent is in a chair and holds a dialogue by taking both parts, which helps the teenager get in touch with the parent's perspective.

Phyllis's Treatment

Phyllis's treatment took place over ten individual therapy sessions, which included Adlerian and Gestalt techniques, followed by weekly adolescent group therapy for 3 months. Her parents were given advice on reactions to Phyllis's behavior and a list of books and magazine articles written especially for parents of teenagers. Phyllis was slow to disclose spontaneously with the therapist, although she was willing to answer questions and negotiate contracts for more appropriate behaviors. She was motivated both by the threat of expulsion from school and by her desire to effect more harmonious relationships with her parents, teachers, and peers. As is often the case with adolescents, a major portion of Phyllis's problems stemmed from inadequate social skills and an inability to communicate feelings in socially appropriate ways. Consequently, individual sessions concentrated on more appropriate assertive behaviors for Phyllis, including contracts for in vivo trials with parents and peers. These strategies dramatically reduced the intense tension between Phyllis and her parents.

The therapy group that Phyllis participated in consisted of eight to ten teenagers who had similar problems in relationships with authority figures, school achievement, and maintaining stable peer relationships. This group functioned like the intimate preadolescent friendships described by Sullivan (1953). Group members assisted one another in problem solving and reality testing within an accepting atmosphere. The group was open-ended—members could enter and then "graduate" as their individual needs were met. Some of the group members became close friends and continued their relationships even after they left the group. Phyllis was more disclosing in the group setting and was relieved to discover similarities with the experiences of other group members.

After 3 months Phyllis's improvement was evidenced by more pleasant interactions with her parents, significant decreases in school detentions, and better grades. She has maintained the friendships formed in the group, enjoys more stable relationships with schoolmates, and is no longer threatened with expulsion. Also, Phyllis now reports that she simply is happier and more confident.

Comment

Phyllis's case is an example of how single, unremarkable life circumstances can in combination predispose adjustment problems in adolescence. The developmental tasks of adolescence are such that teenagers must draw on the experiences of childhood and/or social resources for adequate resolution of the identity crisis (Erikson, 1959). Phyllis's childhood experiences, while superior in many ways, did not include adequate practice in frustration tolerance or in the maintenance of long-term peer relationships. Also, her status as the family's youngest and later as the only child in the home combined with deficits in social skills to restrict her socially. Phyllis did not know how to rely on the support of peers or siblings for credible feedback about her behavior, and she was forced to use the expectations of her parents and teachers as guidelines for judgments. Many teenagers in this position abandon efforts to attain autonomy and conform without protest to the expectations of adults. Such conformity may simply delay rebellion until early adulthood (or even much later), when the social consequences are more serious and the environment considerably less tolerant of oppositional behavior.

Identity Development Crisis or Disorder

The Case of Mr. E. All of us have encountered and endured both adolescents and adolescence. Thus, we have witnessed and experienced the developmental period that is most intense for identity issues. As shown in the following case study, going through this critical developmental period without successfully working through these issues can result in a crisis of identity in the adult years.

The Case of Mr. E.

Mr. E. was born June 15, 1902, near Frankfurt, Germany. He was born to a Danish Jewish mother who had traveled to Frankfurt to be with friends after being abandoned by Mr. E.'s father. Mr. E's father died shortly thereafter.

During Mr. E's first years, he lived alone with his mother, an artist who traveled frequently. When Mr. E. was 3, he became ill and his mother took him to a pediatrician, Theodore Homburger, whom she subsequently married. Mr. E. grew up as a child believing Dr. Homburger was his biological father. He eventually learned differently, but he kept the secret until he was 68 years old that he was the product of an extramarital affair.

While growing up in Karlsruhe, Germany, Mr. E. received other critical identity-related mixed messages. Because his stepfather, Dr. Homburger, was Jewish, Mr. E. went to the temple, where he was referred to as "goy" because of his blonde hair and blue eyes, which reflected his Danish biological parentage. In school, he was referred to as "the Jew" because his stepfather and name were Jewish.

Added to this confusion was the natural role rebellion of adolescence. Although loved and indulged by his parents, Mr. E. rebelled against the "bourgeois" aspects of his family. He even voiced the familiar refrain: "I set out to be different." He decided to become an artist, spent a year or so wandering around Europe, and then enrolled in an art school in Karlsruhe. He soon went to Munich to study art, then to Florence, then back to Karlsruhe.

As often happens in identity development, a pull from the environment rather than a conscious choice provides direction. In his mid-twenties, Mr. E. was asked by a friend to come to Vienna to teach in a progressive school set up for English and American children by Dorothy Burlingham. Burlingham had studied with Sigmund Freud, and this opened up an interest in psychological issues for Mr. E. During Mr. E.'s Vienna years (1927–1933), he came to the attention of Anna Freud, Sigmund Freud's daughter, who was well on her way to becoming a prominent theorist-therapist with children. Mr. E. became one of her training analysands (a combination of student and patient). He then met and married Joan Serson, a fellow analysand-trainee and an artist and dancer.

Because of the political turmoil in Europe in 1933, especially considering Mr. E.'s perceived Jewishness, he and his wife tried to settle in Copenhagen, but, ironically, he was not allowed Danish citizenship, so they traveled to America.

Because of both his ability and also the scarcity of child psychoanalysts, Mr. E. soon received many prestigious academic and medical school appointments. He was Boston's only child psychoanalyst in the early 1930s. He enrolled in the Ph.D. program in psychology at Harvard, but he never finished. Interestingly, although he was soon lauded (and still is) for his academic achievements, he had no degree beyond high school.

Mr. E. moved from Boston to New Haven in 1936, then to the Pine Ridge Sioux Indian Reservation in South Dakota for fieldwork, then to San Francisco in 1939, then to Berkeley, California, then to Stockbridge, Massachusetts, in 1950 (with weekly commutes to Pittsburgh), then back to Harvard and New Haven in 1960. In 1970, Mr. E. retired, dividing his retirement time between Marin County, California, and Cape Cod, Massachusetts, until his death on May 12, 1994.

Identity Challenge

Mr. E.'s life provided much fodder for identity crises: confusion and rejection related to both his parentage and his ethnicity, as well as issues around vocational choice, educational achievement, where "home" was, etc. Thus, it is not surprising that "Mr. E.," Erik Homburger Erikson, himself coined the term "identity crisis" and was the pioneer of this research area (Hopkins, 1995). Even his eventual personal choice for his last name—Erickson—reveals identity questions. He gave some indication that his choice was an attempt to acknowledge his biological father in naming himself after the early Danish explorer Lief Erikson.

Erik Erikson certainly confronted and surmounted his own identity crisis in grand style. He is revered as one of the greatest theorists and synthesizers across theories and disciplines in the behavioral sciences. One colleague described Erikson as "Freud in sonnet form" (Hopkins, 1995). He authored many well-known books and articles, such as the classic *Identity, Youth and Crisis* (1968) and the psychobiography *Gandhi's Truth*, for which he won a Pulitzer Prize.

Treatment

For most of us, physiological maturation, education, contact with mentors, life experience, and time are all the therapy we need for our identity crisis. It is important to remember that, while the majority of the work is done early in life and in bits and pieces, it is nevertheless a lifelong process for us all. In most instances, it is a process of normal development rather than a disorder. This reflects the modern trend to see these issues less as disorder, maybe as crisis, and always as a normal developmental challenge. In this vein, while prior *DSM*s included Identity Disorder as a standard disorder, in the *DSM-IV* there is only an Identity Problem, and the definition is applied only as an "other condition that may be a focus of clinical attention."

However, whether we term it disorder or problem, a number of individuals require some formal intervention to get through the identity challenge. Some high school counselors try to take on this task, but they seldom have enough time to do much. Counseling centers in universities do much of this work. Approaches like client-centered therapy, existential therapy, or the cognitive therapies (see Chapter 1 and Chapter 2) are most often useful here.

15

Organic Mental Disorders and Mental Retardation

The title of this chapter can be a bit misleading in that most mental disorders have accompanying biological conditions, contributing causes, and/or results. What this chapter deals with are those consistent behavioral, affective, and intellectual patterns of disturbance that result when there has been damage to the *normal* brain. Brain cells can be functionally impaired or destroyed by a wide variety of injuries, diseases, and toxic chemicals. Damage to brain structures involved in cognition, affect, and/or impulse control can lead to inadequate psychological functioning. The extent to which a person's psychological functioning is impaired depends on the location and extent of neural damage, the person's prior psychological adjustment, and the quality of the person's lifestyle. The effects of an organic mental disorder can range from mild memory disturbances to severe psychotic reactions.

This chapter presents a rather incredible case in which a person (Harry) had an entire hemisphere (one-half of the brain) surgically removed in his youth. Not only did he survive to live a somewhat normal life, but he actually achieved an overall adjustment at well above the average level. The second case study is a case of Alzheimer's disease in former president Ronald Reagan. The chapter concludes with a discussion of mental retardation.

Recovery of Functions Following Removal of Dominant Brain Hemisphere

**The Case
of Harry**

*Most fighters have some type of trauma. Hey,
we're in the traumatizing business.*

—James Bonecrusher Smith, after being denied
a boxing license in England in April 1994
because of trauma to his brain from boxing

While the human brain can be fragile, it is at the same time a remarkably adaptable organ. People have been known to sustain massive amounts of brain damage due to motor vehicle accidents, tumors, and other lesions, yet show remarkable degrees of recovery. Of course, the eventual level of recovery depends on a number of factors, including age at the time of injury, severity of damage, and the particular region (or regions) of the brain that sustained damage. The psychological assessment of people who have sustained brain injuries should therefore consider changes in performance that are likely to occur for some time after the original insult (Kay and Franklin, 1995). For this reason many clinical neuropsychologists make it a habit to follow up on their clients and to retest them periodically in order to document changes that occur over time.

The processes by which the brain recovers from injury are being studied by a number of investigators, most of whom emphasize the capacity of nondamaged brain areas to help compensate for injury to other areas by assuming new functional roles. This line of reasoning implies that there is not a strict one-to-one correspondence between brain structures and behavioral or mental activity, even though under ordinary circumstances certain regions of the brain appear to exert dominant influence over specific functions.

Many years ago it was believed that there existed a strict correspondence between brain regions and behavior (Harrington, 1985). According to this model, popularly called *phrenology*, discrete regions of the brain controlled very specific behaviors or mental processes. Thus, specific brain regions allegedly were responsible for such states as euphoria, anger, and intellectual superiority. An implication of this view of brain functions is that damage to a given region would be expected to affect only certain psychological functions, leaving others relatively intact. Indeed, early anatomical studies lent some support to this theory. For example, in the late nineteenth century French neurologist Paul Broca discovered that impairment of expressive speech followed damage to a relatively circumscribed region of the left (or dominant) cerebral hemisphere.

Subsequent attempts to localize brain centers that control particular functions have met with varying degrees of success. At present, it is evident that even though there is certainly a general relationship between brain structures and psychological functions, the correlation is by no means exact (Harrington, 1985). It is well known, for example, that the two cerebral hemispheres each control some relatively distinct functions. In healthy and mature right-handed persons the left cerebral hemisphere plays the dominant role in mediating language skills and the right cerebral hemisphere exerts correspondingly more control over what are known as visuospatial abilities, which are manifested in activities such as drawing, finding directions, and being able to visualize spatial arrangements such as one might encounter in geometry problems. At a more general level a distinction between the hemispheres emphasizes the capacity of the left hemisphere for rational, logical, and analytic thought processes, in contrast to the right hemisphere's role in more holistic, intuitive processes.

The axis of the brain extending from front to back is referred to as the anterior-posterior dimension. The front-most regions play a significant role in planning and executing behavior patterns. Structures in the posterior regions appear to be more involved in processing information taken in by the various sensory systems.

A third part of the brain extends inward from the surface of the brain. Surface regions—collectively called the cortical mantle—appear to mediate most of what are called higher mental processes, such as language, abstract thought, and reasoning abilities. Areas of the brain beneath the cortical mantle, by contrast, control a wide range of activities, including vegetative (life support), reflexive, appetitive, and emotive functions. From an evolutionary standpoint, these regions are the oldest, most primitive regions of the brain, collectively referred to as the allocortex, in contrast to the outermost cortical regions, known as the neocortex.

Regarding the functional localization and implications for recovery processes, it is evident that regions, or zones, of the brain are usually responsible for mediating certain psychological functions. These functions can be grouped according to three dimensions—left/right, anterior/posterior, and brain surface/inner regions. Although these dimensions do imply a degree of functional specificity, there is by no means a precise one-to-one correspondence between circumscribed regions of brain tissue and specific behavior patterns or thought processes.

It is interesting to note that this absence of a strict one-to-one correspondence holds true to a greater degree for the so-called higher than for the lower functions. For example, lesions in regions of the visual system concerned with basic perceptual processes may have very pronounced and permanent effects, such as blind spots or reductions in the visual fields (the area of sight from one visual periphery to the other). By contrast, brain lesions in areas controlling cognitive activities such as language may disrupt certain linguistic processes, without such clear-cut effects, however. There are several possible explanations for this. One is that language, because it is such a complex process, is mediated by a greater proportion of brain tissue than are relatively less complex functions. As a result, focal damage is less likely to affect adversely all of the regions involved in this skill. A second possibility is that higher-level functions such as language may be reduplicated in adjacent or even in more distant brain regions. Thus, damage to a zone that ordinarily controls or mediates may be compensated for by other structures, which provide a sort of back-up coverage.

However, depending upon the individual, both the right and left cerebral hemispheres manifest language capabilities, although to different degrees; ordinarily the left hemisphere is considered dominant. Until recently the role of the right hemisphere in language activity was not well understood. However, the results of studies of patients who have undergone certain surgical procedures have made it clear that the right (or nondominant) hemisphere has a capacity for language-related activity. In one such procedure (termed a *hemispherectomy*), an entire cerebral hemisphere is removed, leaving the individual with essentially only half a brain. Understandably, relatively few of these operations are performed. Those that are done have been carried out either to arrest malignant tumors that have infiltrated one hemisphere or as a means of controlling severe seizure activity that has not responded to less dramatic therapy.

The case of Harry is one of the most dramatic instances reported in the literature. Early in childhood the left hemisphere of Harry's brain was removed. The removal was followed by a remarkable recovery of speech and language functions, as assessed by follow-up evaluations years later. Originally described in an article by Smith and Sugar (1975), Harry (not his real name) was briefly seen by the author some 3 years later, at which time a follow-up evaluation was being performed.

The Case of Harry

The product of a full-term pregnancy and a cesarean birth, Harry soon afterward began to manifest signs of significant brain impairment in the form of seizures. These seizures increased to nearly a dozen per day by the time he was 5 years old. A left hemispherectomy was performed shortly thereafter. Within a few months the seizure activity had abated. Testing prior to surgery had revealed distorted speech, doubtless due to the disruptive effects of damage in the left hemisphere.

Remarkably, Harry's performance on tests of language and other abilities improved significantly in the months and years following surgery, despite nearly complete removal of the cerebral hemisphere that normally mediates language skills. In fact, follow-up testing of Harry 15 and 21 years after surgery revealed that he was performing in the high average range of intelligence, with a verbal IQ score in the superior range.

Subsequent contact with Harry suggested that these high performance levels had been sustained and that he was adjusting extremely well. He successfully graduated from college and at last report was working in an executive-level position for an industrial company and contemplating attending graduate school. He had compensated remarkably well for the after effects of surgery, which included loss of sight in the right visual field and motor control problems on the right side (it is characteristic of damage to either hemisphere that control of the contralateral side of the body is affected). Harry was a talkative, quick-witted person who undoubtedly was functioning very effectively with half of his brain intact.

Comment

The case of Harry contains several important implications about the long-term effects of brain injury on behavior. First, the development of above-average language capabilities following removal of the cerebral hemisphere that normally mediates these functions suggests that the nondominant hemisphere may possess greater linguistic capabilities than previously realized. More generally, it is at least evident that brain–behavior relations do not correspond to strict one-to-one functional relations. Instead, compensation for or reduplication of control mechanisms appears to exist for certain cognitive processes.

In Harry's case, it may be concluded that right hemisphere structures were responsible for subsequent development of language skills, despite the fact that the right hemisphere's role in language skills is normally thought to be comparatively minor. Finally, the radical changes and improvements in Harry's mental functions underscore the importance of assessing the effects of brain injury over time and emphasize the recuperative powers of the central nervous system in certain situations. As noted in the introduction, the brain and related nervous system structures make up an incredibly complex yet flexible and adaptive system.

As far as Harry is concerned, it is likely that the early age at which surgery occurred enhanced his recovery potential, as brain structures do become more rigid as one ages. Furthermore, the degree of recovery may indicate that Harry possessed exceptional potential to begin with and for this reason does not provide a truly representative picture of recovery potential. Nonetheless, a discussion of this case is important as a means of counteracting tendencies either to view various functions as being strictly localized in the brain or to assume that any brain damage results in a corresponding permanent loss in psychological abilities.

Alzheimer's Disease

**The Case
of Ronald
Reagan**

Where's the rest of me?
—Ronald Reagan, in the movie *King's Row*, referring to his missing limbs

Alzheimer's disease is a form of dementia caused by the progressive deterioration of brain cells. It is referred to as a "presenile dementia" because the age of onset can be as early as 50. This distinguishes Alzheimer's disease from other forms of neural deterioration associated with the latter phases of the lifespan, which are collectively referred to as the "senile dementias." In actual practice, the distinction between presenile and senile dementias is problematic, because there is some disagreement about the age at which the term "senile" should first be used.

Unlike certain forms of central nervous system (CNS) impairment, Alzheimer's disease involves widespread deterioration of brain tissue so that a broad range of cognitive, behavioral, and physical capabilities eventually become affected. Nerve tissues are invaded by pathogenic structures, known as neuritic plaques and neurofibrillary tangles, that interfere with nerve conduction impulses. The course of the disease is fairly rapid, with death often occurring within 4 to 5 years from the time of onset.

Diagnostic Signs

At the beginning, manifestations of Alzheimer's disease are typically rather subtle. Often the first indications take the form of slight but persisting memory difficulties or of a perceptible loss of efficiency in going about one's day-to-day activities. Gradually a more severe and generalized impairment of intellectual capabilities becomes evident. Cognitive skills such as reading, writing, and reasoning begin to show impairment as an increasing number of brain centers are affected. Signs of neurological impairment begin to become evident, with abnormalities in EEG and visual evoked potentials being reliably reported. Changes in emotional status are evident as well, as bouts of depression, lability (fluctuating mood states), and heightened irritability become increasingly frequent. Eventually the disease progresses to a point at which the patient becomes persistently confused, incoherent, and disoriented. At this stage there is usually a failure to recognize even such familiar family members as spouses and children. Self-care and basic hygiene skills deteriorate, and an almost total dependence on others ensues (Kay and Franklin, 1995).

In some instances a confirming diagnosis can only be made by postmortem examination. However, the functional behavioral and neurological manifestations of Alzheimer's disease become increasingly pronounced as the disease progresses, leaving little doubt as to the presence of underlying CNS impairment.

Psychological Assessment

Psychological assessments of patients with Alzheimer's disease are of greatest help during the early stages of the disorder. There are three major ways in which these evaluations contribute to the diagnosis and management of the disease. First, early manifestations of Alzheimer's disease often include subtle changes in memory, mood, and cognition that can frequently be detected or validated via psychological testing (Kay and Franklin, 1995). In conjunction with a neurological evaluation this information may provide some of the earliest indications of the impending changes in mental status that result from the disease. Second, a thorough assessment of psychological capabilities can help both patient and family develop realistic strategies for coping with the impact of the disease. Significant issues such as employment status and disability determination must be confronted, and psychological assessments can provide useful information to aid in making informed decisions in these areas. Finally, periodic psychological assessments can be useful in helping evaluate the patient's ongoing status, much as repeated physical and neurological examinations do.

Effects on Victim and Family

Victims of Alzheimer's disease, as well as their families, must confront a variety of psychological stressors. The patient must deal with the progressive deterioration of mental capabilities that eventually can turn even routine activities into confusing ordeals. A particularly stressful period comes when a tentative diagnosis has been made while the patient continues to be basically alert and oriented. At this phase the prospect of facing an ultimately fatal illness following the gradual loss of behavioral and mental control is highly stressful and frequently triggers secondary disorders such as depression.

Family members face several key stressors and often need help at this point. Many report that the increasing inability of a parent or spouse to recognize them as the disease progresses is especially disturbing. Related to this is the distress of adapting to the inevitable changes that transform a previously healthy, vital individual into someone who becomes chronically debilitated, frequently depressed and irritable, and eventually totally dependent on others. Finally, families of patients with Alzheimer's disease frequently must endure extraordinary financial hardships as well. This is most evident when the patient has been the chief economic provider and is afflicted with the disease at a point in his or her career when maximal earning power is nearing its peak.

Many of these issues are relevant to a discussion of Ronald Reagan, whose physicians diagnosed him as having Alzheimer's disease 6 years after the end of his second term as U.S. President.

> *Near or above the age of fifty the elasticity of the mental processes, on which the treatment depends, is as a rule lacking—old people are no longer educable—and, on the other hand, the mass of material to be dealt with would prolong the duration of the treatment indefinitely.*
>
> —Sigmund Freud (who was 48 at the time)

The Case of Ronald Reagan

On November 5, 1994, an announcement was made to the American people that Ronald W. Reagan, the fortieth president of the United States, had been diagnosed with Alzheimer's disease. Due to the difficulty of accurately diagnosing Alzheimer's disease in living patients, Reagan's team of five personal physicians carefully administered extensive tests and conducted close observations during the several weeks leading up to the announcement; they had suspected the possibility of Alzheimer's for over a year. After all the tests and observations were completed, the team ruled out virtually all other possibilities. The knowledge that Reagan's mother had died of Alzheimer's disease also aided somewhat in making the diagnosis. According to many newspaper articles in which friends and co-workers were quoted, most of those who had contact with Reagan over the past year were aware that something was not right mentally with the former president.

Ronald Reagan was born on February 6, 1911, in Tampico, Illinois. In his autobiography, he describes his mother as loving and attentive. He credits her with nurturing his acting ability. His father, John, was much loved by Ronald Reagan and was described as "restless, ambitious, and constantly frustrated" by the difficulties he faced as a shoe salesman. John Reagan was an alcoholic, which Ronald Reagan has cited as his father's "only weakness." Although John Reagan was much revered and his alcoholism was written off as a simple weakness, his problem left a deep impression on his son. When he was 11 years old, he came home one winter day to find his father passed out on the front porch of the family home; he pulled his father into the house and put him to bed. Whenever asked to recall memories from his childhood, this is a memory that President Reagan often describes. And although he pleads no resentment toward his father, it is evident by the sheer lasting power of the memory that the alcoholism hurt the President.

Throughout his life, Reagan experienced several illnesses and traumas. As a very young boy, he had bronchial pneumonia; his mother also came down with influenza at about the same time and was delirious with high fevers and chills. Later in his life, at around the age of 37, Reagan developed viral pneumonia and almost died. He too experienced high fevers, delirium, and chills with this illness. On March 30, 1981, President Reagan was shot by John Hinkley, Jr., in an assassination attempt. The bullet struck Reagan in the chest; he lost a great deal of blood and after surgery experienced high fevers and appetite loss. He also underwent surgeries for prostate gland trouble and colon cancer. In 1989, just after leaving the White House and finishing his second term as President, Reagan suffered a subdural hematoma when he was thrown from a horse in Mexico—this too required surgery.

In 1962, Reagan's mother died of Alzheimer's disease after years of torment and pain. It was not known that she had the disease until long after her death. Reagan never hid the fact that his mother was "senile," freely giving the information to reporters who questioned his mental health and age as he campaigned for the presidency. He requested to be tested yearly for senility before he even won the election. Because Ronald Reagan was the oldest president, his health had always been an issue, especially while he was in office. Some experts have said that it is theoretically possible that President Reagan could have been affected by Alzheimer's in his final months in the White House. This idea is vehemently opposed by Reagan's physicians and supporters, who assert that Reagan was monitored and tested yearly for any signs of senility or Alzheimer's disease and that his memory and mental acuity were very sharp during his White House years. Still, rumors were heard that Reagan needed cue cards to get through speeches, would doze off during White House meetings, etc. Whenever President Reagan forgot things or became unsure of himself, however, he would joke or put himself into a flattering position that emphasized his physical fitness.

Nevertheless, the possibility of his Alzheimer's disease beginning toward the end of his second term as president would certainly clarify the confusion felt by many about Reagan's "memory lapses" at the Iran-Contra hearings, at which he failed to recall not only events that occurred, but also the name of an important staff member. Even close friends and associates admit that they detected a slowing of Reagan's mental sharpness and memory much earlier than the doctors' final diagnosis. The general consensus among many friends and associates was that, consistent with Alzheimer's, President Reagan had been fading slowly. Some even claim that as far back as 1986 there was a definite decline in Reagan's mental health. They described him as "less engaged" and "slowing down" and seemed concerned about the "deterioration of his thought processes." During the funeral of former president Richard Nixon in the spring of 1994, many felt that Reagan appeared to be in poor health. President Bill Clinton recalled talking with Reagan after winning the presidency in 1992. He said that they discussed the job of the presidency and in the middle of the conversation, Reagan completely forgot what he was talking about and admitted frustration with himself. During times of forgetfulness, Reagan had been known to wonder if he had inherited Alzheimer's disease from his mother.

It is ironic that, in 1982, President Reagan signed into law a designation of November as National Alzheimer's Disease Month. It was in November 1994, that President Reagan disclosed in a heart-wrenching letter his own diagnosis of Alzheimer's. He called it the start of "the journey that will lead me into the sunset of my life." Ever since that announcement of his illness, he has rarely been seen in public. But he continues a somewhat active life, playing a few holes of golf, and being with his family.

Etiology

Many factors may have played a role in Ronald Reagan's diagnosis of Alzheimer's disease. Definite consideration must be given to the genetic component in his mother having died of Alzheimer's. John Reagan's alcoholism may also be a factor. President Reagan has lived a life of almost constant stress. He lived in an alcoholic and financially struggling home environment, worked for many years as a famous actor, and later went into politics—to end up with the most stressful job of all, president of the United States of America. He also experienced many physical traumas, including several that affected the brain (subdural hematoma, delirium from fevers, etc.). Any of these factors may have caused or contributed to Reagan's Alzheimer's disease.

Issues of both causation and the value ethics of seeking earlier evidence of potential Alzheimer's are highlighted in one of the most elegant "field" studies (see the section on research in Chapter 1) ever devised. Dr. David Snowden and his colleagues (1996) decided to study a group of ninety-three cloistered nuns, all born before 1917 and in their 80s at the time of the study, hypothesizing that nuns who had spent their lives teaching would show less Alzheimer's than those who mainly did household chores. This did not prove to be true.

Fortuitously, all of these nuns had been asked to write a short autobiography 4 years after they entered the convent, just before taking their permanent vows. In a stunning finding that even surprised these researchers, a rating of these autobiographies allowed a prediction, with 90% accuracy, as to whether these nuns would or would not develop Alzheimer's some 50 years later. In addition to this validity, they also assessed the raters' reliability in scoring these autobiographies and found that to be nearly 90%.

Overall, they found that nuns whose sentences were grammatically complex and showed the highest amount of the psycholinguistic feature termed "idea density" did not develop Alzheimer's. Idea density assesses how many ideas are concentrated into a given piece of writing. For example, the two nuns in the study whose writings were at the extremes when rated for idea density were both 20 years old when they wrote their autobiographies, and both had high school degrees. One wrote: "At the time of my entrance, I was in good health and had had no serious illnesses before this time." The other nun wrote: "Now I am wandering about in 'Dove's Lane' waiting, yet only three weeks to follow in the footprints of my Spouse, bound in Him by the Holy Vows of Poverty, Chastity, and Obedience." The first nun obtained a bachelor's and master's degrees and died of Alzheimer's disease about six decades later. The second nun got a bachelor's degree and is still alive, her mind keen and her memory intact.

This study fits with the hypothesis that genetics plays a substantial part in the development of Alzheimer's disease, and correlates with the findings of German researchers headed by Tomas G. Ohm (1996) of J. Guntenberg University in Mainz, who examined 887 brains of people 20 to 104 years old and concluded that neurofibrillary tangles, the pathological changes characteristic of Alzheimer's disease, could be present even when people were 20 years old. The German group concluded that the roots of Alzheimer's disease–related neurofibrillary changes can be traced about 50 years back and may even extend into adolescence.

Snowden's (1996) study has the "natural event" value of all field studies—that is, the lives of these nuns were not manipulated by an experimenter, nor were they asked to write their autobiographies by experimenters, with informed consent, or in a "lab" setting. Yet it has many of the benefits of a controlled experiment: The subjects were all white, female, from similar socio-economic-religious backgrounds, and lived together in the same environment for almost 60 years.

The ethical implications are interesting. Should we examine people early on and tell them the probabilities of developing this or other diseases? Should we examine candidates for political office, especially the presidency, on such early variables? Remember that one of the characteristics many people liked in President Reagan was that his ideas were clear, straightforward, even simple at times.

Outcome Issues

At present, Alzheimer's disease, perhaps the best known of the presenile dementias, is a condition for which there is no known cure. The immediate cause of Alzheimer's involves degeneration of brain cells. So far, the most compelling explanation is one based on hereditary vulnerability.

> *Jesus said, " . . . I tell you the truth . . . when you are old you will stretch out your hands and someone else will dress you and lead you where you do not want to go."*
>
> —John 21:18

Mental Retardation

About 1% of the population falls into the category of mental retardation (American Association of Mental Retardation, 1994). The *DSM-IV* requires indication of significantly subaverage intellectual functioning (Criterion A), an IQ of 70 or below, although testing measurement error, approximately 5 points, would allow a diagnosis up to an IQ of 75 in a standardized, individually administered test, and onset before the age of 18 (Criterion C). Also required (Criterion B) is evidence of significant limitation in adaptive functioning in at least two of the following skill areas: communication, self-care, home living, social/interpersonal skills, use of community resources, self-direction, functional academic skills, work, leisure, health, and safety. (It's good that an IQ score is required, as it appears that many in the population would qualify on Criterion B). The criteria for severity and descriptors and interventions, by age, are found in Table 15–1.

TABLE 15–1 Criteria for Severity of Mental Retardation, by Age

Level	Preschool Age (birth to 5 years)	School Age (6 to 12 years)	Adult (over 21 years)
Mild Retardation (IQ of 50–55 to 70—by *DSM-IV*) (about 85% of retarded persons)	Can develop social and language skills; less retardation in sensorimotor areas. Seldom distinguished from normal until older. Referred to as *educable.*	Can learn academic skills to approximately sixth-grade level by late teens. Cannot learn general high school subjects. Needs special education, particularly at secondary school level.	Capable of social and vocational adequacy with proper education and training. Frequently needs guidance when under serious social or economic stress.
Moderate Retardation (IQ of 35–40 to 50–55) (10% of retarded persons)	Can talk or learn to communicate. Poor social awareness. Fair motor development. May profit from self-help; can be managed with moderate supervision.	Can learn functional academic skills to approximately fourth-grade level by late teens if given special education.	Capable of self-maintenance in unskilled or semiskilled occupations. Needs supervision and guidance when under mild social or economic stress.
Severe Retardation (IQ of 20–25 to 35–40) (3–4% of retarded persons)	Poor motor development. Speech is minimal. Few or no communication skills. Generally unable to profit from training in self-help.	Can talk or learn to communicate. Can be trained in elemental health habits. Cannot learn functional academic skills. Profits from systematic habit training.	Can contribute partially to self-support under complete supervision. Can develop self-protection skills to a minimally useful level in a controlled environment.
Profound Retardation (IQ of 20–25 or below) (1–2% of retarded persons)	Minimal capacity for functioning in sensorimotor areas. Needs nursing care.	Some motor development present. Cannot profit from training in self-help. Needs total care.	Some motor and speech development. Totally incapable of self-maintenance. Needs complete care and supervision.

Source: Adapted in part from J. M. Sattler, *Assessment of Children's Intelligence and Special Abilities* (Boston: Allyn and Bacon, 1982), p. 426.

If there is good reason to believe that significant intellectual retardation is present with functioning at least below an approximate IQ of 70 and for some reason the individual is untestable, the diagnosis Mental Retardation, Severity Unspecified (319) is used. The diagnosis of Borderline Intellectual Functioning (V62.89) encoded on Axis II requires evidence of problems in adaptive coping and an IQ of 71 to 84.

A wide variety of interventions are necessary to deal effectively with mental retardation and its associated problems. Those with less impairment profit most from psycho-educational and social skills interventions, and the greater the degree of impairment, the more necessary are the various behavioral interventions.

16

Legal Issues and Psychological Practice

Legal decisions and processes depend more and more upon psychological information, as has already been suggested by the case studies of O. J. Simpson, Jeffrey Dahmer, Jesse Timmendequas, and several others in this book. There are many ways in which psychology and its related disciplines may provide input or impact into the legal system (see Table 16–1). Some of the most common and important input comes in the areas of evaluating criminal responsibility, competence to stand trial, or competency to handle one's affairs; gauging potential dangerousness and its relationship to involuntary civil commitment; and the appraisal of honesty or truth telling by participants in the criminal justice system (as well as in other areas). The first case in this chapter (Ingrid) provides a ready transition from the preceding chapter on the organic mental disorders, as it deals with the significant and widespread issue of deciding when the psychological and physical ravages of aging require a decision that a person is no longer competent to handle his or her own personal affairs. The other case focuses on the issues of deciding on a defendant's competence to stand trial, level of criminal responsibility and potential for dangerousness through the well-publicized but not always well-understood case of John Hinckley, the individual who attempted to assassinate President Ronald Reagan.

Central Nervous System Dysfunction and Legal Incompetence from Aging and/or Alcohol

The Case of Ingrid

Courtroom: *A place where Jesus Christ and Judas Iscariot would be equals, with the betting odds in favor of Judas.*

—H. L. Mencken, American essayist

TABLE 16–1 Taxonomy of Psycholegal Issues

Reconstructive Context	Contemporaneous Context	Predictive Context
Criminal Context—Defendant Issues		
Competency to Confess (at past arrest)	Competency to Consent to evaluation	Restoration to CST
Criminal Responsibility NGRI, GMBI	Competency to Stand Trial Competency to Plead Guilty	Bond Release: flight danger to community
Mens rea: intent purpose v. reckless	Competency to Waive Counsel Competency to Refuse NGRI	Pre-Sentence Probation risk
Special defenses: Battered wife syndrome	Competency to Waive *Miranda* (at present arrest)	Death Penalty issues: Future danger
Involuntary intoxication	Competency to Testify	Prison adjustment
Duress	Competency to Refuse Medicine	Inmate classification
Infancy (on mental age)	for CSI restoration	Parole release
Death Penalty Mitigation	Competency to be Executed	Juvenile waiver:
mentality (OBS, MR)	Juvenile waiver:	Amenability
under domination of other	sophistication & maturity	for treatment
"emotional disturbance"		Special sentencing: sex offenders youthful offender act
Criminal Content—Victim Issues		
Validation of child's molestation		
Rape trauma syndrome in rebuttal to consent		
Victim impact statement		
Civil Context	Involuntary commitment (need for treatment now)	Involuntary commitment (danger self/others)
Testamentary capacity (testator deceased)	Guardianship	Inpatient disposition
Personal injury (proximate cause)	Conservatorship	d/c suicide watch
Workers' Compensation (work relatedness)	Competency to contract	less restrictive care
Substituted judgment: patient's consent to Rx	Competency to consent voluntary treatment	discharge Parental competence:
Malpractice:	refuse treatment	child custody
Negligent release	research participation	visitation
Failure to commit/warn	Testamentary capacity (testator alive)	foster care/adoption
Liability for suicide	Competency to die (?) (assisted suicide)	after domestic abuse
Abandonment	Competency to testify (child)	Psychological autopsies
Failure to consult/refer	Competency of child to choose custodial parent	Termination of Parental Rights: treatment
Wrongful commitment	Termination of Parental Rights (implementation)	Response to Mediation
Sexual harassment/contact	Child in Need of Supervision	Relicensure of Ph.D., MD
Breach of confidentiality	Malpractice: licence supervision/ revocation	Return to work; duty
Mental illness defenses:		Personal injury: damages (Rx costs)
Impaired professional		
At-fault divorce grounds		
Prior contract(s)		

With permission, from Geoffrey McKee (1994), "Taxonomy of Legal issues," *Bulletin of the American Academy of Forensic Psychology, 15,* 2–4.

There are a variety of areas in which psychologists are frequently called on to address the issue of an individual's mental competence (Melton et al., 1997). "Competence" in the legal arena can refer to competence to manage one's day-to-day affairs, termed "guardianship," as in the case of Ingrid, or can mean competence to make a will, competence to stand trial, or competence to be a witness at trial (often an issue in child abuse cases—see Chapter 13)—even competence to be executed, as required by the Supreme Court in *Ford* v. *Wainwright* (1986) (477 U.S. 399). For the purpose of this case, competence refers to the extent to which individuals are presumed capable of managing their day-to-day affairs, often referred to under the concept of "guardianship." This concept is especially important when applied to older persons. Although the majority of people will remain mentally alert (and presumably competent) throughout most of their lives, the aging process is accompanied by changes that may compromise a person's mental status for any of several reasons, most commonly deterioration of the central nervous system (CNS) (Salmon and Meyer, 1986a).

The term *dementia* is often used to signify the presence of CNS-based mental deterioration sufficient to interfere with a person's functioning; it is more commonly but inaccurately termed "senility." Dementia is diagnosed when there is evidence of significant intellectual decline, plus evidence of more specific cognitive deficits, one of which involves memory loss. Dementia need not have a specific cause; it can result from a wide range of conditions that adversely affect the brain and other CNS structures.

Dementia is often thought of as an essentially irreversible condition, particularly when evident in older persons, but this is not always the case. For example, in many older persons the arteries that supply blood to the brain gradually become occluded due to accumulated deposits of fatty substances (arteriosclerosis). This process curtails blood flow to the brain, reduces metabolic efficiency, and thereby increases forgetfulness, absentmindedness, and a general lowering of behavioral efficiency—in short, common indices of dementia. A significant effect of surgery to help restore brain blood supply (called an endarterectomy) is the often abrupt reversal of symptoms of dementia and the restoration of mental alertness.

The assessment of mental competence thus often involves a determination of whether dementia is present to a significant degree (Melton et al., 1997). This task may be complicated by the fact that other mental disorders—particularly depression—can easily be confused with dementia. This distinction is an important one to make when assessing older persons, who in addition to being more biologically vulnerable to factors underlying true dementia are quite likely to experience events that trigger depressive reactions, such as the death of a spouse or other loved one.

An assessment of mental competence in older persons requires a careful evaluation of events surrounding the reported onset of symptoms. In addition to carrying out formal psychological testing, the psychologist must obtain a detailed history of the client's problems. The following case highlights some of the issues involved in the determination of mental competence. It is a description of Ingrid, a 77-year-old woman who was referred for an extensive psychological assessment to aid the court in a determination of her mental competence.

> *Seventy-year-old Paul Newman became the oldest driver to ever win a major sportscar race—and he did it with the left-turn signal on the entire time.*
>
> —Conan O'Brien, talk show host

The Case of Ingrid

Ingrid's husband Charlie had died 3 years earlier, after a long series of illnesses. They had been a devoted couple, and his death sent Ingrid into a deep depression. For the first time in her life, Ingrid began to drink heavily as a means of washing away her emotional pain. She appeared to others to become absentminded and forgetful, as if lost in a dreamlike reverie. On several occasions Ingrid's neighbors noticed her doing strange things, such as working in her garden in midwinter and taking out the trash when only partially dressed. Charlie had left her a sizeable estate, ample to meet her needs plus an inheritance for the children. On one or two occasions, she talked about giving all the money away to a charity, as if any reminder of Charlie was too much to bear.

Alarmed at these developments—particularly at the prospect of having his inheritance jeopardized—Ingrid's son (aged 53) petitioned to have his mother declared legally incompetent to manage her own affairs. The petition was upheld in a court hearing, and Ingrid's financial holdings were turned over to a court-appointed trustee, who provided her with funds to live on in a local nursing home. At the hearing the attorney retained by Ingrid's son argued that her advanced age made it reasonable to assume that the depression following Charlie's death was only part of a broader picture of mental deterioration indicative of encroaching senility. By way of contrast, expert testimony included the report of a clinical psychologist who, although agreeing that Ingrid showed signs of significant mental impairment, felt that the condition was only temporary and should not be presumed to be accompanied by dementia (senility) merely because of the client's advanced age. He recommended that Ingrid's condition be reevaluated several months hence, should it appear that she showed signs of remission.

Eighteen months later Ingrid herself wrote a meticulously worded, impeccably reasoned letter to the judge requesting that her case be reopened, and at the same time she hired a new attorney. She was in much better spirits and seemed optimistic that they would succeed in overturning the earlier ruling. As part of the proceedings a thorough neuropsychological assessment was carried out. In addition to evaluating global intellectual performance, it assessed five groups of cognitive skills that are sensitive to CNS impairments: speech and language skills, visuospatial abilities, attention and concentration, memory, and sensory-motor areas.

The results of this assessment suggested that Ingrid was mentally competent and that whatever condition(s) had been responsible for her earlier mental relapses were no longer apparent. There was no indication of dementia. Ingrid manifested an IQ in the upper portion of the average range, possessed adequate memory skills, and showed no significant indication of other specific thinking disorders. She appeared to have compensated well for some sensory and motor impairments (poor eyesight, slight hearing loss, plus an obvious motor tremor) and appeared for the assessment as a socially alert, cooperative, well-groomed woman, fully aware of the purpose of the evaluation and related events. As stated in the evaluation (reproduced here in summary form):

> On the Wechsler Adult Intelligence Scale—Revised (WAIS-R), Mrs. A [Ingrid] achieved a Full Scale IQ score that places her at a level slightly above average for individuals of similar age. Her performance was highly consistent, notable for the absence of diagnostic indicators on the WAIS associated with signs of cerebral impairment. These results were obtained despite evidence of sensory and motor deficits including pronounced motor tremor, bilateral cataracts, and possibly transient hearing difficulty. Mrs. A appears to have developed compensatory strategies that included guiding the right hand with the left to minimize tremor; use of a magnifying glass, plus slow visual scanning patterns; and postural adjustments to maximize auditory volume, along with requests for repetition of test items on occasion. Overall, results of the WAIS-R were compatible with the client's educational and job history and reveal normal age-related slowing of response speed and information processing efficiency, without evidence of additional intrusive factors that would interfere with intellectual performance.
>
> Overall, the assessment of this 78-year-old woman reveals intellectual and cognitive capabilities in an above-average range, above-average memory abilities, and a well-focused, organized approach to the tests. Verbal and linguistic fluency appears developed to a higher degree than corresponding skills in visuo-perceptual areas—a discrepancy that may be enhanced by the visual and motor problems apparent to casual observation.

The results of formal testing give only a hint of the range of observations needed to provide a clear picture of Ingrid's mental status. These observations contributed to a three-dimensional image of a competent, well-adjusted individual.

Evaluation

The evaluation was conducted first in the examiner's office and then at the nursing home where Ingrid lived. By carrying out the assessment at two different times and locations, it was possible to evaluate the consistency of Ingrid's behavior. On both occasions, she was neatly groomed and dressed and acted cordial. Ingrid's room at the nursing home reflected active interests. A desk, set up near the bed, contained neatly organized materials—pencils, pens, a work lamp, stationery, plus a vase of freshly cut flowers. She had organized her business papers in a section of the desk; and on one occasion, after stating that she wished to show the examiner some pertinent material, unerringly located it without hesitation or confusion. The material turned out to be a hand-written copy of the letter she had recently sent to the judge requesting a new competency hearing.

Ingrid proved well aware of the purpose of the evaluation and was able to explain clearly the events leading up to the current situation. She was quite frank in discussing the particulars of her history, readily admitting that the grief, fear, and even anger engendered by her husband's death had caused her to do some unfortunate things. Neither her manner and affect nor the details of her account of these events varied appreciably between the two assessment sessions.

Her response to the testing was characteristic of many older persons faced with taking tests—she was anxious. She expressed some trepidation about the nature of the tests and was concerned that her lack of recent experience with similar sorts of activities would compromise her performance. In addition, she was dismayed at the prospect of having to analyze problems without the aid of paper and pencil (or her new calculator, which she had recently learned to use as an aid in analyzing her financial investments). It is important to consider a client's reaction to the tests themselves, as extreme anxiety can have a markedly adverse effect on performance. Ingrid was well aware that the results of the assessment would be used in the determination of her legal competency, yet she managed to master whatever anxiety she felt and performed well on the tests.

During the initial assessment session, Ingrid failed to solve an arithmetic problem involving the computation of a percentage. As a former bookkeeper, she was quite upset at her performance on this particular test item. She remembered the details of the problem, however, and at the beginning of the following session 5 days later she produced the correct solution, along with the results of several similar problems that she had made up. This gave evidence of a number of things, including excellent memory skills, persistence in problem solving, a desire to improve on performance, and perhaps a degree of overcompensation and compulsiveness. It was evident that well into her advanced years, Ingrid had retained a strong desire to both please and impress people. The only difference was that now she found herself trying to please subordinates both in age and experience and to prove to them that she could perform up to standards that people far younger than she had set. Additional indications of mental competency accrue from other sources. A sense of humor, for example, is frequently treated as a sign of mental alertness. Ingrid possessed a mildly self-deprecatory sense of humor and a general attitude that appeared uplifting and optimistic.

These and other indications of behavioral consistency, alertness, and socially apt behavior apparent during the course of two test sessions provided evidence of mental competency that amplified on and individualized the rather bland assertion that Ingrid possessed "average intellectual functioning." A comprehensive description of Ingrid based on these observations took on additional significance in light of the impression that people were prone to form of her based on first impressions. For example, at the onset of the evaluation, she stated that the examiner would have to speak somewhat loudly, and she closed in to a distance that violated usual though unspoken standards of how close two people normally get. Unless able to use a magnifying glass, she resorted to scanning visual materials with her face very close to the page. When writing, she had to steady her right hand with the left in order to lessen the effects of a pronounced motor tremor. Such behavior, from a distance, could easily create a stereotyped image of an incompetent individual. And yet it was precisely this sort of behavior that attested to Ingrid's awareness of her limitations and her successful adaptation to them. It is not uncommon to find individuals of any age who appear superficially competent simply because they are not active and do not behave in ways that might betray their limitations or to find others whose behavior is maladaptive because they are not aware of their limitations. By comparison, Ingrid really was quite competent and well adjusted.

Decision
A court verdict in Ingrid's favor was returned, legally restoring her rights and privileges to manage her own affairs.

Treatment
While certain drug combinations have shown some success in improving memory in persons with problems similar to Ingrid's, it was not deemed necessary here, nor was any formal psychological intervention undertaken. When she learned of the favorable decision, she promptly reinvested a portion of her estate in money market funds, sold the fam-

ily homestead, and purchased a condominium in a progressive retirement community that provided increasing levels of health care as needed by the members. Having quickly dispatched these tasks, she took her first vacation in years, a long cruise. She commented that the outcome of the hearing had given her a new lease on life—at age 78.

Comment

The results of the extensive neuropsychological assessment carried out on this woman corroborated other diagnostic tests. All the tests concluded that Ingrid's mental status was unimpaired and that there were no indications of any underlying CNS impairment that would seriously compromise her ability to think and reason effectively. The assessment did turn up evidence of normal age-related changes in test performance, chiefly a slowing of reaction time and somewhat lower flexibility when confronted with new information. Nevertheless, it was concluded that these factors would not impede Ingrid from competently carrying out her day-to-day affairs, a conclusion amply confirmed by her subsequent behavior.

Beyond merely ruling out the presence of dementia, the thorough assessment of cognitive, intellectual, and social skills highlighted Ingrid's patterns of strengths and weaknesses and individualized her as a person. A most significant aspect of Ingrid's situation concerns the somewhat unusual reversal of a competency ruling in a person of relatively advanced age (Grisso, 1986). The outcome of her case further counteracts the popular tendency to view mental abilities in older persons as suspect (at best) and, if compromised, not readily recovered.

In spite of the positive outcome here, not everyone appreciates the contributions of psychologists to the assessment of competency. In its 1995 session the New Mexico legislature pondered and passed a bill that set limits on the testimony of psychologists regarding competency. Senate Bill 459, written by Richard Romero, included the following language, quoted in the newsletter *Dispatches:*

> "When a psychologist or psychiatrist testifies during a defendant's competency hearing, the psychologist or psychiatrist shall wear a cone-shaped hat that is not less than two feet tall. The surface of the hat shall be imprinted with stars and lightning bolts.

> "Additionally, a psychologist or psychiatrist shall be required to don a white beard . . . and shall punctuate crucial elements of his testimony by stabbing the air with a wand." (Apparently there are only male shrinks in New Mexico.) Before the expert's testimony about competency, the bill specified, "the bailiff shall contemporaneously dim the courtroom lights and administer two strikes to a Chinese gong."

> Although the Senate passed the bill by a voice vote, and the House voted 46 to 14 to make it official, New Mexico Governor Gary Johnson vetoed it.

Criminal Responsibility, Competency to Stand Trial, and Dangerousness

**The Case
of John
Hinckley**

*I feel the insanity defense should be retained. I
bear no grudge against John Hinckley, but I sure
don't hope he wins the Irish Sweepstakes.*

—James Brady, presidential news
secretary and victim of John Hinckley

As violent crime plagues American society, citizens strive to accept judicial decisions while living in a world in which they fear for the welfare of their friends and families. Perhaps no other legal concept raises as many moral ambiguities as the concept of "criminal responsibility," popularly known as the insanity defense. Rightly or wrongly the insanity defense is often portrayed as a choice between liberty and security, for both the accused and society. Despite the behavioral sciences' strongest efforts to draw a firm line of distinction between "madness" and "badness," this boundary continues to shift under the interwoven social, political, economic, and other pressures of our society.

When an individual is charged with a crime and an insanity defense is raised, each juror (or in some cases solely the judge) must determine culpability. Such a determination is never easy, not only because of the real ramifications for the defendant(s), victim(s), family members, and others, but also because the legal concept of criminal responsibility raises the broadest of ethical questions about the limits of one individual's responsibility to another.

Although the issue of criminal responsibility can be reviewed as a singular concept, in judicial application it is nearly always interwoven with the defendant's competency to stand trial. Indeed, the issues of criminal responsibility and competency to stand trial are often confused by mental health experts involved in the judicial process. *Criminal responsibility* refers to the state of the defendant's mind at the time of the alleged crime, while *competency to stand trial* refers to the defendant's psychological state at the time of his or her trial. Such a temporal distinction is of crucial importance in the assessment of these issues.

For a punishable criminal act to occur, two related but independent factors must be present. First, an act or behavior legally defined as illegal must occur—that is, the *actus rea,* or the act itself. Second, the individual committing the act must have the general intent to do so—that is, the *mens rea.* Except for a few criminal statutes, for example, some product liability laws, both an illegal act and guilty mind must be present before a punishable crime has occurred.

Consideration of both the act and the intent has occurred for at least the last 2000 years of recorded history. The American judicial process has historically encompassed a variety of criminal responsibility standards. The McNaughten rule was borrowed from English case law (Daniel McNaughten's Case, 1843) and states the following:

If as a result of mental disease or defect, the defendant did not understand what he did or that it was wrong, or if he was under a delusion (but not otherwise insane), which, if true, would have provided a good defense. Thus, if one does not understand what he was doing at all or did not know that it was wrong, he is excused. He is also excused if due to an insane delusion he thought he was acting in self defense or carrying out the will of God. (Often called the right/wrong test.)

The criminal responsibility standard continued in this form until the irresistible impulse or volition test was added (*Davis* v. *United States,* 1897). The question became whether the individual had been robbed of his free will to control his behavior due to mental disease or defect, despite knowing such behavior was wrong.

In 1954, the Durham rule was set forth (*Durham* v. *United States,* 1954), within which Judge David Bazelon greatly widened the standard. In the face of much criticism, in 1972, Judge Bazelon rejected his own Durham rule (*U.S.* v. *Brawner,* 1972) and adopted the Model Penal Code created by the American Law Institute (ALI) (1962). In general, the ALI standard asserted that an individual is not criminally responsible if, by reason of mental disease or defect, he lacked substantial capacity to appreciate the wrongfulness of his conduct or lacked the substantial capacity to conform his behavior to the requirements of law. The ALI standard thus narrowed the Durham rule but was not as restrictive as the older McNaughten rule. As we will see, the next important change in criminal responsibility came about as a result of the Hinckley trial, via changes in the federal law (see Table 16–2).

TABLE 16–2 Comparison of Insanity Defenses

Test	Legal Standard	Final Burden of Proof	Who Bears Burden of Proof
McNaughten	"Didn't know what he or she was doing or didn't know it was wrong"	Varies from proof by a balance of probabilities on the defense to proof beyond a reasonable doubt on the prosecutor	
Irresistible impulse	"Could not control conduct"		
Durham	"Criminal act was caused by mental illness"	Beyond reasonable doubt	Prosecutor
ALI	"Lacks substantial capacity to appreciate the wrongfulness of the conduct or to control it"	Beyond reasonable doubt	Prosecutor
Present federal law	"Lacks capacity to appreciate the wrongfulness of his or her conduct"	Clear and convincing evidence	Defense

Adapted in part from Norval Morris, "Insanity Defense," *National Institute of Justice Crime File Study Guide* (Washington: U.S. Department of Justice, National Institute of Justice/Criminal Justice Reference Service, 1986).

Competency to Stand Trial

As previously noted, the issue of competency to stand trial deals with the defendant's current state of psychological functioning as related to the judicial process. While the concept of criminal responsibility may trace its roots to English case law and beyond, the principle of competency to stand trial is based firmly in the Sixth Amendment of the United States Constitution, as follows:

> In all criminal prosecutions, the accused shall enjoy the right to a speedy and public trial, by an impartial jury of the state and district wherein the crime shall have been committed, which district shall have been previously ascertained by law, and to be informed of the nature and cause of the accusation; to be confronted with the witnesses against him, to have compulsory process for obtaining witnesses in his favor, and to have the assistance of counsel for his defense.

Case law provides specific guidelines for the determination of competency to stand trial. *Dusky* v. *United States* (1960), which provided the standards used in most jurisdictions after 1960, states that the accused must generally fulfill three broad criteria. First, he or she must have some factual understanding of the judicial proceedings. Second, the accused must have a rational understanding of the proceedings. Third, he or she must also be able to consult with an attorney with a reasonable degree of rational understanding. It should be noted that forensic opinions (i.e., from a psychologist or psychiatrist) regarding competency to stand trial are only clinical opinions and the final determination is a judicial decision.

Other cases have also clarified the courts' position regarding related issues of competency to stand trial. In *Pate* v. *Robinson* (1966) it was determined that the competency issue may be raised at any point during the judicial process. Should a defendant be found not competent to stand trial, then he or she may not be confined for further treatment for an indeterminate period of time, as set forth in *Jackson* v. *Indiana* (1972).

> *Reply to a plaintiff who claims his cabbages were
> eaten by your goat: You had no cabbages. If you
> did they were not eaten. If they were eaten, it was
> not by a goat. If they were eaten by a goat, it was
> not my goat. And, if it was my goat, he was insane.*
>
> —I. Youngner, quoted by J. E. McElhaney (1987)

The Case of John Hinckley

On March 30, 1981, shortly before 2:30 P.M., a gunman aimed and fired six shots from a 22-caliber revolver. Four of the six Devastator bullets found human targets, with tragic results. The first shot struck presidential press secretary James Brady. Although the exploding bullet did extensive neurological damage, Brady lived and began the long rehabilitation process. The second shot struck Washington, DC police officer Thomas

Delahanty; he also survived his back wound. The third bullet hit a building across the street from the Washington Hilton. No human damage resulted. The fourth bullet struck secret service agent Timothy McCarthy. His chest wound was serious, but Agent McCarthy survived. The fifth bullet struck the glass in the presidential limousine but also did no human damage. The sixth and final bullet ricocheted off the rear panel of the limousine and entered the chest of Ronald Reagan, President of the United States. Like the others, President Reagan survived.

The entire attack lasted only a few seconds. A Secret Service agent later testified to his feeling of desperation as he attempted to stop the gunfire. He continued, "I came down on top of the assailant, with my right arm around his head. . . . He was still clicking the weapon as we go down." Understandably such violent and senseless brutality raised many questions about psychological motivation, history, and stability of the gunman, John Hinckley. Testimony in Hinckley's trial indicated his ultimate goal was to capture the love and respect of Yale University student and movie star Jodie Foster. Although unsuccessful in this goal, Hinckley's behavior did lay the foundation for major revisions in criminal responsibility statutes at both federal and state levels.

Background Data

John Hinckley was born in Oklahoma in 1955. His childhood was not unlike many other people's. At the age of 4 he moved to Dallas, Texas. Recreational activities included quarterbacking his elementary school football team and playing basketball in high school. At the age of 9, Hinckley became a fan of the Beatles. His interest in music and possible identification with John Lennon continued into his adulthood. When he was 12, Hinckley moved with his family to a prominent Dallas neighborhood and almost immediately lost social status. He was no longer the "king pin."

Graduation from high school in 1973 prompted a move to Evergreen, Colorado. Soon after, he decided to attend Texas Tech University in Lubbock, Texas. Although Hinckley's future dreams frequently included pursuit of a college degree in Lubbock, repeated efforts over the next 5–6 years were generally unproductive. Around 1974, Hinckley quit school at Texas Tech and moved to Dallas. He wanted to be on his own and "dreamed of future glory in some undefined field, perhaps music or politics" (Caplan, 1984, p. 34). A move to Hollywood in 1976 to sell his music did not have the desired result, but he did see the movie *Taxi Driver* some fifteen times that summer. In the spring of 1977, Hinckley returned to Lubbock.

Roesch (1979) reports that Hinckley's overall adaptation and emotional adjustment were apparently beginning to decline at this point. In the next year he began to experience a number of minor health problems and received medical treatment. In October 1978, he became interested in the American Nazi movement via the National Socialist Party. In August 1979, he purchased his first firearm and in September of that year began to publish the "American Front Newsletter." He appointed himself national director of the American Front and fabricated membership lists from thirty-seven states. By now he had moved seventeen times since high school.

In 1980, Hinckley, who had gained 60 pounds since high school, experienced his first anxiety attack. He bought another gun. In May 1980, *People Magazine* announced that Jodie Foster, star of *Taxi Driver* (later of *The Silence of the Lambs*), would be attending Yale University. This was very important to Hinckley, who believed that he could win the young woman's attention and love. After a disappointing telephone conversation with Ms. Foster on September 20, 1980, Hinckley wrote this in his diary: "My mind was at the breaking point. A relationship I had dreamed about went absolutely nowhere. My disillusionment with everything was complete" (Caplan, 1984, p. 38).

Subsequently the infamous Devastator exploding bullets were purchased, along with six more guns. There were numerous flights to distant places, including Colorado, Washington, DC, Ohio, Nebraska, and Tennessee. Perhaps the most serious development was Hinckley's decision to begin following—perhaps stalking—both President Carter and President Reagan.

During psychiatric treatment by Dr. John Hooper, between October 1980 and February 1981, Hinckley failed to divulge his thoughts, fantasies, or planned activities. Without this information, Dr. Hooper and the patient's family formulated a plan to encourage their son's independence and emotional stability. Despite these efforts, Hinckley took a bus from Los Angeles to Washington, DC, arriving on March 29, 1981. After breakfast on the morning of March 30, Hinckley learned of President Reagan's schedule and, having written a final love letter to Ms. Foster, he loaded his Devastator bullets and began his vigil outside the Washington Hilton Hotel. In seconds his plan to obtain glory and thereby the love of Jodie Foster was enacted.

The Trial

The trial of John Hinckley was well publicized. The thirteen criminal charges included the attempted assassination of the president. Lawyers for the prosecution and defense differed little on the factual events. Considerable disagreement existed over the defendant's true psychological condition. The raising of the insanity defense resulted in a trial that lasted slightly over 7 weeks. The costs incurred were impressive. Mental health experts testifying or assisting the prosecution received over $300,000 in fees. Defense experts received fees in excess of $150,000. Defense attorneys may have received between $500,000 and $1,000,000. Such bills did not include salaries for court officials, ancillary staff, public relations, etc. (Caplan, 1984).

After 3 days of jury deliberation Hinckley was found not guilty by reason of insanity on all thirteen counts. He was automatically committed to Saint Elizabeth's Hospital in Washington, DC for treatment, to stay there until he is viewed by the hospital as no longer dangerous as a result of his mental illness.

Aftermath

In the following weeks twenty-six different bills were introduced to modify the federal statute that covers the insanity defense. As a result of these efforts, two important changes occurred in federal law pertaining to the issue of criminal responsibility. First, the volitional component, that is, the irresistible impulse concept, was removed from the original McNaughten model. At present a successful insanity defense is solely based on the defendant's inability as a result of mental disease or defect to appreciate the criminality of his alleged conduct. Second, the burden of proof, that is, whose responsibility it is to demonstrate the viability of the defendant's psychological state, was shifted from the prosecution to the defense. The level of proof required for the prosecution was also reduced from "beyond a reasonable doubt" to "clear and convincing evidence" when applied to the defense. Thus, the level of certainty required of the jury when viewing the evidence was reduced from an estimated 90–95% to somewhere below that (see the Simpson case in Chapter 1). Although these changes in federal law were significant, they only serve as models to state courts, which hear by far the greater number of insanity defenses each year.

It should be noted that in May and November of 1981, the defense attorneys offered to have their client plead guilty to all counts if the prosecution would agree to recommend to the court that penalties on all counts run concurrently, rather than consecutively. Under this arrangement their client would be eligible for parole in 15 years. The prosecution declined this plea offer because, among other reasons, it was viewed as improper and unseemly to plea bargain a case involving the attempted assassination of the president.

Today, although he is largely free to wander the 300-acre grounds, John Hinckley is still undergoing treatment at Saint Elizabeth's Hospital. He may be released at the recommendation of the hospital and with approval of the presiding judge. Such a recommendation will occur only if the hospital feels that Hinckley no longer poses a threat to society or himself. The political issues amplify the dilemma in all such cases: when to release an individual who has been proven dangerous in the past, may well be dangerous at some point in the future, but who is probably not "imminently" dangerous. Add to that the fact that his degree of mental disorder has likely been lessened by psychotropic medication and other interventions, and we see the complexity inherent in determining to make such a recommendation.

Hinckley's behavior in recent years has generally been without substantial blemish, while in earlier years he provided plenty of material to argue for retaining him in the hospital. In 1986, he exchanged letters with Ted Bundy (see Chapter 10); according to a psychiatrist, Hinckley wrote Bundy to "express his sorrow" for the "awkward position he must be in." Even as late as 1988, his obsession with Jodie Foster was still evident as he wrote a mail order company to order a nude drawing of her; the year before, a search of his hospital room had uncovered fifty-seven photos of the actress.

Hinckley receives regular visits from his parents and from Leslie DeVeau, a 54-year-old Washington woman he has variously called "my fiance" and "the biggest influence in my life." He met DeVeau when she was put in Saint Elizabeth's in 1982, having been found not guilty by reason of insanity of killing her sleeping 10-year-old daughter with a shotgun blast. She had then turned the gun on herself, but succeeded only in blowing off part of her left arm. She was released after 4 years.

In 1984, Hinckley's father, John Sr., sold his oil and gas prospecting company, The Vanderbilt Energy Corporation, reportedly for $26 million. He and his wife spent about $1 million during the 1980s on a national advertising campaign to increase public awareness about both mental disorders and the insanity defense.

> *You couldn't even prove the White House staff*
> *sane beyond a reasonable doubt.*
>
> —Edwin Meese, counselor to Ronald Reagan

Legal Perspectives and Prescriptions for Reform

The case of O. J. Simpson and to a lesser degree the case of John Hinckley highlight several overall perspectives on the legal system. The two primary criteria by which a legal system should be judged are effectiveness and efficiency. Is our legal system effective? The clearest conclusion is that no one knows, because unlike other systems in society such as financial or medical, the legal system has no method of accountability, no way of determining whether it actually finds the truth. Interestingly enough, the percent of time the jurors in the O. J. Simpson criminal trial spent in formal deliberation was 0.06% (4 hours of deliberation divided by 6384 hours in sequestration).

It is clear that many legal maneuvers restrict or void certain pieces of useful information from reaching the jury, thus constricting the potential for gaining any ultimate truth. (During the Simpson trial, 16,000 objections were raised, with approximately 9000 overruled and 7000 sustained. Incidentally the number of other cases completed in some fashion by the Los Angeles Superior Court between the time Simpson was arrested and the end of his first trial was 51,769.) Also, there is very little allowance for interactive assessment, a method used in other systems to maximize effectiveness, in which jurors for example could ask the questions they really wanted answered at about the time they needed the information most. This restricts both effectiveness and efficiency. So a belief shared by many people that the legal system is not especially effective is probably accurate.

As to the other criterion, the criminal trial of O. J. Simpson made it clear that the legal system is appallingly inefficient. Cost accountability appears to be a concept that is foreign to the legal system. Aside from the costs to Simpson himself (estimated at $2.75 million), the costs to the taxpayers of Los Angeles County were absurd, even estimated as high as $9,100,000. Who profited? Certainly the attorneys. The fact is that if any other profession were in such complete control of a system that brought such high profits from such questionably effective endeavors, they would eventually have to answer to people outside their own profession, in claims that went to courts or to state or federal lawmaking bodies. However, any such claims made against attorneys are eventually heard by other attorneys, and lawmaking bodies are dominated by attorneys. Any ultimate reform will likely require that the actions of the attorneys be reviewed by boards in which the great majority of members are not attorneys and are not somehow biased in favor of attorneys.

> In the trial of the century, the specter of mistrial
> arose when it was reported that some jurors, in
> between recesses and sidebar conferences, might
> have heard some actual testimony. An angry Judge
> Ito sternly told them to disregard it.
>
> —Dave Barry, "Windows on the World,"
> *Miami Herald,* Dec. 31, 1995

Our jury system has been referred to as an antiquated legacy from the Vikings, and, as some experts have pointed out, if you were trying to come up with a good system, it's not likely you'd come up with the idea of pulling in twelve people off the street to make the decisions. The jury system had been dropped by a number of countries that once adopted it, such as India and Japan.

Supporters of the system point to Britain's retention of the system. But in that country only about 5% of criminal trials are heard by juries, and only about 1–2% of civil trials are heard by juries. Our own military and the nations of continental Europe rely on panels of professional or lay judges, or just judges.

Assuming the jury system is retained, reform should include:

1. Simplify the language and concepts used in the legal system, and provide uniform definitions to any vague and/or complex terms, e.g., "clear and convincing," "beyond a reasonable doubt."

2. Provide for effective penalties for people who avoid or do not respond to a jury summons.

3. Markedly reduce the number of people (especially those of higher intelligence and/or socio-economic status) who are excused from jury duty.

4. Markedly reduce (or even eliminate) the availability of peremptory challenges, i.e., those that do not require a cause.

5. Expand the types of trials that do not require a jury verdict; i.e., the judge can decide guilt or innocence.

6. Give judges greater powers to reduce or eliminate repetitive or questionably useful testimony.

7. Use very stringent criteria for the admission of expert testimony.

8. Eliminate the requirement for unanimous decisions in all trials except capital cases; and even there consider allowing 11–1 decisions to avoid having the decision controlled by one individual who may be biased, bought, or bent on achieving 15 minutes of fame.

9. Provide for a legal category or easier legal recognition of "frivolous" suits, e.g., by a board similar to a grand jury. When there is such a finding, make the party responsible for bringing such a suit responsible for all of the other party's costs (including some form of punitive damages).

10. Allow juries to order the plaintiff to pay the defendant's costs (e.g., attorney fees, expert witness fees) in any civil trial.

11. Allow jurors to take notes, and to ask questions during the trial, so they can get the information they want, when they want it. Allow them to discuss the evidence together at various points during the trial.

12. Consider "level playing field" requirements; e.g., each side may spend only so much money (including all types of costs), or each may use no more than some maximum allotted time at trial, including the time to have all witnesses, objections, motions, etc., heard.

13. Last, and most important, redesign the system so that jurors are not treated as fragile, gullible drones (e.g., in the Simpson trial when there was concern the jurors might see billboards with the words "guilty" or "innocent" on them). When judges make a guilty or innocent decision in a trial, they are not required to be sequestered or protected. Are they somehow "better" at anything other than a knowledge of the law? If so, then the jury system is a bad system.

17

Postscript: Positive Mental Health

I don't want to achieve immortality through my work, I want to achieve immortality through not dying.

—Woody Allen

The preceding chapters have necessarily focused on negative mental health conditions. However, there are ways that people can improve their psychological functioning, not just as an antidote to psychological disorder but also to get more enjoyment out of life. Many psychologists, writers, and philosophers have tried to communicate what leads to positive mental health. I like this one from a young woman from a small town in rural Kentucky.

> You are responsible for your own happiness, and you can do anything you want to do, no matter what your handicap is. Don't worry about what you can't do, just concentrate on what you can do, and make your life count! . . . I believe that I can choose to use my mental capacity and emotional strength to make my life count, to reach out to others in their time of need, and to share the abundant good God has given me.

This statement was made by a young woman who, 11 years earlier, in the midst of a miscarriage with her first pregnancy, was diagnosed as having amyotrophic lateral sclerosis, more commonly known as Lou Gehrig's disease. As had happened with her, people with this disease gradually lose the ability to move their arms and legs and to talk. Eventually they lose the ability to swallow and to breathe; they usually die in 2 to 5 years. She now spends most of her time using her computer, which she types into by moving her head, to write letters to encourage and support others with difficult diseases.

Throughout this book, a number of facts and opinions may have allowed the reader to infer more specific conclusions as to how a person could lead a happy life across the lifespan. In closing, I present a number of formal principles that may help in that endeavor.

1. The anticipation of a situation is often more distressing or important to us than is the actual situation itself.

2. Our interpretation of our experience is often more important than the actual experience itself.

3. Confronting the sources of our fears until we feel they are mastered is the only way to overcome them, and it's important to keep facing the conflict or disturbing stimulus even if it makes us uncomfortable while doing so.

4. Develop and cherish friendships and other forms of social and moral support. Be there when you are needed, and be quick to ask for help when you need it, and be appreciative of that help.

5. Recognize the importance of relationships in your life. Try to heal any bruised or fractured relationships with significant others (significant in potentiality or by blood). Plan so that people relationships will be in place.

6. Don't ruminate or even focus on missed opportunities and past mistakes. Emphasize your positive achievements and pleasures, and work to accept the fact that you do the best you can.

7. Some problems are best solved by "letting go" and relaxing, adopting a posture of acceptance, humor, and perspective.

8. Some factors in each of us are strongly influenced by genetic (heredity) factors, and it is more effective to develop ways to cope with these factors rather than trying to directly change them.

9. Ambiguity or uncertainty about life situations is anxiety-producing and aversive. Most of us will go to great lengths to impose understanding or meaning on a situation even where there is none or it is not yet available, which may lead us to a quick and sometimes less than optimal solution. As one client put it in a moment of frustration, "I almost wish they would go ahead and tell me I had cancer, rather than making me wait around so long to find out."

10. The belief that we are in control of a situation decreases aversiveness or anxiety, even if that belief is false and even if we have never actually done anything to change the situation.

11. When we expect to fail in a situation, we are very likely to avoid the situation or take inadequate steps to cope with it. The predicted failure is thus more likely to occur. This in turn decreases self-esteem, increases depression, makes us now even less likely to do what is needed, and therefore makes future failure more likely.

12. The spiritual life, in whatever form it takes in your life, affects psychological health. If you are religious, develop an association with a church or synagogue. Make at least a minimal plan for spiritual development.

13. Physical health affects mental health. Get regular exercise, and consider doing it with others, to satisfy your social needs and to fuel your motivation to continue with the exercise. Plan a sound nutritional program and work to change any destructive health habits, such as drinking too much or smoking. Be aware of the side effects of any drugs you are taking.

14. Doing what we can to prevent psychological (and physical) disorder is less costly and distressing, both emotionally and financially, than are the efforts it takes to cure disorder.

15. Purposefully accumulating positive experiences and then preserving them in memory and in symbols (such as photographs) lead to a positive self-image and protect our "self" from the effects of negative experiences.

16. Realize that to learn from your own experience is wisdom; to learn from the experience of others is genius.

Happiness (or at least contentment) and a positive mental health is attained by working directly and purposefully toward the components of positive mental health, which include the following:

1. A clear and accurate picture of our world (good reality testing)

2. An ability to clearly and rationally analyze problems and challenges and a willingness to take well-considered risks in order to meet these challenges

3. Flexibility and the ability to adapt in the face of change and stress

4. Elimination of most emotionally and physically draining internal conflicts by a willingness to take responsibility for one's own life and life choices, and to make sure one's own needs are taken care of; but also to make several selected others a close second to one's own needs (and on occasion, ahead of those needs), with the rest of the world not too far behind

5. Controlling and reducing both internal and external sources of stress, for example, periodically asking yourself, "Will this matter a year from now?", learning meditative relaxation techniques

6. The capacity to sublimate, to direct one's developed or instinctive hostile energy into creative and constructive outlets

7. A positive personal identity that includes a sense of self-worth and some unique competencies

8. Mutually satisfying interpersonal relationships, friendships, and loves

9. A good sense of humor

10. The capacity to relax and enjoy life

11. The ability to be more of a "giver" than a "taker"; the capacity to love, to make commitments to other people, interests, and causes, and to become spiritually and psychologically involved with something outside and beyond ourselves

As you work to develop these or similar principles in your life or in the lives of your children, remember that all of us must strive (although not without relaxation and humor), because we never fully succeed. Yet, as my daughter once said, "The best advice you ever gave me was that you should always try to do your best, but when you do fail, and no matter how great the failure, *always be ready to forgive yourself.* Try to right any wrong you did, and start over again."

> *Once I wasn't*
> *Then I was*
> *Now I ain't again*
> —From a Cleveland cemetery

REFERENCES

Abraham, K. (1916). "The first pregenital stage of the libido." In *Selected papers on psychoanalysis*. New York: Basic Books.

Agras, W. S. (1995). "Treatment of eating disorders." In A. Schatzberg and C. Nemeroff (Eds.), *Textbook of psychopharmacology*. Washington, DC: American Psychiatric Press.

Alford, B., and Beck, A. (1997). *The integrative power of cognitive therapy*. New York: Basic Books.

American Law Institute Model Penal Code, Section 4.01 (1962).

American Psychiatric Association (1994). *DSM-IV: Diagnostic and statistical manual of mental disorders* (4th ed.). Washington, DC: American Psychiatric Press.

Amir, N. (1998). "Anxiety." In H. Friedman (Ed.), *Encyclopedia of mental health*. San Diego: Academic Press.

Arieti, S., and Bemporad, J. (1978). *Severe and mild depression*. New York: Basic Books.

Asher, R. (1951). "Munchausen's syndrome." *Lancet, 1,* 339–341.

Ayllon, T., and Azrin, N. (1968). *The token economy: A motivational system for therapy and rehabilitation*. New York: Appleton-Century-Crofts.

Bandura, A., and Walters, R. (1963). *Social learning and personality development*. New York: Holt, Rinehart.

Barkley, R. (1998). "Attention Deficit Hyperactivity Disorder (ADHD)." In H. Friedman (Ed.), *Encyclopedia of mental health*. San Diego: Academic Press.

Barrett, C., and Meyer, R. (1992). "Cognitive behavioral therapy for inpatient alcoholics." In J. Wright, A. Beck, M. Thase, and J. Ludgate (Eds.), *Inpatient cognitive therapy*. New York: Guilford Press.

Bartol, C., and Bartol, A. (1994). *Psychology and American law*. Belmont, CA: Wadsworth.

Baumeister, R. (1998). " Impulse control." In H. Friedman (Ed.), *Encyclopedia of mental health*. San Diego: Academic Press.

Beck, A. (1976). *Cognitive therapy and the emotional disorders*. New York: International Universities Press.

Beck, A., Freeman, A., and Associates (1990). *Cognitive therapy of personality disorders*. New York: Guilford Press.

Beck, A., and Valin, S. (1953). "Psychotic depressive reaction in soldiers who accidentally killed their buddies." *American Journal of Psychiatry, 110,* 347–353.

Bell, Q. (1972). *Virginia Woolf: A biography*. New York: Harcourt Brace Jovanovich.

Bleuler, E. (1911). *Dementia Praecox oder die Gruppe der Schizophrenia.* Leipzig: Deuticke.

Blouin, A., Blouin, J., Aubin, P., Carter, J., et al. (1992). "Seasonal patterns of bulimia nervosa." *American Journal of Psychiatry, 149,* 73–81.

Bongar, B., and Beutler, L. (Eds.) (1995). *Comprehensive textbook of psychotherapy.* New York: Oxford.

Boss, M. (1963). Psychoanalysis and Dasein analysis. New York: Plenum.

Bowlby, J. (1973). *Attachment and loss: Separation anxiety and anger* (vol. 2). New York: Basic Books.

Briere, J. (1997). *Psychological assessment of adult posttraumatic states.* Washington, DC: American Psychological Association Books.

Bruch, H., Czyzewski, D., and Suhr, M. (1988). *Conversations with anorexics.* New York: Basic Books.

Buckley, P., and Meltzer, H. (1995). "Treatment of schizophrenia." In A. Schatzberg and C. Nemeroff (Eds.), *Textbook of psychiatry.* Washington, DC: American Psychiatric Press.

Campbell, L. C. (1993). *The royal marriages.* New York: St. Martin's Press.

Caplan, L. (1984). *The insanity defense.* Boston: Godine.

Chambless, D., Sanderson, W., Shoham, V., and Johnson, S. (1996). An update on empirically validated therapies. *The Clinical Psychologist, 49(2),* 5–18.

Chiles, J., and Strosahl, K. (1995). *The suicidal patient.* Washington, DC: American Psychiatric Press.

Clayton, R., and Heard, D. (1994). *Elvis up close: In the words of those who knew him best.* Atlanta, GA: Turner.

Cleckley, H. (1964). *The mask of sanity* (4th ed.). St. Louis, MO: Mosby.

Clum, G. (1998). "Phobias." In H. Friedman (Ed.), *Encyclopedia of mental health.* San Diego: Academic Press.

Cohen, S., Kessler, R., and Gordon, L. (1995). *Measuring stress.* New York: Oxford University Press.

Colby, K. (1977). "Appraisal of four psychological theories of paranoid phenomena." *Journal of Abnormal Psychology, 86,* 54–59.

Coleman, R. (1994). *The Carpenters.* New York: HarperCollins.

Craigie, F., and Ross, S. (1980). "The use of a videotape pre-treatment training program to encourage treatment-seeking among alcoholic detoxification patients." *Behavior Therapy, 11,* 141–147.

Crowther, J. H., Wolf, E. M., and Sherwood, N. E. (1992). "Epidemiology of bulimia nervosa." In J. H. Crowther, D. L. Tennenbaum, S. E. Hobfoll, and M. A. P. Stephens (Eds.), *The etiology of bulimia nervosa: The individual and family context* (pp. 1–26). Washington, DC: Hemisphere.

Curtin, J. E. (1992). *Unseen Elvis: Candids of the King.* Canada: Little, Brown.

Dangel, R., and Polster, R. (1986). *Teaching child management skills.* New York: Pergamon Press.

Daniel McNaughten's case, 10 C1, and Fin. 200, 8 Eng. Rep. 718 (1843).

DeBattista, C. (1998). "Mood disorders." In H. Friedman (Ed.), *Encyclopedia of mental health.* San Diego: Academic Press.

Diliberto, G. (1985). "Karen Carpenter was killed by over-the-counter drug some doctors say may be killing many others." *People Weekly, 23,* 67–70.

Doctor, R. (1998). "Sexual disorders." In H. Friedman (Ed.), *Encyclopedia of mental health.* San Diego: Academic Press.

Duncan, M., Bregman, J., Weller, E., and Weller, R. (1995). "Treatment of childhood and adolescent disorders." In A. Schatzberg and C. Nemeroff (Eds.), *Textbook of psychopharmacology.* Washington, DC: American Psychiatric Press.

Durham v. *United States, 214 F. 2d 962,* 874–875 (D.C. Circuit, 1954).

Durkheim, E. (1951). *Suicide.* New York: Free Press.

Dusky v. *United States,* 362 U.S. 402 (1960).

Endicott, J., Nee, J., Cohen, J., Fliess, J., and Simon, A. (1986). Diagnosis of schizophrenia. *Archives of General Psychology, 43,* 13–19.

Erikson, E. (1959). "Identity and the life cycle." *Psychological Issues, 1,* 18–64.

Escobar, J. (1998). "Somatization and hypochondriasis." In H. Friedman (Ed.), *Encyclopedia of mental health.* San Diego: Academic Press.

Esposito, J., and Oumano, E. (1994). *Good rockin' tonight.* New York: Simon & Schuster.

Eysenck, H. (1985). "Incubation theory of fear/anxiety." In S. Riess and R. Bootzin (Eds.), *Theoretical issues in behavior therapy.* Orlando, FL: Academic Press.

Fawcett, J. (1992). "Suicide risk factors in depressive disorders and in panic disorder." *Journal of Clinical Psychiatry, 53* (suppl.), 9–13.

Feldman, J., and Kazdin, A. (1995). Parent management training for oppositional and conduct problem children. *The Clinical Psychologist, 48(4),* 3–5.

Fenichel, O. (1945). *The psychoanalytic theory of neurosis.* New York: Wiley.

Fenigstein, A. (1998). "Paranoia." In H. Friedman (Ed.), *Encyclopedia of mental health.* San Diego: Academic Press.

Fernald, D. (1984). *The Hans legacy.* Hillsdale, NJ: Erlbaum.

Ferster, C., and Culbertson, S. (1982). *Behavior principles* (3d ed.). Englewood Cliffs, NJ: Prentice-Hall.

Finkelhor, D., and Dziuba-Leatherman, J. (1994). "Victimization of children." *American Psychologist, 49,* 173–183.

Ford, B., and Chase, C. (1978). *The times of my life.* New York: HarperCollins.

Ford, B., and Chase, C. (1988). *A glad awakening.* Boston: Hall.

Frankl, V. (1975). *The unconscious god: Psychotherapy and theology.* New York: Simon & Schuster.

Friedman, M., and Brounell, K. (1995). "Psychological correlates of obesity." *Psychological Bulletin, 117,* 3–20.

Frost, R. (1998). "Obsessive-Compulsive Disorder." In H. Friedman (Ed.), *Encyclopedia of mental health.* San Diego: Academic Press.

Garfield, S. (1981). "Psychotherapy: A 40-year appraisal." *American Psychologist, 36,* 174–183.

Garner, D., and Garfinkel, P. (Eds.) (1997). *Handbook of treatment for eating disorders.* New York: Guilford Press.

Gilmore, J. (1991). "Murdering while asleep." *Forensic Reports, 4,* 455–459.

Glasser, W. (1980). "Two cases in reality therapy." In G. Belkin (Ed.), *Contemporary psychotherapies.* Chicago: Rand McNally.

Goodwin, F. K., and Jamison, K. R. (1990). *Manic-depressive illness.* New York: Oxford University Press.

Goodwin, G. M. (1994). "Recurrence of mania after lithium withdrawal." *British Journal of Psychiatry, 164,* 149–152.

Gottesman, I., and Shields, J. (1972). *Schizophrenia and genetics: A twin study vantage point.* New York: Academic Press.

Hare, R., Hart, S., and Harpur, T. (1991). "Psychopathy and the *DSM-IV* criteria for Antisocial Personality Disorder." *Journal of Abnormal Psychology, 100,* 391–398.

Harrington, A. (1985). "Nineteenth-century ideas on hemisphere differences and 'duality of mind.'" *The Behavioral and Brain Sciences, 8,* 617–660.

Harsh, J., and Ogilvie, R. (Eds.) (1995). *Sleep onset: Normal and abnormal processes.* Washington, DC: American Psychological Association.

Hillebrand, M., and Pallone, N. (Eds.) (1995). *The psychobiology of aggression.* Binghamton, NY: Haworth.

Hopkins, J. R. (1995). "Erick Homburger Erikson (1902–1994)." *American Psychologist, 50,* 796–797.

Ingram, R. (1998). "Depression." In H. Friedman (Ed.), *Encyclopedia of mental health.* San Diego: Academic Press.

Jackson v. *Indiana,* 406 U.S. 715 (1972).

Jaffee v. *Redmond,* 116 S. Ct.; 64 L.W. 4490, June 13, 1996.

Janofsky, J. (1994). "The Munchausen syndrome in civil forensic psychiatry." *Bulletin of the American Academy of Psychiatry and the Law, 22,* 488–489.

Johnson, A., Falstein, E., Szurek, S., and Svendsen, M. (1941). "School phobia." *American Journal of Orthopsychiatry, 11,* 702–711.

Jones, M. C. (1924). "A laboratory study of fear: The case of Peter." *Journal of General Psychology, 31,* 308–315.

Kanner, L. (1943). "Autistic disturbances of affective content." *Nervous Child, 2,* 217–240.

Kansas v. *Hendricks* (117 S. Ct.; 65 L.W. 4564, June 23, 1997).

Kantor, S. (1978). *Who was Ruby?* Bethesda, MD: Everest House.

Katon, W. (1993). "Somatization disorder, hypochondriasis, and conversion disorder." In D. Dunner (Ed.), *Current psychiatric therapy.* Philadelphia: Saunders.

Kay, J., and Franklin, S. (1995). In R. Mapor and J. Spector (Eds.), *Clinical neuropsychological assessment.* New York: Plenum.

Kellam, A. (1969). "Shoplifting treated by aversion to a film." *Behavior Research and Therapy, 7,* 125–127.

Kelly, G. (1955). *The psychology of personal constructs* (2 vols.). New York: Norton.

Kelly, W. (Ed.) (1985). *Post traumatic stress disorder and the war veteran patient.* New York: Brunner/Mazel.

Kendler, K., Heath, A., Martin, N., and Eaves, L. (1986). "Symptoms of anxiety and depression in a volunteer twin population." *Archives of General Psychiatry, 43,* 213–221.

Kernberg, O. (1984). *Severe personality disorders.* New Haven, CO: Yale University Press.

Kluft, R. (1998). "Dissociative Disorders." In H. Friedman (Ed.), *Encyclopedia of mental health.* San Diego: Academic Press.

Kluft, R., and Fine, C. (1993). *Clinical perspectives on multiple personality disorder.* Washington, DC: American Psychiatric Press.

Knable, M., Kleinman, J., and Weinberger, D. (1995). "Neurobiology of schizophrenia." In A. Schatzberg and C. Nemeroff (Eds.), *Textbook of psychiatry.* Washington, DC: American Psychiatric Press.

Kohut, H. (1977). *The restoration of the self.* New York: International Universities Press.

Kraeplin, E. (1899 [1919]). *Dementia praecox and paraphrenia* (8th Ger. ed.). R. Barclay and G. Robertson (Trans.). Edinburgh: Livingstone.

Kroll, J. (1993). *PTSD/borderlines in therapy.* New York: Norton.

Kronenberger, W., and Meyer, R. (1996). *The child clinician's handbook.* Boston: Allyn & Bacon.

Lazarus, A. (1971). *Behavior therapy and beyond.* New York: McGraw-Hill.

Lehmann, J. (1975). *Virginia Woolf and her world.* New York: Harcourt Brace Jovanovich.

Lezak, M. (1995). *Neuropsychological assessment.* New York: Oxford University Press.

Lo Piccolo, J. (1993). "Paraphilias." In D. Dunner (Ed.), *Current psychiatric therapy.* Philadelphia: Saunders.

Ludwig, A. (1996). *The price of greatness.* New York: Guilford Press.

Lydiard, B., Brawnmen-Mintzer, O., and Ballenger, J. (1996). Recent developments in the pharmacotherapy of anxiety disorders. *Journal of Consulting and Clinical Psychology, 64,* 660–668.

Lykken, D. (1995). *The antisocial personalities.* New York: Erlbaum.

Margolis, R., and Zweben, J. (1998). *Treating patients with alcohol and other drug problems.* Washington, DC: American Psychological Association.

Marsella, A., De Vos, G., and Hsu, F. (Eds.) (1985). *Culture and self: Asian and western perspectives.* New York: Tavistock.

Maslow, A. (1954). *Motivation and personality.* New York: HarperCollins.

Massie, R. K. (1967). *Nicholas and Alexander.* New York: Atheneum.

Masters, W., Johnson, V., and Kolodny, R. (1991). *Human sexuality* (4th ed.). Glenville, IL: Scott, Foresman, Little, Brown.

Masters, W., Johnson, V., and Kolodny, R. (1994). *Heterosexuality.* New York: Harper Collins.

Maultsby, M. (1998). "Behaviour therapy." In H. Friedman (Ed.), *Encyclopedia of mental health.* San Diego: Academic Press.

May, R. (1981). *Existential psychology.* New York: Random House.

McElhaney, J. E. (1987). *Trial notebook* (2 ed.). Chicago: American Bar Association.

Meichenbaum, D. (1977). *Cognitive behavior modification.* New York: Plenum.

Meichenbaum, D. (1986). *Stress inoculation training.* New York: Pergamon Press.

Meister, R. (1980). *Hypochondria.* New York: Taplinger.

Melton, G., Petrila, J. Poythress, N., and Slobogin, C. (1997). *Psychological evaluation for courts* (2d ed.). New York: Guilford Press.

Meyer, R. (1992). *Practical clinical hypnosis.* Lexington, MA: Lexington Books.

Meyer, R. (1995). *Preparation for licensing and board certification examinations in psychology: The professional, legal, and ethical components* (2d ed.). New York: Brunner/Mazel.

Meyer, R. (1998a). "Antisocial Personality Disorder." In H. Friedman (Ed.), *Encyclopedia of mental health.* San Diego: Academic Press.

Meyer, R. (1998b). "Personality disorders." In H. Friedman (Ed.), *Encyclopedia of mental health.* San Diego: Academic Press.

Meyer, R., and Deitsch, S. (1996). *The clinicians' handbook: Integrated diagnostics, assessment, and intervention in adult and adolescent psychopathology* (4th ed.). Boston: Allyn & Bacon.

Miklowitz, D., Strachan, A., Goldstein, M., Doane, J., Snyder, K., Hogarty, G., and Falloon, I. (1986). "Expressed emotion and communication deviance in the families of schizophrenics." *Journal of Abnormal Psychology, 95,* 60–66.

Milner, J. (1998). Personal communication.

Mischel, W. (1969). "Continuity and change in personality." *American Psychologist, 24,* 1012–1018.

Mischel, W. (1986). *Introduction to personality* (4th ed.). New York: Holt Rinehart & Winston.

Mitchell, S. (1817). "Mary Reynolds: A case of double consciousness." *Transactions of the College of Physicians of Philadelphia.* Third Series 10, 1888.

Monahan, J. (1981). *Predicting violent behavior.* Thousand Oaks, CA: Sage.

Money, J. (1985). "Gender: History, theory and usage of the term and its relationship to nature/nurture." *Journal of Sex and Marital Therapy, 11,* 71–79.

Money, J. (1987). "Sin, sickness, or status: Homosexual gender identity and psychoneuroendocrinology." *American Psychologist, 42,* 384–399.

Morel, B. (1857). *Traite des degenerescences physiques, intellectuelles et morales.* Paris: Bailliere.

Morton, A. (1992). *Diana: Her True Story.* New York: Simon & Schuster.

Morton, A. (1994). *Diana: Her New Life.* New York: Simon & Schuster.

Nathan, K., Musselman, D., Schatzberg, A., and Nemeroff, C. (1995). "Biology of mood disorders." In A. Schatzberg and C. Nemeroff (Eds.), *Textbook of Psychiatry.* Washington, DC: American Psychiatric Press.

Oren, D., Moul, D., Schwartz, P., and Brown, C., et al. (1994). "Exposure to ambient light in patients with winter seasonal affective disorder." *American Journal of Psychiatry, 151,* 591–593.

Pallis, C., and Bamji, A. (1979). "McIlroy was here, or was he?" *British Medical Journal, 1,* 973–975.

Pate v. *Robinson,* 383 U.S. 375, 86 S. Ct., 83C, 15 L. Ed. 2d 815 (1966).

Perkinson, R. (1997). *Chemical dependency counseling.* Thousand Oaks, CA: Sage.

Perls, F., Hefferline, R., and Goodman, P. (1958). *Gestalt therapy.* New York: Julian.

Peselow, E. D., Fieve, R. R., Difiglia, C., and Sanfilipo, M. P. (1994). "Lithium prophylaxis of bipolar illness." *British Journal of Psychiatry, 164,* 208–214.

Petraitis, J., Flay B., and Miller, T. (1995). "Reviewing theories of adolescent substance abuse." *Psychological Bulletin, 117,* 67–86.

Phillips, D. (1974). "The influence of suggestion on suicide." *American Sociological Review, 39,* 340–354.

Phillips, D., Lesyna, K., and Paight, D. (1993). "Suicide and the media. " In R. Maris, A. Berman, J. Maltsberger (Eds.), *Assessment and prediction of suicide.* New York: Guilford Press.

Pike, J. (1993). "The death of rock'n'roll." Boston: Faber and Faber.

Pitman, R., and Orr, S. (1993). "Psychophysiologic testing for PTSD." *Bulletin of the American Academy of Psychiatry and the Law, 21,* 37–52.

Pitman, S., and Orr, S. (1993). "Psychophysiologic testing for PTSD." *Bulletin of the American Academy of Psychiatry and the Law, 21,* 37–52.

Post, R. M. (1993). "Issues in the long-term management of bipolar affective illness. " *Psychiatric Annals, 23,* 86–93.

Pressman, M., and Orr, W. (Eds.) (1997). *Understanding sleep: The evaluation and treatment of sleep disorders.* Washington, DC: American Psychological Association Books.

Prochaska, J., DiClemente, C., and Norcross, J. (1992). "In search of how people change." *American Psychologist, 47,* 1102–1114.

Reynolds, D. (1984). *Constructive living.* Honolulu: University of Hawaii Press.

Rice, M., Harris, G., and Cormier, C. (1992). "An evaluation of a maximum security therapeutic community for psychopaths and other mentally disordered offenders." *Law and Human Behavior, 16,* 399–412.

Robins, L., and Regier, D. (1990). *Psychiatric disorders in America.* New York: Free Press.

Roesch, R. (1979). "Determining competency to stand trial: An examination of evaluation procedures in an institutional setting." *Journal of Consulting and Clinical Psychology, 47(3),* 542–550.

Rogers, C. (1961). *On becoming a person.* Boston: Houghton Mifflin.

Rosenhan, D. (1973). "On being sane in insane places." *Science, 179,* 250–258.

Salmon, P., and Meyer, R. (1986a). "Neuropsychological assessment: Adults." In M. Kurke and R. Meyer (Eds.), *Psychology in product liability and personal injury law.* New York: Hemisphere.

Salmon, P., and Meyer, R. (1986b). "Neuropsychological assessment: Children." In M. Kurke and R. Meyer (Eds.), *Psychology in product liability and personal injury law.* New York: Hemisphere.

Schmidt, C. (1995). "Sexual psychopathology and *DSM-IV.*" In J. Oldham and M. Riba (Eds.), *Review of psychiatry.* Washington, DC: American Psychiatric Press.

Schuckit, M. (1996). Recent developments in the pharmacotherapy of alcoholism. *Journal of Consulting and Clinical Psychology, 64,* 669–676.

Schwartz, J., Stoessel, P., Baxter, L., Martin, K., and Phelps, M. (1996). Systematic changes in cerebral glucose metabolic rate after successful behavior modification treatment of obsessive-compulsive disorder. *Archives of General Psychiatry, 53,* 109–113.

Scott, P. D. (1994). *Deep politics and the death of JFK.* Los Angeles: University of California Press.

Seidman, S., and Rieder, R. (1994). "A review of sexual behavior in the United States." *American Journal of Psychiatry, 151,* 330–341.

Seligman, M. (1995). The effectiveness of psychotherapy. *American Psychologist, 50,* 965–974.

Seltzer, L. (1986). *Paradoxical strategies in psychotherapy.* New York: Wiley.

Shneidman, E. (1985). *Definition of suicide.* New York: Wiley.

Silverman, I., and Geer, J. (1968). "The elimination of a recurrent nightmare by desensitization of a related phobia." *Behavior Research and Therapy, 6,* 109–111.

Silverman, L., and Weinberger, J. (1985). "Mommy and I are one: Implications for psychotherapy." *American Psychologist, 40,* 1296–1308.

Slovenko, R. (1995). *Psychiatry and criminal culpability.* New York: Wiley.

Smith, A., and Sugar, O. (1975). "Development of above normal language and intelligence 21 years after left hemispherectomy." *Neurology, 25,* 813–818.

Smith, M., Glass, G., and Miller, T. (1980). *The benefit of psychotherapy.* Baltimore, MD: Johns Hopkins Press.

Snowden, D. (1996). *Journal of the American Medical Association.*

Spanos, N. (1996). *Multiple identities and false memories.* Washington, DC: American Psychological Association Books.

Spanos, N. P., Weekes, N. P., and Bertraud, L. D. (1985). "Multiple personality: A social psychological perspective." *Journal of Abnormal Psychology 94(3),* 362–376.

Stanley, D., and Loffey, F. (1994). *The Elvis encyclopedia.* Santa Monica, CA: General Publishing Group.

State v. *Grieg* (Yellowstone County, Montana, 1977).

Striegel-Moore, R., Silberstein, L., and Rodin, J. (1986). "Toward an understanding of risk factors for bulimia." *American Psychologist, 43,* 246–263.

Strupp, H., Lambert, M., and Horowitz, L. (Eds.) (1997). *Measuring patient changes in mood, anxiety and personality disorders.* Washington, DC: American Psychological Association Books.

Sullivan, H. S. (1953). *The interpersonal theory of psychiatry.* New York: Norton.

Summers, A. (1980). *Conspiracy.* New York: McGraw-Hill.

Taylor, W. S., and Martin, M. (1944). "Multiple personality." *Journal of Abnormal Psychology, 39,* 281.

Thigpen, C., and Cleckley, H. (1984). "On the incidence of multiple personality." *International Journal of Clinical and Experimental Hypnosis, 32,* 63.

Tollefson, G. (1993). "Major depression." In D. Dunner (Ed.), *Current psychiatric therapy.* Philadelphia: Saunders.

United States v. *Brawner,* 471 F. 2d. 969 (D.C. Circuit, 1972).

Van Oppen, P., Hoekstra, R., and Emmelkamp, P. (1995). "The structure of obsessive-compulsive symptoms." *Behavior Research and Therapy, 33,* 15–23.

Wachtel, P. (1997). *Psychoanalysis behavior therapy, and the relational world.* Washington, DC: American Psychological Association Books.

Walker, E. (1998). "Schizophrenia." In H. Friedman (Ed.), *Encyclopedia of mental health.* San Diego: Academic Press.

Watson, J., and Rayner, R. (1920). "Conditioned emotional reactions." *Journal of Experimental Psychology, 3,* 1–14.

Weidenfeld, S. R. (1979). *First Lady's lady: With the Fords at the White House.* New York: Putnam.

Weissberg, M. (1993). "Multiple personality disorder and iatrogenesis: The cautionary tale of Anna O." *International Journal of Clinical and Experimental Hypnosis, 41(1),* 15–34.

Welch, M., and Kartub, P. (1978). "Socio-cultural correlates of incidence of impotence: A cross-cultural study." *Journal of Sex Research, 14,* 218–230.

Wender, P. (1995). *Attention-deficit hyperactivity disorder in adults.* New York: Oxford University Press.

Whybrow, P. (1997). *A mood apart: Depression, manic depression and other afflictions of the self.* New York: Basic Books.

Widiger, T., Frances, A., Pincus, H., Davis, W., and First, M. (1991). "Toward an empirical classification for the *DSM-IV*." *Journal of Abnormal Psychology, 100,* 280–288.

Winer, D. (1978). "Anger and dissociation: A case study of multiple personality." *Journal of Abnormal Psychology, 87,* 368.

Wolman, B. (1998). *Adolescence.* Westport, CT: Greenwood Press.

Wolpe, J. (1958). *Psychotherapy by reciprocal inhibition.* Stanford, CA: Stanford University Press.

Wolpe, J. (1973). *The practice of behavior therapy.* New York: Pergamon Press.

Wrangham, R., and Peterson, D. (1996). *Demonic males: Apes and the origins of human violence.* New York: Houghton Mifflin.

Zuercher, E. (1996). *An end to panic.* Oakland, CA: New Harbinger.

INDEX